RUSSIA

The Once and Future Empire from Pre-History to Putin

PHILIP LONGWORTH

St. Martin's Press New York

www.stmartins.com

Library of Congress Cataloging-in-Publication Data

Longworth, Philip, 1933–
Russia : the once and future empire from pre-history to Putin / Philip Longworth.
p. cm.
Inlcudes bibliographical references and index.
ISBN-13: 978-0-312-36041-2
ISBN-10: 0-312-36041-X
1. Russia—History. 2. Soviet Union—History. Russia (Federation)—History.
I. Title.

DK40.L66 2006
947—dc22

2006048494

First published in Great Britain by John Murray (Publishers), a division of Hodder Headline, under the title *Russia's Empires: Their Rise and Fall: From Prehistory to Putin*

First U.S. Edition: December 2006

10 9 8 7 6 5 4 3 2 1

Contents

Illustrations

The author and publishers would like to thank the following for permission to reproduce illustrations: Plate 7, From the Hakluyt Society's *Yermark's Campaign in Siberia,* ed. Terence Armstrong, London, 1975, reproduced by permission of David Higham Associates; 16, Add.5523 fol.7, the British Library; 24, Laurence Kelly; 28, Getty Images, AFP/Maxim Marmur. Plates are also taken from the following publications: 2, S. Vysotskii, *Svetskie freski Sofuskogo Sobore v Kieve [Secular Frescos in the St Sophia Cathedral in Kiev]*, Kiev, 1989; 3, I. Toskaia et al., *The State Architectural and Historical Museum of St Sophia Cathedral*, 2nd edn, Kiev 1996.

Acknowledgements

This book owes much to many helpers, but I alone am responsible for any errors it contains. I am grateful to former colleagues in three faculties of McGill University for advice in areas in which I lack expertise, and to the Department of History for granting me writing leave in the winter term of 2003. My debts to scholars in both Russia and the West go back many years, and are to some extent acknowledged in the references. I have also benefited from discussions with colleagues in the British Universities' Association of Slavists' Study groups on medieval and eighteenth-century Russia, the University of Budapest's biennial seminar on Russian history, and the Royal Institute of International Affairs in London. McGill's McLennan Library has a rich collection in the Russian area, and when it lacked an item I needed it readily obtained it for me. I am also grateful to the British Library and to the library of the School of Slavonic Studies in University College, London.

I am indebted to Bill Hamilton for the idea, to my conscientious and perceptive editor Gordon Wise, to Catherine Benwell and other members of the helpful John Murray team who saw the book through to its finished form, and, as always, to Ruth for her patience, encouragement and the critical eye which she applied to the entire text.

Philip Longworth

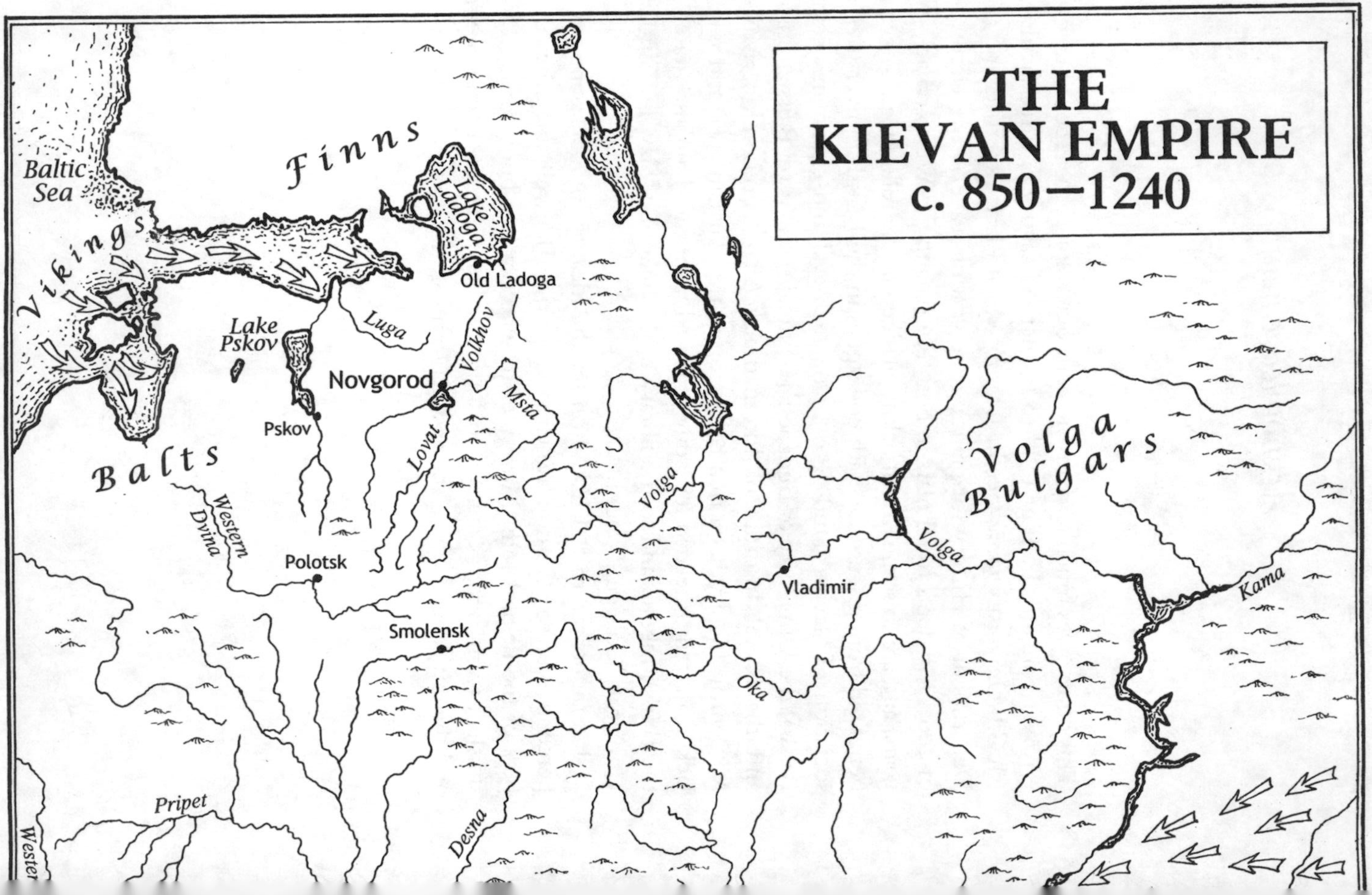
THE
KIEVAN EMPIRE
c. 850–1240
Baltic Sea
Finns
Vikings
Lake Ladoga
Old Ladoga
Luga
Volkhov
Lake Pskov
Novgorod
Msta
Pskov
Lovat
Balts
Western Dvina
Volga
Volga Bulgars
Polotsk
Vladimir
Kama
Smolensk
Oka
Pripet
Desna
Wester

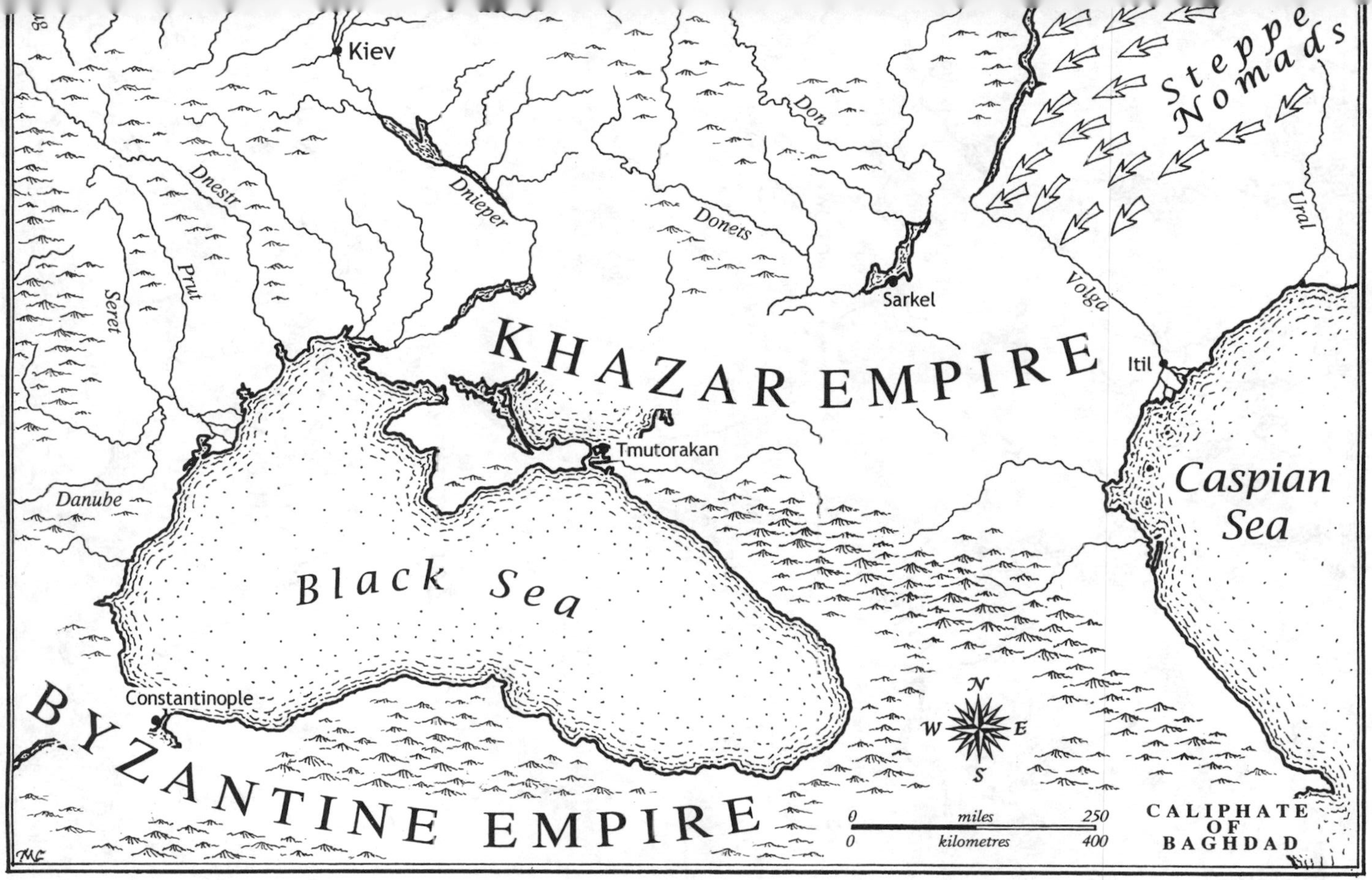
Steppe Nomads
Kiev
Dnestr
Dnieper
Don
Donets
Sarkel
Volga
Ural
Itil
KHAZAR EMPIRE
Tmutorakan
Prut
Seret
Danube
Caspian Sea
Black Sea
Constantinople
BYZANTINE EMPIRE
N
W
E
S
0 miles 250
0 kilometres 400
CALIPHATE OF BAGHDAD

England
Arc
Baltic Sea
Narva
Novgorod
Vologda
Riga
Pskov
Torzhok
Kostroma
Uglich
Iaroslavl
LITHUANIA
Polotsk
Volga
Rostov
Vitebsk
Trinity - St Sergius Monastery
MOSCOW
POLAND
Smolensk
Kaulga
Oka
Minsk
Riazan
Tula
Orel
Kursk
Kiev
Peremyshl
Pereislavl
Putivl
Don
Zaporozhian Cossacks
Dnieper
Don Cossacks
Nogai
CRIMEAN KHANATE
Black Sea
CAUCASUS
Istanbul
GEO

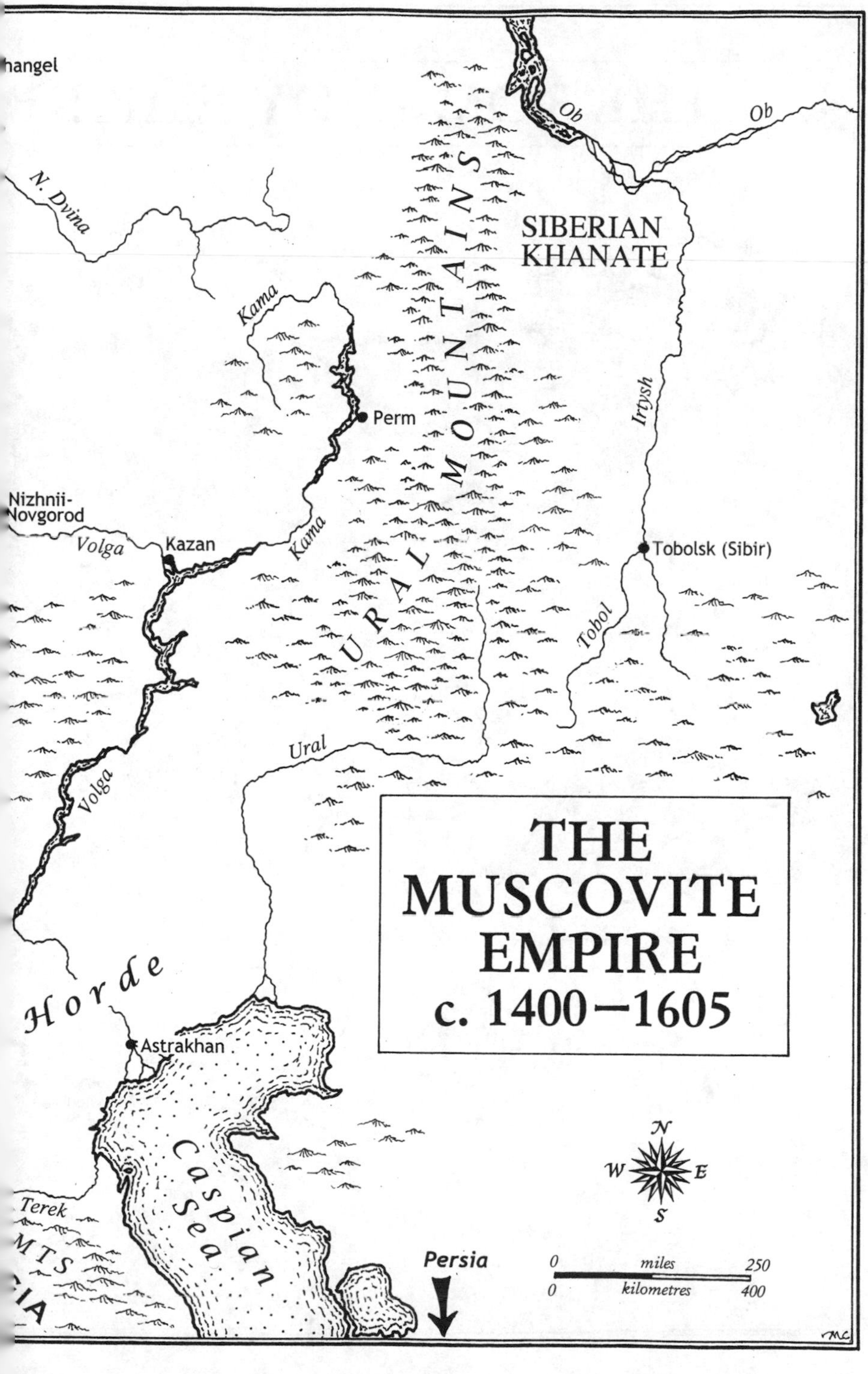

hangel
N. Dvina
Kama
Ob
Ob
URAL MOUNTAINS
SIBERIAN KHANATE
Perm
Irtysh
Nizhnii-Novgorod
Volga
Kazan
Kama
Tobolsk (Sibir)
Tobol
Ural
Volga
THE MUSCOVITE EMPIRE c. 1400–1605
Horde
Astrakhan
Caspian Sea
Terek
MTS
IA
N
W
E
S
Persia
0 miles 250
0 kilometres 400

THE ROMANOV EMPIRE
North Sea
NORWAY
SWEDEN
Barents Sea
DENMARK
Stockholm
Baltic Sea
Kara Sea
Berlin
Pskov
Riga
St Petersburg
Archangel
HABSBURG EMPIRE
Vienna
Vistula
Warsaw
Minsk
Novgorod
Ustiug
N. Dvina
URAL MOUNTAINS
Ob
Volga
Smolensk
Moscow
Iaroslavl
Budapest
Dnieper
Kiev
Nizhnii-Novgorod
Irtysh
LITTLE SERBIA
ROMANIA
Riazan
Kama
Kharkov
Voronezh
Kazan
ALBANIA
BULGARIA
Odessa
Ochakov
Saratov
Samara
Ufa
Cheliabinsk
Tobolsk
GREECE
Constantinople
Rostov
Don
Volga
Orenburg
Tobol
Tara
Sevastopol
Azov
Tsaritsyn
Black Sea
Kaban
OTTOMAN EMPIRE
Astrakhan
Terek
Batumi
CAUCASUS MTS
Caspian Sea
Irtysh
Kars
Tiflis
Derbent
Baku
Aral Sea
Krasnovodsk
Khiva
Tashkent
Bukhara
Kokand
Andijzhan
Samarkand
Tehran
Kushk
Kabul
PERSIA
AFGHAN-ISTAN
INDIA
MC

1613—1917
ALASKA
Bering Strait
Arctic Ocean
Anadyr
Kolyma
Indigirka
KAMCHATKA
SIBERIAN PLAINS
Lena
Yenisei
Okhotsk
Sea of Okhotsk
Iakutsk
LOWER TUNGUSKA
Lena
Aldan
SAKHALIN
Yeniseysk
Angara
Tomsk
Lake Baikal
Amur
Nerchinsk
Kuznetsk
Irkutsk
MANCHURIA
Harbin
Vladivostok
MONGOLIA
JAPAN
CHINA
KOREA
Port Arthur
N
W
E
S
strategic railways
0
miles
1000
0
kilometres
1600

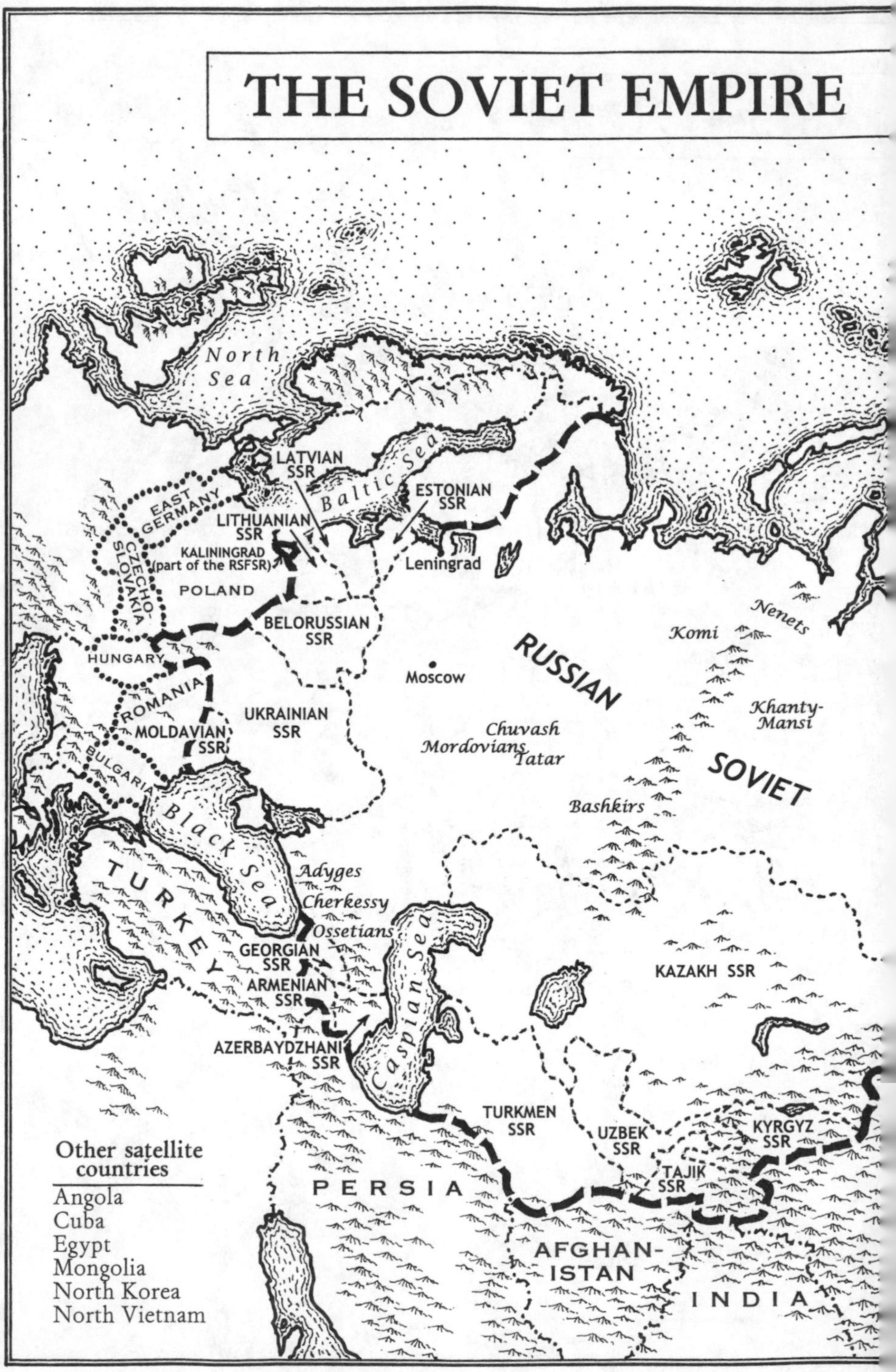
THE SOVIET EMPIRE
North Sea
Baltic Sea
LATVIAN SSR
ESTONIAN SSR
LITHUANIAN SSR
EAST GERMANY
KALININGRAD (part of the RSFSR)
Leningrad
CZECHO-SLOVAKIA
POLAND
BELORUSSIAN SSR
HUNGARY
ROMANIA
MOLDAVIAN SSR
UKRAINIAN SSR
BULGARIA
Moscow
RUSSIAN SOVIET
Komi
Nenets
Khanty-Mansi
Chuvash
Mordovians
Tatar
Bashkirs
Black Sea
TURKEY
Adyges
Cherkessy
Ossetians
GEORGIAN SSR
ARMENIAN SSR
AZERBAYDZHANI SSR
Caspian Sea
KAZAKH SSR
TURKMEN SSR
UZBEK SSR
KYRGYZ SSR
TAJIK SSR
PERSIA
AFGHAN-ISTAN
INDIA
Other satellite countries
Angola
Cuba
Egypt
Mongolia
North Korea
North Vietnam

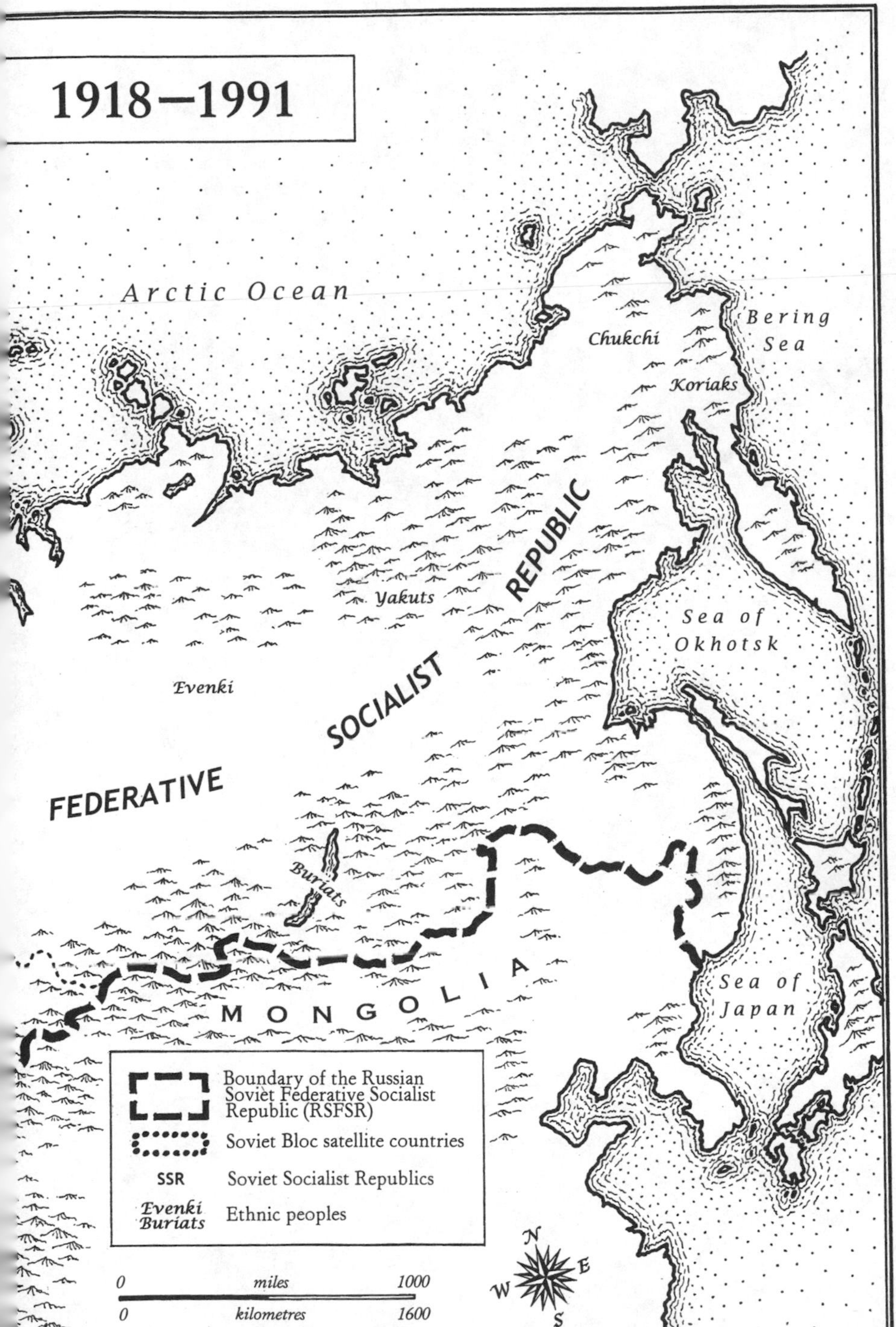
1918–1991
Arctic Ocean
Chukchi
Bering Sea
Koriaks
REPUBLIC
Yakuts
Sea of Okhotsk
SOCIALIST
Evenki
FEDERATIVE
Buriats
MONGOLIA
Sea of Japan
Boundary of the Russian Soviet Federative Socialist Republic (RSFSR)
Soviet Bloc satellite countries
SSR Soviet Socialist Republics
Evenki Buriats Ethnic peoples
0 miles 1000
0 kilometres 1600
N
E
W
S

Introduction

MOST EMPIRES RISE, expand and then collapse – and once collapsed do not revive. But Russia's case is different. Russians have built no fewer than four empires. The first, the medieval commercial colonial empire of Kievan Rus, was destroyed in the 1200s. But some time later a new absolutist *imperium*, which tried to replicate something of the glory of the later Roman Empire, arose. It was centred on Moscow, the 'Third Rome' of legend. In the later sixteenth century, under Ivan the Terrible, it began to expand vigorously towards the Baltic, the Caspian and, across the Urals into Asia. Then, in the early 1600s, the state which was the motor of this empire suddenly seized up; Russia dissolved into confusion, and the neighbouring Poles were able to install their own tsar in the Kremlin. Yet out of the debris of Russia's imperial collapse a third, more conventional, European dynastic empire soon emerged, rooting itself in the remains of its predecessor.

This Romanov Empire came to serve as the epitome of Russia's power and aggression. It expanded into Ukraine, extended its hold on Siberia as far as the Pacific and the gates of China, and, having humbled Poland-Lithuania, proceeded to demolish the two great powers which dared to challenge it: Sweden and Napoleonic France. Having established itself as the strongest land power in Europe, it continued its expansion – through the Balkans towards the Mediterranean, across the Caucasus, and, to the consternation of the British, into the heights of Central Asia. It became a sea power to reckon with in the north Pacific, and even came to exert a certain influence in China. The Romanov Empire suffered reverses in the Crimean War and against Japan in 1904, though it lost little territory and influence as a result. Soon afterwards, however, during the First World War, this empire, too, disintegrated.

The Soviet state which supplanted it seemed unlikely to survive. Russia was racked by civil war, and was promptly invaded by British, French, Japanese and American troops. It lost a war with Poland too. Bankrupt, friendless and besieged, it nevertheless contrived, within the remarkably short span of a quarter of a century, to recover sufficiently to inflict a comprehensive defeat on Hitler's Germany, Europe's strongest military and economic power, together with its allies, and to dictate the shape of post-Second World War Europe. This Soviet Empire – more centralized and ideological than any of its predecessors – became the most extensive and powerful of all. It was also the most short-lived.

The purpose of the book is to examine the phoenix-like nature of Russian imperialism and improve our understanding of it. Why the strange alternation between aggression and fragility? Why the tendency for Russian empires to disintegrate as they did around the years 1240, 1600 and 1918, but then to rise from the ashes stronger than before? Why, for that matter, do Russians, as a society, tend to alternate between torpor and manic energy, and what are the sources of their resilience? What has enabled them to withstand invasions by numerically and technologically superior armies; to spring back and gain the strength to conquer immense tracts of territory and exercise dominion over millions of subjects of diverse cultures?

To find adequate explanations for these phenomena we need to describe the rise and fall of each Russian empire and inquire into its strengths and weaknesses. But we also have to delve back to times before the modern era which most general histories treat either cursorily or not at all,[1] for it is only there that we can hope to find evidence that might illuminate some basic questions concerning the character of Russians: their psyche, habits and the singularities of their institutions, all of which were formed over time and in relation to physical conditions. And here we encounter a problem, because the early chronicles were composed to sustain the legitimacy and claims of princes rather than to provide objective records of circumstances and events. Nor are the earliest travellers' accounts always reliable. Furthermore, such accounts begin too late in time. Since, as we shall see, there are good, scientific, reasons to believe that the Russians' ancestors were explorers and colonizers for some time before the fabled founding father Riurik and his band of Viking venturers ever established themselves in their land, a way must be found of establishing relevant developments in periods unrecorded by conventional history.

To trace the origins of Russian imperialism, then, we need a wider range of tools than is offered by conventional history. The first chapter of this book will therefore exploit the findings of non-historical science – genetics, anthropology, archaeology and linguistics – to explore the roots of the phenomenon: the making of the landscape which formed the Russians' habitat, their diet, physiognomy, migratory patterns, habits, capacities and disposition. Readers should discover that some of these findings will resonate from time to time throughout the book. However, those who prefer conventional history should start with Chapter 2 (where for their benefit I have repeated a few essential points made in Chapter 1).

Some new material appears in later chapters, though they are mostly based on the work of specialist historians who are acknowledged in the endnotes. There is no shortage of general books on Russia and Russian imperialism, of course, and each one represents a view. But this book differs from all of them in its perspectives. It examines the formative stages in the development of the land and its people which took place *before* the era of written record to which historians generally confine themselves. Some of the material it uses is new, and confronts some popular prejudices which are based on outdated readings of the evidence or which obscure the truth. No doubt I have made mistakes, but my conclusions have been based on evidence rather than preconceived ideas, whether pro- or anti-Russian.

Chapter 2 describes the rise and fall of Kievan Rus. The three that follow consider the rise of Muscovy, its attainment of imperial status under Ivan the Terrible (who adopted the insignia of the double-headed eagle from the defunct Roman Empire) and its subsequent collapse. The next group of chapters deal with the new imperial expansion under the Romanov rulers Alexis, Peter the Great and Catherine the Great – an advance that was slow at first, but which, despite fierce resistance, gained steadily in tempo. They also describe the apogee of Romanov power which followed the Napoleonic Wars, the first great and bloody campaigns against the Chechens and Circassians in the Caucasus – wars which inspired some great romantic and imperialistic literature – and the subsequent decline and collapse in 1917–18.

The last set of chapters traces the astonishing rise of Soviet Russia, the burgeoning of its empire following the defeat of Nazi Germany, and its no less astonishing and precipitous collapse. Chapter 15 describes post-Communist Russia, while the Conclusion summarizes the results of the inquiry and also assesses Russia's place and prospects in the world in 2004.

I

The Russians: Who are They?

IN JANUARY 1547, within days of the deaths of Henry VIII of England and Francis I of France, at the other end of Europe a sixteen-year-old youth was crowned tsar of Russia. The ceremony took place in the Kremlin's Cathedral of the Assumption, one of most richly decorated of all Europe's cathedrals, and when the Tsar emerged, crowned and holding orb and sceptre, to be showered with gold to symbolize prosperity, all the bells of Moscow pealed out and the huge, enthusiastic crowds roared as if in expectation of great things to come. The youth they acclaimed was Ivan IV, first titular emperor of Russia, self-proclaimed descendant of the Viking Riurik and of the Roman Emperor Augustus. He was to prove himself a dedicated empire-builder, whose possessions came to extend right across Eurasia, from Sweden to Persia and from the Baltic to the Pacific. It was the largest imperial heartland in the world.

Most accounts of the Russian past begin here – or even later, with Peter the Great – and give only cursory treatment to the preceding periods, despite their relevance to the development of Russian imperialism. This history, however, will begin at the beginning. But what was the beginning? Russian tradition suggests the arrival of Riurik and his band of Vikings in the ninth century, but since they found the land inhabited should one not begin earlier? And should one begin with the people or with the land of Russia? Common sense suggests the land, but, since the Russian environment and ecology were formed to an extent simultaneously with human settlement, there is reason to deal with them together. Either course presents a problem, however, since this story begins long before the written records on which most history is based, and since no historical records of those times survive (even supposing they were ever made). We shall therefore have to reconstruct our account of what happened by inference, from the conclusions of sciences other than history.

Anthropologists, archaeologists, experts in linguistics and others have all contributed to our understanding of what happened, but there are questions on which there is, as yet, no consensus – the live areas of scholarship fired by dispute. Even when written sources appear, they cannot be taken at their face value. The early chroniclers worked for princes. They recorded what was of interest to their masters and, like public-relations staffs today, did so in ways which showed them in the best light, suppressing inconvenient facts. They justified their princes' actions, supported their claims, and blackened the reputations of their enemies.

Despite these problems, the data unearthed by scholars in a variety of fields allows us to construct a picture of even the earliest past of human society and its environment. The information is patchy, disputed at points, and tells us little or nothing about some things we would like to know – such as the stories of individual human beings. The best picture we can build of the Russians' earliest past, then, will resemble an old, imperfect silent movie. It will describe a long-drawn out process in a series of brief rushes; the definition will often be indistinct, and the film will break off altogether at certain points. Yet there are *some* certainties about human existence in what is now Russia from as early as twenty millennia ago, and even a sweeping survey of this difficult prehistoric ground may yield clues that could prove vital to later conclusions about the nature of Russians and their expansionist tendencies.

The territory of European Russia had been populated before the Ice Age. Among the earliest remains that have so far been discovered is a grave at Sungir, near Vladimir in central Russia. It dates from between 20,000 and 26,000 years ago, and contained the bones of a twelve- or thirteen-year-old boy and a girl of six or seven. The dead wore garments similar to modern anoraks and leather trousers that were sewn directly to their moccasin-like shoes – a device which Siberians still use to fight the cold. Their clothes had been decorated with thousands of shell beads. These and the variety of stone tools, pierced antler rods, ivory bracelets, and the two spears made from straightened mammoth tusks found with them suggest that the children were the offspring of a chief.[1]

The Sungir remains mark an end rather than a beginning, of societies as well as of individuals, for the people of Sungir disappeared along with the mammoths and the population of almost all the rest of Europe. As the cold became more intense, they either died or moved to the warmer climes of the continent's southern peripheries. However, the territory was resettled after the Ice Age, and so our story resumes after a lapse of several millennia about 10,000 to 16,000 years ago.

One basic certainty is that the Russians are Europeans by descent. We know this from the work of the geneticist Dr O. Semino and his associates. In the year 2000 they published a major study which has extended knowledge of the genetic history of Europeans. They had analysed blood samples from over 1,000 men from all over Europe, and their findings, which focused on the Y chromosome, which is carried only by males, led them to conclude that when Europe was struck by the Ice Age, about 24,000 years ago, its Stone Age inhabitants withdrew in three directions, taking refuge in the warmer climes of southern Europe: Mediterranean France and Spain, the Balkans, and what is now Ukraine. The Russians are descended from this last group.

The Ice Age ended very slowly, and the global warming was interrupted by phases when the great cold returned. Eventually, however, the glaciers retreated, and the earth warmed somewhat, although permafrost continued to hold the tundra of the far north and large tracts of Siberia in its deadening grip. It does so to this day. There are still immense tracts of tundra where the subsoil is permanently frozen, which makes for problems in maintaining rail beds for Siberia's railways. But elsewhere, as temperatures became milder, the atmosphere became moister. As it did so, life gradually returned – at first in the form of plants, then of insects and animals. As larger areas became habitable once more, descendants of the three groups of refugees began to repopulate those regions of Europe which their ancestors had abandoned when they became ice-bound.

By the time of the return, each group of humanoids carried a genetic specific that differed significantly from the others. We also know that most of them belonged to blood group B, and were predominately rhesus positive. But the blood of the Ukrainian group, to which the Russians owe their origins, was now distinguished by haplotype Eu 19. This genetic marker was to be bestowed on the generations of Slavs and other Europeans who were to follow.[2]

At first, these ancestors of the Russians, Ukrainians, Poles, Hungarians and others (for scholars know of no characteristics which distinguished them from one another until very much later) were confined to a swathe of territory to the north and west of the Black Sea. Much of the country beyond, later known as Russia, was still covered with icy marsh, and conditions over large areas even further south did not allow life to flourish in any form. The atmosphere was as dry as the temperature was cold, and, since life depends on humidity, the vast terrain was bleak, forbidding. Before humans could survive there, an ecological system with the potential to sustain human life had to develop.

The first need was for plant life. The earliest species to appear were those with the highest tolerance of cold. Tiny, rudimentary plants pioneered the taming of the wastelands, then successively larger plants, including trees – the aspen and the birch (still characteristic of northern Russia), the pine, the larch, the hazel and the willow. Where the warming produced excessive wetness, the spruce helped make the area more hospitable. As the climate became milder 7,000 to 8,000 years ago, the hornbeam and linden appeared, and, where conditions favoured them, deciduous oak and elm took root and flourished. The famous Russian forests were in the making.

Towards the milder south, however, the forests gradually thinned out into the rolling steppe. The vegetation there was thick, but rainfall was less certain and the winds which blew across from Asia were so fierce that, except in deep ravines which afforded some protection, trees were comparatively rare.

The moister conditions had already created an environment hospitable to insects, including the productive bee. As water temperatures rose, more and more species of fish appeared, eventually including pike, perch and salmon, and it became warm enough to accommodate the water chestnut too. Ducks and other water fowl arrived, and larger, more complex, animals moved into what had been wasteland – hares, beavers, red deer, roe deer, and a variety of predatory species including the fox, the wolf, the lynx, the glutton (similar to the American wolverine) and the lumbering, honey-loving brown bear. And, now a suitable environment had been created, human beings also entered the scene.

They had begun to exploit certain wild creatures in the south country where they had sheltered during the Ice Age, and they followed them northward into their new habitats as the ice receded. They hunted deer and wild pigs and horses for food, and in time they were to domesticate some of them. Primitive man understood breeding. He also learned to cultivate certain grasses for their seeds, and to crush them into flour, which could be cooked and eaten. The descendants of the first practitioners of this systematic crop-raising and animal-rearing were to carry these techniques northward. However, the movement of humans from the southern lands into the virgin lands to the north was gradual and exploratory. People moved cautiously, edging little by little into the new environment, and the yields from farming were, as yet, sparse and unreliable. Hunting, fishing and gathering whatever edible plants nature provided in season remained essential to human sustenance.

Indeed, the hunters led the way into the virgin territories, penetrating to the edge of the northernmost areas that were free of ice in summer, tracking animals and birds to kill, not only for food, but also for their fur, feathers, horns and bones, from which all manner of useful things could be made. Others trekked upriver and explored lakes to find the points where fish could be found in abundance and caught most easily, and seasonal gatherers (mostly women and children, one imagines) came with the men, searching for edible grasses, berries, nuts and other forest fruits like mushrooms. Normally they would retreat to base at the onset of winter, carrying their spoils. But as populations grew, so did pressures to extend the areas of permanent settlement. Similar pressures affected the primitive societies of central Europe too, so that migrants from the west, including those who were subsequently to be identified as Balts and Finns, also moved into fringes of the north-land.

The people who explored and eventually made homes in the Russian lands belonged to the species *Homo sapiens sapiens*. They were, as we have seen, genetically distinct, Caucasoid in anthropological type, and capable of speech and language. Their culture was of the Stone Age, but of the later, more sophisticated, palaeolithic kind. We can infer that they were by nature curious, venturesome, ingenious and adaptable.

Their adaptation to their new homeland took two forms: conscious and unconscious. The conscious process involved learning from experience, collectively as well as individually, and the recording of experience through memory and storytelling down the generations. Unconscious adaptation took place over a much longer timescale, as it still does, and was genetic. The DNA of the Russians' ancestors gradually changed in response to climate and environment. In more northerly areas, where they had less exposure to sunlight, their hair grew fairer and their skin lighter. In colder areas their noses tended to grow longer, allowing the air they breathed in a longer time to be warmed in its passage to the lungs; and, thanks to the processes of natural selection, they developed resistance or immunity to some diseases. Their genetic structure was to change somewhat as they encountered other groups and mated with them, but their essential characteristics are broadly identifiable and have persisted into our own times.

Although we can relate no personal stories from these earliest, formative, times, we can begin to picture representative Russian men and women. A huge research project mounted by the Soviet Academy of Sciences in its heyday was devoted to describing the Russians in terms of physical type and to investigating the historical origins of their physical characteristics. The work, carried out in the later 1950s by Dr V. Bunak and his team of ethnographers, examined no fewer than 17,000 adult men and women in over 100 regions of Russian settlement. The large sample made it statistically possible to map an anthropological type in all its variations. Whereas earlier research had concentrated on the geographical spread of head shapes and body height, this study also registered face size (breadth and height from the brow), complexion, hair colour, shape of nose, thickness of lip, body height, strength of beard growth, and other indicators including blood group. Variations in each characteristic were mapped, and combinations of them were grouped according to geographical area.

It was found, for example, that in north-west Russia people were moderately brachycephalic, or short-headed with rather broad skulls, and had fairish hair, broad faces, comparatively weak beard growth and, often, a high base of nose, though all these characteristics varied in intensity within the region. To the west the Russians were found to have longer faces, darker hair (by contrast to their fair-complexioned Finnic, Balt and Mazurian Polish neighbours), lower nose-bases, and a higher incidence of folded eyelids. In the south-east, by contrast, people were mostly mesocephalic, with medium-shaped skulls and skull capacity. They had bright complexions and dark hair; and again these characteristics were more pronounced in some parts of the region than in others.[3]

Variations in build and appearance reflected intermarriage with neighbouring groups, but also natural selection in response to differences in diet and climatic conditions. The better nourished people are, the taller they tend to be; the greater their exposure to the sun, the darker their colouring; the greater the cold, the more Mongoloid their faces; the less their exposure to light, the fairer their hair.[4] To this extent the appearance of the Russians, as with all humanity, is partly a response to their environment, which continues to change.

The northward movement of people from what is now Ukraine to colonize territory which is now known as Russia had not been even. Extensive marshlands made access to some areas difficult or impossible. Dense forests had a similar effect. On the other hand, rivers often provided convenient routes for the explorers. Similar factors account for linguistic development. Old Slavonic diversified into a variety of languages just as the physical characteristics of Russians varied in response to geography and ecological conditions. Interestingly, geneticists suggest that linguistic variations are roughly in line with genetic variations. The Russian language and the genes that make Russians what they are physically are evidently inseparable.

Geographical barriers sometimes promoted differences in language. Areas of bog and marsh have tended to be as effective as mountains in keeping societies separate and distinct. The Carpathian Mountains separated the ancestors of the Czechs and Poles from those of the south-Slav Serbs and Croats; the Pripet Marshes constituted a no less effective a barrier between the west Slavs and the east Slavs whose descendants were to become Ukrainians, Belarusans and Russians. Such physical barriers facilitated separate linguistic development. It could even be said that the traditional enmity between Poles and Russians has its origins in geography.

The ancestors of the Russians were not conscious of their genetic make-up, of course, and were still less able to control it. But, though genetic adaptation is unconscious and slow, human intelligence and ingenuity make for a faster track of adaptation. That these people could make tools, use them, and domesticate some animals suggests that they were conscious actors, capable – collectively – of shaping their own culture. The Russians of the future, then, were to be the creation both of their ancestors and of the developing environment of the Russian land. Some characteristics we associate with Russians nowadays originated in the rigours of those prehistoric times: tolerance of cold, endurance of privation, and a readiness to adopt new technology from other peoples they were to encounter. This last we know from the work of archaeologists.

By the year 4000 BCE conditions for civilization were fast being created. Tools had become more varied and sophisticated. People had learned to make nets, hooks and needles as well as awls and scrapers – bows and arrows too. Indeed, the remains in several grave digs of the period suggest arrows to have been a relatively common cause of death. Society was being organized on a larger scale than hitherto; exploitation of the wild was becoming more specialized. A new kind of economy was in the making. It was based largely on farming, of both crops and domesticated animals, including the horse (though wild horses were to survive into the eighteenth century). And, as farming and artisanal skills developed, settlements grew in size – a few of them considerably.

One site, at Talyanky, east of the river Dnieper, is reckoned to have housed as many as 10,000 inhabitants. Yet, despite its size, it could hardly be called a town. Rather, it was an agglomeration of largely self-sufficient farmsteads. The buildings were oblong, timber-framed, clay-and-wattle structures with wooden floors reinforced with baked clay, and with low-pitched roofs. Most structures were divided into three or four rooms, each with a stove or hearth, which suggests what might be termed industrial use. Many of them were certainly used for baking clay objects. Settlements in Ukraine of the so-called Tripolye type, dating from approximately 5,000 to 6,000 years ago, belonged to people who grew wheat, barley, millet and fruit, and raised pigs, sheep, goats and cattle.[5]

The size of such settlements suggests that there had been something of a revolution in food production. This had led to a marked improvement in diet, and hence in female fecundity. If the consequent population increase made for larger settlements, it probably also created pressure on resources which, as we have noticed, encouraged migration northward. The hunting bands that had led the way, also pioneered settlement, at first by erecting seasonal encampments, for summer or winter depending on the prey sought: deer, fish or wildfowl or furry animals. Such temporary settlements had similar characteristics to those of Sredny Stog in northern Ukraine, a place associated with the domestication of wild horses, and permanent settlements of later date. They were usually sited on a raised shelf of land above a river, this being convenient for transportation and communication as well as for fresh water and for fishing, yet safe from flooding.[6]

One great advantage of the cold times had been the ease with which the meat of hunted creatures could be frozen. The popular Russian dish *pelmeni* is a reminder of this fact: at the onset of winter (a popular time for slaughtering animals), pasta shells filled with meat are thrown out of the kitchen window to freeze. Then, during the winter months, they are taken inside as needed, a shovelful at a time, to be boiled up for dinner. In warmer conditions, however, people learned to preserve meat, and fish, by air-drying or, more commonly, by salting.

The need for large quantities of salt to preserve both meat and fish was to promote both trade and industry. It encouraged searches for saline lakes and marshes, and the development of evaporation techniques. Excavations of sites in Ukraine have demonstrated that the trade in salt became extensive and far-ranging, and this helped to develop culture contacts with other budding societies.

While late Stone Age society had been developing in what is now southern Russia and Ukraine, hunter-gatherers with stone technology had been developing to the north, towards Finland and the Baltic. A cemetery excavated by Soviet archaeologists in Karelia and dating from about 7,500 years ago tells us quite a lot about these people. Most were Europeoid, though a few had Mongoloid features derived from the climate their ancestors had endured. That most of the buried bodies faced east and were sprinkled with red ochre has persuaded archaeologists that they may have venerated the sun. The knives, fish-hooks and harpoons found along with animal remains show that they lived by hunting elk, beaver and seals as well as red and roe deer and wild pigs.[7] Climate as well as the availability of materials dictated the form of clothing they wore.

Human life, even in these early times, was more than a struggle for subsistence and self-preservation, however. The settlers had a taste for pretty things like ivories or amber brought from the Baltic. Archaeologists have found a range of decorative jewellery, some of which rings or rattles beguilingly when the wearer moves, and a variety of primitive musical instruments – pipes, drums and bells – that suggest that these people did not lack amusement, nor noisy means of conjuring up spirits. Other finds suggest a yearning for immortality: the remains of animal sacrifice, for example, and the care taken of the dead. In many cases the bodies of the deceased were ritually positioned and buried together with votive statuettes as well as objects that might be useful in an afterlife, or of which the dead had been fond.

The prevalence of pregnant-woman sculptures – talismans of productivity and growing riches – may suggest a society in which women were valued more than men. Certainly, the women were productive in ways other than child-bearing. They gathered food, made yarns, and engaged in a variety of other handicrafts as well as providing care and comfort. However, any such superior valuation is unlikely to have lasted into times when the men's brute strength and strategic sense were needed for defence – whether against the elements or against other men. It was this need that put men at a premium and precluded the development of matriarchy, and there is evidence that it coincided with the advent of metal technology. From this period on the idols are of men rather than women.

The technological revolution associated first with copper and then with bronze occurred about 3,500 years ago in the Russian land. Evidence of copper ore and copper-smelting, as well as a range of objects including copper knives, ornaments and sickles, has been found in the Volga basin of eastern Russia. Bronze axe heads and spear heads have been found both near the Baltic and in the south – and male figures are characteristic of the votive objects and ornaments found.[8] Then, about 3,000 years ago, the Iron Age arrived in Russia, and the pace of change quickened.

Trading networks, usually running along rivers, connected Russia both with the Mediterranean and with western Europe, which shared in the Iron Age culture. Even so, iron metallurgy is thought to have developed more or less independently in Russia. In any case, traders did not necessarily travel long distances – although some of the objects they traded in did. Commerce tended to be incremental, one group trading with its neighbours, and they with others, until commercial chains were formed along which travelled the commodities from which traders profited. A chain lasted until a cheaper or better alternative source was found, or until the consumers in the market learned to produce the goods themselves.

Though old technology often persisted alongside the new, metal technology speeded the pace of agricultural development. In areas where the use of such iron implements as the sickle caught on, more land could be cultivated and the community became richer. At the same time the makers of sickles forged swords, spear heads and axe heads, and made armour, allowing war to be waged more effectively. Iron culture made a society more attractive to predators; it also permitted a more effective defence. Certainly, with the advent of iron both settlements and society changed. Forts, albeit rudimentary at first, began to appear on hills overlooking farming land, and society became more differentiated both in function and in status. A variety of specialists appeared – metalworkers, people skilled in handling heavy weapons (like large axes), and organizers. But the new and larger society became more dependent on farming.

At the same time iron helped speed the extension of settlement northward into the forest zone, thanks to the iron axe head, which allowed trees to be felled more efficiently. It also contributed to swidden agriculture. This method of taming the forested wilderness and extending the area of farming was suggested by nature itself. Late-summer storms accompanied by lightning occasionally set fire to tracts of dried-out scrub and trees. The ashes provided a nutritious seedbed for plants, and the proto-Russians learned to exploit the phenomenon.

The swidden (or, more dramatically, 'slash-and-burn') method of farming, though simple, required patience and, in the initial phase, some heavy work. This would normally begin in early summer, when axe-men would hack down trees in a selected area of forest – probably near a river where the ground was flat and firm – and leave the timber to dry out until late the following spring. Techniques changed according to conditions: in conifer forests the bark was often stripped off to dry out the trees before felling. Such wood as was needed to make tools, build huts and use as fuel would be taken out; the rest would be burned, together with the undergrowth. The women and the weaker men would then set to with the sowing. Sometimes they scattered the seed directly into the ashes once these had cooled, though more often they used wooden hoes and forked scratch-ploughs, fashioned on the spot, to prepare a tilth before sowing.

At first the crops would be good. The ground, after all, was rich in potash and humus. Meanwhile wild plants, which had colonized the uncultivated parts of the clearing, provided good fodder for the newcomers' domesticated animals. The method was comparatively cheap in terms of energy invested. However, after two, three or at most four seasons the harvests became sparse and poor, so the little community which depended on it had to move on and start the process again. Since the land had to be left fallow for at least fifteen years (and in some areas as long as thirty) before it regained strength, slash-and-burn agriculture demanded a large area of prospective as well as actual cultivation. It could not support a population of any density, though it certainly encouraged expansion of the land area farmed. Swidden farming was practised in Russia as early as 1000 BCE, and it was to be used by colonizing venturers for centuries afterwards in the course of taming the Russian land.

And swidden agriculture also had implications for private landownership. What point could there be in owning land when one's family moved on regularly (if not necessarily far) every few years and there was no shortage of land anyway?[9] The angry protests in Russia against the denationalization of land at the beginning of the present century may not be directly attributable to the historical effects of swidden farming, but the technique may have left a mark on the Russian mentality. Indeed, there is reason to believe that the distinctive character of certain Russian institutions originated in the particular nature of Russian farming, developed in response to difficulties posed by soil and climate.

The swidden farmers who had moved northward and those who remained in the Ukraine area shared much the same culture as well as much the same blood. However, differences in conditions and the availability of materials dictated variations in the houses they built for themselves. To the north, where timber was plentiful, houses came to be built entirely of logs, rather than the use of timber being confined to frames and battens; and the pitch of the roofs was much steeper, to facilitate the shedding of snow. And if differences of environment promoted change in aspects of physical culture, they are associated with developments in language too.

What is now northern Russia was inhabited at that time by small groups of people speaking Finnic dialects. The Russians-to-be were only beginning to penetrate these areas, and their language came, as they themselves had done, from the south. Scholars are still divided over the issue of whether cereal-farming was introduced at the same time as the Indo-European group of languages (to which Russian belongs but Finnish does not) by people who had originated in the so-called 'fertile crescent' of the Near East (the area of modern Iraq); the views of Sir Colin Renfrew on the spread of Indo-European languages have been challenged by another brilliant anthropologist, J. Mallory.[10] But it is certain that the proto-Russians, like the proto-Ukrainians and proto-Poles and others, spoke Slavonic.

Linguistics experts can tell how, and roughly when, modern languages diverged from a common root like Latin or Old Slavonic. Thanks to them we know that Slavonic, like Latin, derived in its turn from a common Indo-European ancestor. Where Slavonic actually originated, however, has long been disputed: several Slavonic-speaking nations, from Russia to the Czech Republic, insist that it was on *their* territory. In effect the issue has become a point of modern nationalistic pride. It seems certain, however, that speakers of Slavonic in its earliest form centred on areas east of the river Vistula and west of the river Dnieper in what is now eastern Poland and Ukraine. But, as Russia's earliest chronicler knew, all Slavs spoke the same language, and other sources from Byzantium confirm the fact. Differences were to set in with the movement of populations and the passage of time, creating distinctive Russian, Czech, Bulgarian and other forms of Slavonic. But whereas another Indo-European language, Latin, began to dissolve into Italian, Spanish, French and the other Romance languages between 1,200 and 1,600 years ago, Old Slavonic was not to disintegrate into the variety of different eastern-European languages we know today until much later.[11]

As they moved north to the Baltic and east to the foothills of the Urals, the east Slavs, including the proto-Russians, were not alone in the wilderness they were reclaiming. They had encountered people speaking Finno-Ugrian dialect in the north, and to the south and south-east they were to encounter peoples who had originated in the Caucasus and in the steppes of Asia. Traces of these contacts are seen in traded objects found by archaeologists, in physical (especially facial) characteristics recorded by physical anthropologists, and in singularities of language studied by philologists.

Yet barriers of ice and wetland continued to impede settlement long after the global warming got under way. The 'Black Earth' belt of rich, loamy soil which made Ukraine the breadbasket of Russia – and for a time around 1900 of Europe too – extends from the margin of European Russia, the core of the original Russia, into the Urals and western Siberia. But the quality of arable land in the rest of the country is inferior, and most of the land mass is not cultivable at all. Marshes and bogs still preclude agriculture over large areas, though some were drained in the Soviet period; and until relatively modern times, seemingly dense forest impeded development.

And always the Russian climate has been unstable, largely unpredictable. It has been a major influence on Russians, and made them unlike other peoples. Severe though the North American climate can be, Russia's is worse. Even the south is cold – colder than central Europe. Summers there may be mild, even hot, but, as Baedeker warned, 'Sudden variations in temperature are very frequent . . . The traveller must always be on his guard against sudden falls in temperatures.'[12] Climate variations can cause havoc, and have often done so in Russia. On the North American prairies one expects snow to fall before the ground freezes, which insulates autumn-sown crops. But on the Russian steppes severe ground frosts not infrequently precede snow falls, in which case the seed freezes – and until a few decades ago that could spell famine. As for rainfall, it is adequate in the north, where soils are poor, but poorer where the soil is good. And not only does the climate tend to extremes: so do the seasons. Winters are long and dark, summers hot but short, and in the north it remains light throughout the month of May.

In the west of Europe spring comes in March and farmers can continue working the fields into December. In Russia, by contrast, it is still as if the Ice Age has not quite concluded: the growing season lasts barely five months rather than eight or more. Moreover, to produce enough for subsistence the poor soil demands more labour than in, say, France or North America south of the 52nd Parallel. These conditions were to have huge implications for the way in which both Russia and the Russians developed. They influenced the Russian temperament, and even the nature of Russian institutions.

For example, the very short growing season made for haste in both sowing and reaping. This encouraged interdependence between farmers to get things done, and even a tendency to share resources. But it also discouraged farming on an individual basis. Individualism involved risk; co-operation was a form of insurance. Russians may not have been natural communists, as romantic socialists used to claim, but the landscape and the harsh environment from which they have had to wrest a living seem to have developed in them a capacity for suffering, a certain communalism, even a willingness to sacrifice the individual for the common good. Circumstances made it impossible for the Russian economy and the Russian state to develop as England, France or, in due time, the United States were to develop.

The pressure to prepare the soil for spring sowing as soon as the ground was safe from frost, and to harvest all one's crops before the rains came, required frenetic, strenuous effort, long hours in the field, and the mobilization of children. On the other hand in winter, when days were short and there was little work to do outdoors, and little indoors either apart from whittling wood, Russians tended to indolence and lethargy. In short, temperamentally they inclined to extremes – or at least the men did. The demands on women were different. Not only were the domestic chores left to them, so too was the care of the homestead's domesticated animals – and cows and goats, of course, not to mention children, need attention on a daily basis. Such tasks induced a different approach to work, a different temper.

As Professor L. Milev of Moscow University has argued, the low level of surplus encouraged the emerging elite to control wider areas and ever more farmers, in order to increase their income. This helps to explain the tendency of the Russian state to expand, or so it has been claimed. Moreover the fact that farmers had little incentive to work harder to produce a surplus without compulsion, or the threat of it, was at the root of the violent tendency in Russian life, the autocratic nature of Russian governments.[13] But there was another source of Russian violence, deriving from defence needs. At first the northern forest zone had been too thinly peopled to promote much competition between groups of settlers. Nor had there been much risk of attack by outsiders in the zone of wooded steppe to the south in the area of modern Ukraine, around the upper and middle reaches of the river Dnieper and its tributaries, which was the region of densest proto-Russian settlement 3,000 years ago. But the open steppe further to the south could be dangerous. This was where groups of nomads – incomers from the Caucasus and Central Asia – grazed their horses and their herds. Their interests were different from those of the agricultural settlers. Not only did they chase would-be colonizers of the open steppe off their grazing lands, they encroached on their areas of settlement.

The first such nomadic group we know of arrived about 1000 BCE. These were the Cimmerians, who figure in the *Odyssey* and who are described by the Greek historians Herodotus and Strabo. The Cimmerians spoke an Iranian language; they swept over the whole region, from the northern Caucasus to the Carpathians, and extended their conquests into Thrace and Asia Minor. King Midas of Phrygia was evidently one of their victims. Archaeologists have concluded that for four centuries, until about 600 BCE, the agriculturalists in Ukraine traded food for Cimmerian copper and bronze goods, but otherwise kept themselves at a respectful distance.[14]

The Cimmerians fell victims to another aggressive people from Asia: the Scythians. The Scythians ranged even further afield than the Cimmerians had done, becoming a menace in the Middle East as far away as Egypt. They were to brush with both Darius and Alexander the Great, and with Mithridates, king of Pontus, and they were to influence the Slavs of what is now Ukraine. Archaeologists tell us that the Scythians were warlike, loved horses, imported goods from the ancient Greeks, and employed Slavs who provided them with food. These, presumably, are the

Scythian husbandmen to whom Herodotus refers to in his Book 4.[15] Later still the Sarmatians arrived, and both they and the Scythians left a mark on the imagination of the Slavs. Some latter-day Russians thought that the Scythians represented the quintessence of their supposedly Asian heritage, and the Polish gentry of the seventeenth century imagined the Sarmatians to personify the noble class, and even claimed to be descended from them.

As we shall see, other predatory peoples were to storm into the area from Asia later, but we may suppose that the Cimmerians' occupation of the open steppe stimulated agriculture in the forest steppe just to the north. Certainly it was on the forest steppe that plough technology, as well as a fallow system of land use, was developed – rather than in the forest zone or the open steppe. More than one kind of implement was devised. Some were fitted with iron parts which could cut through the tangled root systems in the comparatively shallow soils which predominated in the cultivable areas north of the Black Earth zone. The black earth itself is among the most productive soils on the planet and, once tamed for cultivation, promotes fast population growth and social development. However, the land there was heavy to work, and called for something more effective than a human-powered scratch-plough, which would have to be pushed over a field not once but several times. The more effective ploughs had the disadvantage of being heavier and difficult to propel, although in time ways were to be found to harness oxen or horses to pull them.[16]

Archaeologists have unearthed evidence of homes and artefacts more advanced than those found on the earlier site at Talyanky, and with iron and copper objects as well as pottery. These settlements consisted of typically fifteen or twenty dwellings, each equipped with a kitchen and living room, in which a variety of goods has been found – axes, sickles, fish-hooks, needles, jewellery and, not least, weapons: axe, spear and arrow heads, and daggers. Some of the artefacts had been made elsewhere. From this, archaeologists have deduced that the inhabitants had trading contacts not only with peoples to the north, where some of the jewellery came from, but also with the Urals, which was a source of iron ore, and towards the Caucasus and Crimea across the treeless prairies where feather grass and wormwood grew.

Despite these developments, and despite increasing sophistication in both their material life and their social organization, the proto-Russians could not yet be said to possess a civilization. Civilization was a preserve of warmer climes, where productivity was greater, population denser, and society more complex. So, in examining the development of what was to become Russian civilization and in enumerating the causes, the most prominent place must be accorded to global warming.

Some 900 years before the Christian era, average temperatures began to rise again. So did the rainfall (or snowfall). This trend, which culminated in what is known as the 'little climatic optimum', was to continue with only minor interruptions for over 2,000 years. It created the conditions in which the Roman Empire was to develop; it also laid the foundations of Europe's medieval glory. Out of warmth grew riches. Some pale reflection of such prosperity was seen even in the less-favoured peripheries, and these provided the backdrop for developments among the east Slavs. In particular they prompted the development of more complex settlement patterns and of northward expansion into the forest zone.

Rather than simply counting village settlements consisting of anything from four households to twenty, archaeologists consider the development in this period of clusters of five to fifteen villages spaced between 12 and 18 miles apart to be significant. These clusters, they tell us, suggest some form of tribal organization. Furthermore, most of the larger villages provided a social focus of some kind, whether a smithy to supply precious iron tools or fittings, a shrine for an idol, or simply fortifications which could provide shelter to tribal members under attack. As time passed, these more important villages were more often sited at the confluence of rivers and were progressively better fortified, with earthworks and wooden palings. These protected settlements represent the birth of towns, which were essentially tribal headquarters – places from which a leader and his aides would organize defences, the collection of food surpluses and, if and when the volume of trade warranted it, the collection of duties too.[17]

By the eighth century CE this primitive Russia had been 'discovered' by outsiders, and it was they who first put the Russians on the map. Trade had prompted the interest. This Russia was rich in honey, wax and tallow, for which there was growing demand. It was also a region where furs could be had cheaply – and, which were still more valuable, slaves. A quickening commercial tempo helps to explain coin hoards that have been found, and that many of these comprised Islamic silver coins dating from the seventh century testifies to the fact that Russia was already becoming a commercial staging post between the Orient and western Europe. They are found in their greatest concentrations in the regions of the upper reaches of the rivers Don and Dnieper and along the southern and western coasts of the Baltic, but there were also impressive concentrations in what is now central Russia.[18]

At the same time, the pace of forest colonization from the south quickened, aided by the development around the year 800 of the hardy bread grain which was to become Russia's staple, the foundation of the healthy Russian diet and of its remarkable cuisine – winter rye, a grain which has generated a great deal of Russian lore.[19] This fast spread of population to the north suggests that population was outrunning food production, and the first signs appear suggesting that cities and even states were in the process of formation.

The first evidence of social associations larger than the tribe points to tribal unions. The names of some of these have reached us thanks to the earliest Greek and Roman sources on eastern Europe. Among these were the Krivichie tribes of what is now west Russia; the Slovenie and the Viatichi to the north and east of them respectively; and the Derevlians (or 'old settlers'). The Severiane and the Poliane lived in the territory we now know as Ukraine, the last-mentioned in the neighbourhood of what was to become its chief city, Kiev. These tribes all shared the same Slavonic language. Nevertheless, they did not constitute a state, even though centuries later their descendants were to speak differentiated, albeit similar, languages and populate three different nation states: Ukraine and Belarus, as well as Russia. Nor were the tribes to remain settled in the same areas. Archaeologists have traced significant movements. The Slovenie moved east and south in the late 800s, while some northward movement by the southern tribes has been noted.[20]

Cities in Russia owed their origins to two very different developments. On the one hand there was the headquarters of the super-chief, head of a tribal confederation, its organizer, defender and (insofar as he extracted income from it) oppressor too. This sort of city was a military and administrative centre which acted as a magnet for people simply because men who took decisions and exercised power were to be found there. The other kind of city was in origin a commercial centre, a defensible point along a route which joined two or more emporia. This helps to explain the different settlement pattern in northern Russia, where strongholds were established without a populated hinterland capable of supporting them, by contrast to Russian settlement in the south.

Archaeologists argue that strongholds – most of them positioned by important river crossings and often on a periphery of any settled region in order to control trade routes and tax the value passing through – preceded settlements in northern Russia. But the distinction soon became theoretical rather than practical, because the surplus goods the super-chiefs had to sell attracted merchants, and the commercial centres needed both craftsmen and protection. The functions of the city-in the-making soon became mixed. And the creation of cities and the advent of merchants operating over long distances implied the end of isolated, tribal life. It also indicated some exposure to outside influences, heralding a new kind of life with a potential for civilization. However, it also implied the loss of that self-contained, self-supporting realm of blood-related family rooted in a place (the mythic realm of which all nationalists dream), and threatened the old beliefs associated with the old ways of life.

Russia's famous store of fairy tales includes some that date from ancient times, and these provide our only evidence of the spiritual world of the Russians before it was influenced by outside agencies, including Christianity. Unfortunately, the provenance of these traditions is inextricably bound up with the early history of the Christian Church in Russia, which was intent on eradicating them and the magic beliefs many of them reflected. Some dimly reflect real historical heroes and events and must be relatively late inventions, but others are more ancient, and it is reasonable to infer that some, at least, have pre-Christian origins. Such tales reflect the natural world the early Russians inhabited. They stress the importance of water to life and death to a greater extent than the folklore of other peoples, and purport to explain such mysteries as the placid river which hides dangerous rapids, the sudden, death-dealing storm, the relative who becomes a burden or who turns nasty (as Little Red Riding Hood's nice grandmama turns into an all-devouring wolf).

In doing so they created a magic realm for children and for us, conjuring up a world of forest sprites which appear as wolves, bears or even whirlwinds; of girls called *rusalki*, water-spirits that float on streams or lakes decked out in wreaths and garlands like live Ophelias; of tree- and spring-spirits; of wild animals which talk, and water-demons who are the spirits of people who died by drowning and who, by beckoning watchers on the bank, cause more young men to drown. And, the most powerful and fundamental of them all, Perun the Thunder God, bringer of rain, fertility and hence prosperity.[21]

This magic world of early Russia was not only to inspire literature and the theatre; it also helped form the Russian national character itself. However charmingly presented, these tales reflect an essential realism rooted in the land of Russia and in all the peculiarities of that land. They acknowledge both nature's bounty and the price in hard labour and risk that nature often demanded for it. They recognize the dangerous streaks of unpredictability both in weather and in humankind; and they teach the importance of going with nature, not against it.

But though the original, isolated, magic Russia was to leave its imprint on the people, it was not to survive the impact of the outside world. As those caches of Islamic coins demonstrate, the outside world had discovered Russia even as early as the 600s. From then on commercial pressures were to play an important role in moulding Russia's development. And the first such important influence seems to have been the Khazars.

Starting in the seventh to eighth century, the Khazars formed a commercial state. With their capital first at Itil on the Volga (not far from the present-day city of Tsaritsyn, once Stalingrad), and later at Sarkel on the river Don, Khazar warriors commanded all the routes between Russia, Central Asia, Persia and the eastern Mediterranean. They both taxed and protected all the trade that passed through. In this period the Roman Empire was in decline, the Arab Empire on the rise. At the same time Russia was becoming more important as a European trade route, now that the Mediterranean was no longer the safe Roman lake it had been. The Khazars found themselves poised between two worlds aside from the pagan Russians – the world of Christendom and the world of Islam. The two worlds were locked in combat, yet Khazar prosperity depended on trade with both. In order, therefore, to preserve their ideological integrity and discourage missionaries from both Christian Byzantium and the Muslim Caliphate (Ummayad and later Abbasid), the Khazar elite chose to become Jews. The fact that Jewish traders were among the most enterprising and well connected in the wider commercial world was another reason for this apparently eccentric decision. And the decision proved sound.

The Khazars made subjects of the Russian tribal confederations known as the Poliane, Severiane and Krivichie, requiring each household to pay them a silver coin and a squirrel pelt each year. They exacted tolls on Russian traders passing through their territory, developed their own system of weights and measures, minted their own coins, and provided other models that were to serve the first Russian state (or kaganate). Thanks to Khazar influence and protection, Russian merchants were soon ranging as far afield as Baghdad. A contemporary Arab writer, Ibn Khurdadhbih, reported in a geographical handbook for merchants he wrote around the 840s that Russians were taking black-fox pelts, beaver furs and swords from the north lands to the Black Sea, paying tolls there to Byzantium. They also went through Sarkel in Khazar territory to the Caspian, and sometimes they brought their goods thence 'by camel . . . to Baghdad, where Slavic eunuchs serve as interpreters for them'.[22] But these Russian traders in the south brought with them swords that had been forged in the north by a quite different people, the Vikings.

★

The Vikings – sometimes referred to as Varangians or Norsemen – acted as a commercial catalyst for the Russian tribes in the north just as the Khazars did for those in the south. They lived by trade and plunder. Active in the Baltic, they had come into contact with the Finns and Slavs of north-west Russia. From them they learned about the river routes to other Slav communities far to the south and to the Khazars' territory beyond. Through forays into the Mediterranean they already knew that the Khazars held the gateway to the riches of both the Orient and the Mediterranean world. It was in order to capture some of this trade that they decided to build a base at Ladoga, and then another close to what was to become the city of Novgorod.

This was a bleak region with very poor soil and very sparse settlement, inhabited by Finno-Ugrian fishermen, themselves not very long established, and by a few Russians who had come in later. It was here that the classic trading city was developed. The Vikings who made a base at the site now known as Old Ladoga in the 750s were trader-warriors dealing in furs, beads and blood. They built a fort there to protect themselves, their craftsmen and their wares. Archaeologists who have carefully investigated the remains of the settlement have found and dated wickerwork walls and conclude that the building of such a fort required labour in the form of slaves. The Vikings either brought these with them or found them locally. But if there was an initial labour shortage, it did not last long.

Once the fort was in existence people came from afar to marvel and to sell fish or other food or a few pelts gathered in the forests, and so an emporium of sorts arose, which became something of a magnet for Slavs migrating from the south.[23] But the Viking settlers were interested in more than petty local trade. Their eyes were set on the long-distance trade in more valuable commodities – honey, weapons and above all slaves to trade in Byzantine markets for the silks, spices and precious stone of the Orient. It is likely that, in time, traders came from as far afield as the Caucasus and Caspian.

The archaeologists' finds are puzzling, because they comprise the remains of not one settlement but two. Like the first scraps of information found in the Latin and Arabic sources of the period, these have been seized on by scholars, who like few things better than a good dispute. The result has been a sizeable literature on the origins of towns in Russia, and an impressive variety of theories. Did towns develop from tribal centres or from fortified strong-points? Or were they created from scratch because of a sudden need? Were they formed by nobles, or by traders and artisans? The consensus seems to be that most of these elements played a part. Still, the fact that Novgorod boasted two such settlements within a mile or so of each other by the river Volkhov is intriguing, and excavations at Kiev and Smolensk have revealed that these cities also grew from two distinct but associated settlements. Perhaps the two settlements had different functions. At any rate 'Riurik's town' or hill settlement (*gorodishche* in Russian, or *holmgarthr* in Scandinavian), sited close to the point where the river Volkhov flows out of Lake Ilmen, was much the more important of the two. Twenty-five acres in area, Riurik's town was the more easily defensible site and stood clear of the spring floodwaters (which persuaded an Arab visitor that it was in fact an island in the river).[24]

If the cities of the Russian south originated as tribal headquarters and agricultural centres, the city of Novgorod owed its origins to trade and was associated with the Vikings. The Vikings had been trained in a hard school. They knew that they must expand their trade, their settlements and their conquests or perish. And they represented the commercial world at its most ruthless and greedy. 'Even the man who has only modest wealth,' remarked the tenth-century Arab writer Ibn Rusta, 'is . . . envied by his brother, who would not hesitate to do away with him in order to steal it.'[25] Their intelligence system was well developed. They had learned of the Khazars and of the Russians who were taking their cue as traders from them. And they had soon found their way to both.

Since their natural element was water, they searched for – and found – water routes to where they wanted to go. Since they now wanted to cross the great land mass of Russia, they followed the rivers. Their first important settlement in Russia, at what was to become known as Novgorod, provided access to the river Volkhov, and this eventually gave them access to other rivers. Local knowledge and information extracted from men who had made the journey, or part of it, served as their maps. They also knew how to build the boats they needed – boats capable of negotiating shoals and rapids, or of construction light enough to be hauled on to the shore and dragged around the obstacle or over portages, those hopefully short stretches of land which separated the headwaters of one river from another that flowed in a different direction.

At first such journeys tended to be slow and hazardous, but, as the commercial tempo picked up and the traffic became somewhat heavier, settlements appeared at the more popular landing points; people offered the venturers food, and sold them their services as guides, carriers and hauliers. By such means a trading system was established, and the country began to be opened up to the international commerce of the day. The most important axis was between Kiev and Novgorod. According to legend, the first Vikings to rule there were the adventurers Askold and Dir, though they were soon dispatched by local Russians. In fact co-operation, not conflict, was to be the mark of Viking–Russian relations. Mutual interest and dependence evidently outweighed natural caution and resentment of outsiders. The Vikings were to leave their imprint on Russia. Yet, rather than replacing or absorbing the Russian elites, within a very few generations they themselves were to be absorbed by them. Perhaps the Russians were already developing the capacity to control and integrate peoples of different language and culture which was to help them build empires in later ages.

The Russians themselves had already acquired definition. Fundamentally European in their genetic structure, they had been shaped by climatic and ecological conditions in their wooded steppe and forest habitat. These conditions helped to feed the Russian imagination and religious sensibility, and the dependence on agriculture in seasonally demanding, harsh conditions also contributed to the Russians' distinctive 'national' profile.[26]

By the ninth century, however, they had encountered, and begun to intermarry with, Finns and Balts as well as Vikings in the north-west; with Chuds and Cheremis (or Maris) in the north-east; and in the south with Khazars and a variety of other incomers from the Caucasus and the steppes of Central Asia. These circumstances seem to have encouraged an open-mindedness about strangers and a surprising absence of xenophobia compared to other European peoples (the Russians' latter-day prejudice against blacks constitutes a glaring exception). A readiness to accept strangers into one's ranks was to remain characteristic of them. In this respect Russian expansionism was to differ from that of the English, Dutch or pre-revolutionary French, and this attitude was to give Russia a certain advantage in empire-building. However, an empire presupposes a state, and a state had yet to be constructed.

This earliest Russia is visible only darkly. Our history so far has been a reconstruction by inference from disciplines other than history. The proto-Russians who inhabited the world we have described left no records that survived. In time they were to be encountered by other peoples, who did leave accounts of them, though these were scrappy at first, mostly based on hearsay, and often inconsistent with more reliable evidence.

Then, suddenly, in the ninth century, a Russian state burst on to the historical stage. Its emergence was due to a symbiosis of the agricultural elites who controlled the tribal confederations and the Viking traders from the north, but a third factor was to be of immense importance: Constantinople, capital of the later Roman Empire and the greatest city in the world. The

Vikings had established themselves in Russia partly in order to gain better access than they already had to Constantinople and its riches. And when these two elements – the Vikings and Constantinople – came into contact, an electric charge was created which was to shake historical Russia into existence.

2

The First Russian State

FROM THE NINTH CENTURY onward written sources on Russia and the Russians become more plentiful. They come mostly from Imperial Constantinople, which, despite the rise of the Arabs and the appearance of a rival emperor, Charlemagne, in the West, was still the great power of eastern Europe and Asia Minor. But Icelandic sagas, the writings of Arab and Jewish merchants, and the first Russian chronicle also yield information. Together they allow us to reconstruct the process by which Russians became Christian (a term most of their descendants used to describe themselves a thousand years later) and the political implications of their conversion. They also describe the people who helped construct the first Russian state – the shrewd and vengeful widow Olga; Vladimir the sainted slave trader; the vain, resentful Sviatoslav; and Iaroslav the Wise.

The first Russian state – often referred as Kievan Rus – was essentially a commercial undertaking. It developed out of the mutual needs of Russians in the neighbourhood of what became the city of Novgorod and a band of Vikings in search of employment and plunder. The traders of Novgorod had been prospering and the population of their settlements had been growing, so a bigger food supply had to be assured. Since the soil of the area was poor, however, they had to take control of food producers over a large enough area to ensure an adequate supply. They also needed to protect their settlements and their growing commercial interests from predators. It made sense, then, to retain the services of a band of Viking military specialists.[1] From such a beginning, it seems, these Vikings in conjunction with the local Russian elite groups soon gained control of the transcontinental trade between Scandinavia, Constantinople (capital of the Roman Empire now that Rome itself had fallen to the barbarians) and the Orient.

Until the middle of the ninth century their operations were confined to the northern part of the complex network of rivers that crossed the vast expanses of Russia. The southern part, already discovered by Arab traders in the seventh century, was controlled by the Khazars, a Turkic-speaking people whose territory centred on the Volga estuary and the northern

Caucasus and whose rulers were to convert to Judaism in the 860s.[2] Yet emergent Russia was not fated to be part of a Jewish empire. It was the Vikings who eventually gained control of the long river route with all its portages, and who, intermarrying with women of the Russian tribes with whom they dealt, were to become rulers of the Russian lands.

Their first, legendary, leader was a Jutlander called Riurik. He had made a reputation raiding in western Europe, including the British Isles, but then decided to turn east to seek his fortune. Around 856 he and his followers established a base at Ladoga in northern Russia. Subsequently, however, he decided that the area of Novgorod (which the Vikings knew as Holmgarthr) was better situated, and so he built a fort there. Novgorod was to be the key access point to the Russian river route for traders coming from the west. But, as these Vikings probably already knew, Kiev was the key point in the south. It had access to the Dnieper river system, which led to the most populous areas of Russia at that time. Kiev was ruled by the Khazars, but in 858 a Viking war band led by Askold and Dir took command of it. The ambition of these two adventurers soon extended further, and two years later, accompanied by a large force of Russians, they raided Constantinople. The city was heir to the imperial as well as the newer Christian traditions. Its language was now Greek rather than Latin, and since it is commonly referred to nowadays as the Byzantine Empire that is what we shall call it.

The raid of 860 was the first known encounter between Constantinople and the Rus. We do not know precisely who organized it and how, but a book written by the emperor Constantine VII nearly a century later provides evidence about a Rus trading expedition. His account, intended as a brief for his heir, vividly describes the preparations required and the perils of the route. The essential vessel for the enterprise was a dugout ship (*monolyxa* in Greek) fashioned out of a tree trunk. The trees would have been cut in the forest zone of central Russia during the preceding winter, then dried out and launched into the lakes which ran into the river Dnieper when the ice melted. They would then be ribbed, widened with side-planks, and taken down to Kiev to be sold to the expedition's organizers, who saw to their fitting out with rowlocks, oars and tackle. In June they would have moved off from Kiev to a gathering point downsteam. Then, when all the boats and men were ready, the expedition set out.

Danger threatened almost at once, at the first of the infamous Dnieper rapids, a defile as narrow, Constantine tells us, 'as the polo ground' in Constantinople, full of high rocks. 'Against these . . . comes the water and wells up and dashes over the other side, with a mighty and terrific din.' Here there was no alternative but to put into the shore and disembark most of the men with their slaves in their chains. The remaining men then negotiated the rapids, some with punt-poles, while others, ranged round each boat, felt for hidden rocks with their bare feet, and walked the vessel through. Having negotiated this set of rapids, six more had to be negotiated. The third set was so dangerous that the boats had to be taken out of the water entirely and dragged or carried a distance of 6 miles overland. The fourth set had to be skirted in a similar manner. And from this point the expedition had to watch out for raiding parties from the fierce Pecheneg people, who would come in from the steppe on the prowl for booty.

The most dangerous point of all was a wide ford used by merchants of Kherson to access a river island with a huge oak tree. This was the Pechenegs' favourite ambush point. So, on reaching the island, members of the expedition would leave food to propitiate their gods and kill some cocks as sacrifices. Four days later they would have reached an island in the Black Sea where they would fit out the boats with the masts, sails, ropes and tackle they had brought with them, for from that point on sail-power could supplement rowing.[3] Now at last they were ready.

The great Rus – Viking raid on Constantinople in 860 was a masterpiece of the genre. Two hundred boats and up to 8,000 men took part. They struck with savagery as well as in force, and they achieved complete surprise. 'The unexpectedness of the attack,' wrote a distinguished eyewitness, 'its strange swiftness, the inhumanity of the barbarous tribe, the harshness of its manners and the savagery of its character proclaim the blow to have been discharged like a thunderbolt from God.' The civilized inhabitants of the city were pious Christians, and so they saw the Viking attack as a punishment for their sins. And it was shaming as well as surprising to have been hurt by unknowns – by 'an obscure people, a people of no account, a people ranked as slaves'.[4] In this way, the Rus leaped to the front of the political stage and into the history books. Then they disappeared from it just as suddenly as they had arrived.

Recovering from the surprise, the government took action to forestall any similar attempt. Imperial diplomats were dispatched to the Khazars. Presumably it was assumed that these Rus were subject to them. It is not clear if this was the case or not, though Vikings did contract themselves out as mercenaries as well as trading and plundering on their own account. Nor do we know if Khazar intervention had anything to do with it but in 882, nine years after Riurik's death, his grandson, Oleg, gathered and took his war bands south against Askold and Dir and killed the two 'renegades', as they were to be called henceforth.[5] We cannot be sure that these 'renegades' were the same people as those who had taken possession of Kiev in 858, but we can infer that the victory of 882 secured Oleg effective control of the entire commercial network from the Baltic to the Black Sea, and since he now had access to Kiev, over which the Khazars still claimed sovereignty, he was able to operate over much more extensive territory than formerly, collecting honey, furs and slaves to trade with Constantinople, albeit under Khazar tutelage.

From the later 800s Rus were selling furs, especially black fox and beaver, swords and slaves to distant Baghdad. Using the Volga route to the Caspian Sea, they negotiated their way past the Khazar customs posts or else traded their merchandise there for resale to the realm of the Caliph. They brought back beads and oriental cloths, double-headed axes, buttons, and coins – chiefly dirhams, the currency of the caliphs of Baghdad, which Russian merchants, lacking a coinage of their own, were to adopt. Over the next fifty years or so shortage of labour and a surplus of cash generated a steady demand for slaves, especially female slaves, from both the Caliphate and the Byzantine Empire, which the Rus were happy to meet. They were not alone however. Chains and neck shackles have been found in archaeological digs along all the more important Mediterranean and European routes. Not only Constantinople but papal Rome had a thriving slave market, and Spain was a major supplier as well as Rus.[6]

Then the Russians fell out with the Khazars who claimed lordship over them. Constantinople sided with the Khazars, but when Oleg led a succesful Rus' assault on the city in 907 it thought again. The upshot was an agreement of 911, by which the Emperor agreed to pay a money tribute both to those Rus who took part in the expedition and to the princes who had sent them. Oleg also obtained permission for Rus merchants to stay for up to six months at a house, or *fondaco*, set aside for them at the St Mamas quarter of Constantinople, and won agreement that they would be fed at the imperial expense when they visited the city. Yet the Khazars, who had married into the local Rus elite, still reigned as kagans of Kievan Rus, and they were to keep control of Kiev itself till about 930.[7]

The exact nature of Oleg's relationship with them in this period is not yet clear. He may have been their partner or their tributary, but whatever the relationship it must have been tense. And so long as the situation held it seems that many unfortunate tribesmen had to pay tribute both to the Rus and to the Khazars. Eventually, however, Oleg's son Igor was to displace his former overlords and rule Kiev as kagan.

Igor proved to be no less rapacious than his forebears and predecessors. In 914 he decided to increase the tribute he demanded of the Rus tribes known as Derevlians. Thirty years later he raised it again – only this time the Derevlians resisted. As Russia's first chronicle recalled, Igor

> attacked the Derevlians in search of tribute, and to the old tribute he added a new tribute and collected it by violence from the people . . . On his way home . . . he said to his followers, 'Take the tribute home. I shall turn back and collect more.' . . . Hearing of his return the Derevlians consulted with Mal, their prince, saying 'If a wolf comes among sheep it will take the whole flock one by one, unless it is killed . . . If we do not kill [Igor] now, he will destroy us all.[8]

And so they killed him.

But the Derevlians had not reckoned with Igor's widow, Olga. Prince Mal offered to marry her, but Olga refused, determined to take personal charge, to rule on behalf of Sviatoslav her baby son, and to take vengeance on the Derevlians. A call went out to her warriors, and they were soon moving against Mal's stronghold, Ikorosan, about 100 miles upstream from Kiev. They burned the place and rounded up the Derevlian leaders. The vengeance Olga exacted was a model of how to discourage resistance. She had some of them tortured, slaughtered many, and enslaved the rest.

Yet this same fierce, empowered Olga is now revered as a saint, for she became a Christian as well as an historical figure of the first importance.[9] Her conversion was prompted by political calculation as well as by spiritual yearning, however. She proved a good and energetic organizer, doing away with the anarchic, ad-hoc, ways of raising taxes which had provoked the Derevlians. She regularized the amount of tribute to be paid – whether in honey, furs or feathers – and journeyed extensively along the main tributaries of the Dnieper, seeing that her order was imposed on the inhabitants. She also visited Novgorod, where she set up an administrative centre. Her reforms have been represented as marking a transition from the ways of a robber economy to a regime based on norms. If so, they were a significant contribution to state-building.[10]

The Viking elite were fast losing their Nordic identity as they intermarried with their Rus tributaries. In any case, they were too few to build a state alone. They needed local knowledge and men to organize an economy, to gather in food and marketable goods like honey, furs and slaves on a systematic basis. The indigenous chiefs organized the provision of these things for them. But, just as the Vikings needed the chiefs, the chiefs needed them – for their military prowess and their knowledge of the wider world. The first Russian state was founded on the interdependence of a group of sea-going colonizers and tribes of Slavonic-speakers who used the rivers as avenues for colonization. Intermarriage cemented the alliance and extended the ruling family. At the same time the Scandinavian element was fast being absorbed linguistically and culturally into the Slavonic-speaking mass, though characteristic Scandinavian burial mounds have been found in central Russia from up to a century after Vikings and Slavs established their alliance.[11]

In 941 Prince Igor, son of Olga, mounted another large-scale raid on Constantinople. Only this time the previous successes were not to be repeated. The imperial forces were prepared, and were able to exploit their superior technology – ships equipped with rams, grappling chains and a devastating secret weapon known as 'Greek fire', an incendiary device containing naphtha, one form of which ignited on contact with water. Scholars do not yet know how it was launched, but it could be extremely effective. Invented in the late 600s, Greek fire had helped save much of the Empire from the Arabs. Had the Emperor been able to deploy it in 860 or against Oleg in 907, the city might have been spared the depredations of the Viking-led Russians. Presumably sheer surprise or unfavourable weather or water conditions prevented its use. But now the weapon was deployed with devastating effect. A graphic account written by a Western envoy about a century afterwards reflects the memory of the great victory:

> Having become surrounded by the Rus', the Greeks [that is, the subjects of the Emperor] hurled their fire all around them. When the Rus' saw this, they at once threw themselves from their ships into the sea, choosing to be drowned by the waves rather than cremated by the fire. Some, weighed down by their breastplates and helmets . . . sank to the bottom . . . Others were burned as they swam on the waves.

No one could escape except by sailing into the shallow inshore waters where the deep-draughted imperial ships could not follow.[12]

An apparently earlier source, a Viking saga, records the same traumatic event from the raiders' point of view, and with some convincing detail. It tells, for example, of a brass tube from which a great spark flew to reduce one of the ships of its pagan hero Yngvar to ashes within seconds. This story, however, was to be changed under Christian influence to put Yngvar on the right side and cast the Emperor as a villainous creature. In this version Greek fire assumes the form of Jakulus, a terrifying flying dragon which spits venom, to which Yngvar has an antidote: arrows bearing 'consecrated flame'.[13]

Byzantine diplomats eventually persuaded Igor/Yngvar and the Rus that they could gain more from negotiation and trade than from naked force. Certainly, by the time the Emperor Constantine VII wrote his account of the Russians in the middle of the tenth century a regular commercial relationship had been established between them. Cargoes of slaves would be brought in for sale in Constantinople's market, and, once their summer's venturing was over, the Russian traders would return to Kiev until November, when they would disperse in various directions upstream to the regions they had come from.

> The severe manner of life of these same Russians in winter-time is as follows. When the month of November begins, their chiefs together with all the Russians [that is, the Vikings and the Russian tribal chiefs associated with them] go off on . . . [their] 'rounds', that is to the Slavonic regions of the Vervians and Drugovichians and Krivichians and Serverians and the rest of the Slavs who pay . . . [them] tribute. There they are maintained throughout the winter, but then once more, starting in the month of April, when the ice on the Dnieper river melts, they come back to Kiev . . .[14]

And the cycle would begin again.

The organizational centre had moved from Novgorod to Kiev. Even so the frontiers were too stretched and the strategic points too scattered for one man to control the entire operation effectively.[15] Kings of England would take their courts on tour round their domains, but in Russia this was impracticable – the distances too great, the climate too difficult. To overcome this difficulty, the first Russian state devised a working system more like a family business. Riurik's successors ruled in Kiev, their heirs apparent in Novgorod, while younger brothers and other close relatives ruled centres like Smolensk or Chernigov, according to their seniority and the town's relative importance. Family could be trusted, and the system (often termed 'apanage') had the advantage of giving future rulers experience of governing an important region before acceding to the top position. However, though the system had advantages in co-ordinating commercial operations on a basis of trust, it had disadvantages in respect of the integrity of a state. In Russia the system was to break down in the twelfth century, largely, as we shall see, because of its inherent weaknesses. This has led some historians to argue that Kievan Rus was not a state at all.[16]

However, the subjects of Kievan Rus paid taxes, they were defended from outside enemies, and they were subject to common laws. These characteristics qualify Kievan Rus as no less a state than some other imperfect political structures of that age. The particular problem of Kievan Rus was that, though imperial in territorial extent, it lacked appropriate imperial institutions. But it soon began to import models and ideals to remedy these deficiencies. The source was the city of Constantinople, and one of the chief carriers of this late Roman influence to Russia was the same Princess Olga who had massacred the Derevlian elite and imposed a semblance of administrative order on the Rus.

Olga travelled to Constantinople in 955 or 957 (the sources differ on the date), and the imperial authorities there, impressed with Russia's potential, laid down a red carpet for her. She was taken to view the many wonders of the imperial city – the three fortified walls which guarded it; the great cistern which could supply the large population with water in the event of a long siege; the hippodrome, which was used for imperial ceremonies as well as for games and racing. The city's central market sold every imaginable commodity from every corner of the world. This scene of plenty was presided over by a great column surmounted by the gilded head of the city's founder, the first Christian emperor, Constantine I. The city's fine marble buildings and statues, wonderfully carved, and the extraordinary variety of peoples and dress amazed all who saw them for the first time. But only special guests entered the imperial palace. Olga was so privileged.

Inside the palace, plume-helmeted guardsmen punctuated the spaces, and there were astonishing things to see: clockwork metal songbirds that sang like real birds; a pair of gilded lions which rolled their eyes and roared; a throne harnessed to hydraulic power which could lift the Emperor to the ceiling of his audience chamber, making him appear godlike to people beneath. The court protocol was elaborate, with much pomp and many formalities. Some 400 years earlier the wife of the Emperor Justinian – Theodora – had been both influential and visible, but subsequently the Christian Church had whittled away much of the women's former privileges and freedom. As a result, women were less visible and less powerful than they had once been – even well-regarded women whom the Emperor was wooing. Empresses were still important, but their formal engagements proceeded for the most part separately from those of the men. And so Olga was entertained by the Empress to a separate dinner, though held at the same time as the Emperor's, and only met the Emperor informally, when he visited the Empress and the imperial children in their quarters.

But the grandeur and exotic unfamiliarity of court life could hardly have been lost on Olga. Even informal meals would be taken at a golden table, though diners reclined on couches in the old Roman style. The food served was wonderfully different. The cooking – based on olive oil – featured not only familiar fish, meats and fowl, mushrooms, apples and honey, but unfamiliar aubergines, figs and pomegranates, anchovies and calamari. Ingredients were transformed by unfamiliar spices, wine marinades, exotic stuffings and amazing creations of filo pastry. And Olga would have learned to cope with small unfamiliar eating implements made of ivory and precious metal rather than tearing the meats placed before her with her fingers or her teeth.[17]

Most impressive of all, though, was the Church of the Holy Wisdom, or Santa Sophia. Inside this splendid pile with its immense dome, built by Justinian four centuries or so before, were mosaic portraits of emperors, saints and archangels attending the figure of Jesus and, high above this, a magisterial depiction of God the Father. Through this huge space, crowded with worshippers, came black-cowled deacons swinging censers of pungent incense. Priests and bishops in richly patterned vestments followed – and then choirs struck up, echoing each other's ethereal music from all directions. Like so many other newcomers to the experience, even the hard-headed Olga must have wondered for some moments whether she was in heaven or on earth.[18]

The chronicles present Olga as a pious candidate for sainthood. Yet, amazed though she must have been by the unimaginable wealth and strange beauty of it all, her actions suggest that she remained a calculating, political woman. To understand the Russians' conversion one must discount the tales about Olga's piety and recognize the deeply political nature of her choice. She knew the Byzantine Church had competitors, and she was to use the German Church as a lever to get what she wanted. She well understood the implications conversion would have for Russian princely power. She learned that the Christian Church, administered by the Patriarch of Constantinople (who also received her), worked 'in symphony' with the emperor and helped the secular authorities in many ways – as spiritual arm, moral authority, provider of social services, and mobilizer of the Christian populations. She also observed the effectiveness of Christianity in holding the people in thrall.

Olga is reckoned to have become a Christian before going to Constantinople, indeed to have had a priest in her retinue when she went. Nevertheless, she decided to be baptized there again, this time in a more political way, with the Emperor himself serving as her godfather at a carefully orchestrated ceremony which gave her a new name: Helen. Helen had been the mother of the first Christian emperor, Constantine the Great, so an analogy was suggested: Olga/Helen as mother of a new Russian state. And the memory of Olga was later to suggest a link between ancient Rome and the no less extensive Russian Empire of the future.

However, Olga had gone to Constantinople to negotiate better trading terms, and in this she was evidently disappointed, because shortly after her return to Kiev she sent an embassy to the German king, Otto I, asking him to send her a bishop and priests. She knew very well that, though Christendom was formally united, there were three competing Christian organizations, each with its own traditions, and that the German Church, though under the Pope, was effectively owned by the prince who had power of ecclesiastical appointments. Such power was an attractive option, but Olga used her flirtation with the Germans as a warning to Byzantium. When the Emperor became more accommodating, the German bishop was sent away.[19]

Olga's visit inspired a desire to re-create in her own land some of the wonders she had seen. It also encouraged an expansion of Byzantine missionary activity among the Russians, and established a conduit through which cultural influences began to flow. Byzantine designs and Byzantine artisans penetrated Russia in increasing numbers, and some Russians even began to hanker after literacy – for missionaries had invented an alphabet to represent the sounds that Slavonic-speaking peoples made when they spoke. Invented for the Balkan Slavs, it was to serve the Russians equally well, for, as Constantine VII recorded, all Slavs, whether in the east, west or south, spoke the same language at that time.

Yet Olga/Helen's personal commitment to Christianity did not imply the Christianization of Russia. The opposition was far too strong for that. Most Rus were addicted to their own gods – gods who represented the forces of nature. Christianity, with its faith in the Son of God, who suffered to save the whole community and was resurrected every year, had undoubted attractions. But it could not easily replace the familiar sprites that had power over woods and streams. And was the Christian god as powerful as, say, Perun, the god of thunder, bringer of rain and of prosperity, by whom Russians swore their most solemn oaths? How could the memory of a crucifixion be as effective as the sacrifice of human beings in propitiating a god? And would these chanting black-garbed foreign priests be as effective as the Rus shamans in their magic clothes sewn with tinkling bells? Whatever their personal preferences, Olga and her successors had to take account of their subjects' feeling if they were to survive.

The Christian priests who came to Russia were persuasive missionaries. They intoned the liturgy in fine voices, learned the local vernacular, and were able to relate and explain the stories of the Bible, the significance of every feast and fast day, and the merits of every saint in their calendar with reference to powerful and captivating visual aids called icons. Above all, they spread a vision of hell and the prospect of bliss through salvation. They also exploited the advantages of superior technology, bringing bigger, more resounding bells with them, and incense that smelled stronger and more interesting than the shamans' concoctions. The number of Christian converts increased steadily. Yet, as more Rus became Christians, divisions and conflicts arose.

Resistance to the new religion was fed by interest as well as by affection for the familiar. Christianity threatened the shamans with loss of power and social standing, and also loss of income. Moreover, many members of the ruling elite were themselves pagans or were cautious enough not to alienate the people of their district by challenging their gods. Olga/Helen, though a Christian herself, dared not proclaim Christianity to be the religion of her people. That fateful step was to be taken by her grandson Vladimir some twenty years after Olga's death. Meanwhile her son Sviatoslav ruled, a determined warrior and a pagan.

It was Sviatoslav who finally eliminated the Khazars, who had for so long controlled the commercial networks of the south. He drove them from their strong-points on the Sea of Azov and then from Itil, their strategic trading centre on the Volga. At the same time he overcame the Volga Bulgar tribes. Then, presumably in return for a favour or in expection of one, he answered a call from the Emperor to campaign against the Bulgars of the Balkans. The experience evidently whetted his ambition to control the delta of the river Danube, so great was its commercial value. There, in the words of an early Russian chronicler, 'all the good things of the world converge: gold, precious silks, wine and fruit from Byzantium, silver and horses from Bohemia and Hungary, furs, wax, honey and slaves from Russia.'[20]

Indeed, in 971 Sviatoslav decided to establish his capital in the delta. From that point on the Danube seems to have been embedded in the Russians' collective imagination as a source of fascination. Long afterwards, popular folk songs were to reflect a yearning to possess it.[21] But, though Sviatoslav was at first succesful, he soon ran foul of Byzantine interests. The Emperor John Tzimisces, a former general who had killed his predecessor in a palace coup, found Sviatoslav's initiative intolerable and resolved to drive him out. Sviatoslav proved to be no match for him in strategy. John led his army in a dramatically fast march which trapped the Russians in the stronghold they called Pereiaslavets on the Danube. Despite frantic resistance, Sviatoslav was forced to concede. The parley that ended the fight occasioned a pen-portrait of him by a Byzantine observer.

According to this, Sviatoslav was a man of medium height, broad shouldered, blue-eyed, bushy-browed and snub-nosed. He had a thick neck, long moustachios and a shaven head – except for a lock of hair on one side, the mark of his nobility. In one ear he wore a gold ring set with two pearls and a ruby, and he wore a suit of golden armour. Yet he seemed 'gloomy and savage', no doubt because his imperial hopes had been dashed.[22] Sviatoslav would not adopt an appropriate mien of humility, however, and this did not please the Emperor, whose agents soon arranged for the Pechenegs to ambush Sviatoslav and kill him. In this way, glittering ambition met a mean and dusty end.

Politics continued in its bloody tradition. Sviatoslav's three sons, who had been acting as his viceroys in Kiev, Novgorod and Derevliania, fell out with one another, and two of them lost their lives. The survivor was Vladimir, the ruler who brought Russia into the Christian fold and became its founding saint. His image, created by a grateful Church, gives a misleading impression of the man, however. The real Vladimir was visibly his father's son: a commercial slave-owner who became the proud possessor of several hundred concubines; a ruthless politico, little moved by considerations of brotherly love. With the help of a band of Viking mercenaries he had disposed of his brother Iaropolk of Kiev, who favoured Christianity, and promised to maintain the cause of paganism. Many years were to pass before he recanted, and then only for compelling political reasons.

Vladimir had sent a contingent of warriors to help Emperor Basil II defeat a rebellion, and the grateful Basil had offered his own sister Anna to Vladimir in marriage – an alliance which would confer considerable prestige. No princess born in the purple had ever before been offered in marriage to a foreigner, however useful, however powerful. The price was conversion, but it seemed a price worth paying. Then the Emperor and his entourage began to have second thoughts about the merits of the match. This hitch led Vladimir to launch a campaign against Byzantine holdings in the Crimea. Only when Anna was finally delivered did Vladimir fulfil his side of the bargain.

The statue of Perun the Thunderer and the other idols he had had erected on a hill that dominated Kiev were now pulled down. They were then subjected to a humiliating ritual flogging by twelve men as they were dragged to the river Dnieper and then hurled into it.[23] The entire population of the city is said to have been driven into the river too – to be baptized. Russia now was part of Christendom.

A splendid monument celebrating the conversion still stands in Kiev: the cathedral church now known as St Sophia, though the original foundation had been dedicated to Kiev's carefully chosen patron saint, Elias. Vladimir's sponsor, the Emperor Basil, was, after all, a devotee of St Elias.

Moreover, the saint was associated with thunder and lightning, which made his cult particularly attractive to worshippers of Perun.[24] The choice was calculated both to ingratiate Russia's ruler with the great Emperor and to help wean pagan subjects from their addiction to Perun. The pressing need for St Elias eventually passed, however, and so when a new cathedral was built it was dedicated to Santa Sophia, the Holy Wisdom.

It was not Vladimir who built it, however, but his son Iaroslav the Wise, who lies buried in it still, in a white stone sarcophagus. Begun in 1017 and dedicated in 1037, a year after Iaroslav inflicted a decisive defeat on the Pechenegs, the cathedral in Kiev has thirteen domes – one for Christ, and one for each of the Apostles. Its impressive massing recalls Justinian's basilica of the Holy Wisdom in Constantinople, and Byzantine masons, engineers and artists were undoubtedly involved in its creation, as they were in the cathedral of Santa Sophia which Iaroslav built in Novgorod. Aspects of the Kiev structure, indeed, recall Novgorod rather than Byzantium, and are said to represent something distinctively Russian in style.[25] The building, on which so many nameless craftsmen lavished their skills, symbolized both Russia's coming of age as an independent state and its membership of what has been called 'the Byzantine Commonwealth' of Christian Orthodoxy. The first priests there had been Greek, but now that more Russians were becoming literate and ordained priests a Russian church hierarchy was being formed. Indeed some of the more able of them were to serve the Grand Prince and help him build an efficient administration for his far-flung realm. The new cathedral symbolized Russia's membership of Christian civilization, just as it reflected the state's considerable wealth.

Riurik may be the legendary progenitor of Russia's ruling house; Vladimir may have brought Russia into Christendom; Iaroslav the Wise has a good claim to be regarded as a founding father of the Russian state. He issued its first code of laws, and he created a family cult that was to have political as well as spiritual value: the cult of Boris and Gleb. The youngest sons of Vladimir, they had been murdered in 1015 by their older brother, Sviatopolk, in a bid to gain his father's throne; they were already regarded as saints by many people for having, as they supposed, faced death with Christ-like submissiveness. Iaroslav now ordained the celebration of their feast day, and arranged for them to be commemorated no fewer than six times a year.[26] In this way the blood of the innocents came to sanctify the men of power related to them, and the Byzantine concept of divinely sanctioned, albeit sinful, rulers set the seal on the ruling family's authority.

With the missionary priests who had been moving into Russia came books – Bibles, psalters, compilations of civil as well as canon law – and literacy. These introduced elements of a distinct political philosophy which was to infuse Russian political life down the generations. The views of the great law-giver Justinian on the divine origin of political authority and relations between state and Church lay at its foundation: 'God's greatest gifts to men . . .' he wrote, 'are the priesthood and state authority (*imperium*). The former serves the divine interest, the latter controls and cares for human interests.' A legitimate ruler was given by 'Christ, our God, who directs this great vessel of the present world . . . [as] a wise priest and pious tsar, a true leader giving the right words in judgement, guarding the truth for eternity . . . If anybody should upbraid . . . a pious prince without justification may he be punished. If a cleric he may be deposed, if a layman excommunicated.' The ruler was appointed by God, and represented Christ on earth. He carried out priestly functions, promoted the Church's interests, and supervised the clergy. Many such ideas, promoting symbiosis of Church and state, concludes one expert, 'were merged into the political structure of the State of Kiev, and . . . became the basis for Russia's further evolution'.[27]

More than that, Russian rulers sought legitimation by presenting themselves ceremonially in the manner of Byzantine emperors, as well as by virtue of their Christianity. Ilarion, whom Iaroslav had appointed metropolitan of Kiev in 1051, made the connection in a treatise on law and grace which contains a remarkable paeon of praise for Vladimir and by implication for his son Iaroslav: 'You are similar to Constantine the Great, you are equally wise, and you love God as much, and therefore you equally deserve respect from his servants [the Church] . . . Let us praise . . . our leader and instructor, the great khagan of our land, Vladimir.'[28]

Iaroslav not only ordered the compilation of Russia's first code of law (*Russkaia pravda*), he issued his own coinage (presenting an image of himself enthroned in majesty) rather than continuing to use imported currency like Byzantine drachmas or oriental dirhams, and he was recognized as the peer of most other European rulers. Iaroslav had married a daughter of the King of Sweden; his son Vsevolod married into the Byzantine imperial family; his daughters married the kings of France, Hungary and Norway. Magnus the Good, the future king of Denmark, was raised at his court; so was Harald Hardrada, who had been a mercenary commander in Russia and Byzantium, and was to be Harold Godwinson's challenger for the crown of England in 1066.[29]

The wealth, power and influence that Russia enjoyed in the time of Iaroslav held out every prospect of an even greater future. Russia's territory was immense, its population had burgeoned, its commerce thrived, its ruler had European stature. Almost every augury pointed to a brilliant future. And yet this first Russian Empire was to shrivel and collapse within 200 years, and Iaroslav bears some responsibility for it. There was a flaw in the succession system which was serious enough to undermine the state, and Iaroslav was aware of it.

The fatal flaw was the 'apanage' system, the practice by which an estate was divided between one's offspring. The eldest might get more than his brothers, but the others also inherited portions. This was the custom of the Slavs as it was of the Irish – princes and peasants alike. It seemed to carry some advantages in Russia, where both commercial and political success depended on unitary control of the immense river system from Novgorod in the north to Kiev in the south and from Polotsk in the west to Tmutorakhan (present-day Taman) in the east. Family interdependence implied trust, while also providing sufficient devolution of authority to facilitate effective regional control. Even the practice Iaroslav initiated of lateral succession, from brother to brother, rather than vertical succession, from father to son, had the advantage of entrusting the most important cities with their hinterlands to the most senior, and therefore most experienced, members of the ruler's immediate family. However, as time passed and the family tree ramified, it became increasing difficult to determine the right pecking order, and the succession eventually became the object of almost perpetual dispute and feuding.[30] Common blood does not necessarily imply harmony. Family members can fall out, especially when power is at stake.

Belatedly, Iaroslav himself recognized the danger and tried to avert it. According to a chronicler, before he died in 1054 he summoned his sons and begged them, much as Shakespeare has the dying Edward IV beg his courtiers, to love each other and his heir. If they did so, said Iaroslav, God would vanquish their enemies and peace would prevail. But, he warned, 'If you live in hatred and dissention, quarrelling with one another, then you will ruin the country your ancestors won with so much effort, and you yourselves will perish.'

Though Iaroslav had had the authority to create a more centralized administration, he had failed to challenge the apanage principle. Perhaps he was too much of a traditionalist; perhaps it was politically impossible for him to do so. At any rate, his will was set in the traditional mould. He bequeathed the throne of Kiev to Iziaslav, his first-born, and four other cities to his other sons, Sviatoslav, Vsevolod, Igor and Viacheslav. If any of them violated the boundaries of another's territory or tried to oust him, the others were to join together to help the brother who had been wronged.[31] Beyond that, Iaroslav had only exhortations for them. It was not enough. The falling-out was not long delayed.

The masters of the steppe, which ran eastward of the Kievan frontier, were now the Polovtsians, otherwise known as Cumans or the Kipchak horde. Anxious to break into the profitable slave trade and to filch such plunder as they could from Russian territory, their raiding parties were becoming a nuisance, and to the more exposed cities even a danger. In 1068 these Polovtsians succeeded in routing a Russian army trying to keep them out, and this precipitated a revolt against Grand Prince Iziaslav of Kiev. The rebels evidently thought Iziaslav was failing them over the issue of defence. The invaders were turned back by Sviatoslav's forces and order was restored to Kiev. However, the divisive issue of the succession remained. Iziaslav's three brothers joined forces to remove him, and Sviatoslav gained control of Kiev. But he died in 1077, at which Iziaslav returned from refuge in Poland and took over again.

When he was killed in the following year, a chaotic period of family infighting followed – only briefly interrupted by war against the Polovtsians. The premier city passed into the hands of Iaroslav's last surviving son, Vsevolod, but he died in 1094, and from then on the crisis deepened. Attempts were made to find an accommodation between rival members of the family, and it was agreed to abide by Iaroslav's will by giving Kiev to Iziaslav's son Sviatopolk as a patrimony, Chernigov to the sons of Sviatoslav, and so on. But, as generation succeeded generation and the lines of precedence among Iaroslav's numerous descendants became more and more blurred, the spirit of family solidarity withered, and the tendency to civil strife grew.

Apanages became patrimonies, and the Rus state came to resemble a ramshackle collection of little independent duchies. Pressure from the Polovtsians increased, and some of them joined in the Russians' family fights. Fear of the steppe people and a sense of the common interest sometimes made for co-operation, but family conflict always flared up again and the fear of civil war was pervasive even in quiet times. 'Why', wailed a chronicler, 'do we ruin the land of Russia by continual strife against each other?'[32]

The answer was ambition, aggressive individualism, resentments enshrined in family memories, the prevailing sense of honour – familiar enough in western Europe at that time, where they also led to rebellion and civil war. Then in 1113 Vladimir Monomakh became grand prince of Kiev, and the old sense of family solidarity briefly reasserted itself.

Vladimir was born in 1053, a year before the death of Iaroslav, his grandfather. The offspring of Vsevolod of Chernigov and a Byzantine princess, he liked to boast of his toughness and prowess. In his autobiographical testament he wrote that

> I [have] captured ten or twenty wild horses with my own hand . . . Two bison tossed me and my horse on their horns, a stag gored me, an elk trampled me underfoot, another gored me with his horns, a wild boar tore my sword from my thigh, a bear bit my saddle-cloth next to my knee, and another wild beast jumped on to my flank and threw [down] my horse with me . . . [Yet] God preserved me unharmed. I often fell from my horse, fractured my skull twice, and in my youth injured my arms and legs, not sparing my head or my life.[33]

Vladimir was literate as well as courageous. An heir to both the Slavonic tradition of Russia and the Greek tradition of Byzantium, it was in his reign that Slavonic replaced Greek on his official seal. Yet he treasured his Roman-Byzantine heritage too, having frescos painted in Santa Sophia depicting an emperor presiding over games in the hippodrome. Vladimir sponsored public works, building a bridge over the Dnieper and erecting Kiev's 'Golden Gate', celebrated in one of Mussorgsky's *Pictures at an Exhibition*; and he was also a loyal and generous son of the Church.

The Church in return was his staunch supporter. Though its head, the Metropolitan, was appointed by the Patriarch of Constantinople and was, as yet, usually a Greek rather than a Russian, the Grand Prince's wishes on ecclesiastical appointments were heeded. The Church also provided a major source of political advice and administrative skill for him to draw on. The reinterment of Boris and Gleb – in effect their canonization – took place in 1115, the centenary of their murder, and must have been the fruit of deep discussion between Vladimir and his ecclesiastics. Vladimir and his son Oleg attended the ceremony, which was clearly intended to bolster their legitimacy. They were, after all, blood relatives of the infant martyrs (albeit also of their murderer).

When Oleg died, however, it proved impossible to keep the state together. The solidarity of the Riurikid clan on which the first Russian state, Kievan Rus, had been built was crumbling, and the descent into ruin became steadily faster. In large part this was because the narrow interests of each patrimonial principality began to outweigh consideration of the general good, and because of the bickering of the various princes. But secular changes were also important.

Between the years 1000 and 1200 Russia's population is reckoned to have doubled.[34] At the same time its centre of gravity, both demographic and economic, had begun to move north from Kiev. Novgorod was expanding into the vast, rich hunting grounds of Perm, and by the end of the century it was extracting tribute from native peoples in the Urals. Yet the chief beneficiary of the demographic change was not Novgorod but the new city of Vladimir, which ruled over the east-central region known as Suzdalia. By 1200 even the proud princes of the south looked up to the Prince of Vladimir as first among equals.[35] Long important for the access it gave to the Caspian and the Orient, the mid-Volga valley had become a major source not only of food but also of furs, honey and other commercial products. And its population had been multiplying, both by natural increase and through immigration. It was coming to be seen as a land of opportunity, and it was also safer from predatory raiders than some districts further south.

These demographic changes led to some towns losing importance and the appearance of new ones: Iurev-Polskii, Dmitrov, Moscow. The prince most associated with developing and exploiting this trend was Monomakh's son, Prince Iurii Dolgorukii ('Long-Arm') of Rostov and Suzdal. He invested in Vladimir, fortified the little commercial settlement of Moscow, and in 1155 ascended to the throne of Kiev. He died two years later, but his successor as prince of Vladimir was the doughty Andrei Bogoliubskii. Andrei was both a great builder (his Church of the Intercession on the river Nerl bids fair to being the most perfect in all Christendom) and a competitor for the throne of the Grand Prince in Kiev. He actually captured and plundered Kiev in 1169, though he could not hold it. For the moment the rival clans of the south, of Volhynia and Pereiaslav, held Kiev, but they enjoyed only a nominal pre-eminence. Kiev had lost the control of Russia it had exerted a century earlier.

As Andrei's career suggested, Russia's economic strength was coming to be based more on the middle Volga region and less on the lower Dnieper and the Black Sea. The relative decline of the south coincided with, and may have been related to, Byzantium's increasing commercial difficulties. By contrast, the rising prosperity of Vladimir, and of Pskov, was based in part on trade with Germany. And Andrei's domains also profited from trade with the Caucasus, the Caspian and beyond. Indeed, this connection was so important that in 1197 a marriage was arranged between Andrei's son and Queen Tamara of Georgia.[36] These economic trends tended to accentuate the northward drift of population.

Despite the long-standing influence of Byzantium on Russia, Andrei Bogoliubskii was the first Russian ruler to assume the authority of a Byzantine autocrat. Here at last, it seems, was a potential grand prince who could make Kievan Rus work as a state. He would not pander to the people; nor did he respect the conventions of family inheritance – indeed, he recognized its inefficiency. He lavished gifts on the Church, but insisted on the last word even on some clerical issues (and dismissed a bishop who disagreed with him). Yet the Church inspired his autocratic impulses and justified them. It sang his praises, compared him to King Solomon, said that he interceded with heaven in the interests of the Russian land. A cabal of disgruntled retainers led by a princely relative assassinated him in 1175. His enemies rejoiced at the deed, but the Church pictured him as a martyr.

Andrei's brother Vsevolod III – known as 'Big Nest' because he had so many children – succeeded him and eventually challenged Roman of Volhynia for the throne of the grand prince. He gained possession of it in 1205, but his rivals would not concede and he proved unable to establish his authority over all Russia. For the remaining seven years of his life Vsevolod concentrated his attentions on his vast northern patrimony, which stretched from the Neva to the Volga. But he shared his brother's political philosophy and practised it insofar as he was able. When investing his son Constantine with a cross and a sword symbolizing his right to rule in Novgorod, Vsevolod told him, 'God has given thee the seniority over all thy brothers, and Novgorod the Great [now] possesses the seniority [and right] to rule over all the Russian lands.'[37]

After Vsevolod died in 1212, however, even his own sons fell out with one another. Prince Vsevolod Rostislavich took over in Novgorod. In 1221 the people there rejected him and asked Prince Iurii of Vladimir to send them a Suzdalian prince instead. Fifteen years later, just such a prince was sent there. He bore the famous name of Alexander, and tried to emulate his namesake.[38]

Fourteen years later civil war erupted yet again in the south, and over the next five years Kiev changed hands seven times. Well might the Novgorod chronicler bewail 'the accursed, ever-destructive devil who wishes no good to the human race [who] raised up sedition among the princes of Rus' so that men might not live in peace . . . The evil one rejoices in the shedding of Christian blood.'[39]

Kievan Russia was at the point of collapse. The descendants of Riurik had become so numerous that serious genealogical skills would have been needed to establish where sovereignty and precedence should lie, but by the early thirteenth century it hardly seemed to matter. The state was collapsing amid the almost constant war for the possession of Kiev, when a series of hammer blows shattered it beyond hope of recovery. This *coup de grâce* was delivered by a new enemy: the Mongols.

In 1222 Mongols had routed a poorly co-ordinated force of Russians and Pechenegs on the river Kalka. But they were only a reconnaissance party, which soon turned back. Ten years later, however, they returned, this time in full force, commanded by Baty, grandson of the dreaded Chingiz Khan. Ironically, they came at a time when Prince Alexander of Novgorod was demonstrating that there was still fight left in the Russians. He defeated a Swedish army on the river Neva in 1240 (which is why he is known as Alexander Nevskii), and then destroyed a force of Teutonic Knights in a battle on the ice of Lake Peipus near the Baltic. These victories were to be trumpeted by Russian propagandists in many a dark day over the following centuries, but even Alexander had no answer to the Mongols. And when they returned this time they came intent on subduing all Russia.

They were terrifyingly efficient,[40] and killing aroused few qualms in them. Indeed, they used terror deliberately to weaken their enemies' will to resist. Their original purpose in moving west had been to claim large tracts of grassland on which to feed their herds. A spell of global warming had struck their grazing grounds, which had suffered from a succession of droughts. This had spurred them to go out in search of fresh pastures for their horses, which represented food and drink as well as mobility to them. But they killed and terrorized for booty too, and for regular income in the form of tribute. The Russians were no match for them.

From this point on, however, we should refer to the Mongols as Tatars, for, although the Tatars were not Mongols but Turkic-speaking tribes who followed Chingiz Khan and his successors, they came to represent Mongol power to the Russians. The Tatars sacked Riazan in 1237, Vladimir and Suzdal in 1238, and Pereiaslav and Chernigov in 1239. In 1240 they took Kiev itself. Then they put Russia's princes to the rack, demanding their submission.

In 1243 Iaroslav of Vladimir submitted; in 1245 Prince Daniil Romanovich of Volhynia followed suit. Baty Khan confirmed both in office. When Grand Prince Mikhail Vsevolodovich of Kiev demurred, in 1246, they executed him. From then on the Khan was in control. The internecine fighting between the princes continued, but the Tatars learned to manage and manipulate it. They also enforced the taking of a census and the regular payment of considerable taxes. Beyond that they were content to govern at a distance, allowing the princes to administer their new subjects on their behalf. They only demanded that the princes visit their capital, Sarai on the Volga, to obtain confirmation of their appointments from the Khan, that they leave hostages as sureties for their good behaviour, and that they obey orders. Any infraction met with swift retribution, any protest with harsh reprisal. Otherwise the Russians were left alone.

Kievan Rus was destroyed; no Russian principality – not even Novgorod, which the Tatars had not reached – remained sovereign, and the Tatars were to make vicious punitive raids thereafter on various parts of the Russian land. The destruction and the loss of life was considerable; the sense of shame deep. Yet the impression nourished by Cold War historians that the Mongols 'orientalized' Russia is exaggerated. Apart from lending Russia a few institutions like the *yam*, or postal service (which is not peculiar to the Orient), and words for money, treasury and customs duties, their influence was chiefly psychological. Russia recovered demographically, the economy eventually revived; the Church was virtually unaffected; and relations with Byzantium were not interrupted.[41] And the seeds of the next, more successful, imperial Russia had already been sown.

3
Reincarnation

THE POLITICAL SYSTEM of Kievan Rus had crumbled, never to be revived. The ultimate authority for the Russian lands was now the Tatar khan and his court at Sarai on the Volga. Yet over the course of the next two and a half centuries a new centre of authority was to emerge, more viable than the last – and in Moscow, a fortified settlement hardly heard of in the year 1200. It was the consequence of many causes, of both long-term trends and actions by individuals. To the extent that some recognizable elements of the old Russia were involved in creating the new entity it can be termed a reincarnation, but new factors also came into play, and the Tatars themselves unwittingly contributed towards it.

Some important trends noticeable in the late Kievan period continued. The drift of population northward, which had already given Vladimir pre-eminence among the principalities, resumed after an interval.[1] So did the extension of agriculture, especially towards the east. This increased food production and hence human fertility. A rising birth rate evidently compensated for the increase of mortality due to war, and, although outbreaks of bubonic plague were to cause setbacks, the population soon resumed its healthy tendency to expansion. The territorial extent of the hunting-and-gathering economy also spread steadily eastwards and towards the north-east, bringing in more wealth in furs to sell. By the later 1300s it was also bringing more people of different ethnicity into the Russian orbit, including Maris and Mordvs, strengthening a colonial tendency which had begun long before when Russians and Riurik's Viking band had first encountered Finnic fisher-folk in the neighbourhood of Novgorod. But it was Moscow, rather than Vladimir or Novgorod, that proved best able to capitalize on these changes. This was chiefly because of its advantageous location commanding the portages, and hence the commerce, that passed between rivers in the basin of the mid and upper Volga, between the smaller rivers Kostroma and Sokhma, the Sukhna and the Vaga.[2]

The Russian princes, particularly of the north-central regions, benefited from these accretions of wealth, but so did the Tatars, who used the princes to collect taxes for them. Immediately following the conquest the Khan had sent in officials, called *baskaks*, to control each prince and each domain. The *baskak* ensured the payment of taxes and supervised a census, begun in 1257, to establish a systematic basis for revenue collection. The *baskak* also supervised the maintenance of order and ensured that the prince toed the correct political line. Quite soon, however, the Khan began to delegate some of these functions to co-operative Russians. So it was that Alexander Nevskii, hero of wars against the Teutonic Knights and Sweden, and grand prince of Vladimir from 1252 to 1263, came to impose the Tatars' census on Novgorod, where he had begun his career. After a time all the *baskak*'s functions were transferred to the Grand Prince, and, as the Khan's chief tax agent, the Grand Prince came to exercise a substantial advantage over rival rulers of the Russian lands. In this way a servile practice was transformed into a means of accreting power.

The imposition of Tatar power eventually contributed to a more effective Russian unity. It also stimulated institutional development, both directly (insofar as the princes' courts borrowed some Tatar practices) and indirectly. The role of the Church in particular was much enhanced – not only as a source of spiritual solace and welfare, of literacy and political wisdom, but as an economic organizer. The Church became steadily wealthier as pious notables, merchants and landowners showered it with assets to ensure forgiveness for their sins and places in the world to come, and the assets were put to profitable use; and it developed a new dimension, helping to organize the territorial expansion into the interior which was already under way, and promoting further colonization. Its principal agency for this was the monastic movement, which was to make a considerable contribution to the territorial and economic development of the new Russia. So, by salvaging something from the ruins of Kievan Russia, and developing new agencies, Russians were eventually able to exploit more favourable ecological and demographic trends and to start rebuilding.

There were obstacles, of course. For a century and a half the Tatars continued to exploit Russia, creaming off its assets, and they regularly meddled in its affairs thereafter, diverting its energies. There were new outbreaks of fraternal strife among the Russian princes, most seriously between Tver and Moscow, and a new power, pagan Lithuania, emerged to the west and began to expand vigorously not only to the south but also eastward, threatening central Russia. Faced with these circumstances, Russians reacted in various ways: by migrating to avoid the challenges (though often confronting new ones in so doing), by exploiting the situations to their best advantage, but on occasion by confronting them. The chief actors in this bleak period were the princes.

They negotiated the best terms they could for themselves and their people with the Khan. They met him, his officials and each other at the periodic conferences he convened at Sarai, so that even their intrigues against each other were supervised. In personality the princes, though always represented as God-fearing, were mostly unattractive. They were arrogant and servile by turns according to the context in which they acted out their schizophrenic roles; cruel, and perforce sly. They could hardly have been much different, for theirs was a hard age and they faced cruel circumstances. Ivan I emerges as something of a hero among them, devious and grasping though he was, because his modest achievements proved to be a foundation stone of a new and successful political structure.

Prelates also played significant political roles. When the princes met at Sarai, metropolitans went with them to safeguard the Church's interest, and at least one bishop was entrusted by the Khan with a mission to Constantinople.[3] Churchmen helped to guide the long-term destiny of Russia by their decisions. Metropolitan Petr of Kiev, for example, noticing that the location of power in Russia was moving northward, decided to move his seat of operations from Kiev to Moscow at the invitation of its prince. It was an interesting decision, for at the time Moscow was subordinate to the Grand Principality of Vladimir, even though it had potential to become the strategic centre of the Russian lands. Petr was to develop the see of Moscow into the premier seat of the Orthodox Church in Russia. Buried in the Kremlin's Cathedral of the Assumption, which became the traditional resting place for Russian primates, he was to be venerated as one of Russia's more significant political saints.[4] For Russians, faith and politics were never to be far apart.

Another saint of the age, though more obviously spiritual, was hardly less important for Russia's development. This was the charismatic hermit Sergius, who blessed Russia's champion Dmitrii of the Don before he led his warriors to Russia's first famous victory over the Tatars, at Kulikovo in 1380. But Sergius accomplished something much more significant for Russia in the long run: he inspired the boom in monastic development. The age also produced Russia's finest painter, Andrei Rublev, and Stephen of Novgorod, who wrote a cheerful account of a pilgrimage to Constantinople.

Such people contributed in their different ways towards Russia's revival. But so did the collectivity of souls who for their own individual reasons moved in directions that turned out to be historically significant. And, ironically, the same rapacious Tatars who plundered, disrupted and lorded it over Russia also contributed unwittingly to Russia's reincarnation by introducing more effective methods of exercising economic and fiscal authority. The Tatars never interfered in the religion of their tributaries. Soon after the conquest they had confirmed the status of the Orthodox Church and confirmed its rights. This policy was not to change when, in the early 1300s, the Tatars abandoned Buddhism for Islam. Indeed, becoming part of the Muslim world expanded the range of Russians' commercial connections – to the Arabian peninsula and through central Asia to India and China. Yet the old links with western Europe were not severed. The markets for the gleaming glutton pelts, Russian sable and fox furs grew, and prices rose. So, although the conquest disrupted the Russian economy, in the longer term it afforded some compensation.[5]

The old connection with Christian Constantinople, on the other hand, lost some of its former commercial importance. The imperial city had become a pale image of its former glory after the crusaders sacked it in 1204. Exchanges still took place, but for the most part they involved churchmen rather than merchants, and, instead of Russians shopping in Constantinople for superior art and technology, Greeks came to Russia holding begging bowls in outstretched hands. When the great dome of St Sophia, the Church of the Holy Wisdom in Constantinople, collapsed in 1346, it was the Russian grand prince Simeon the Proud, the son of Ivan I, who contributed most for the repairs. And this was only one of the grand princes' many charitable disbursements. The mentors had become the supplicants.

The Tatars had jolted Russians out of their old mould, and by denying them access to the steppe they forced their energies into other directions. What happened as a result is not a question specifically addressed in the chronicles of the time. Yet an enterprising historian at the Academy of Sciences in Moscow, A. A. Gorskii, devised an ingenious method for tracing changes in the relative importance of Russia's cities which throws light on the problem. He counted the number of times each one is mentioned in the chronicles of each region of Russia over a lengthy period. He found that some place names cease to be referred to, others are mentioned with increasing frequency, and that new place names appear. If frequency of reference reflects importance, then these records indicate the rise and decline of cities and regions over time. In the chronicles of north-eastern Russia, for example, the city of Pereiaslav-Zalesskii is the most mentioned in the first half of the thirteenth century, but in the second half Moscow eclipses it, as does its parent city, Vladimir. Gorskii also found that Kiev is mentioned 44 times in the period 1200 to 1250 in the chronicles of the north-east, and that Halych is the second most frequently mentioned southern city. However, by 1300 Novgorod leads, and it holds its lead into the 1300s. A count of fortified settlements in the century after 1250 has shown that the principality of Chernigov had most, followed by Smolensk in the west, and then Kiev. However, the walls of Volyn and of Suzdal enclosed the largest areas, suggesting a greater concentration of population. Some of the detail may be confusing, but the general trend is clear: whereas the most populous and important cities had been in the south, they were now in the north. The political configuration confirms this finding. The four strongest principalities in the early thirteenth century had been Chernigov, Halych-Volynia, Smolensk and Vladimir-Suzdal. By the early 1300s the first three had ceased to exist, but a new state was being formed on the territory of the fourth.[6]

The rising star was the Principality of Vladimir-Moscow. Yet by no means all parts of the first Russia were to cohere around it. One result of the Tatar impact was to send several old Russian centres in the south and west into a different orbit. They were to become part of the rising power of Lithuania. In time the influence of western neighbours on their language and culture caused them to diverge from the remaining Russians. Ultimately their peoples were to become those we know today as Ukrainians and Belorussians. However, despite these substantial losses of territory and population, and the attrition of Tatar rule, Russians were to make a good recovery demographically and go on to settle an area quite out of proportion to their numbers. How this came about is a question that fascinated one of Russia's most interesting, and neglected, historians, Matvei Liubavskii,[7] and it is related to the problem of why first Vladimir and then Moscow became the political centre of Russia.

Liubavskii noticed that the migration was confined to the forest zone. The colonizers avoided the Tatars' stomping ground, the steppe. He also noticed that settlements were unevenly distributed, scattered, bounded by marshes and impenetrable tracts of forests, Russia's natural frontiers. The great spread and dispersed character of Russian settlement helps to explain the lack of political cohesion in the old Russia and the failure to create an integrated state. Thanks to the Tatars and the northward movement of population, a new concentration of population allowed a more integrated state to be constructed. However, this did not explain why the principalities of the north-east should have become the fastest-growing sector in all Russia, or why Moscow, a neophyte among Russian cities, in a region that was relatively poor in natural resources and with little transit trade, should become the country's capital, rather than Novgorod, Russia's oldest city.

Liubavskii explained this in terms of Novgorod's lack of an agricultural hinterland. This made it difficult for the city to secure food supplies for a large army, and this precluded its attaining pre-eminence in Russia. Moscow, on the other hand, had come to command a strategic central sector of Russia's great network of rivers and portages, and developed an adequate agriculture and food supply. It was part of the Grand Principality of Vladimir, 'a complex of . . . valuable territories, which were the source of great military and financial resources'. This strength derived in large measure from population growth, and from the extension of colonization, organized by the princes, boyars (their elite retainers) and clergy. But it also owed something to the aggression of its princes, who had to fight for a share of the commercial resources which more prosperous cities like Tver, Novgorod and Pskov already enjoyed,[8] and to a new form of monastic development, which, as we shall see, was a reaction to the invasion.

The political coherence of Russia depended on the princes, especially on the grand prince of Vladimir-Moscow. By the fourteenth century the Tatars had relaxed their grip sufficiently to allow the princes to pursue policies that were rather less subservient. The first hint of change came when Ivan I was the leading Russian prince.

Historians customarily picture Ivan as cruel, sly and hypocritical, even though the chronicles yield virtually nothing about his character or personality except that his nickname (coined by an unappreciative brother) was *Kalita* – 'Money-Bag'. This suggests that he was a good money manager, ungenerous, perhaps, and greedy. Inferences from actions, difficult though these sometimes are to reconstruct,[9] suggest that he was also a canny strategist and a tough negotiator. His chief concern was unheroic: to maintain and, if possible, enlarge his heritage. He seized his opportunities, but only when it seemed safe to do so. Otherwise he prudently observed convention, kept the Church on his side, and never offended the Khan. The complexity and dangers of his predicament hardly allowed him to play the hero. Ivan is remembered as a significant historical figure in Russian history because he stumbled on opportunities. He happened to live at a juncture when he could exploit the Tatar khan's dependence on his services and establish Moscow as the pre-eminent centre for the Russians.

A grandson of Alexander Nevskii, Ivan was born around 1288 and came to prominence in his forties, when he was enthroned as grand prince of Vladimir as well as prince of Moscow. Vladimir, to the east of Moscow, had been founded in 1108 on the river Kliazma, a tributary to the Volga. He reigned for only nine years. Yet one of his more significant achievements belonged to the period before he became grand prince. In 1325 he persuaded the Metropolitan of Kiev, Petr, to move permanently to Moscow. As an extra inducement he built the Cathedral of the Dormition, one of the four famous cathedral churches enclosed along with the palace within the walls of Moscow's castle, the Kremlin. The expense was justified as well as affordable, for the new church added religious lustre to the place, and by extension to the Grand Prince. To have the head of the Russian Church based in his own city rather than Kiev was a great coup. It gave Moscow spiritual pre-eminence in Russia, and lent its prince particular prestige and clout.

Though their titles suggested authority, every Russian ruler of the time was a Tatar underling and had to accept regular humiliation. On the death of his predecessor a prince had to apply to the Khan at Sarai for permission to rule his inheritance. If his appointment was approved by the grant of a *yarlyk*, the Khan's men would take the prince to his capital, enthrone him, and monitor his activities thereafter. Ivan took good care to please the Khan. When, therefore, Prince Dmitrii of Tver murdered his brother, Grand Duke Iurii, in a revenge killing in 1326, Ivan no doubt expected to be made grand prince. He was to be disappointed.

The Khan eventually executed Dmitrii for the murder, but then made Dmitrii's brother, Aleksandr, grand prince. Aleksandr was evidently in the Khan's good graces too.[10] Ivan had no alternative but to acquiesce, and wait. Then, in 1327, an anti-Tatar uprising erupted in Tver. Many Tatars were lynched, and Ivan rushed off to Sarai with the news. Uzbek Khan responded by entrusting him with a Tatar army 50,000 strong, telling him to punish Tver. He also authorized him to rule the western districts of the grand principality. But he did not appoint him grand prince. Instead he chose Aleksandr of Suzdal, who ruled the eastern districts, including Vladimir. Aleksandr is said to have carried off the cathedral bell from Vladimir and reinstalled it in the cathedral of his own city, Suzdal, but, according to one (presumably pro-Muscovite) chronicler, it refused to ring there.[11] This was a way of suggesting that Aleksandr's appointment lacked divine sanction. However, after Aleksandr's death, in 1331, Ivan was finally confirmed as grand prince of Vladimir 'and All Russia'.

The Khan's reluctance to appoint him earlier had not been based on favouritism or whim. Nor was his preference for the princes of Tver and Suzdal. The decision reflected a sober appreciation of the fact that the Principality of Moscow had come to command more resources than any other principality. It had become altogether too mighty. That was why the policy-makers at Sarai had promoted Tver, Moscow's rival. But then Tver had rebelled. So another counter-weight to Moscow had to be found. This explains the division of Tver's territories between Ivan and Aleksandr. By 1331, however, the Khan's priorities had changed. A grand prince of Vladimir 'and all Russia' was needed now to guard the Khan's western territories, which were threatened not only by Sweden, but also by the fast-rising Grand Duchy of Lithuania. Its ruler, Olgerd, had been expanding vigorously towards the south and west, vying with Moscow for control of Novgorod, and threatening Smolensk and Pskov. Suddenly Sarai saw a strong Moscow as an asset rather than a danger.

Ivan recognized his chance and seized it. Some years previously his brother the grand prince Iurii had taken responsibility for the collection of tribute for the Tatars from all north-eastern Russia. Now the indispensable Ivan turned the Khan's rising dependence on him to good account by having the *baskaks* removed and charging all the princes with collection under his supervision.[12] In practice this made the Grand Prince governor of all the princes. Nevertheless, Ivan was far from confident that his patrimony would remain intact or that his descendants would inherit it. This much is evident from his several wills.

In one of them, made within a year of his death and witnessed by three priests, he declares himself to be 'the sinful, poor slave of God' and bequeaths his patrimony, Moscow, to his three sons. He proceeds to specify every property precisely, and in stating which towns and villages each son should have, he mentions that he has already given the eldest, Semen, 'four golden chains, three golden belts . . . a golden plate set with a pearl and precious stones . . . my red fur coat with pearls and my gold cap'. Yet he is by no means certain that his wishes will be honoured, that the Tatars will not intervene. 'If for my sins the Tatars should covet any of these . . . [properties] then you, my sons and my princess, should divide . . . [those that remain] among yourselves.' Nor, anxious though he is that memory of him and of his ancestors should not be extinguished, is he confident that his work, his patrimony, will be perpetuated.[13] Yet his tomb and those of his descendants in the Kremlin's Cathedral of the Archangel still witness to the fact that it was.

The reign of Ivan 'Money-Bag' marks a watershed not only for Tatar rule in Russia, which was never again to be as firm and assured as it had been in the first quarter of the century, but for Moscow as the centre of Russian political life. By the end of the century the Grand Principality had come to be regarded as the patrimony of the princes of Moscow. This was the foundation on which the new Russia was to rise.

★

The metropolitans had played a vital role in developing Moscow's political role, and none more so than Metropolitan Petr. The future saint's hagiographer assures us that Petr 'foresaw the future glory of Moscow' even 'while it was yet poor'. Yet when Ivan pressed him to move there he seems to have implicitly insisted on a condition: 'If thou wilt build a temple here worthy of the Mother of God,' he told Ivan, 'then thou shalt be more glorious than all the other princes, and thy posterity shall become great.'[14] The Cathedral of the Dormition was started, Petr duly arrived, and the continuing close co-operation between the grand princes and metropolitans of Moscow did much to ensure the fulfilment of Petr's prophecy.

Circumstances encouraged metropolitan and grand prince to co-operate. Olgerd of Lithuania was fast absorbing western and southern Russia into his domains, and was pressing for a separate Lithuanian Church hierarchy, headed by its own metropolitan. The Lithuanian advance posed many churchmen with a choice of allegiance. Those who distrusted the Lithuanians, who had so recently been pagans and who were open to Catholic influences from the German and Polish Churches, opted for Russia. So did the Patriarch of Constantinople, who was becoming dependent on Muscovite subsidies. These factors and the steadfastness of Petr's successors as metropolitan of Moscow – particularly Aleksei who was subsequently canonized – were to help Moscow beat off several challenges to its ecclesiastical jurisdiction, and to steady society when it was ravaged by the Black Death.

Aleksei's family had served the father of Ivan I, so he had connections at the Grand Prince's court and was familiar with affairs of state. Even so, his responsibilities as metropolitan were daunting. He had to start by going to Constantinople to negotiate with the Patriarch to secure his see; he had to guard it against inroads by the Lithuanians; and then he had to make his mark with the Khan (he earned a reputation as a healer in the process). Finally installed in Moscow, with an ecclesiastical jurisdiction more extensive than the Grand Prince's political jurisdiction,[15] he had to rescue the incapable Ivan II – the weakest of 'Money-Bag's' sons, but the only one to survive the plague – from the consequences of his ineptitude. Things might very easily have descended into civil war. It was thanks largely to the adroit Aleksei that they did not. He made peace between fractious princely families; calmed anti-Muscovite Tver; advised on policy towards the Tatars; and acted as mentor to Ivan's son and successor, Dmitrii, and as regent during the boy's minority. In short, Metropolitan Aleksei held the Russian centre together and guided it through a period of crisis. He also prepared the way for a dramatic change in relations between the Russians and the Tatars, for in 1378 young Dmitrii – now of age – led a Russian army to victory over the Tatars on the river Vozha; two years later he trounced them again at the famous battle of Kulikovo.

These victories did not end Russia's subjection, but they showed that the Tatars could be defeated, and hence that the subjection need not last. They also showed that Russian princes could sink their differences in a common front against the enemy, for warriors had come from all over northern Russia 'like eagles' to Dmitrii's aid. By the time of his death, in 1389, Dmitrii had also doubled the territory of the Grand Principality. The new circumstances also made it more probable that his descendants would succeed him. Yet a venerable monk named Sergius, who attended his funeral, was to do as much as Dmitrii to enlarge the Russian land.

The times encouraged piety of more than one kind. In 1349 a pious but feisty citizen of Novgorod made a pilgrimage to Constantinople with a group from his native city, and left a cheerful account of everything he saw. The journey took many months and required considerable resources, but pilgrim Stephen could afford the expense. The Tatars had hardly touched his home city of Novgorod. It had remained a prosperous commercial centre, with good connections with central Europe as well as with the Russian hinterland and with access, through it, to the eastern Mediterranean. In his description of Constantinople, Stephen expressed the pious conventionalities of a pilgrim, the innocent excitement of someone who took relics seriously, awe at secular as well as religious wonders long heard of and now seen, and credulity at every tale a guide told him:

> I arrived at the city during Holy Week, and we went to St Sophia where stands a column of wondrous size, height and beauty; it can be seen from far away at sea, and a marvellous, lifelike Justinian the Great sits on a horse at the top . . . [holding] a large golden orb surmounted by a cross in one hand . . . [while] his right hand stretches out bravely . . . towards the Saracen land and Jerusalem . . .

He toured the Cathedral of St Sophia, with its icons, mosaics and relics; lit a candle; kissed the remains of St Arsenius and the live hand of the Patriarch; and proceeded on a tour of the city's shrines and monuments which lasted several days. He walked up the imperial road to Constantine's purple column, which had been brought from Rome ('Noah's axe is there'), and to the Monastery of St George, where a set of the relics of

Christ's Passion was locked away 'and sealed with the imperial seal'. He kissed the body of St Anne there, the head of St John Chrysostom, and the head of St Basil in another monastery, and joined a procession which was following the icon of Mary 'the Virgin Mother of God . . . [painted] by St Luke . . . while she was still alive . . . '

'You go from there to the Monastery . . . Church of the Nine [Ranks of Angels] . . .' he continued. The '"Palace of the Orthodox Emperor Constantine" is there . . . as large as a town . . . [which has] walls higher than those of the city . . . The Monastery of St Sergius and Bacchus . . . is near by.' He kissed their heads too, and went on to the Hippodrome, and to kiss the hand of St John the Baptist, the remains of Gregory the Theologian, and the tomb of the prophet Daniel and of St Romanus . . . So the catalogue continues, enlivened by tales of stabbed icons which bled, comments on the beauty of the marble and of the singing – even the occasional confession. On visiting the tombs of the emperors he kissed them too, 'even though they are not saints'. His account concludes with advice that has application to the modern tourist too: visiting 'Constantinople is like entering a great forest. It is impossible to get about without a good guide, and if you try to go around on your own you will not be able to see or kiss a single saint, unless it happens to be that saint's day.'[16]

The happy pilgrim Stephen's contemporary, Sergius, was moulded by quite different circumstances. He was born in a less prosperous, more troubled, part of Russia at a time when, as in many other parts of Europe, despair was widespread and social values were changing. The unpromising outlook was encouraging migration out of towns, which were targets for the tax collectors and the war bands of rival princes, as well as Tatar raiders. Visitations of the Black Plague also encouraged movement to safer settlements and into the forests. There was a parallel tendency to avoid exposure to earthly risks and invest more in the spirit. Such were the disturbed conditions that shaped the early life of St Sergius.

Born in or around 1322,[17] the second of three brothers, he was christened Bartholomew. His parents were on their way down in the world. His father, a boyar who served the Prince of Rostov, belonged to the local elite. But Rostov was an enclave surrounded by the Principality of Moscow and being swallowed by it. In the course of his wars with Tver, Ivan had sent men to occupy parts of it and collect resources from its hapless people. But Ivan's government was offering tax exemptions to people who would settle on wastelands north of Moscow, so the family moved there, to a place called Radonezh.[18]The boy's life there began when he was seven, but he was a child of the outdoors, physical rather than bookish. He learned to read only years later. The state of the world was soon borne in on him, however, through both hearsay and experience.

His elder brother, Stefan, a widower with two small sons, entered a nearby monastery (what happened to his little boys is not recorded). Then his parents died, at which Bartholomew settled what remained of the family's assets on his younger brother and set out into the forest, accompanied by Stefan the monk. The hagiographer states that Bartholomew had long wanted to become a monk, but he was not tonsured immediately. Perhaps he could not afford to enter a monastery. He had no assets to bring, and his older brother's decision to leave his monastery and go with him may also have been prompted by the family's straitened circumstances. The brothers decided to live as hermits in the wilderness, fending for themselves. Why they did so is not entirely clear. A sense of adventure may have counted; they may have felt an urge to escape the world.

They erected a brushwood hovel to shelter in, then built a little church. But Stefan could not stand the solitude, and soon headed off to Moscow. There he entered the Monastery of the Apparition. Its abbot, Aleksei, was to become metropolitan. Stefan himself was to rise to become an abbot and chaplain to the Grand Prince. He was in the world now, if not of it. But Bartholomew remained a hermit in his wilderness, living a life of hard physical toil, prayer and meditation. He was to remain there in solitude for two years. A vision of the Devil he had about this time reflected concerns which were as much political as religious, however, for 'the evil forces' appeared before him 'clothed and hatted in the Lithuanian style' – the style, that is, of the Catholic West. The future saint was a patriot.

Word of the pious hermit spread, and people came to him in the forest bringing little gifts. Three or four even came to join him. He built 'cells' for them. But he also began to make occasional forays into the world he had forsaken. On one he persuaded a monk, who was also a priest, to shave his head and rechristen him a monk. His new name was Sergei, or Sergius. More and more young men came to live near Sergius as hermits, until, – reluctantly, so we are told – he agreed to the transformation of the settlement of separate hermitages into a monastery, and to his own installation as its abbot. He was to supervise the community and enforce strict discipline over the monks. The year was 1353–4 and he was thirty-one or thirty-two.

This would hardly have been done without the blessing of Metropolitan Aleksei. The Church had recognized the popularity of Sergius's initiative, and set out to capture and direct the trend. Sergius was encouraged to organize an expansion of the movement, to found new monasteries further out into the Russian 'wilderness'. Aside from the benefits of charity and piety that it would bring, putting the energies of so many displaced or undirected young men to productive account turned out to be of strategic economic significance too. So monks were sent out to form communities of their own, and all the time fresh recruits came in wanting the peace of mind and solace that came of prayer and physical labour. A twelve-year-old orphan of Sergius's brother became a novice, then a monk with the name of Fedor. He was later to found a monastery in Moscow and become archbishop of Rostov. But most of the monks who went out founded monasteries in the 'wilderness' of the countryside, not, as convention until that time dictated, at the edge of towns.

Sergius the hermit-turned-organizer became political. In 1358 he was sent to the Prince of Rostov, to the territory where his own family had hailed from, to persuade him to concede in his dispute with Moscow. Seven years later he undertook another mission as peacemaker, between two warring brothers over which of them should be prince of Nizhnii-Novgorod, which controlled an important confluence further down the Volga. He not only blessed Grand Prince Dmitrii before his victory over the Tatars at Kulikovo in 1380, he is reputed to have given him strategic advice, though he was also among those who fled Moscow at the approach of the vengeful Tatar leader Tokhtamysh, who sacked the city two years later. Sergius died in 1392. The site of his first hermit's cell at Zagorsk, north of Moscow, had already grown to be the Trinity–St Sergius monastic centre. It was to become the administrative centre for the Patriarch of All Russia, and a patriotic symbol for all Russians.

The story of St Sergius helps to explain how Russia relocated itself further to the north in the thirteenth century. It also throws light on how it came to occupy so vast a territory. The policy of princes, particularly Moscow's prince, of encouraging settlement on unfarmed land in strategic areas was significant in this respect, but the foundation of monasteries in 'the wilderness', as Sergius had done, was fundamental to the process.

The Church had become a refuge for peasants who had uprooted themselves from unsafe areas, and a major agency for their resettlement. This helps to explain the popularity of 'wilderness' monasteries, many of them founded in distant places where conditions were harsh but which were safe from the Tatars and other human predators. The monastic foundations kept the young men safe and productive. They seem also to have helped to increase population. Monks are, or should be, chaste, of course, but the demographic imperative was satisfied by novices who decided not to take their vows, and by peasants, artisans and service people who attached themselves to monastic communities, creating little suburbs around them.

The new monastic foundations tended to avoid land owned by princes, so people in monasteries' dependent settlements could live more freely than elsewhere and benefit from privileges and benefits that would not otherwise have been available to them. Yet the monastic colonization movement suited the princes – especially the Prince of Moscow, who made over great swathes of undeveloped territory to the Church, knowing that if it could find peasants to settle on it and make the land productive it would ultimately yield taxes and benefit the state, albeit through the Church. This and the continuing disposition of young Russians to take up the life of pioneers was to have continuing importance for Muscovy's development, particularly over the following two centuries. The development coincides with what Liubavskii identified as a period of sharp population growth associated with the development of colonization during the half century following the death of Ivan 'Money-Bag',[19] and monastic communities were founded at an increasing pace from the later thirteenth and fourteenth centuries, with several practical, as well as spiritual, purposes in mind.

Political centres had long attracted monastic foundations. No fewer than sixteen foundations were established around Moscow in the period by grand princes, metropolitans, abbots and the disciples of monastic saints.[20] But most were founded further afield – to win more virgin land for the plough, to convert pagan tribespeople, to profit from commercial crossroads, to access natural resources like salt. They were founded for these and a dozen other reasons, but, above all, monasteries were the organizational heart of the ongoing colonization process, whose tempo so accelerated in the fourteenth century. And when, in the mid-1500s, a Western visitor was to marvel at the fact that monasteries owned one-third of all land in the entire country[21] it was largely to the legacy of St Sergius that he was pointing – a multifaceted legacy of economic and political as well as spiritual and patriotic significance.[22]

Despite all this building, striving and achievement, in 1400 there was no obvious prospect that the Grand Principality of Moscow-Vladimir would develop into a great European power. It controlled only a fraction of the territory inhabited by Russians. Most of what it did control was within 50 to 350 miles of Moscow, though some of this territory was interspersed with the apanages of other princes. True, the Grand Prince took precedence over all other princes, but his titles did not imply authority. Although the apanage (*udel'*) had originally been a temporary allocation of property from a prince's inheritance for the upkeep of a family member, since about 1350 apanages had been granted to subordinate princes in perpetuity. Every prince guarded his apanage, his inheritance, and proud, prosperous city states like Pskov, Novgorod and Smolensk only took orders from the Grand Prince if it were in their interest to do so, or unless he compelled them. The Metropolitan, who still had spiritual authority over the Orthodox of Lithuania, had more communicants than the Grand Prince had subjects. Furthermore, the grand princes themselves were less than confident in the future they were trying to build, and were by no means certain that their descendants would inherit their property. A phrase recurring in their wills makes that much plain: 'if God brings about a change concerning the Tatars'.[23]

On the other hand metropolitans provided grand princes with substantial political support. The Orthodox Church believed that it should always work 'in symphony' with the legitimate, God-given, ruler. But circumstances made it particularly anxious to do so. Since the Great Schism in the Church, the Latin West, led by the Pope, had been trying to encroach on the ecclesiastical territory of the Orthodox Church, and – especially now that the struggle for the spiritual destiny of Lithuania loomed so large – the Church needed the Grand Prince's support. Even so, the Grand Principality of Moscow itself was in a difficult strategic position, repeatedly in danger, placed as it was between the pincers of two dangerous enemies: the Tatars to the east and the Lithuanians to the west.

Besieged by Lithuanian armies in 1368 and again in 1370, it was captured and laid waste by Tatars in 1382, and besieged again in 1408 by the Tatar Yedigei, who extracted a large ransom for it. A Tatar army reached Moscow again in 1439, though by then its walls were built of stone and brick rather than of earth and timber. And the Tatars would still return thereafter, even though the city was no longer easy prey. Abandoning Moscow and fleeing with one's treasure at the approach of an enemy was to become an almost routine practice for Moscow's rulers. Yet somehow they survived the repeated assaults of external enemies. But then civil war erupted.

Grand Prince Dmitrii was to be succeeded by his eldest son, Vasilii I, and his grandson, Vasilii II. But, though their combined reigns lasted almost three-quarters of a century – from 1389 to 1462 – they were to be less fortunate than Dmitrii. From the beginning of his reign Vasilii I was overshadowed by the high-riding Grand Duke of Lithuania. Nevertheless, he seized opportunities when he could. When the Tatars were diverted by their enemies in the east, he annexed the strategic principality of Nizhnii-Novgorod further down the Volga, though he failed to impose effective rule over all of it. In 1398 he tried to seize another strategic asset, (this time from Novgorod the Great): the valley of the Northern Dvina. He was repulsed. He tried again, without success, in 1401.

While Moscow struggled against its neighbours to the east and west, restive subordinate principalities tried to wriggle their way towards greater autonomy. The dreaded Khan Tamerlane created panic by leading his army towards Moscow. Then he swung away towards the east and the panic subsided. Moscow was at war with Lithuania from 1406 until 1408, and that same year Yedigei's Tatar army returned to pillage Vladimir. Russian renegades as well as Tatars took part in that operation. At the same time Vasilii was faced with a determined Lithuanian attempt to supplant Moscow as centre of the Orthodox Church. Vasilii I was a successful ruler only in the sense that, though he suffered many reverses, he managed to avoid disaster. His son Vasilii II did not fare so well.[24]

Vasilii II was only ten when, in 1425, he acceded to his father's throne. Provision had been made for his minority: a council of regents was to govern till he came of age. His mother and her father, Grand Duke Vitovt of Lithuania, were among its members. So were his uncles Andrei and Petr, his future father-in-law Prince Iaroslav of Sepukhov, and his brother Semen, both of them great-grandsons of Ivan 'Money-Bag'. The regency was knitted together by close kinship and political interest. But someone of account had been excluded: the boy-prince's eldest uncle, Iurii, whose power base included the profitable salt-producing region around Galich and Chukhloma and also Zvenigorod only a few miles to the west of Moscow. Iurii immediately claimed the throne on the ground of traditional, lateral succession in the House of Riurik. Moral pressure from the Patriarch Photius persuaded him to drop his claim – but not for long. When Photius and Grand Duke Vitovt died, he reasserted it and was soon in command at Moscow. Vasilii was forced to swear homage to his uncle and content himself with the Principality of Kolomna as his inheritance. The year was 1433; Vasilii was eighteen.

Many Muscovite notables would not accept Iurii as grand prince, however, and the upshot was civil war. An army of Vasilii's supporters sacked Iurii's base at Galich, but the following year Iurii counter-attacked and Vasilii himself was defeated and taken to Moscow, this time as his uncle's prisoner. Fortunately for him, Iurii died suddenly; but then his sons took up their father's claim. In 1436 Vasilii captured the elder of them, his cousin Vasilii Kosoi, and blinded him. But he was not secure as grand prince, and for the next several years he was absorbed in trying to exert an effective grip on his domains, keeping the Tatars out, and reacting to a crisis in the Church.[25]

The throne of the metropolitan had remained empty since Photii's death. It was eventually filled by Isidore, a Greek from Constantinople. But Isidore soon accepted an invitation to attend a Church council in Italy sponsored by the Pope. The papacy had long wanted to unite the Eastern and Western Churches on his own terms. With the Ottoman Turks pressing in on Constantinople from every side, the Emperor was desperate for aid and all for compromise. So was Russia's Greek patriarch. But most Russians found the idea appalling. For them the only true Christian faith was their faith. The 'Latins', such as the crusaders from north-west Europe, who had exhibited such greed, depravity and lack of sexual restraint when they had sacked Constantinople in 1204, no longer observed the practices, still less the morality, of the Orthodox Christian faith. And so, when Isidore returned to Russia from Ferrara in 1441, having agreed to acknowledge the Pope, Vasilii ordered his arrest. A more reliable Russian bishop eventually took his place, but not for seven years. For that period the cruel, unfortunate, Vasilii lacked the support his predecessors had come to rely on in difficult times. And before the situation was resolved his former enemies returned to haunt him.

A substantial fraction of what remained of the Golden Horde, led by Ulug-Mehmet, had taken to regularly pillaging Muscovite territory. Vasilii had tried to counter its raids without much success, and when, in 1445, he was confronted by it before all his forces could be mustered he suffered a disastrous defeat and was taken prisoner. Ulug-Mehmet thought of replacing Vasilii with Dmitrii Shemiaka, Vasilii's cousin, but eventually he sent 500 warriors to escort the Grand Prince back to Moscow. Vasilii returned in shame to a capital which had suffered a disastrous fire in his absence. Worse, Dmitrii now managed to raised support from among the Muscovite elite, and when the Grand Prince left town on a pilgrimage to the Holy Trinity Church and the shrine of St Sergius at Zagorsk, Dmitrii and his friends took possession of Moscow.

Soon afterwards, Vasilii was taken prisoner, whereupon Dmitrii, in revenge for his brother Vasilii Kosoi, had his eyes put out. Thenceforth the victim was known as Vasilii the Blind. Surprisingly, perhaps, the act did not emasculate him politically, but this was chiefly because of Dmitrii's mistakes. Rather like Richard III as pictured by Shakespeare, Dmitrii imprisoned Vasilii's young sons. This alienated many Russians, and when Vasilii journeyed to Tver people of many camps, including two of Ulug-Mehmet's own sons, came to join him on the way. By the time he turned back towards Moscow his following had grown into an army. Seeing no hope, Dmitrii abandoned the city. There ensued a slow but inexorable pursuit, and Dmitrii eventually submitted, and swore loyalty to Vasilii, in 1448. But as soon as Novgorod decided to lend him its power he reneged. By now he represented the interests of some of the more important principalities which were resisting the imposition of Moscow's supremacy, but within two years his forces had been overcome, his city of Galich had been captured, and he himself had been forced into exile in Novgorod, where, many months later, Vasilii's agents succeeded in poisoning him.

At last Blind Vasilii ruled unchallenged. But Muscovy was in a debilitated condition, and he was heavily dependent on the Church to exert moral pressure on political dissidents, even to threaten them with excommunication (as it had threatened Dmitrii in 1447). Smooth transfers of power could not be expected, and it became his urgent priority to establish a succession to his throne that would be regarded as legitimate. The recent civil wars had shown that claims based on genealogy could still be backed by force, and cities like Pskov, Tver and Novgorod could still assert themselves against Moscow. Besides, in theory at least, the Khan still decided who the Grand Prince was to be, granting him legitimacy with the issue of his *yarlyk*, his licence to rule. However, Vasilii's chancery had a strategy which it implemented with vigour.

It made great strides in claiming back apanages. It bought some, and took others by force, but that still left princes and cities which hankered after a remembered independence and bygone privileges. Determined to reinforce his power, which had been so much eroded, Vasilii did not spare those who stood in his way. Cities that had supported his enemies were punished. Novgorod was disciplined; compelled for the first time to use the Grand Prince's insignia in its official correspondence, and to swear never to enter into relations with foreign powers on its own initiative, it was also forced to pay a sizeable indemnity. A new prince of Pskov, which had hitherto been neutral, was forced to swear an oath of loyalty to the Grand Prince as well as undertaking to uphold the customs of Pskov. By 1460 Pskov was referring to itself as Blind Vasilii's 'hereditary property' (*otchina*), addressing him as 'Sovereign' (*Gosudar'*), and pledging loyalty not only to him but to his descendants.[26] Following the precedent set by Grand Prince Iurii Danilovich, who had annexed Mozhaisk in 1303, a Muscovite governor was imposed on it. In the same way the Principality of Tver became an hereditary property of the Grand Prince. The Principality of Riazan was also annexed. In effect all princely rights were becoming subject to the Grand Prince's will.

The brisk way in which these measures were taken suggests that policies were already in place, awaiting the opportunity to implement them, and that the Grand Prince had enough trained functionaries ready to carry them out. Policy was formulated by the blind ruler's executive council, or *duma*, consisting of five or six boyars – experienced executives drawn from the ranks of the princes, like I. Iu. Patrikeev, or untitled servitors, like F. M. Cheliadnia.[27] But implementation depended on a cadre of literate and numerate functionaries from the subjected principalities themselves and on servitors of former enemies as well as on the Grand Prince's own staff. This can be safely inferred from our knowledge of the reign of Blind Vasilii's son and successor, Ivan III, who was to continue the work. So the Grand Prince began to interpose himself between the subject princes and their people. A quasi-feudal, hierarchical ruling structure was beginning to give way to a more direct and absolutist regime.[28]

To the extent that the new governmental trend cut across traditional vested interests, it was unpopular; but society was tired of civil war, and Vasilii's strict regime promised to end it. The new metropolitan, Jonah, backed these policies to the hilt. The Church felt besieged and in particular need of the Grand Prince's support. Jonah had been installed by the Russian bishops, without reference to the Patriarch of Constantinople. This was an alarming breach of precedent, but the circumstances were extraordinary. It was generally recognized that Constantinople must soon fall to the Turks. Besides, most Russians were convinced that the senior patriarch, who had supported the Council of Ferrara/Florence had fallen from the faith. The installation of Metropolitan Jonah, therefore, signalled the independence of the Russian Church, but also isolated it. Furthermore, largely Orthodox Lithuania and Catholic Poland, united by a dynastic marriage in 1386, had begun to merge politically after the Treaty of Horodlo of 1413, and on terms which discriminated against non-Catholic nobles and gentry.

Vasilii was also helped by the break-up of the Golden Horde, creation of the Tatar khan, into the separate Tatar khanates of Kazan, Astrakhan, Siberia and the Crimea. The threat from Tatar raiders hardly diminished, but the possibilities of managing the problem by diplomatic as well as military means became greater. Now that the Tatars were in decline and the Golden Horde had split, they could no longer dictate who the grand prince was to be, and henceforth grand princes tried to assert their independence by seeking an additional, more impressive, title. They also began not only to nominate their chosen successors, but also to adopt the long-standing Byzantine practice, by which an emperor would co-opt his successor with him. In 1448 Vasilii the Blind co-opted his son, the future Ivan III, into government with him, formally investing him as co-ruler.

As well as striving to establish a legitimate succession, the grand princes had for some time been trying to bequeath incontestable title to their territories as personal property, and to eliminate the titles of lesser princes to their apanages. They went so far as to claim to have purchased lands they had in fact conquered, and willed their titles to their sons, hoping to secure the succession and inheritance of their property down the generations. Vasilii II succeeded in eliminating almost all apanages, though he also created new ones for his own offspring. The historian A. E. Presniakov argued that in the last resort Vasilii survived not because of any formal powers but thanks to the popular support he received. But Vasilii was aggressive, and the people expected him to be aggressive; the interests of the grand princes and their subjects happened to coincide. Such, implicitly, was the judgement of Liubavskii too. He attributed Moscow's success to power rather than territory – the grand princes' strengthening hold over the military class, their command of taxation resources and of landed assets.[29] But it was civil war which inspired the rise of Moscow and, according to some, the inception of the Russian autocracy.

Russia's political fractiousness in the period was paralleled in many other parts of Europe. England was riven by the Wars of the Roses for longer than the Russians were by their civil wars, and the states of Italy seemed to be locked in almost perpetual struggles. Petrarch had regretted Italy's lack of unity a century earlier, and the hard political advice that Machiavelli was to give in the century following was born of the bitter experience in the interim. Russians were exercising their minds about the problem too. Indeed, within a few decades, under Ivan III, they were to develop a more durable political entity in Moscow than the more brilliant Lorenzo de' Medici was to build in Florence, and begin to flex their muscles in a wider world.

4
The Foundation of an Empire

RATHER THAN STRIVING for an imperial role, Muscovy stumbled into one. The impetus came from the fall of Constantinople to the Turks in 1453. This long-expected but none the less traumatic event was immediately interpreted by the Russian bishops as a punishment for apostasy – Constantinople's dalliance with the Pope at the Council of Ferrara/ Florence. The work of legitimizing Russian imperial power began at that point, and again churchmen took the lead. The Legend of the White Cowl, suggesting that Moscow had become the seat of true Orthodoxy in religion, and the idea of Moscow as the 'Third Rome', the new capital of the Roman Empire, were both elaborated in monastic think-tanks. However, there was also a more tangible kind of transfer from Constantinople to Moscow: both before and after 1453, Greek refugees trickled in. They included churchmen, noblemen, artists and functionaries of every sort, and they brought with them the diplomatic, administrative and military expertise essential to the building of empires.

Moscow's rulers began to hanker after imperial dignity, both to boost their authority in their own domains and to enhance their standing abroad. They did not aspire to rule the world, however. Nor is there evidence that they contemplated ruling a multiplicity of different peoples as the Romans had done. Muscovy could double its territorial extent and power merely by extending its rule over linguistic Russians who were Orthodox Christians, through 'the ingathering of the Russian lands' as it came to be called. But the first priority was to complete the task that Vasilii the Blind had begun: to establish direct control over the subject princes and exploit their lands and people in a systematic way.

From this point of view the reign of Vasilii's twenty-two-year-old son, Ivan III, did not begin auspiciously. Within a year of his accession in 1462, Novgorod had applied to King Casimir of Poland-Lithuania for support against him, and the Knights of the Sword had invaded the Principality of Pskov from Livonia. Yet eventually he was to succeed on almost every front. He was to become the great centralizer of the Russian principalities, and an historical figure of comparable weight to his contemporaries Henry VII of England and Louis XI of France.

He resolved the ambiguous status of the more important apanage principalities. Their lords ruled on their own account, and although he was grand Prince – their acknowledged superior – in practice they could defy him. He might call on them to join him with all their force to repel an invader or to attack an enemy's stronghold, and they might very well comply, like those princes who had joined Dmitrii of the Don in his famous battle against the Tatars years before. But again they might not. Their assessments of necessity and advantage were not necessarily the same as his, and, even though they had a formal and moral obligation to the Grand Prince, they had the power to act as they pleased. And as long as they retained that power, Muscovy would be vulnerable to foreign enemies. Furthermore, the perpetuation of a subordinate prince's command over his own forces allowed the possibility of civil war. As the reign of Vasilii II had proved, a grand prince was ill-advised to trust even his nearest kith and kin. And so Ivan III determined to be 'sovereign over all the sovereigns of the Russian land'. His aim was to subordinate the princes to his will, absorb their private armies into his own army, and transfer such of their boyars as might be useful – and unconditionally loyal – into his own service. In short, he wanted to monopolize, and rationalize, power over the Russian lands. He also set out to solve the perennial succession question, to make possession of the throne hereditary, the permanent property (*votchina*) of himself and his descendants, requiring oaths not only to himself but to his chosen heir.[1]

In terms of Muscovy's territorial expansion the results were dramatic. In the 1470s Muscovy secured all Novgorod's northern territories as far as the east and west banks of the White Sea, and the lands of Great Perm eastward to the river Ob, which bordered on the frontier with the Khanate of Siberia. This brought more native peoples under Ivan's rule: Voguls and Ostiaks, Votiaks and Cheremis. The city state of Tver, which had hitherto blocked Moscow's way to the north, had been incorporated; Novgorod was crushed, and its constitution, which incorporated liberties for the propertied element, was overridden. Ivan had already annexed Iaroslavl (1463) and Viatka to the south. He stood firm against the Golden Horde's last attempt to bully Muscovy in 1480, and in 1493 he adopted the title 'Sovereign of All Russia'.

But territorial advance did not end there. Towards the west, Toropets was secured, and the important area between the rivers Ugra and Desna as far as the Berezina; and towards the south-east, also at Lithuania's expense, the towns of Briansk and Chernigov were taken. Muscovy's power now extended to not far short of Kiev itself. More than this, by the time of his death in 1505, Ivan had increased his country's military power, placed the state's finances on a sounder footing, and laid the foundations of a system by which property and status depended on service to the Grand Prince. Inheritance was still to count, but it came to apply as much to obligations – particularly obligations to serve the Grand Prince – as to property and privilege.

These achievements may be enough to justify Ivan's sobriquet 'the Great', but there was also another: it was he who made Muscovy a European power to be reckoned with. He established diplomatic relations with Ottoman Turkey as well as with Poland-Lithuania and the Tatars, and exchanged embassies with Denmark, Venice, Georgia, Hungary and the Holy Roman Emperor. Nor did Ivan behave like a respectful newcomer among Europe's heads of states. When the Emperor, anxious to please him, offered him the title of king, Ivan summarily rejected it. He would not be patronized. He had a better estimation of his dignity than that.

Ivan, more than any other individual, was the architect of the Muscovite state, and he gave it the capability of becoming an empire. But there were costs. His rule was exacting and oppressive. He crushed Novgorod and its autonomous institutions; he carried out dispossessions on a large scale; and his reign has been described, with some justice, as one of 'cultural depression and spiritual barrenness'. In all these respects Ivan III resembles Ivan the Terrible, Nicholas I, Stalin and all the other Russian tyrants. But is this fair? Were the Tudor rulers of England less tyrannical than he? Were their exactions less demanding? Did Catholics and humanists not suffer under them? Should not historical figures be judged in context, and according to the standards of their own times rather than of ours?[2]

There is no doubt that Ivan's reign saw a marked upward surge in Russia's fortunes, and that he was in large measure responsible for it; but, like so many great historical figures, he enjoyed a good share of luck. The death of his first wife, Maria of Tver, in April 1467, is a case in point, for the sad event opened up an unexpected opportunity. In 1469 a Byzantine Greek called Iurii Trakhaniot arrived in Moscow bearing a letter from Bessarion, an eminent scholar from Constantinople who had taken refuge from the Turks in Rome. The letter proposed marriage between Ivan and Zoe Palaeologue, the daughter of the Despot of Morea and niece of Constantinople's last emperor.[3] Whatever the lady's personal attributes, politically the offer was tempting. A union between the house of Moscow and the imperial dynasty would bring prestige and open up tempting prospects of aggrandizement.

Yet there were dangers attached. The Palaeologues were virtual beggars. A kinsman of the girl was known to have been touting his titles round the courts of Europe for sale. Worse, Zoe's Orthodox credentials were questionable. She was a ward of the Pope, Paul II. As for the intermediary, Bessarion, he had played a prominent part in the notorious Council of Ferrara/Florence, had subscribed to the union with Rome, which Muscovy had rejected, and now wore a cardinal's hat. Clearly the Pope was offering Zoe as bait, hoping to bring the Russian ruler into communion with Rome. If it came to marriage, the Orthodox Church might withdraw its support and the Grand Prince could well be rendered powerless in the face of a popular rebellion. Nevertheless, Ivan responded positively to the overture. Evidently he and his closest advisers thought they could take the bait and avoid the trap. Negotiations began. They were to last the better part of three years.

At last, in 1472, Zoe and her suite arrived in Moscow, accompanied by a papal legate who brought her a handsome dowry of 6,000 gold ducats donated by the Pope. The marriage took place in Moscow in November – though not before Zoe had been renamed Sofia, presumably in order to emphasize her commitment to the Eastern Church and distance her from her Catholic connections, rather as a novice would be renamed on taking holy orders as a nun. Nevertheless, the Metropolitan and other prelates excused themselves from the ceremony on canonical grounds, so an arch-priest and Ivan's personal chaplain officiated. Obviously carefully instructed and monitored, the bride was to observe every behavioural rule and convention of a strictly Orthodox grand princess, and, for the moment at least, there was to be no obvious public reaction. However, Ivan lost no time in exploiting his wife's imperial association in support of his own imperial pretensions. He adopted the double-headed eagle as his insignia, using it on his seals and emblazoning it on the backrest of his wooden throne.[4]

The matter came, or was brought, to the attention of foreigners too. The Senate of the Republic of Venice wrote to him in 1473 suggesting that 'The Eastern Empire, captured by the Ottoman, will with the ending of the imperial male line belong to your illustrious self, thanks to your fortunate marriage.'[5]

Ivan was developing a much clearer and firmer sense of his status. But he had not yet imposed his imperial will over all the Russian principalities.

*

The rulers of Novgorod had seen the danger that Ivan of Moscow posed for them and had moved to pre-empt him. It was this that had precipitated the Muscovite assault.[6] Opinion in Novgorod was divided. The Boretskii faction wanted to guard what was left of Novgorod's independence against any further encroachment and to recover privileges already lost. Since the city could not muster sufficient power to resist the Grand Prince, it asked King Casimir of Poland-Lithuania for assistance. This was tantamount to treason and gave Ivan good cause to intervene. According to a Muscovite chronicler, 'the entire city became restless and behaved as if drunk.'[7] But Ivan knew he could count on the support of those opposed to the Boretskii faction: the people who saw Moscow as the city's only reliable source of food and of defence. Rising food prices and anti-war sentiments in Novgorod lent them support. Each party had its stone-hurling street mob to back its cause.

War came, but did not turn out the way Boretskii hoped. King Casimir was preoccupied with affairs in Bohemia and Hungary and failed to send the expected support. Pskov, despite a treaty obligation to Novgorod, joined Ivan against it. The Archbishop of Novgorod advised the army not to resist the Grand Prince's troops but only those of Pskov who were with him, and the operations of Novgorod's own army were badly co-ordinated. The campaign was almost a walkover. Ivan appeared magnanimous in victory: his terms were lenient, and he returned to Moscow in triumph to be greeted 4 miles outside the gates by the merchants and the artisan elite as well as by the princes and boyars, and the people of the city.[8]

Four years later he returned to Novgorod with more demands. The city's assembly and the post of mayor were to be abolished. There would be no potential power base for any future Boretskii. And Ivan wanted land too – a great deal of it. Novgorod's initial response was rejected, but eventually a deal was reached. Ivan would get the lands of Torzhok, an area of strategic importance that included an important portage, and which not only gave access to Novgorod but allowed him to seal off Tver. He was also to receive over 30,000 acres belonging to Novgorod's archbishop and half the landed property of its six largest monasteries – a total of over 100,000 acres aside from the Torzhok lands.

The opposition would not be reconciled, however, so in 1478 Ivan returned to bombard Novgorod into submission. This time there were arrests, and a hundred men were executed for treason. The Archbishop was implicated too. He was imprisoned in a monastery, and all his property confiscated.[9] The acreage at the disposal of the state was now huge, and it is here that a wider aspect of Ivan's grand strategy becomes apparent. To secure this strategic region on Muscovy's western frontier, Ivan needed to settle his own men, his own servitors, there. The Grand Prince appropriated about 2.7 million acres of land at a stroke. He retained nearly half of it for himself or the state (no distinction was drawn between the two); on the remainder he settled 2,000 of his people – some of them loyalists from Novgorod, the others outsiders. The idea, which anticipated that of the Irish plantations, had a similar purpose: to establish a politically reliable element of sufficient size to secure the region. The inspiration almost certainly came from Constantinople. Under the late-Roman/Byzantine *pronoia* system, state land was leased in small parcels in return for service to the state, and was heritable by a son who followed his father into state service.

Ivan seems to have imitated this practice. Under the system he laid down in Novgorod, a servitor was allotted land to support himself in service in the form of a conditional lease, which was heritable on the same condition. The institution, called *pomestie* in Russian, was to be extended subsequently with a series of deportations and resettlements. Good coin was relatively scarce in Muscovy, and an estate allowed a servitor to support himself and his family without need for cash. Furthermore, transportations and resettlements on a grand scale, especially in vulnerable frontier areas, had also been a late-Roman practice.[10] *Pomestie* was to allow Ivan to field an army three or four times the size of that which his father, Vasilii, had commanded. It was certainly a practice that was to be much used in Russia in the future. Indeed, it became the mainstay of both civil and military servicemen for generations to come – a major Russian institution: the cornerstone of the Muscovite service state.

It had administrative implications, however. Some time after the state took possession of the land on which servitors were to be settled, a small army of officials descended upon it. In effect they mapped each area, recording its extent, its settlements, its rivers, and the quality and lie of the land in cadastral registers. And the allotments to servicemen were also recorded. Indeed a new office had to be founded in Ivan's reign to administer the servicemen who held the land, so that they could be called upon, properly armed and equipped, when they were needed. This came to be known as the Muster Office (*Razriad*), and so vital was it to a Russian ruler that from the beginning it was run not by a boyar, however trusted a counsellor, but by experienced senior secretaries responsible directly to the ruler.

Once affairs in Novgorod were settled, a harder line was imposed on Pskov, and then on Tver, whose Grand Prince Mikhail had sworn loyalty to Casimir of Poland. In the late summer of 1485 Muscovite forces descended on Tver in strength and with a powerful artillery train directed by an Italian in Ivan's service, Aristotele Fioravanti. The show of overwhelming strength was sufficient to achieve Ivan's purpose without being used. After suburbs had been set on fire, Tver capitulated. Prince Mikhail fled to Lithuania; the rest of the elite swore oaths of loyalty to Ivan. The oath-taking was not reciprocal. Allegiance to Ivan was not a matter of mutuality; furthermore, it was to extend to his heirs.[11]

Nevertheless, authority was imposed in ways that would not arouse more hostility than necessary, and the Grand Prince took care to show grace and favour to those on whom he most depended. As with other principalities that Moscow absorbed, steps were taken to reconcile those who mattered and put them to use, but at the same time the old elite were not neglected. The most important members, including some princes in their own right, were accorded the rank of boyar or of senior counsellor (*okolnichii*). These were the most senior people in the Grand Prince's entourage. Such designations carried with them great prestige and privilege. They also gave the heirs of those so honoured the expectation of a similarly high place in the pecking order for court ceremonies as well as for judicial and administrative positions, and even military campaigns. There were no more than a dozen members of this exclusive order at this juncture.[12] Subsequently it was to develop into a great council of state. Muscovy was already acquiring some institutions that were to facilitate the running of an empire.

While Ivan was extending and strengthening his government's hold over territories settled by Russians and ruled by other descendants of Riurik, he was also establishing Russia's position as a European power. The fact that he succeeded in making his mark with most other crown heads seems truly astonishing, given the obstacles. Russia, after all, was relatively isolated from the rest of Europe, which was mostly Catholic; the Orthodox Church encouraged an aversion to things foreign, including languages and learning, and there was a substantial and growing culture gap separating Russia from western Europe. True, foreign powers – including the papacy – made part of the running, trying to involve the Grand Prince in alliances and other schemes to promote their interests, but Ivan was always firmly engaged in pursuit of his own interests, which often placed him in an adversarial relationship with others. How, then, did he succeed in mediating these problems, conducting a successful foreign policy, and, in the process, creating an efficient diplomatic establishment?

The culture gap was bridged in the first place by Greek immigrants from Constantinople (some of whom had arrived in the entourage of Ivan's new wife) who were engaged to serve the Grand Prince. The two Trakhaniot brothers – who had served the Byzantine emperor – the Rhallis, the Angelos, the Laskaris and others were familiar with imperial protocol and institutions. They also had practical knowledge of how Europe's rulers dealt with one another, and brought their understandings of late-Roman statecraft to Russia. Iurii Trakhaniot served as ambassador to the Holy Roman Emperor Frederick III and to the King of Denmark, helped organize the reception of the imperial ambassador to Moscow, and was to rise to the dignity of treasurer (*kaznachei*), the Russian official in charge of foreign relations at that time.[13] Other immigrants were ethnic Italians, notably Gianbattista della Volpe, who has been credited with suggesting the match between Ivan and Zoe/Sofia. He was engaged as Ivan's master of the mint, and some of his relatives were hired too. Volpe himself eventually became an Orthodox Christian, but it is not certain if all 'Latin' incomers did, and the Grand Prince employed at least one German and even a Jew, a merchant called Khoja Kokos, whom he used as an intermediary in the Crimea.[14] But many more of the first Russian diplomats were home grown.

Most of these originally had other, lesser, functions at court, several of them as clerks or falconers. Falconry was an elite sport in late medieval Europe, not least in Russia, and the Grand Prince ran a large falconry establishment. Since well-trained falcons made princely gifts for foreign potentates, some of these falconers came to be used in diplomatic functions. One such was Mikhail Iaropkin, who was sent as an envoy to Poland four times. But the work was directed and processed by officials, secretaries and under-secretaries – some of them specialists like Andrei Fedorovich Maiko, who dealt chiefly with Polish-Lithuanian affairs – and there was a team of translators to handle the correspondence. By 1500 there were to be more than twenty translators, including Bakshei, who dealt with correspondence in Turkish with the khans of the Crimea, the nomadic Nogais, and with the Ottoman sultan. From 1504 there was a permanent German translator, Istoma Maloi.[15]

The small but variegated cadre of officials translated documents from and into foreign languages (mainly Latin), acted as interpreters, served as envoys and messengers to foreign courts, saw to the reception of foreign emissaries in Russia, and advised the Grand Prince on the wider world. They drew up letters of credence for outgoing embassies, ensuring they presented the Grand Prince's titles accurately and sealing them with the appropriate seal – from 1497 both the ancient symbol of the Roman Empire, the double-headed eagle, and the image of St George slaying a dragon.[16] They also established a record-filing system which was to prove essential not only for establishing protocol and precedence but as a back-file on policy and a source of knowledge on anything from philosophy to firearms. The staff resources must have been stretched as the Grand Prince's foreign relations became more widespread and complex. In the last quarter of the fifteenth century links were established with Milan and Hungary, Kakhetia and Vienna. An alliance was formed with Denmark against Sweden, and new policies were formulated towards the Hanseatic League of north-German commercial cities and towards the Livonian Knights, as well as the successor states of the Golden Horde.[17] True, there were no permanent embassies at that time: one ruler would send a mission to another only as occasion demanded. Even so, we can infer that staffing such missions must have constituted a problem.

Educated immigrants in Ivan's service were relatively few, so Russians had to be sent out. However, most Russians of the time lacked not only knowledge of a foreign language but also the required degree of sophistication and self-discipline; hence rules were laid down for them to follow. The instructions to an embassy to Poland, which was headed by a senior counsellor (*okolnichii*) and included one of the above-mentioned falconers, began with exhortations to members of the embassy to respect each other. It went on to explain protocol, particularly relating to the drink with which their hosts could be expected to regale them after dinner:

'You should drink moderately, and not to the point of drunkenness. Wherever you happen to drink you should watch yourself and drink carefully, lest your carelessness bring dishonour to Our name. Any misbehaviour on your part will dishonour both Us and yourselves, so watch yourselves in all things.' Finally came rules regarding precedence within the embassy, and the enforcement of discipline: 'Reprimand anyone who disobeys you, and hit him.'[18]

The repetition and the violence reflect a largely oral culture and a boorish society with a tendency to anarchy. Despite this, the routines put in place for managing Ivan's foreign relations, with their meticulous paperwork, their care for precedent, and their tendency never to take anything for granted, were to help Russia keep abreast of the European diplomatic system, which by 1500 was still in the process of formation.[19]

Cynics may define a diplomat as someone who goes abroad to lie for his country, but diplomats have usually been spies too, in the sense of being used to gather intelligence. The Russians were no exception. One embassy was instructed to gather political intelligence not only on Austria and Hungary but also on France and Brittany, to establish what the Habsburg emperor Maximilian's intentions were towards Hungary. (Maximilian had asked

Muscovy for help when Matthias Corvinus, king of Hungary, captured Vienna in 1485.) But Moscow also wanted to know what the Emperor's present marital status was, and what suitable brides for the Grand Prince's sons might be available at his court. A mission sent to Poland in 1493 was charged in particular with finding out about Conrad of Mazovia. Was he now subservient to King Casimir, with whom he had been in conflict? What dues and services did he owe Casimir? What were his relations with Prussia? What was his position in the princely pecking order? And how populous and powerful was the principality he ruled? The list went on.[20]

How quickly Muscovy learned the language of diplomacy and how to seize advantage and avoid the pitfalls of the diplomatic game is illustrated by the handling of a seemingly flattering overture from the Holy Roman Emperor. In 1489 an emissary called Nicholas Poppel arrived with a letter of credence from the Holy Roman Emperor Frederick III. He proceeded to outline a proposal for a dynastic marriage between Ivan's daughter and one of three candidates: Duke Albrecht of Padua, Count John of Saxony, and Sigismund, margrave of Baden. He also asked if Ivan would accept the title 'king' from the Emperor. The proposal might seem flattering, but the next day Poppel was told that Ivan would send his reply to the marriage proposal to the Emperor with his own emissary. As for the offer of a royal crown, Ivan affected outrage at the implication that he was not the Emperor's equal: 'By the grace of God we have always been sovereign in our territories, since the first of our ancestors.' He did not hold his titles thanks to anyone else, nor had he purchased them: 'We can be regarded as no one's subject by any authority. We hold our title only from Christ. We reject rights deriving from others.'[21]

Clearly the Emperor was underinformed about the Grand Prince. Indeed, Poppel's instructions had included a charge to find out whether Ivan was a vassal of the Polish king, and Ivan's men had to explain to Poppel that, so far from being his vassal, Ivan was both richer and more powerful than Casimir.[22] The response to Frederick's marriage proposal was delivered by an embassy headed by Iurii Trakhaniot. It explained that Russia's rulers had long had relations of 'love and alliance' with the Roman emperors, 'who had given Rome to the Pope and themselves ruled from Byzantium even until the time of my own father-in-law John Palaeologue'. It was therefore inappropriate for Ivan's daughter to marry princes of such low rank as had been proposed, although a match with Frederick's son, the recently widowered Archduke Maximilian, might be possible.

Although Muscovy's department of foreign affairs, the Ambassadorial Office, was not formally established until the 1500s, the late 1400s saw the foundation, of Muscovy's foreign service and intelligence-gathering system. It was to develop into an essential and most effective instrument in the building of Russian empires.

Military development was also proceeding apace. Indeed Ivan's envoy to the Duke of Milan in 1486 took care to make it clear that Muscovy boasted a well-armed and well-organized army. The cavalry were plentifully supplied with horses from Tatary as well as Russia. They carried scimitars as well as lances, and wore light body armour like that of the Ottoman sultan's Mamelukes. The infantry, by contrast, were equipped with the latest Western technology, including the latest type of crossbow out of Germany and firearms. Indeed the Grand Prince's servicemen had 'grown accustomed' to using firearms identified as matchlock arquebuses.[23] By the beginning of the sixteenth century as many as a thousand of these could be deployed in an operation, and soon they were being distributed among units at commanders' discretion to provide firepower where needed. They were used to defend Pskov against attacks by the Livonian order of the Knights of the Sword, and on the southern frontier against incursions by Crimean Tatars.[24] Ivan also invited German gunsmiths to Moscow to establish firearms manufacture and save the cost of importation.

Moscow had been casting cannon since the 1300s, and the size and effectiveness of its artillery had grown incrementally thereafter.[25] Cannon had pounded the walls of Novgorod in the 1470s, helping to reduce the city to submission, but their deployment in battle and at sieges required effective logistical support. Guns were transported on rafts along river routes, but were also hauled overland by teams of men and animals; lines of supply were guarded by manned posts. All this required a considerable organizational effort, and the mobilization of the necessary manpower and equipment along the lines of march.

At the same time, the nature of warfare against Tatars in areas where the Russian population was relatively thin on the ground and the enemy highly mobile required a constant state of high alert and led to a less conventional military response. It was in the 1400s that the government began to retain the services of independent or renegade Tatar groups like those of Riazan to give early warning of a raiding party's approach and to slow down their advance. This was the origin of the Cossack hosts, which were to play so significant a role in Russia's imperial advance later. The cost was relatively modest, and it helped to extend the area safe for agriculture, so indirectly it brought an economic benefit too.

Even so, the rising expense of the military establishment, and of the court (which was also the centre of governmental administration), required marked increases in taxes and duties. Although they occasioned rising discontent among those who had to pay, these impositions seem to have encouraged growth. Rising taxes are often said to be bad for the economy, yet in the Russian context of that time they actually stimulated it. Because landlords increased their demands of their serfs and tenants, the peasants had to work harder, and more land was brought under the plough. Because Ivan's increased demands had to be paid in coin, the subject princes and their boyars had to produce a surplus for sale from their estates rather than consuming it, and deploy the labour at their command more rationally. Yet the fact that the population grew at a healthy rate suggests that people as a whole were no worse fed as a result of all this.

Facing such diverse adversaries as Kazan and the Crimea, Sweden, Livonia and Poland-Lithuania, and the danger of engaging too many of them simultaneously, Ivan III needed an astute foreign policy as well as a strong and flexible army. With his good timing and readiness to break off a fight if the outcome looked unpromising, he proved equal to the challenge. He also made a shrewd choices of allies.

The break-up of the Golden Horde did not end the Tatar threat, which lasted well into the sixteenth century. But it radically changed the balance of power in the south, allowing Muscovy to set the successor states to the Horde against each other and against Poland-Lithuania. Ivan played this game with great skill. He backed the claims of Muhammed-Amin to supplant his father, the Khan of Kazan. He befriended Mengli-Girei, the Crimean khan, and the Nogai Tatars, using them to counter both the Golden Horde and Poland-Lithuania. Thanks to the alliance with the Crimean Tatars, Ivan was able to take the great city of Kazan, emporium of steppe trade, for a time, and eventually to draw the sting from the Great Horde itself altogether.

As the eighteenth-century historian Prince Mikhail Shcherbatov noted, Ivan III's foreign policy interacted closely with his domestic centralizing policies. The Golden Horde's assaults on Muscovy in 1472 and 1480 were the occasions of 'agreements' between Ivan and his brothers Boris and Andrei which spoke of brotherly support and their common blood but which in fact destroyed their younger brothers' capacity for independent action. Ivan was equally firm with his own sons. He deprived them of their former right to dispose of their apanages as if they were their personal property rather than lands allotted for their maintenance during their father's pleasure, which had been the original purpose of the apanage. And he forbade all the princes to coin their own money.[26]

Ivan's policy of subjecting apanage princes to his authority led some of them to seek the support of Poland-Lithuania, and, as we have seen, Novgorod's attempt to do so precipitated Ivan's campaign against the city. On the other hand, his firm centralization measures of the 1480s and '90s, which subjected Novgorod and other principalities of the north-west to his direct rule, were a necessary prelude to a three-year struggle against both Alexander of Poland-Lithuania and the Knights of Livonia, beginning in 1500.[27]

Contrasting strategic motives were involved in these wars. Ideology, as well as interest, inspired Muscovite hostility to Poland-Lithuania. Perhaps because Lithuania had been pagan until comparatively recently, the Catholic Church in Poland adopted something of a crusading attitude towards it, but its concern to convert pagans was soon transmuted into a concern to convert Orthodox Christians, of which there were considerable numbers in Lithuania. This angered Moscow, as did Poland's attempts to separate the Orthodox hierarchy of Lithuania from the Metropolitan of Moscow. It also alienated many of Lithuania's noble class (boyars), many of whom defected to Moscow in the 1490s, helping Muscovy seize Viazma and occupy the strategic area westward to the Berezina, and opening the road into Ukraine.

The Russians were less vigorous and adept missionaries than the Latins. Nevertheless, they had acquired a missionizing legacy from Byzantium and were encouraged to pursue it by a delegation of Orthodox notables from Constantinople, who had arrived in Moscow just before their own city fell. They had suggested that 'the great Patriarchal rank of this imperial city will be given over . . . to bright Russia, for in bestowing these gifts God wants the Russian lands to fulfil the glory of the Orthodox mission'.[28]

When war with Poland came, it took on the character of a crusade for both sides. This made it easier to justify cruelty, although terror had had respectable credentials in war since the time of the Romans. It could induce panic among the enemy, and its devastation could be used to empty an area of people and crops, rendering it incapable of sustaining enemy forces. To that extent terror was a defensive tactic.

Although Ivan's motives in fighting the Knights of Livonia were in part religious, they were chiefly economic and strategic. With its expanding connections with the rest of Europe, Moscow recognized the advantages that would flow from having direct access to the Baltic and through the Baltic to the West. It was also beginning to realize that there was more profit to be made from trading with the West directly rather than through intermediaries like the Hansa. Such considerations figured in Ivan's decision in 1492 to build a fort (which he called Ivan's town, Ivangorod) opposite Narva, on the left bank of the river that flowed north from his loyal city of Pskov into the Baltic, and to close down the Hansa's operation in Novgorod. Here was the genesis of both Russia's search for 'a window on the West' and its struggle to come to terms with the nascent world economy.

War with the Knights continued intermittently from 1490 to 1510. It resumed after an interval in 1501 at the Knights' initiative. They were able to field 2,000 German mercenaries – both cavalry and men-at-arms – in addition to their own numbers, and had a commitment from Alexander of Lithuania, brother of King Casimir of Poland, with whom they had signed an offensive alliance. Hostilities began with the Knights marching on Izborsk and winning a victory against such Muscovite troops as could be mustered. But then Alexander was diverted by the death of his brother, King Casimir, and the need to secure his crown. In the event, the Knights, under their Master, Walter von Plettenberg, had to fight on without him. Then a force of Russians arrived, and between them the two armies devastated the country.

Perhaps because of the crusading spirit, wars on this front had long been fought in a vicious manner. In the 1470s, for example, the Knights had burned Kobyle on the east shore of Lake Peipus, together with 3,985 people. On this occasion Moscow sent in a force of Tatars and a new terror weapon, 1,600 dogs (the memory of which may have inspired Shakespeare's reference a century later to letting loose the dogs of war). The Knights retaliated by attacking Pskov, where both sides fought each other to a standstill. In 1502 the Livonian war was subsumed into a larger conflict between Muscovy and Poland-Lithuania, and in 1503 Ivan and von Plettenberg concluded a peace at Pskov.[29]

The Knights had repeatedly asked Rome to endorse their crusade against the Orthodox Russians, but the Pope was more concerned with the Turkish threat and anxious, if he could, to enlist Ivan's support against it. But Poland-Lithuania was soon taking up the cry. By 1515 its king was assuring the Pope that the Grand Prince of Moscow was 'a Sarmatian Asiatic-tyrant, a blasphemer and schismatic' bent on 'the downfall of the Roman Church'.[30] Certainly the war inspired the publication of the first of a long series of German flysheets (*Flugschriften*) proclaiming anti-Russian sentiments in increasingly vitriolic terms. Cold War rhetoric was of ancient provenance, and had its beginning here, in Russia's first imperialist push towards the west.[31]

*

Despite the Polish king's aspersions, Muscovy no longer humbled itself before the Asiatic Tatars. Indeed, it now sought to subdue them, but its face was already turned Janus-like towards the West as well. Greeks and Germans had been recruited for Ivan's service, and he seems to have now exploited contacts with the Byzantine émigrés in Italy to bring Italians with modern skills to Moscow. They included the architect Pietro Antonio Solari of Milan, who designed the new Saviour Gate to the Kremlin and the magnificent reception hall known as the Hall of Facets, and the brilliant engineer, coiner and Renaissance jack of many trades Aristotele Fioravanti of Ferrara.

Meanwhile, although the Church had been uneasy about Ivan's second marriage and his association with Rome, with the Latins and the ways of the Latins, the Grand Prince had had his way. But tensions had continued to simmer under the surface, and now they erupted. It was whispered that there was a conspiracy to undermine the purity of Russians' Orthodox faith, and that several prominent figures very close to the Grand Prince were part of it. So was Metropolitan Zosimus. These were the so-called 'Judaizers'.

There was nothing Jewish about them. 'Judaizer' was simply a term of ideological abuse, like 'Trotskyist' in the 1930s. To label one's enemies as heretics was to establish a correct political line, and, as in the 1930s, this process was associated with purges. The nearest the Judaizers came to the heresy they were accused of was, perhaps, to borrow a form of rationalism from humanists in the West, but the controversy was strongly informed by political interest. Ivan himself seems to have been attracted by one aspect of the so-called heresy, because it opened up the possibility of secularizing church lands,[32] which, as we have seen in regard to the Novgorod appropriations, he was anxious to do. Like Henry VIII of England, who presided over the dissolution of the monasteries, Ivan was anxious to place the Church's assets at the disposal of the state.

The purgers' first target, however, was Metropolitan Zosimus. Zosimus's public reference to Ivan as 'the new Emperor Constantine of the new Constantinople – Moscow' had justified the confidence which had Ivan to appoint him.[33] Yet such was the current extent of feeling against Zosimus that the Grand Prince, ever the sensitive politician, allowed him to be sacrificed. Zosimus was ousted in 1496, and was subsequently relegated in official church history to the status of 'a wicked heretic' for his alleged 'Judaizing'.[34] But that was not the end of it. Fingers pointed to several other important figures close to the Grand Prince – to Fedor Kuritsyn, one of Ivan's leading diplomats and foreign-policy advisers; to the Greek Trakhaniot brothers; even to the Grand Princess Sofia.

She had, after all, been a Uniate and a ward of the Pope. Ivan protected them, at least for a time.

In 1497 Ivan presided over a council of bishops and officials which issued a law book (*Sudebnik*), but this civil triumph was soon overshadowed by palace conspiracies. In a dramatic turn of events, the Grand Prince's eldest surviving son, Prince Vasilii, was disgraced and disinherited. The following year Ivan invested his grandson Dmitrii, who was only a few years younger than the disinherited Vasilii, as his co-ruler and heir. Vasilii's supporters tried to organize a *coup d'état*, but were discovered and executed. At issue was more than the question of which of the Grand Prince's progeny should succeed him when he died; related developments suggest that policy was also at stake. The Trakhaniots fell out of favour and Sofia herself, who was implicated in the coup, fell under a cloud. So did Ivan's personal secretary, Ivan Volk Kuritsyn, whose brother Fedor may have served the opposition as a surrogate and scapegoat for the Grand Prince himself.

Kuritsyn was a nickname, meaning 'hen', perhaps because the family's heraldic sign was a cockerel. The Kuritsyns had aristocratic connections, and formed a veritable dynasty of top officials. Ivan Volk had led a 1492 embassy to the West, which had provided a mass of invaluable information on European affairs; he was associated with the Grand Prince's centralizing policies, and had served as the senior civil official on the Novgorod campaign of 1495. Clearly he had a great many enemies. He was hated by those who had lost hereditary family privileges and property through the Grand Prince's policies, by the losers in the succession crises of the 1490s, and by those who were disturbed by the importation of foreigners and foreign things.

In 1499 the disinherited Vasilii was suddenly back in favour, though not reinstated as co-ruler, but the Kremlin remained in the grip of intrigue. In 1500 Vasilii raised an armed rebellion against his father, but then came to some accommodation with him and submitted. In 1502 Ivan had Vasilii's rival, Dmitrii, arrested and accused of impertinence. Disobedience and even disappointment received short shrift at the hands of an old and probably ailing ruler determined to keep control. But Ivan had to contend with fierce resentment on the part of the disinherited, and from conservatives who feared the modernization implied by the dawning age of absolutism. Ivan's secretary, Ivan Volk Kuritsyn, became a lightning rod for all their hatred and resentment. Even the Grand Prince, by then well into his last illness, could not save him, and so, in 1504, Ivan Volk was burned alive in a cage as a Judaizer.[35] The Grand Prince himself, whom his secretary had served so well, died a year later. Their work, however, was preserved. Ivan III had presided over a revolution of a kind, and every revolution has its victims.

Vasilii III succeeded as Grand Prince, and ruled for twenty-eight years. Despite his conflicts with his father, he continued Ivan's policies, exhibiting the same principles of statecraft. How much these principles were due to the rulers themselves and how much to advisers such as Vasilii Dolmatov – diplomat, registrar, oath-giver and personal secretary to (and, according to Habsburg ambassador Sigismund von Herberstein, favourite of) the Grand Prince – is impossible to determine. But certainly caution prevailed. Whenever possible, objectives, were achieved incrementally rather than all at once, and by negotiation and conciliation rather than confrontation. Battle was offered only if the Muscovites had clear superiority. Both Ivan and Vasilii took care to reward their servitors and show their subjects a pious, kindly and pleasant face – yet were sudden and ruthless in punishing those who fell out of line. Together they tripled Muscovy's territorial extent.[36]

In 1514 Vasilii captured the important city of Smolensk to the west. Only a few years before, he had abolished Pskov's former liberties. It was by then safe for him to do so. He had made peace with both Lithuania and Livonia in 1509. Until that point he could not afford to antagonize Pskov, which was so important for mobilizing troops on the western frontier, by threatening what remained of its autonomy. But once he no longer needed to placate it, its offending institutions were eliminated.[37] Having strengthened Muscovy's position in the west, he then turned to the south. In 1523 he tried and failed to take the Tatar city of Kazan, but then found an inventive way of bypassing it and achieving a large part of his purpose by building a fort near by. He called it Vasilievskaia, after himself. The project was expensive, but soon repaid the investment, for not only did Vasilievskaia threaten Kazan, it sheltered a fair which succeeding in stealing most of the trade of the nomadic Nogai Tatars, which had formerly gone to Kazan.[38] Meanwhile he cultivated relations with Europe's great powers, especially the Emperor. In 1514 Vasily's diplomats scored a triumph: their master was actually referred to as '*Keyser*' in the German version of an agreement, and '*imperator*' in the Latin: Vasilii had achieved recognition as a ruler of equal rank to the Emperor Maximilian.[39]

This triumph was also somewhat ironic, because (as has been noted before) though Muscovy had an emperor it was not yet an empire. Apart from tribesmen incapable of making a state of their own, Vasilii ruled over virtually none but Russians. In any case Maximilian soon came to a rapprochement with Poland and his officials reverted to their former manner of addressing the Grand Prince. Nevertheless the idea had been aired. The Emperor's embassy to Moscow of 1517 – led by Sigismund von Herberstein, a Slovene nobleman who was to write one of the earliest published accounts of Russia – did not refer to an imperial title. However, Vasilii had allowed a resumption of relations with Constantinople, broken off after the Council of Florence, and the Greeks were always ready to point to a continuity between their imperial heritage and that of Vasilii, whose mother, after all, had been a Palaeologue.

In 1518 Vasilii received a large delegation from the patriarch of Constantinople, which included an interpreter called Maxim, a learned scholar who was to remain in Muscovy. And that same year an emissary, Nicholas Schonberg, arrived from Pope Leo X in the hope of negotiating a five-year truce between Muscovy and Poland, a united front against the Turk, and a union of the Muscovite Church with Rome. And once again the matter of the Constantinople inheritance was raised.

The monk Filofei, otherwise known as Philotheus of Pskov, developed the idea of Moscow as the 'Third Rome' in a letter to Vasilii III around 1523. This germ of an idea was to be developed into the Legend of the White Cowl. The cowl, the headdress worn by a patriarch, symbolizing the purity of faith that, according to the story, had once characterized St Peter, had moved from Rome to Constantinople (the Second Rome), which, as events had proved, was unworthy of the honour. For this reason it had now migrated to the 'Third Rome', Moscow. It has been argued that the purpose of the myth was to promote Moscow as the chief centre of the Orthodox world rather than support its pretensions to empire.[40] Nevertheless, it was to provide the state with a religious justification for uniting not just the Russians but all Orthodox Christians, whether in Russia, Ukraine, the Balkans or the Levant.

Year after year passed, and still Grand Princess Solomonia did not bear a child. For twenty years her husband, Vasilii, showed patience, but he also took precautions. He forbade his younger brothers from marrying until he had an heir. Eventually, in 1525, he dispatched Solomonia to a nunnery and obtained permission from the Church to remarry. Then, immediately after his second marriage, to Elena Glinskaia, Vasilii did something strangely untraditional. He shaved off his beard. His appearance clean-shaven shocked many Russians, and not surprisingly. They believed that a man was made in God's image, and that his beard was an integral part of him. A clean-shaven man was a heretic or, worse, a Latin, someone who had betrayed his heritage. Indeed, one of the most intense expressions of hatred by one Russian for another was to try to cut off his beard, for to lose one's beard was tantamount to losing one's place in the world to come.[41] Vasilii's gesture, however, suggests that he believed he must have the appearance of a Roman emperor if he were to realize his imperial ambitions.

Religious conservatism, which harked back to the Great Schism of the Christian Church in the twelfth century, implied cultural isolation. It was not compatible with the social and technological advances of the Renaissance age. The issue of beards, which symbolized the tension between the modernizers and traditionalists, was not to be resolved for almost two centuries, and even then the tension did not entirely disappear. The problem touched on identity, patriotism and, ultimately, the nature of Russian nationalism. Russians knew who they were: Christians. Every peasant defined himself as such. And their idea was quite compatible with the centralized state that Ivan III had created. But if the cosy womb of Orthodoxy were to be breached, its customs and values challenged, what would a Russian be? And if it were not and Russians were trapped in the past and the isolationism that that implied, how could Russia become an empire?

5

Ivan IV and the First Imperial Expansion

On 16 January 1547, at a glittering ceremony in the Kremlin's Cathedral of the Assumption, the sixteen-year-old son of Vasilii III was solemnly invested with a bejewelled cross and collar, with the cap of Vladimir Monomakh, which had been brought from Constantinople, and with a cloak of imperial purple. In this way young Ivan IV became the first tsar, as well as autocrat, of Russia. The long-sought imperial title had finally been approved by the supreme head of the Orthodox Christian Church, the Patriarch of Constantinople, who for Russians was the only legitimate ecclesiastical authority. It may seem ironic that Ivan, who was to parade his piety as a most Christian monarch, should have received his imperial dignity from a subject of the Muslim Ottoman sultan. But the title was to be justified by temporal events.

As the investiture ceremony made clear, more than titles were involved – more even than demonstrations of legitimacy – for the ceremony linked Ivan's Russia with the Roman Empire. The country's new imperial status was proclaimed in the blessing: 'Grant [Ivan] long life . . . Seat him on the throne of righteousness . . . [and] bring all the barbarian peoples under his power.'[1]

The reign of Ivan IV is one of the great climacterics of history. It marks the emergence of an imperial power in fact as well as aspiration, and Ivan justified Russia's use of the double-headed eagle by ordering expansionist drives southwards into the Caucasus, and westward to the Baltic, launching a third, into Siberia, for good measure. The new imperial status was also supported by a fresh, and violent, effort to make government autocratic in practice as well as in theory, by the emergence of a colonial administrative system, and by the systemization of Russia's foreign relations.

The hectic period saw a series of other innovations and changes. The first printing press was set up in Moscow; the laws were to some extent reformed and an attempt was made to codify them; new technology was applied to both the army and its armament; and the revolution was capped by institutional developments of lasting importance: the establishment of a system of granting landed estates on condition of service to the state, and of modern, absolutist, practices of government. It is curious, however, that Ivan – who is associated with Russia's emergence as a great European power – should also be held responsible for its subsequent collapse, and doubly paradoxical that historians should claim that his own actions both undermined the empire he had created and helped to ensure its longer-term recovery. However, the crucial changes of his tumultuous reign can hardly be understood without reference to the man himself in all his eccentric brilliance.

Ivan's image is clouded by controversy. He is both an object of hate and a folk hero. Since his own time he has been regarded as an ogre in the West, but his epithet 'the Terrible' is a misleading translation of the Russian *Groznyi*, 'the Dread' – bestowed by his propagandists for his punishing of wrongdoers – and he is still revered by many of his own people as a truly Christian ruler. One of his successors was to find it necessary to atone posthumously for Ivan's sins; yet his image was to be resurrected as a morale-booster when Russia was beleaguered during the Second World War.

Furthermore, Ivan's reputation has been shaped to suit political interests abroad as well as in Russia. Germans, frightened by Ivan's drive towards the Baltic, used their new printing presses to blacken his image with sensational reports of his atrocities. More than sixty German news-sheets recording Ivan's outrages, real and alleged, both in Russia and abroad, appeared between 1560 and 1580 alone. They included hair-raising stories of how the Russians not only butchered their enemies, severed people's limbs, and led thousands away in chains, captive, but also spitted and roasted young girls, impaled babies, and burned old people in their houses. Atrocities *were* committed – though they were not the monopoly of one side – but exaggerated and invented tales about the Russians were disseminated in a deliberate attempt to enlist the sympathy of the German-speaking world and the help of the Habsburg Emperor. The Polish government and Counter-Reformation publicists added their voices to the anti-Ivan chorus (although the papacy, still hoping to bring the Orthodox Churches within its fold, and interested in Russia as a possible route to China, held its fire). So the notion was propagated that Russians were savage heretics and their tsar a classic tyrant. It was the foundation of a tradition which was to inspire President Reagan's definition of the Soviet Union as an 'evil empire'.[2]

During the Cold War, Western propaganda presented Ivan as the precursor of Stalin: a paranoid imperialist, and creator of a reign of terror. But we should not judge him before the accretions of myth, both for and against him, have been stripped from his image. Nor should he be judged outside the context of his own turbulent and violent times. Ivan was a Renaissance prince and an Orthodox Christian in that confusing and pitiless age of Protestant Reformation and Catholic Counter-Reformation whose attendant wars were also to draw in the Christian Orthodox world to which Ivan and his people belonged. The invention of printing sharpened polemic, and the military revolution forced all monarchs who took their responsibilities seriously to take draconian measures to modernize their realms. Ivan was indeed responsible for terrible massacres, as were his contemporaries. Pizarro and the Spanish conquistadores did not shrink from killing; Lorenzo de' Medici was ruthless in dispatching his political rivals; Louis XI of France sanctioned the St Bartholomew's Day massacres; Queen Mary of England condoned the burning of the Oxford martyrs. The blood these rulers shed was as much a measure of the forces they were pitted against as of any sadistic impulses they may have had. Ivan was no less cruel than his peers, but that did not make him an Asiatic despot.

All this said, Ivan presents as a quirky figure. He married seven times – once more than Henry VIII – regardless of the canons of his Church, which permitted no more than three marriages. He quit his own capital in an apparent huff when thwarted, engaged personally in a theological disputation with a Jesuit sent to him by the Pope, had the Metropolitan of the Russian Church done to death, and killed his own eldest son in a fit of rage. In search of the real Ivan, his remains have been disinterred and subjected to scientific tests; there have even been attempts to psychoanalyse him in retrospect. Yet the controversy remains. Was he hero or devil, paranoiac, sadist, or just and concerned ruler? Contemporary historians are divided on the question.[3] To get the measure of this man who was both maker and breaker of an empire, we need first to consider his formation and then follow his career as empire-builder in the context that shaped his actions.

Ivan was born in 1530, and succeeded to the throne in 1533, on the death of his father, Vasilii III. A council of regents ruled Russia in his name until he came of age. But the government was unstable, and the period stormy. When his mother, Elena Glinskaia, the central figure of the government, died, allegedly of poison, in 1538, Prince Vasilii Shuiskii took her place; and when Shuiskii died shortly afterwards his brother Ivan took over – only to be was ousted by a rival, Ivan Belskii, who was soon deposed in his turn and executed. Meanwhile successive heads of the Russian Church were ousted and replaced. This traumatizing phase of political instability came to an end when members of Ivan's mother's family staged a coup in his favour in 1543. The occasion was his thirteenth birthday, which marked the coming of age for sons of emperors in the Byzantine Empire, and, according to the Nikon Chronicle, Ivan himself gave the order. So the presiding regent, Prince Andrei Shuiskii, was seized and handed over to the palace kennel-men, 'and the dog-keepers took him and killed him . . . And from that time the boyars began to fear the sovereign.'[4]

Thus Ivan's early years were marked by political instability, and possibly personal insecurity too (as Sergei Eisenstein, the famous Soviet film-maker, suggests in his classic but unfinished film treatment of Ivan). It is also said that he grew up wild and violent, but the source was a close friend who became a bitter enemy and cannot be trusted.[5] Nor was it as easy for the young ruler to establish his authority as the chronicle makes out. However, we can infer from his own writings and contemporary accounts that Ivan had received an excellent education for his time and station. He was both highly literate and musical, interested in the outside world, and, as befitted a monarch, both a keen huntsman and dutiful in matters of religion. He received instruction from senior officials concerned with legal administration, military and foreign affairs, and, of course, the Church, so that he was well apprised of Muscovite policies and statecraft and knew something about the lands beyond his frontiers.

Crowned at his own instance in January 1547, the sixteen-year-old tsar was also seized of new ideas. If he did not actually read Machiavelli, evidence suggests that he was acquainted with many of the Italian's precepts. A German immigrant, Hans Schlitte, fired his interest in German science, and he seized eagerly on information about new technology. The Tsar sent Schlitte back to Germany with commissions to recruit doctors, artisans, and experts in explosives and other Western arts. A Dutchman called Akema and a citizen of Hamburg called Marselius were soon to found a firearms manufactory at Tula, which was to be developed into the centre of Russia's arms industry. In 1550 Ivan founded a corps of musketeers (*streltsy*) – six companies of them in the first instance. His other acts suggest that he was intent on shoring up his legitimacy and on acting as a new broom (a symbol he adopted later for his most notorious institution, the *oprichnina*) in reforming the administration. In his first months as tsar no fewer than thirty-nine new saints were canonized, including many of his ancestors in the House of Riurik – enlargers of the state of Muscovy, and protectors of the Orthodox Church. Not only did these canonizations proclaim the values of the new regime, they invested it with an aura of sanctity.

Others of Ivan's immediate concerns were to extend and enforce the law, to root out corruption, and to stamp out the factionalism which had marred his boyhood. Above all, he wanted to enforce obedience. In 1550 a new law book was issued. Besides repeating previous legislation, this co-ordinated the operations of central and local government, laid down rules for due process, and required court decisions to be recorded. Ivan's first months in power were also marked by the expansion of the ministerial council, which reflected the use of patronage to bolster his authority. However, critical decisions were pondered by a kitchen cabinet of close advisers – the 'Chosen Council' – among them a learned monk called Silvestr, who did duty in one of the Kremlin churches; a foreign-policy specialist, Daniil Adashev; and a military specialist from the western provinces, Prince Andrei Kurbskii. It was with this group that in 1551 Ivan decided to mount his first great campaign the following year – against Kazan.

The Khanate of Kazan occupied a strategic location adjoining Muscovy's southern frontier, and Moscow had interfered in its affairs for decades past. However, the influence exerted was only intermittently effective. Control over Kazan needed to be secured. A phase of political instability there encouraged Ivan and his advisers to launch a major campaign to seize the city.[6] Kazan was defended by walls the height of three grown men and more, and by 30,000 Tatars. But young Ivan brought 150,000 troops to the scene, as well as siege equipment, explosive devices, and a train of 150 guns. A siege began on 23 August 1552.

The preparations had been thorough, and steps were taken to maintain the troops' morale. Immense drums were pounded by a battery of drummers to give the Russians encouragement; shawms and trumpets brayed in alarming unison to inspire the Tatar defenders with dread. Standards bearing images of Christ or of warlike saints like Demetrius and George, or pious slogans prophesying victory, waved and billowed over the serried regiments, demonstrating the Russians' view that their army was the visible army of Christ and its every campaign a holy mission. For them, as for the Byzantines, every war they fought was a crusade, and every enemy – Polish, Swedish or Livonian as well as Tatar – was heathen or heretical.[7] Tsar Ivan himself presided over the siege in style. As the Englishman Richard Chancellor, who came to Russia soon afterwards noted, 'his Pavillion [i.e. tent] is covered eyther with Cloth of Gold or Silver, and so set with stones that it is wonderfull to see it. I have seene the Kings Majesties of England and the French Kings pavilions, which are fayre, yet not like unto his.'[8] But, unlike Henry VIII's meeting with Francis I on the Field of the Cloth of Gold, this was no meeting between equals. Forty days after the siege began, explosives breached the walls, the Russian troops stormed in and after a bloody fight secured the city.

Kazan did not become a client state of any kind. That approach had been tried and had failed. Nor was it accorded any autonomy or separate administration to suit the ethnic and religious preferences of its conquered population. (However, some members of the Tatar elite threw in their hand with Russia and were soon employed in fighting Ivan's wars on other fronts.)[9] Kazan simply became a Russian province, administered by a Russian governor responsible for both civil and military affairs, and by a supporting staff of government clerks and servicemen. Russians were soon being encouraged to settle there. Before long, thanks to this and outward Tatar migration, the population of the city itself was soon overwhelmingly Russian. Kazan became an archdiocese, and its energetic archbishop was soon administering big church-building and missionary programmes.[10]

The impetus of this southward drive for empire did not end at Kazan. Ivan's eyes were already focused on the country beyond, on the Khanate of Astrakhan, which commanded the estuary of the river Volga and the roads to Central Asia and to the steppe lands at the approaches to the Caucasus, where the Nogai Horde roamed. In order to realize his strategic plan in the south, Ivan needed to ensure Nogai compliance. But he knew that the Nogais depended on trade with Muscovy, supplying it with as many as 50,000 horses a year. Partly for this reason, many Nogais welcomed Russia's taking control of the strategic commercial roads between Asia and Europe which the Khazars had once commanded.[11]

These considerations help to explain a letter that Ivan sent to the Nogai Horde a few weeks after the capture of Kazan. In it he gave implicit warning of what the price of resistance would be. When Kazan had fallen, he wrote, its defenders had been slaughtered and the women and children taken as slaves. The Khan himself, however, had been spared and deported to Russia, where he had been allotted an estate for his maintenance. The Nogai Tatars were welcome to trade, but were made to understand that the Tsar would brook no attempt to challenge the political arrangements he proposed for the region. The city of Astrakhan was annexed, securing control of the Nogai steppe and providing access to the Caucasus, the northern gateway to Asia. This had immense implications for Russia's imperial future.

As is often the case with expanding empires, some people in Russia's expected line of march rushed to offer their allegiance even before the would-be conqueror arrived. Some Christian princelings of the Kabarda region of the Caucasus did so even before Ivan's victory over Astrakhan. In 1555 Prince Kudaduk and Prince Sisak formally submitted to the Tsar's representative, along with with 150 of their warriors. Two years later more did so. These Kabardinian chiefs and their followers were known as Circassians (*Cherkessy*). The Russians thought they were pledging allegiance in the hope of support against hostile neighbours, but they made similar overtures to the Crimean khan and to the shamkhal of Dagestan, so they may have been seeking insurance or simply making a gesture of recognition – Caucasian politesse. In any case, in 1560 Ivan sent 500 musketeers and 500 Cossacks there, ostensibly to help the Circassian Prince Temriuk. It proved to be the beginning of a fateful relationship that has lasted to this day.

A people accustomed to flatlands, the Russians now confronted the most mountainous and exotic region of Europe. For sixteenth-century man, mountains lacked the romantic aura they were to attract in the late eighteenth and the nineteenth centuries. They were difficult of access, and harboured dangerous peoples. Yet Russia was already becoming involved in the very centre of the Caucasus, the Kabarda. The chief lure was commerce. The Kabarda straddled the roads from the Crimea to the town of Derbent on the Caspian, and from the river Terek in the north to Georgia in the south.

Russians seeing this land for the first time were awed by the immensity of the lowering mountains – the highest in Europe – and by the precipitous valleys that harboured isolated communities that spoke a kaleidoscopic variety of languages and dialects. Some settlements grew crops or reared horses; others boasted smithies where chain mail was made and swords of wonderful workmanship and sharpness were crafted. Others again lived by trade and robbery. And all bred fighting men, skilled in ambush and raiding. In 1561 Ivan – who had lost his wife, Anastasia, a year earlier – married one of Prince Temriuk's daughters. Two years later the leader of the Nogais, Mirza Din-Ahmed, married another of Temriuk's daughters. This little web of dynastic marriages was to further Moscow's ambitions in the south, and before long its advance was marked by the erections of fortresses in the Kabarda (1563) and at Terka on the river Terek (1567).

The social scene there was totally strange to Russian eyes. The Kabardinians were congeries of warlike clans, each headed by a landowning prince, each with his vassal gentry, all of them sustained by peasants and slaves. There was no overall chief, no hierarchical system of a sort familiar to Russians or Tatars. Seniority and fighting prowess earned deference, however. Raiding for slaves and trading in them was not uncommon (Istanbul provided a good market). As for religion, allegiance varied. Some of the mountain men were Christian, others were Muslim (at least nominally), a few were Jews (perhaps survivals from the Khazar Empire), and a good many were pagan animists. In fact religion was largely a political issue, a matter of alliances: of Ivan's new in-laws, one brother became a Christian, most of the others remained Muslims, but religion and political allegiance were as yet quite independent.

And the Kabardinians were only one loose tribal grouping among many. There were also the Adyge to the west; the Darghins and Laks, the Kaytaks and Lezghins of Dagestan; and, beyond them to the south, the Tabasarans, Tsakhurs, Rutuls and Chechens – not to mention the Ingush, Ossetians and others. All were singular, all were warlike, and, like the Swiss in the time of William Tell, all were difficult (and sometimes impossible) to govern. If the Russians fully comprehended this variegated, seemingly anarchic, scene, they left little evidence of the fact at the time.[12] Wisely, they did not attempt to control it. Instead, they set out to further their interests incrementally, by agreement. But, if they found the fragmented tribal political scene difficult to fathom, they understood the broader strategic realities very clearly indeed. Behind some of the Muslim tribal groupings of the Caucasus stood the might of the Ottoman Turks, who controlled the Crimean khan, the ally of hostile Poland. Moscow needed help to counter the power of this Turkish alliance, which was blocking its lines of advance to the west as well as to the south, and help could come only from Ivan's nominal rival, the Holy Roman Emperor, Maximilian II of the House of Habsburg.

The Kremlin soon decided that practical strategic considerations must outweigh Russia's theoretical claims to imperial primacy, and so Moscow's relations with the Habsburgs became more cordial. Sacrificing its own unpromising claims to the elective throne of Poland, in the 1570s it supported the Habsburg candidate, Ernest. At the same time Moscow's calls for the Emperor to join Russia in an alliance against 'the enemies of Christ's name', the Muslim Turks and Tatars, became insistent.[13] It was the beginning of a long-term strategy directed against the Ottoman Empire that was eventually to give rise, three centuries later, to the notorious 'Eastern Question'.

The Cossacks employed to shore up Russia's position in the Caucasus – and, more particularly, to secure a line along the river Terek – were irregulars. The word 'Cossack' (*kazak*) had originally denoted a freelance Tatar warrior, but by now the Cossacks were chiefly rootless Russian, Lithuanian and Polish subjects who had moved south to the new frontier lands, where they made a living as traders, robbers, mercenaries and colonists. Ivan's government engaged them in increasing numbers because they were tough, cheap and biddable. For a patch of virgin land and an annual allotment of gunpowder and grain, or a few coins, they would do any patron's bidding.

The Lithuanian magnate Dmitry Vishnevetsky established an entire colony of them on an island beyond the Dnieper rapids, just short of Crimean Tatar and Ottoman Turkish territory. In 1557 he offered his allegiance to Tsar Ivan, and so the Zaporozhian Cossacks became the Tsar's subjects too. Four years later Vishnevetsky returned to his former Polish allegiance, but Moscow regarded the Zaporozhian Host as a Russian asset and protectorate. So did some of its members. The Cossack community of the Don also became subject to Moscow, and proved rather more stable in its allegiance than the Zaporozhians. Even so, it was regarded as overzealous in mounting raids against the Turks, for Moscow was held responsible for them. This could be dangerous as well as embarrassing, and so Moscow found it convenient to disown the Cossacks at times. Nevertheless their links, based on mutual interests, remained close. East and south of the Volga, too, the Tsar was again the biggest patron and beneficiary of Cossack activity.

Three categories of Cossack were soon discernible. One comprised members of autonomous communities, like the Don and Zaporozhian Hosts, which were defined by their own rules and customs, and acknowledged an obligation to the Tsar in return for subsidies. Another was the 'town' Cossacks, who, having kissed the cross in sign of loyalty to the Tsar, were allotted a salary and assigned for policing, defence and other duties to a particular town or dependent village. Cossacks of the third type were engaged as groups collectively. Usually pioneers or frontier settlers, they were given annual allotments of gunpowder, food and other necessities, and rights to farm a stretch of virgin land in return for defending the locality and turning out on campaign when required. Such were the men who were to guard the line of the river Terek, the frontier to the Caucasus, and the river Don to the west, on the far side of the Crimea.

The imperial implications of the conquest of Kazan and Astrakhan were not fully appreciated at the time, even though the strategic importance of the northern Caucasus was clearly understood. Indeed, it very soon brought Russia into confrontation with the great power south of the Caucasus, the Ottoman Empire. Hearing of Ivan's intervention on the Terek, Sultan Selim II mounted an expedition to Azov, hoping to cut a canal through to the Volga and take Astrakhan, but this soon proved to be overambitious. Nevertheless, the Crimea to the west was an Ottoman client and allied to hostile Lithuania. These two powers blocked Ivan's advance in both directions.

Although Russia valued Astrakhan as an emporium for silks from China and gems from India, the desert steppe of central Asia to the east was inhospitable and unwanted. Some groups of Bashkirs, who roamed the country to the east of the Urals and the north of the steppe, volunteered their submission soon after the conquest of Kazan, and the Russian government was to establish the fortress of Ufa in northern Bashkiria in 1586, though almost two centuries were to pass before colonization developed in that direction.[14] Meanwhile the significance of Siberia, with all its riches, was hardly appreciated at all. Indeed the beginning of that great venture can be traced to the state's granting exploitation rights to a private individual – a most unusual act by a regime whose characteristic administrative style was brutally direct.

On 4 April 1558 the Tsar granted a petition from Grigorii Stroganov, whose family had already grown rich through exploiting the salt pans of Solvychegodsk in north-eastern Russia and trading with the native peoples of the Great Perm region. Grigorii had established himself there only a few years before, but now he was given the rights to exploit the deserted region along the river Kama some 50 miles and more beyond Perm. Stroganov's vision was as bright as that of any Western merchant venturer in the first decades of the new colonizing age, eminently practical and surprisingly entrepreneurial. He wanted to fell the region's dark forests, and exploit its fish-teeming lakes and streams. He wanted to prospect for salt and other minerals, to encourage trade, and to make large tracts of the territory agricultural by encouraging the settlement of homesteaders not already registered for tax elsewhere. The scheme appealed to the Tsar.

The population of the region was sparse, consisting of small communities of tribal hunters – Voguls and Ostiaks – though Tatars were beginning to penetrate the area from the south. Understanding that predators and traders tend to gather wherever wealth is generated, the Tsar authorized the Stroganovs to establish a fort at some appropriate point along the river, to equip it with cannon, and to man it with arquebusiers. In 1563 the concession was extended along both banks of the Kama and up its tributary, the Chusovaia. Furthermore, the regional government of Perm was warned not to interfere with any homesteaders in the region and to leave its defence to the Stroganovs. These grants of imperial property to a private individual, though rare in Russian law, were not unlike the charters granted by the kings of England or France to Western merchant venturers in that age.[15]

From this one seed grew a great regional enterprise, the basis of the Stroganov family fortune, and the conquest of Siberia. Despite its immense extent, Siberia was very sparsely populated and the material culture of its natives was mostly stuck in the Stone Age. Only one of its peoples posed any serious opposition to Russian colonization – a group of Tatars descended from a branch of Baty Khan's White Horde. However, their khan, Kuchum, offered spirited resistance until the Stroganovs' private army of hired Cossacks finally overwhelmed him.

In 1579 a messenger was to be ushered into Ivan's presence. He bore a trophy for the Tsar – a splendid fur robe. It had belonged to Kuchum Khan. Stroganov's man Yermak had fought his way through to the Khan's camp on the river Irtysh with 500 men, and had routed Kuchum's army.[16] Although Kuchum returned to get his revenge by killing Yermak and many of his band, he was eventually forced to flee, and from then on there was little to impede Russia from extending all the way to the Pacific – except vast distances, difficult terrain, and weather conditions which could be vicious. The immense economic and strategic implications of the Stroganov grant, however, could hardly have been foreseen by Russia's government of the time. But nor did the kings of England and of France realize that the little overseas colonies they founded in that age would one day be recognized as the beginnings of great empires.

Flushed with his victories in the south, Tsar Ivan had immediately turned his attention westward to Livonia. Russia had long been probing westward, of course, but the scale and force of the 1558 campaign was new – as was its purpose: to secure Russia a base on the Baltic and direct access to the West.

This was despite the fact that a Western country had just found a new route to Russia. It was while trying to find a north-east passage to China that an English expedition led by Richard Chancellor had landed on the White Sea coast at the mouth of the Northern Dvina river. As a result, direct diplomatic and commercial relations were established between England and Russia. Trade soon developed sufficiently to merit the establishment of a trading house for the English at Kholmogorii, on the way to Moscow, and in 1584 the port town of Archangel was founded to service the trade in the summer months when the ice receded sufficiently to allow ships to make the perilous voyage round North Cape. The significance of the link had early been noted by the Polish government, which became alarmed by the possibility that Russia might be able to obtain up-to-date military equipment from England and tried unsuccessfully to stop it. The link was also significant in providing the English with first-hand reports of Muscovy, and not least in giving Moscow up-to-date intelligence about England and developments in western Europe[17] – matters in which Ivan took a keen personal interest. All this strengthened his resolve to gain access to a more convenient sea route to the West from a warmer Baltic port.

The Livonian campaign was fought in the area of what are now Estonia and Latvia, and was well timed. The region had long been ruled by the Knights of the Teutonic Order and the Knights of the Sword, displaced crusaders whose *raison d'être* had long been questioned, and whose hold was now undermined by the popularity of Lutheranism and by military threats from Sweden and Denmark as well as Russia. Nor were the Russians any longer at a technological disadvantage, as once they had been; they attacked in force, deploying large numbers of soldiers and hauling a large siege train with them. They were assisted to some degree by native Letts who hated their German masters and did what they could to sabotage their operations. Stronghold after stronghold submitted without a fight. Narva fell in May, Derpt in July, and then Wesenberg. Wesenberg was soon recaptured, but the Russians held on to Narva and Derpt as well as many other strong-points. As was the case with the newly acquired territories in the south, Muscovite governors were immediately installed, backed by government clerks.[18]

But then success became more elusive, and its price higher. The German Knights of Livonia and the former autonomous Hansa cities of the region soon recognized that they could not withstand the might of Russia's army alone, and so they sought the protection of other powers. Reval submitted to Sweden, Riga and the Duchy of Courland to Poland-Lithuania; another part of Livonia fell to Denmark. Hostilities dragged on from months to years, the area of operations broadened, and the war became more intense.

In 1563, when Ivan's troops, opening up a new front, stormed the Polish city of Polotsk, it was said that they ordered 'twenty thousand people, first to have their arms and legs chopped off, and then to be strangled . . . No words can express the outrages they committed among Matrons, Maidens and Children . . . [Then the victims] were stripped naked and . . . led chained into captivity . . . [This] created an exceeding terror into the whole of this province.'[19] Terror had long been used as a means of scaring an enemy into headlong retreat, but this account is reminiscent of descriptions of the Mongol terror in central Europe three centuries earlier, and it may have repeated conventional literary tropes. Nevertheless, well founded or not, hate literature concerning Russia and the Russians was gaining wide currency in the West, especially in Germany.

Though locked into this war in the west, Ivan also needed to maintain a strong military establishment in the south, to safeguard earlier successes and contain the Crimean khan and his mighty overlord, the Ottoman sultan. The strains of this huge effort in two directions eventually precipitated a crisis for the Russian state. The crisis was associated with the creation by Ivan early in 1565 of a seemingly weird institution. Known as the *oprichnina*,[20] which suggests something apart or separate, it was a kind of state outside the state, owning extensive properties and run by Ivan's trusties, who wore black cowls and carried brooms and dogs'-heads at their saddle-bows.

The *oprichnina* is associated with a reign of terror. This strange and bloody episode in Russia's history has been attributed to Ivan's paranoia – to his belief that many of the elite, including ministers, former trusties and prelates of the Church, were plotting against him. On the other hand, proponents of Ivan have adduced evidence of plots, and the Tsar is commonly, and accurately, portrayed as lashing out angrily against those who stood in his way. Even so, the psychological and political interpretations are not entirely satisfactory.

It is only when account is taken of the financial demands of war and the determined opposition of vested interests to Ivan's exercise of personal power, not least within the court itself, that the *oprichnina* and the terror become explicable in rational terms. The cause of strife had little to do with personalities, but a great deal to do with the state's attempt to extend its fiscal base and secure suffient income for all the servicemen it needed.[21] It also had to do with the primitive character of Russian social institutions. Other states could use or mould existing institutions to serve its needs. Russia often had to create them. Even such apparently quintessentially Russian institutions as the liquor-house (*kabak*), notorious haven of the heroic Russian drunk, and the village commune (*mir* or *obshchina*), fabled proof that Russians were natural democrats, were the inventions of Ivan's state.[22] The first was a means of exploiting the state's monopoly of spirits in the most profitable way; the second was a means of imposing a collective obligation to pay taxes.

However, the Church, which had originally been established by secular authority and had long been the staunch supporter and protector of Russia's secular rulers, constituted a major obstacle to Ivan's plans. It was absorbing too many resources, in that its landed property comprised a major, if not the largest, proportion of Russia's total cultivated surface, and its wealth had been extended by legislation of 1550 which the twenty-year-old Ivan did not want but could not at that time resist. By mid-1563 his relations with the Metropolitan, Makarii, had reached breaking point, and when Makarii left Moscow for a monastery it was taken as a sign that he disapproved of the Tsar. The Tsar, however, was soon to show that he, too, could exert moral pressure in a similar time-honoured way. The Metropolitan had support among the elite, and even some of Ivan's closest advisers, including his former friend Prince Andrei Kurbskii and Boyar Mikhail Repnin, who had invested Ivan with his crown at the coronation ceremony.

The Tsar's attempt to restrict the Church's wealth and to challenge its property rights breached precedent, but it should not be supposed that even the Metropolitan's opposition was founded solely on moral, still less legal or constitutional, grounds. Protecting property was a major concern of both clerics and laity, and it should be borne in mind that an alternative model of government, which respected traditional rights and especially property, was evident in neighbouring Poland-Lithuania. Kurbskii himself was of Lithuanian descent (his family, like many others, espoused Russia because it defended the Orthodox religion against the inroads of the Catholic Church), and now that Poland was wooing his like he soon availed himself of its protection, fearing for his life in Russia.

The murder of Ivan's opponents and suspected opponents had begun in 1563. Its purpose was to secure the throne from challenge, but opposition persisted and the Church still tried to restrain the Tsar. The pressure was maintained even after the death of Metropolitan Makarii, in December 1563, and then, a year after Makarii's death, Ivan himself played the moral blackmail card. In December 1564 he swept out of the Kremlin together with his family and a strong force of armed retainers. He went briefly to Kolomenskoe, a short distance downstream from Moscow, where he celebrated Christmas, and then moved on to the suburb of Alexandrova. He had taken with him his entire treasury and many of the most precious icons and liturgical objects from the Kremlin churches. It was as if he were trying to strip the Metropolitan and other prelates who were opposing him of their legitimacy. In turning his back on Moscow, Ivan was metaphorically shaking the dust off his feet, as the Apostle Matthew and Saint Paul had done. Interpreting the symbolism of the occasion, Professor Floria explains that 'In effect the Tsar was giving the ruling elite an ultimatum: either they must abandon their traditional ways which obstructed the Tsar's freedom of action, or else they would have to go to war against their legitimate ruler – a war in which the Tsar could call on the armed service gentry and would enjoy the support of the population of Moscow.'[23]

Ivan timed his move shrewdly. Servicemen, who now fulfilled civil as well as military functions, could not function without the Tsar's authority, so there was a danger that the administration of the realm might suffer a progressive collapse.[24] Those opposed to him did not relish a fight at a time when the country was engaged in war on two fronts and the Tsar was so evidently popular. Besides, state and Church were supposed to work in symphony, and the evident breakdown in their relationship redounded as much to the Metropolitan's discredit as to the Tsar's – even more so in the mind of the people. A vast crowd of concerned Muscovites followed Ivan to Kolomenskoe. Before long a delegation of top-level clergy and members of the Tsar's own council[25] of top administrators and advisers made their way to Alexandrova to beg him put his anger aside and rule as he wished. In effect Ivan was given carte blanche to punish those who disobeyed him and anyone he considered a traitor – without the formality of a trial. Boyars Mikhail Repnin and Iurii Kashin were soon numbered among the victims; Kurbskii had fled.

The purge was not the whim of a half-crazed paranoiac, which is the line of one popular genre of literature about Ivan. His plan was to eliminate opposition to his exercise of autocracy, which he deemed essential if Russia were to fulfil its imperial potential.[26] He justified this in a letter to the defector Kurbskii, who had upbraided him for abusing his authority. In it he accused Kurbskii of calumny and of advocating 'the rule of servants over the heads of their masters [whereas he, Ivan, was trying] zealously to lead people to the truth . . . so that they may know the one true God . . . and . . . cease from internecine strife . . . which causes kingdoms to crumble . . . If a tsar's subjects do not obey him they will forever be at war with one another.'[27] This was written in the same spirit as Thomas Hobbes was to write *Leviathan* a century later. What Ivan was advocating was closely related to what came to be known in western Europe as absolutism.

Ivan's method, however, was not simply to appropriate the estates of the wealthy hereditary aristocracy and deprive the aristocrats of influence, as some popular histories have suggested. The aristocracy was to remain wealthy and powerful. Rather, he wanted to disperse its landholdings, to render the aristocrats incapable of mobilizing a power base against their ruler, which they could have done if their estates had remained concentrated. It was, in fact, a safeguard for the state and for good order. In neighbouring Poland-Lithuania, by contrast, the magnates were in fact able to mobilize against the king, and this ability was soon to be transformed into a legal right to rebel – a tradition which was to render the country ungovernable.

The reign of terror had the effect of transforming the old hereditary aristocracy – the princes descended through so many genealogical lines from Riuruk and the so-called 'non-titled' aristocrats, scions of those families who had distinguished themselves through service to ruling grand princes through the generations – into a service aristocracy. From now on Russian noblemen, high as well as low, needed the tsar's approval, or at least his toleration, and it became the convention for younger aristocrats to serve at court and seek the ruling tsar's patronage.[28] In order to assuage the feelings of the old nobility and to encourage the new service class, a new practice called *mestnichestvo* was tolerated by the state. According to this, appointments to commands were allotted partly on the basis of the family's past association with those commands, so that they tended henceforth to be perpetuated in particular families. But the noble class, which in any case had no autonomous corporate tradition, became the servants of the tsar. The revolution was not accomplished overnight. But Ivan succeeded in establishing the principle, and it is curious that the devices used by Louis XIV to counter localism at his grand court at Versailles had been initiated over a century earlier at the other end of Europe

Ivan ensured that Russia would be able to administer an empire. However, he used draconian means. The image of his black-cowled *oprichniki* sweeping through a locality in an orgy of killing – and there were such occasions – draws attention to the purpose of that singular institution the *oprichnina*. On the one hand it was an instrument of permanent purge, a means of maintaining tension and fear of the Tsar; on the other hand it was a means of overcoming the convention which regarded all Church endowments as sacrosanct and hence untouchable by the secular power. Given the practice of pious (and increasingly prosperous) Russians making over large gifts to monasteries for the salvation of their souls, huge resources were going to the Church which might otherwise have produced revenue for the Tsar. The government's concern about this had been evident as early as 1551, when a general review of all charters granting property to monasteries had been carried out.[29] However, no way had been found to obviate the problem by legal means. In England the problem had been solved by the dissolution of the monasteries, but in Holy Mother Russia such a Protestant solution was unthinkable.

However, one school of thought considers the *oprichnina* itself to have been modelled on a monastic order, with a rule laid down by the Tsar himself. Funded initially by a huge allocation of 100,000 rubles from state funds, it eventually came to absorb the revenues of a large part of his realm. Its assets enjoyed the same protection as did the Church's property, and were subject to no taxes. All other property continued to be administered by the normal agencies and was taxed to provide income for the state, but

Ivan's 'separate realm' was his own, untrammelled by any institution, including his own bureaucracy. The foundation of the *oprichnina* proved to be the first of several attempts by Russia's rulers to bypass normal channels and find a more direct, efficient instrument of asserting their will. From this perspective the black-cowled *oprichniki* were merely the first of the state's special agents.

The *oprichniki* themselves included many leading members of the old elite, and they were organized as a quasi-monastic community. The Tsar was its abbot; its headquarters was the surburb of Alexandrova, to which Ivan had moved in 1564 shortly before founding the order, and its rule derived in part from that of the Basilian Order and was influenced, apparently, by the Dominicans (whose coat of arms also features a dog). Curiously enough, the unicorn adopted for the *oprichnina*'s coat of arms was also the symbol of the Jesuits.[30] Ivan was nothing if not eclectic.

The ruthless depredations of the *oprichniki* are proverbial. In effect they represented government by terror; and all the while the ruinous war for Livonia continued. Ivan invoked the people in support of his purpose, and in 1566 the first representative 'Assembly of the Land' (*Zemskii Sobor*) endorsed the continuance of his policy. The only opposition came from the Church. That same year Metropolitan Afanasii resigned after an incumbency of only two years. His successor was sacked after only two days, and *his* successor, Filipp, was deposed two years later by a synod at the Tsar's insistence (and was murdered within months by a leading *oprichnik*). Filipp's successor, Pimen, was himself to be deposed in 1570. The times were fraught, the struggle desperate.

By the Union of Lublin of 1569, Lithuania formally merged with Catholic Poland. Lithuanian noblemen were now eligible for the same legal and political privileges as their Polish counterparts, provided they were, or became, practising Catholics. From that point on the Orthodox elite of Lithuania began to desert to Catholicism in increasing numbers. The same year King Erik XIV of Sweden was deposed in a coup, altering the political balance in the Baltic region, and the citadel of Izborsk fell. The fact that Izborsk was well defended, and the force that captured it small, suggested treason. Rumour reached the Tsar that Archbishop Pimen of Novgorod was preparing to hand Novgorod and Pskov to the Polish king, and that all sectors of the Novgorod population were involved in the plot. If true, it would not have been surprising. Novgorod had been squeezed very hard for taxes in recent years; Muscovite officials had replaced local men, and so many peasants had fled that there was a labour shortage too.

Once again, then, a tsar's fears of holding the line in the west centred on Novgorod, and so in 1570 the *oprichniki* descended on the city, sacked it, and butchered as many as 30,000 of its inhabitants. A huge number of hereditary estates were taken over, the surviving owners being banished to other parts of Russia and the land which was once theirs redistributed to state servitors.[31] Two years later, however, in the autumn of 1572, the Tsar abolished the *oprichnina*. It may have served its original purpose, but as a seven-year experiment in government by tension it had been an expensive disappointment. An experiment bred of desperate impatience, designed to strengthen the state, turned out to have wasted its resources and dissipated its strength. Its assets were returned whence they had come. The revolution, if revolution it was, was over.

The Livonian war was now directed against Sweden as well as the Knights, while the Crimean Tatars remained a perennial menace in the south. Indeed, on one occasion they were more than a threat. In 1571 their army had looted Moscow and burned it, though it had failed to take the Kremlin. The strains on Ivan and Russia were severe. Yet there were successes too. In the summer of 1572 another onslaught by the Crimean Tatars was broken at Molodi; in 1573 the Swedish fort of Pajda in Livonia was captured, and a faction of Poland's nobility even canvassed the name of Ivan's son, Fedor, as a candidate to Poland's throne. But not until 1577 could the necessary resources be gathered for yet another major offensive in Livonia. By September of the same year the region was all in Ivan's possession except for the port cities of Riga and Tallin which he desired so much.

Then the tide turned. In 1578 Russian forces were defeated at Wenden, and other Livonian towns were lost. A new king of Poland, the able Hungarian strategist Stefan Bathory, was sweeping all before him. Then Ivan's former ally King Magnus of Denmark deserted the cause and in 1579 the city of Polotsk was lost. Ivan had been driven back almost to the point where he had started. Within months he was suing for peace, prepared to surrender everything that he had gained at so much cost in the north-west.

To what extent internal strife had contributed to the reversal of fortune it is difficult to say. Ivan's purges were over. There had been nine terrible bouts of executions. Indeed, they had become an almost routine mark of that period of Ivan's reign. He expressed indignation at the massacres in France to his ally the Emperor Maximilian II, but he himself was no gentler than the King of France. Some of his most successful generals were among his victims. So was the keeper of his Great Seal, the brilliant diplomat Ivan Mikhailovich Viskovatii. Nevertheless Viskovatii bequeathed a legacy that was to be of lasting value to the Russian state.

The work of establishing protocol for dealings with foreign countries, already begun, had been extended under Viskovatii's supervision, at a time when the European diplomatic system was still in process of formation. And he had also established a practice for keeping records in a systematic way.[32] Every embassy, of whatever rank, sent to another country (as yet no state maintained permanent missions in other capitals) was equipped with detailed instructions about what to say and even in what circumstances to say it. It was also given specific questions to ask, and lists of matters it should seek intelligence about. As a result, a large database was built up on all previous dealings with a country and of accurate intelligence about its geography, resources, society and mores. Russian diplomats may have taken protocol and record-keeping to tedious lengths, but the tradition carried with it some inestimable advantages. Russian decision-takers tended to be better informed than their rivals, and, though their representatives abroad often seemed slow and their method cumbersome by contrast to their often more brilliant opposite numbers, they were more careful, painstaking, professional.

This was a less glorious achievement than the capture of Kazan and Siberia, perhaps, but none the less significant. Advantage was also gained from Ivan's massacres, for they had helped to complete the revolution in landholding begun by the Tsar's predecessors. Henceforth the entire elite of Russia served the tsar, and knew that their privileges and their advancement depended on him alone. Although his reign coincided with a demographic upswing, it also saw a major haemorrhage of the kind of talent and expertise which is of value in building empires, and the massacres left a blot on his reputation. They stirred deep resentments at the time. Yet they may also have added to the Tsar's popularity as the supporter of the common man (a reputation which the Tsar's own court may have helped to create by spreading positive rumours about him). History's verdict on Ivan has not yet been agreed.

Among the victims of Ivan's executioners was his personal physician and astrologer the Cambridge-educated Dr Elisei Bomel. The learned Bomel may have borne some responsibility for the increasingly uncontrollable fits of rage that Ivan suffered from in later life. An autopsy on Ivan's remains has revealed that he suffered from the acutely painful condition known as ankylosing spondylitis – that is, his spine was locked in a stooping position. Inhalation of mercury vapour was evidently prescribed to excess in order to help him with the pain, and scholars have recently suggested that, over the years, this medication resulted in neurological damage which produced insomnia and contributed to his rage attacks.[33] It was in one of these bouts in 1581 that he unintentionally killed his son Ivan, who was being groomed to succeed him. But for that, the succession crisis, and the political destabilization, which followed Ivan's death on 18 March 1584 might well have been avoided.

Meanwhile, the strains and costs of Ivan's wars of imperial expansion and the internal upheaval he created in his attempts to pay for his campaigns contributed to an economic crisis which struck Russia in the latter part of the sixteenth century. As a result, many urban settlements were abandoned by their inhabitants, who fled to the countryside, and there was a large-scale movement of population from central and north-western Russia to the south and south-east.[34] The effect was not only to diminish tax revenues but also to pauperize many servicemen who depended on their peasants for their income. The government tried to combat this trend by restricting the right of peasants to move except during a brief period after the autumn harvest, and by allowing their lords to pursue and reclaim those who flitted. This was the beginning of the oppressive system known as serfdom.

At the root of the problem was the fact that the Russian state could not accumulate sufficient specie to issue good coin in sufficient quantity to pay its servicemen in cash. It therefore had to supply them with land in lieu. But the land was useless without labour, and small landlords, such as the holders of service estates, were not able to attract labour in competition with the great landowners, who could afford to offer peasants better terms of tenure. So the state had to intervene to save the servitors from their predicament at the expense of the peasants' freedom. Serfdom did not yet exist formally as an institution, but from Ivan's reign it became progressively inevitable.

In the long term, the oppressive effects of serfdom were to aid Russian expansion by encouraging a steady flow of people ready to pioneer newly discovered or recently secured territories at the periphery of the state. However, by the 1580s Ivan's main expansionist thrusts had all been halted. Poland and Sweden had blocked Russia's roads westward and to the Baltic; the Turks blocked the advance to the south. And Ivan himself seemed a broken man. He had finally conceded failure in the war for Livonia; he had brought ruin to much of his realm, and destroyed many of its best human assets. Compared with such costs, his achievements seemed slight indeed. In his last testament, redolent with quotations from the Bible, he gave vent to despair and self-pity: 'My spirit is afflicted, my spiritual and bodily wounds have increased, and there is no physician to heal me . . . I have found no comforters, they have repaid me with evil for my kindness and hatred for my love.'[35]

Resentful and full of foreboding, one imagines, both for his empire and for the state of his soul, Ivan confronted death. He died in 1584, and Russia did indeed fall into ruin. Before long, the pretensions to imperial status were to seem almost risible.

6
The Crash

HISTORIANS OFTEN ATTRIBUTE Russia's descent into anarchy in the early 1600s to Ivan's misrule, yet the tyrant's death did not mark the onset of what Russians call 'the era of confusion' and we in the West know as the 'Time of Troubles'. Indeed, there was something of a recovery. However disappointing the terms that ended the Livonian war may have been politically, the conclusion of hostilities the year before Ivan's death eased the economic pressure on the country. Recognition that the terror of Ivan's *oprichnina* had gone for good gave hope to many; there was a breathing space, a chance to stabilize the country after the disruptions of the *oprichnina* – and the new tsar's government seized the opportunity.

Economic activity revived; the outward migration of population from the Moscow region ceased. Abandoned villages were gradually resettled. Service gentry, in despair at losing their peasant tenants, who had been leaving for the freedom of the frontier areas or for large estates which offered them terms that mere gentry could not afford, were mollified by new laws. These banned the departure of peasant tenants before St George's Day (the end of the autumn harvest), and authorized their recovery by force for a period thereafter. At the same time, the weight of government demands on the peasantry was lightened.

The new domestic policy sought to establish internal calm after all the recent storms. It was paralleled by a foreign policy which guarded Russia's essential interests without requiring any massive mobilization of resources. Dangerous ambition was abandoned, and feelers were put out to countries far and near offering co-operation for mutual benefit. The defences of the southern frontier were shored up; a twelve-year peace was concluded with Poland-Lithuania in 1591; diplomatic relations were established with the Ottoman Empire, and commercial relations with Holland and France. Only the confrontation with Sweden continued – but it was to result in the recovery of central Karelia and territories on the Gulf of Finland and Lake Ladoga which had been lost in the Livonian War. Another triumph, achieved by peaceful means, was the raising of the metropolitan see of

Moscow, hitherto subject to the Patriarch of Constantinople, to the status of an independent patriarchate in 1591. This made the Russian Church effectively a national church, increasing both its authority and that of its partner, the state.[1]

If Ivan's misrule had made a collapse inevitable, the measures taken under his successor kept disaster at bay, and when the reckoning eventually came it was to be precipitated and deepened by factors independent of Ivan's actions – by 'acts of God' that were quite unforeseeable.

The new tsar, Fedor, was the elder of Ivan's two surviving sons. The younger, Dmitrii, was to die an accidental death in 1591. Years afterwards this event was to precipitate a crisis, but not at the time. True, Tsar Fedor was rumoured to be of limited ability – he was probably mentally retarded – but he served well enough as a figurehead, and he soon gained a reputation for piety, a critical indicator of legitimacy in that age and therefore a real political asset. Besides, it transpired that he was capable of siring an heir. His policies, however, are associated with those who managed affairs for him – the regents, his ministers.

These included the brothers Shchelkalov – Andrei, who had headed the Foreign Office (*Posolskii prikaz*) from 1570 to 1594, and Vasilii, who as head of both the Musketeer Office (*Streletskii prikaz*) and the Felony Department (*Razboinii prikaz*) was effectively in charge of state security.[2] Two other leading lights were Dmitrii Godunov, a former *oprichnik*, and his brother Boris, who made a reputation as a financial manager. The Godunovs hailed from Kostroma on the Volga, where they were generous benefactors of the riverside Trinity Monastery. Both had been members of Ivan's council of ministers; both were shrewd politically, and when Boris persuaded the Tsar to marry his sister his prospects were much enhanced.

The policies that Boris and his colleagues pursued were judicious. One of the new regime's first measures was to abolish the tax privileges of hereditary estate-holders. It also gave effective relief to the hard-pressed service gentry by giving them seigneurial rights over their ploughland, as well as allowing them to pursue and recover their runaway peasants. Tradesmen, craftsmen and other productive commercial people – another vital constituency – were helped too, by exempting the suburbs and settlements where they lived from taxation. These measures promoted social peace and encouraged commerce especially in central Russia, but the government also took radical measures to develop the south and south-east, chiefly by building new towns.

Samara and the stronghold of Ufa in northern Bashkiria (founded in 1586), Tsaritsyn, later Stalingrad (1589), Saratov (1590) and Tsivilsk – forts and future cities with alliterative, romantic names – were all founded on the middle and lower reaches of the Volga at this time. The government's hold of the steppe was furthered both by founding new towns and by refortifying others: Voronezh and Livny (1586), Kursk (1587), Yelets (1592), Kromy (1595) and in 1598 Belgorod on the river Donets. The purpose was to create strong defensive points and governmental centres to administer the growing population of those parts, for since Tsar Ivan's time Russian settlement had been growing denser south and east of the centre. In pursuing this policy, therefore, the state was trying to catch up with its own population, and at the same time to promote, protect and control commerce. But it also probed regions beyond. In 1586 an emissary was sent to spy out the land of Kakhetia south of the Caucasus Mountains. He returned with an envoy from the local king. This proved the beginning of a long, close association between Russia and Georgia.[3]

Before the end of the century Moscow was also in touch with the Kazakhs of the southern steppe, and further north, across the Urals, it was extending its authority into Siberia. Tiumen was founded in 1585, Tobolsk in 1587, as well as Pelym, Tara and other strong-points, including eventually Verkhoturia. This was a remarkably swift follow-up of Yermak's conquest of the Tatar state of eastern Siberia and the Stroganovs' exploitation of it. The building boom extended to established towns too. Astrakhan and Kazan were given new stone citadels at this time, and Smolensk on the western frontier was developed into the strongest fortress of all.[4]

The chief purpose of the government's extension into Siberia was to secure that invaluable source of furs – a major export – and to administer the native population, the hunters and trappers, who all paid their taxes in furs. Russia was creating an immense colonial empire in Siberia and the southern steppe. But it did so innocently, without realizing the world significance of the fact,[5] its long-term strategic significance in giving Moscow control of the world's most extensive land mass. But, though the motive was short-term and practical, the policy was systematically pursued. Every strong-point, whether built of logs upon earthworks, of brick or of stone, was strategically sited and provided a serviceable district centre for the government's representative, who acted as both civil governor and military commander.[6]

Scattered as many of them were, it would be the work of decades to develop these strong-points into an integrated system of defence. In the meantime older expedients still had their uses, like that of which the

Elizabethan venturer Jerome Horsey wrote in 1588: 'The moving Castle [*gulaigorod*] . . . so framed, that it may be set up in length . . . two, three, foure, five, sixe or seven miles'. A double wall of timber spaced with three yards in between and closed at both ends, the structure could be dismantled, transported and re-erected where needed, and was an effective block to Tatar and other raiders from the steppe.[7]

Careful thought as well as improvisation lay behind these essentially expansionist developments – as behind the stabilization programme and the economic and foreign policies – and Boris Godunov was the moving spirit behind all of them. He had a particular interest in the south-east, and some relevant expertise, having earlier run the department which administered Kazan, Astrakhan and Siberia. He knew all about running a central financial department and how the palace was administered, was supported by some very able helpers, and made it a principle to promote and exploit talent. Apart from the Shchelkalov brothers, he furthered the careers of men like Foma Petelin, the treasury specialist whom the English merchant Giles Fletcher considered outstandingly efficient and politically astute, and Eleazar Vyluzgin, chief administrator of the department of service estates, who seems to have headed the regents' private office and who, in 1591, was sent to Uglich with the commission of inquiry into the sudden death of the Tsarevich Dmitrii.

The untimely death of the Tsar's younger brother is popularly attributed to Boris, but the charge is unjust. Boris had no motive to kill Dmitrii in 1591, when Tsar Fedor, whatever his mental strength may have been, was in good health and expected to sire heirs. Generations of good historians from V. I. Klein to Ruslan Skrynnikov have sifted the evidence and concluded that Boris was innocent and that, as the investigation report concluded, Dmitrii died by accident or misadventure while playing with a sharp instrument in the courtyard of the palace at Uglich.[8] Why, then, has the contrary view prevailed?

The rumour that the Tsarevich had been murdered was first put about immediately after his death by his mother's kinsmen, the Nagois. But the Nagois hated Boris. They had tried to displace Tsar Fedor, and Boris had thwarted them, sidelining the heir apparent and his entourage. After the death they sought revenge, spreading derogatory rumours about Boris and trying to organize opposition to him. They had little immediate effect, although, as we shall see, they were to gain ground later. The myth that Boris had had Dmitrii murdered was furthered fifteen years later by the young prince's canonization (for cynical political reasons) as an innocent 'sufferer for Christ's sake', like the popular boy saints Boris and Gleb. Later still, and for their own purposes, the Romanovs were also to exploit the myth.[9] The leading nineteenth-century historian Soloviev followed the Nagois' line, giving an account of 'the saint's murder' which was dramatic, sentimental and disgracefully tendentious, and the famous Vasilii Kliuchevskii followed him uncritically – although both historians wrote before essential evidence was published in 1913.

Meanwhile Russia's greatest poet, Pushkin, and the composer Mussorgsky had used the myth to create a popular Shakespearian-type tragedy and a famous opera. Since then the lie about Boris's implication in Dmitrii's 'murder' has been perpetuated by the Church, which would find it embarrassing to de-canonize the saint, and by the financial interests of those who profit from the pilgrims and tourists attracted to Dmitrii's shrine. Boris Godunov has been traduced. There is no evidence that he plotted to murder his way to the throne as Shakespeare pictures Richard of York doing; no evidence that he was more scheming than any other politician anxious to preserve his position near the top of the pile. But there is evidence that he was an able minister concerned to promote the country's interests, treating its subjects no worse than necessary.[10]

In 1588 Terka, Russia's stronghold in the north-eastern foothills of the towering Caucasus, was rebuilt on a new site. In the following year Prince Andrei Khvorostinin was appointed its governor. The region had been identified as particularly important, and the government sensed that its politics were complex, so Khvorostinin was instructed to follow the situation there particularly closely. In 1589 he reported that Shevkal, the shamkhal of Tarku, was being wooed by the Ottoman pasha of Derbent. The shamkhal was chief of the Kumukhs, who had originated in the mountains of Dagestan but had come to dominate the Kumyks of the coastal plain west of the Caspian. But if the Turks wanted the shamkhal to declare for them, the Russians wanted him on their side and the Turks out of the region. The motive was control of the profitable trade route between Moscow and Persia, the source of rich silks and other oriental luxuries.[11]

Besides, the Tarku area was adjacent to the most convenient road south across the mountains to the exotic lands of Georgia and Armenia. Moscow was now particularly interested in the little successor states to the united Georgia that the Mongols had undermined, for their peoples were Orthodox Christians and natural allies. So in April 1589 an embassy left

Moscow for the south, returning a mission from the King of Imretia which accompanied them. The importance of the mission can be gauged by the presents it took.

For King Alexander himself there were:

Forty sables worth 100 rubles,
A thousand ermine pelts worth 30 rubles,
Fifteen fish teeth [probably walrus tusks] worth 70 rubles,
A cuirass worth 20 rubles,
A helmet worth 20 rubles

as well as three falcons, which were not valued[12] – perhaps priceless – one of which specialized in catching swans. Valuable gifts were also taken to present to princes and *mirzas* (to use the Persian term for prince) of the neighbouring Avars and Kabardinians. But the shamkhal of Tarku was to be given only a warning to send hostages for his future good behaviour if he did not want war.

This particular attempt to expand into the eastern Caucasus was to end in failure in 1594 when a Russian force, deserted by its Muslim allies, was routed. A joint attempt with Georgian forces was also to come to grief in 1605, though the attempts did not end there. In any case the 1594 mission had other aims, including cultural penetration. The mission, which was given an escort of nearly 300 soldiers and 50 Terek Cossacks, also included priests who were experts in liturgy and canon law and three icon painters. Clearly Moscow wanted the Georgians to conform to its version of the religiously correct. This had become all the more important now that the see of Moscow had been raised to patriarchal status, and the Catholic Church was campaigning not only against the Protestants, but against Orthodox Christians too.

The Catholics were to register another victory with the foundation in 1596 of the Uniate Church of Ukraine, a communion which retained most of the Orthodox liturgy and permitted parish priests to marry, but which recognized the Pope's authority and (albeit with greater misgivings) the Gregorian calendar. At the same time the Orthodox Church ceased to have any official existence in Lithuania, of which Ukraine then formed a part. After most of the Lithuanian elite had been lured away from Orthodoxy by the promise of all the privileges of the Polish nobility if they became Catholics, the new confession threatened to suborn much of the Ukrainian clergy and the peasants too.

There was resistance. The immensely wealthy Prince Konstantin

Ostrozhsky championed the cause of Orthodox Christianity. He funded a school and a Slavonic printing press, sponsored writers, and summoned up moral support from the patriarchs of Alexandria and Constantinople. Orthodox merchants organized confraternities and also founded schools, and Cossacks raised violent protests against Polish influence and Polish rule. In time the various strands of opposition were to combine and the movement was to gather a force which Moscow was able to exploit (See Chapter 7). However, the mobilization of these different interests was slow and their co-ordination was difficult. Besides, the Orthodox cause boasted too few educated polemists to be able to compete with the barrage of propaganda mounted by the Jesuits, and by the turn of the century the Tsar was pre-occupied with other problems.[13]

In 1598 Tsar Fedor died, and his death precipitated a crisis for the state. Fedor was the last of his line. The Riurikid dynasty, which had produced too many claimants to the crown when lateral succession was allowed, produced too few now that claims were confined to vertical succession. It was an unexpected misfortune. Of the three sons whom Ivan IV had fathered, Ivan, the eldest had died accidentally. Ivan had struck him in a fit of temper, and, falling awkwardly, the child fractured his skull. The youngest, Dmitrii, had died of misadventure playing with a knife. Now, seven years later, Fedor had died without leaving an heir. As a church historian put it, the royal house of Russia was left without a tenant.[14] Who, then, should succeed?

There were several hopefuls. Some, including the Romanovs and Nagois, were related to Ivan's wives; others, like Prince Vasilii Shuiskii, claimed both distinguished ancestry and ministerial experience. Boris Godunov, though not of princely descent, was also a candidate. As the late Tsar's brother-in law, a senior minister and a senior courtier he was well-positioned, though Shuiskii and Fedor Romanov also sat on the boyar council. Boris's particular advantage was the powerful support of his friend Patriarch Job (whom he himself had been instrumental in appointing); he was also well qualified in terms of both native ability and personal qualities, and, insofar as he was known, popular. The distinguished historian A. A. Zimin describes him as resolute and far-sighted, as capable of dissembling and cruelty when circumstances demanded, but also generous and charming.[15] In fact he was the obvious choice for tsar, and an Assembly of the Land duly endorsed his election.

Boris made a decent show of reluctance, refusing the crown three times. The official record of the meeting has its members clamouring long and loud for him to change his mind:

> 'We want Boris Fedorovich [Godunov] to be Tsar. There is no other [candidate]. God himself has chosen him . . .' And . . . the most holy Patriarch . . . said: 'Blessed be God who willed this. The Lord's will be done, for the voice of the people is the voice of God.' And therefore . . . by the grace given us through the Holy Ghost we have all installed . . . Boris Fedorovich [as] Autocrat of all Russia, Sovereign of the Russian land.

Boris's lack of hereditary credentials, was acknowledged, but it was pointed out that the Bible recorded cases of kings 'invested with the purple of sovereignty who . . . were commoners . . . and yet ruled . . . according to God's will honourably and justly'.[16]

So on 3 September 1598 Boris was enthroned as tsar amid general acclamations. Huge cannon boomed out their salute, and embassies were sent out far and wide to announce the accession. Yet he took no chances. Potential rivals – including several Nagois and Romanovs – were taken under escort to distant prisons, an amnesty for common criminals was declared, a tax holiday was granted, and largesse was distributed to widows, orphans, foreigners in Russia's service and the people of Moscow.[17] So Russia acquired an able, legitimate tsar. A succession crisis had been averted.

Russia's prospects seemed good. Tsar Boris was experienced in all the major branches of state policy; he commanded the loyalty of state servants, both military and civil; and, in early middle age, he was at the height of his powers. Moreover, his son Fedor was a healthy and intelligent boy. Russia seemed destined to prosper under the new regime. Yet the seven lean years that followed were lean indeed, and by the time they ended Boris was dead, his heir murdered, the realm in ruins, and the enemy at the gate.

The cause was not the legacy of Ivan the Terrible, though this contributed to the disaster, and the supposed murder of the Tsarevich Dmitrii was merely incidental. The fundamental reason was a change in weather patterns known as the Little Ice Age. Bad weather caused repeated famines and associated ecological problems and epidemics. These in turn affected agriculture, and promoted migrations and public discontent. Soon social distress spilled over into political protest, giving space to the political climbers and entrepreneurs who are always ready to profit personally from public disasters. Events unfolded inexorably, as in a Greek tragedy.

They began with a severe drought in the first summer of Boris's reign, and then fire struck the dried-out timbers of the still largely wooden city of Moscow. The winter of 1600 was long and very cold, particularly in the south and west, and then there was a spate of unusually heavy storms. The consequence was famine, but not disaster. Russians were no strangers to cruel weather and the destructive forces of nature. They resowed, repaired, eked out what they had left, borrowed if they had to. The urban population suffered when the price of bread rose, but, like the government of ancient Rome, the Russian tsardom made provision when hunger threatened. There had been localized famines before, and a widespread one in the winter of 1587–8, without causing any long-term trauma. This time it was different.

Disaster struck not once or twice, but year in, year out. The summer of 1601 was extremely wet. Day after day 'rain fell without stopping, and the rye and the spring wheat got sodden and lay on the ground all winter.' Around Moscow itself there were heavy frosts in late July, and every type of grain and vegetable was frozen. Nor was the disaster localized. It hit Pskov in the west, and also Kaluga and Livny in the south-east. In 1602 there was another drought, followed by violent storms and floods so great that even the very old could not remember their like. Then blights struck and epidemics, and every year now seemed a year of famine.[18] Well might the religious have recalled the ten plagues that God sent to afflict the Egyptians, and concluded that Tsar Boris must have committed dreadful God-offending acts. Historians who attribute Russia's collapse to the dynasty dying out are just as mistaken as those who attributed it to Boris's 'sin'. Climate change and the series of weather disasters precipitated a social catastrophe, and political debacle flowed from it. Tales about the infant Dmitrii and the 'usurper' Boris only gained currency in the wake of the great hunger.

Far from being to blame, Boris did everything within his power to alleviate his people's sufferings. He campaigned against speculators who hoarded grain waiting for the price to rise; he sold grain cheaply from his own granaries; he sent out messages of encouragement; he arranged for the indigent dead to be given decent burial, and doled out large sums to the needy from his own treasury. But luck had deserted him: the grain he sold cheaply was often resold for private gain; as news of his largesse spread, more and more poor peasants crowded into the city in expectation of his charity, compounding the problems. Whatever was done was never enough. An eyewitness described the scene:

> I swear to God that this is the truth. I saw with my own eyes people lying on the streets, eating grass like cattle in summer and hay in winter. Some were already dead, with hay and dung in their mouths and also (pardon my indelicacy) had swallowed human excrement . . .
>
> Many dead bodies of people who had perished through hunger were found daily in the streets. . . . Daily . . . hundreds of corpses were gathered up at the tsar's command and carried away on so many carts, that to behold it (scarcely to be believed) was grisly and horrible.[19]

The continuing period of abnormal weather precipitated not only famine and disease, but also a social and demographic crisis. Marginal farmers, peasants no longer able to pay their rents and taxes, or even feed themselves, abandoned their holdings and took to the road. The number of beggars, vagabonds and robbers multiplied, and they became more desperate. There was another, relatively sharp, population shift – this time from north to south, and particularly to the frontier lands. And it was from the south-west frontier that the first political challenge emerged in the autumn of 1604: a claimant to the throne who called himself Dmitrii and said he had escaped death at Uglich. From then on Boris's days were numbered.

In July 1604 the Tsar received an ambassador from England, Sir Thomas Smith, who subsequently reported to Sir Robert Cecil on his reception. Great care had been taken to hide any sign of social distress from him, and Boris treated him warmly and 'in great state, [seated] in a throne of gold, with his Imperiall Crowne on his head, his sceptre in his hand, & many other ornaments of state . . . his sonne [Fedor] who sat by him, inquired of the healthe of my King [James I], and invited me to dine with them together with Fedor.' After dinner and taking wine with the Tsar, Smith was dismissed, but was informed that 'I should have . . . very shortly audience, agayne, for ye dispatche of businesse, but in ye meane time, newes came of certaine rebels risen in armes, against ye Emperor, in his borders towards Poland, which hath hindered my speedy dispatch [of business], and therfor must stay here, and returne ye same way I came.'[20]

Quite how a popular political rebellion got under way in a country governed by a relatively efficient, centralized monarchy, among a people that was largely illiterate, has never been satisfactorily explained. It has been suggested, however, that rumour served as a substitute for modern media in early modern Russia, and that many if not most of the political rumours that gained currency were started by politicians anxious to manipulate popular opinion and, indeed, to trigger popular protests.[21] But several elements were needed to get the rebellion started.

As we have seen, a series of natural disasters was disrupting the Russian economy and society. It was also bleeding the state of funds and raising doubts about the legitimacy of its government. But a rebellion against a God-sanctioned emperor had somehow to be justified. Hence the appearance of a pretender – someone claiming to be the Tsarevich Dmitrii miraculously rescued from death in 1591 and therefore Russia's legitimate God-given ruler in this time of troubles. Who the pretender actually was is disputed. Tsar

Boris thought he was a defrocked monk from the Miracle Monastery in Moscow, called Grigorii Otrepev. Chester Dunning, in his recent, massive study of the subject, suspects he was a protégé of the Nagois, who brought up a child to believe he really was the infant Dmitrii. Whoever he was, the role he was cast in required ambition, nerve, intelligence and histrionic skills. 'Dmitrii' possessed them all. He had all the bravado of a chancer.

But personal qualities were not enough. He also needed sponsors – people to train and brief him, to provide contacts for him, and to fund him. Circumstantial evidence suggests that these backers were prominent Russians, enemies of Boris. The finger of suspicion has pointed not only to the Nagois but, among others, to the Romanovs as well. The pretender soon gained a powerful backer in Poland-Lithuania too: the wealthy magnate Adam Vyshnevetski who had extensive property interests in the frontier area near Seversk and was in dispute with the Muscovite government. It was Vyshnevetski who provided the pretender with a base, helped him recruit the nucleus of an army (a few hundred Cossacks, many of them recent immigrants from Muscovy), and introduced him to other helpers, notably Jerzy Mniszech, the Polish palatine (governor) of Sandomir, who agreed to serve 'Dmitrii' as military commander.[22]

The pretender Dmitrii's invasion was launched against the frontier fortress of Moravsk in October 1604. The garrison mutinied, and the place surrendered without a fight. The invaders moved on to the substantial town of Chernigov. Here there was resistance, but, thanks again to a rebellion by servicemen and townspeople, the city was captured and the troops in the citadel soon surrendered. News of these successes, and of 'Dmitrii' gaining more support, encouraged further defections from the Muscovite side – particularly from discontented servicemen, for the government was by now critically short of cash to pay them.

Then Peter Basmanov, whom the Tsar had charged with the defence of the region, succeeded in stopping the advance. He summoned up various detachments of musketeers, town Cossacks, service people of various ranks and recruits to his headquarters at Novgorod-Seversk, which boasted a useful battery of artillery. The town held, forcing the rebels to lay siege to it. But then Putivl declared for 'Dmitrii', and this prompted more defectors from all ranks – less out of love for 'Dmitrii' than from fear they might be lynched if they remained loyal. But Basmanov and his men held firm at Novgorod-Seversk giving time for a strong force from Moscow to approach it. When the armies met, however, the pretender's forces got the better of the inconclusive contest.

In the weeks that followed, 'Dmitrii's' supporters continued to increase, but then, perhaps afraid of what might happen to the likes of him if the common people got the upper hand, Mniszech deserted. In January 1605 Shuiskii arrived with reinforcements from Moscow and elsewhere, and at the battle of Dobrynichi the superior firepower of the Tsar's army forced the enemy into a disorderly retreat. The insurgency might have ended there. It did not.

Shuiskii's men ravaged the areas they recaptured, partly as punishment for the rebellion, partly to compensate themselves for the privations they had suffered at the enemy's hands. But their behaviour made the Tsar no friends, and by the spring of 1605 most of the service ranks in southern Russia were angry. Boris's tired troops broke off their siege of Rylsk and concentrated on trying to secure the strategic fort of Kromy, where the garrison had gone over to the enemy. Large forces were brought up to retake Kromy, but a spirited defence in which a Cossack ataman called Korela distinguished himself kept the Tsar's forces at bay.

Then on 13 April Tsar Boris, who had been ill since January (probably with heart disease), died – and this precipitated the disasters which followed. So long as the Tsar lived he could probably count on the loyalty of most Russians. Now he was dead the chances were recalculated. Most of the troops from central Russia remained loyal, but not the men from the southern frontier, and a carefully planned mutiny among many of them stationed with the loyalist army at Kromy changed the balance of forces. Suddenly the loyalty of many senior commanders began to erode. Boris's heir was a youth of sixteen with little experience and no personal following. And, thanks to the rumours that Boris's enemies had been spreading, many doubted his right to succeed. People had been whispering that the Tsarevich Dmitrii was planning to take revenge on Tsar Boris; that Boris was not the legitimate tsar; that his son and successor, Tsar Fedor, was so frightened of 'Dmitrii' and the vengeance of the Russian people that he planned to flee to England.

As for the personable 'Dmitrii', whom rumour said was the true tsar – son of the grim but popular Ivan – events in the south showed him to have support. A trickle of notables, including the commander Basmanov, began to drift into 'Dmitrii's' camp, and the trickle soon became a flood. Boris's reign had been marred by catastrophes of every kind. With the false Dmitrii as tsar the people hoped for better. They were not to get it.

In May 1605 a crowd began to gather around the high point of Red Square outside the Kremlin in Moscow, the place used for official proclamations and state executions. Soon it was a multitude, including many servicemen. Letters from the pretender were brandished, and the crowd grew more restive and threatening. Ministers concluded that the situation was beyond their powers to control alone, and sent for Patriarch Job. According to the 'New Chronicle', composed around 1630,[23] Job – a Godunov loyalist, who had already pronounced anathema on the pretender – tried every wile he knew, using sweet reason in an attempt to calm the throng, and threatening them with the judgement of God. But nothing worked. The mob wanted 'Dmitrii'. Tsar Fedor, his mother, his sister, other Godunovs, relatives and the people reputedly loyal to them were seized and taken away, their houses looted. The Patriarch was seized too, and led off to imprisonment. Then 'Dmitrii' was sent for.

The pretender was already on his way, making a triumphal progress towards Moscow, receiving the plaudits of the people and the homage of virtually every potentate. As he approached, Prince Vasilii Golitsyn ordered the young Tsar and his mother to be suffocated. On 20 June 1605 'Dmitrii' entered Moscow, heading a large parade. He was solemnly crowned tsar on the following day. But his own days were numbered, and he was not to last a year.

The arguments about the false Dmitrii – who and what kind of man he was, and what he stood for – continue to this day. The sources are mostly *parti pris* and allow great scope for speculation. However, the fact that the chronicles favour one interest or another, that official documents contain propaganda, and that reports by contemporaries reflect rumour suggests that Russia was awash with political talk at that time – talk that reflected attempts by interested parties to justify their cause or discredit an enemy, and to bring opinion to their side. And now Dmitrii was in power the tenor of the rumours changed. Instead of questioning Boris's legitimacy, they attacked Dmitrii. It was said that he was really Grigorii Otrepev, a defrocked monk; that he was a puppet of the Jesuits; that he was executing Orthodox monks who were hostile to him; that he had promised to cede Russian territory to the King of Poland; that he intended to massacre the clergy and convert Russians to the Catholic religion; that he was a sex maniac; that he practised magic with devils.[24] One may suppose that many of these rumours were put about by friends of Vasilii Shuiskii, who was plotting against Dmitrii. On 17 May 1606 his plot succeeded.

Dmitrii may not have been as evil as most Russians came to paint him, and Chester Dunning has recently argued that he had merit as a ruler.

However, his association with Poles and Jesuits was regarded with deep suspicion, as was his marriage to the Catholic Marina, his supporter Mniszech's daughter. A scuffle between wedding guests in which a Russian met his death at the hands of the visitors triggered a violent reaction. In the ensuing fight both Dmitrii and Basmanov met their deaths. Their naked corpses were publicly displayed for three days, inviting excoriation and ridicule. But Marina escaped. They said she turned herself into a magpie (like a witch) and flew away.

Vasilii Shuiskii became tsar (as Vasilii IV), and a new patriarch, called Hermogen, was installed. The twin pillars supporting the state were in place again, and for the first time in seven years the weather was normal. But the effects of the revolutions in climate and politics were still evident in endemic discontent, and the new tsar failed to establish his legitimacy in the eyes of the people. Rumours that Dmitrii still lived took hold again. A fearful Shuiskii turned to public relations to shore up his position. He or his minions dreamed up two master-strokes. First, the false Dmitrii's body was 'rediscovered' at a site far from where it had been buried, prompting another set of rumours to circulate – that the Devil was playing tricks on Christian folk; that Lapps had taught Dmitrii how to die and come alive again; that he had been so evil that the earth would not accept him. So his remains were publicly burned on a wooden float adorned with pictures of hell. The second device, intended to make assurance doubly sure, was the 'discovery' of the real Tsarevich Dmitrii's allegedly uncorrupted remains at Uglich.[25] Nevertheless, another pretender calling himself Dmitrii was soon to appear.

In the summer of 1607 crowds gained the upper hand over the forces of law and order as another great rebellion welled up from the south under a new leader, a former galley slave and Cossack called Ivan Bolotnikov. They 'threw the governors into gaol, plundered their masters' houses . . . looted their property, raped their wives and virgin daughters . . . and committed . . . unspeakable outrages'.[26] Russia, in fact, was at war with itself. The south was in perpetual revolt, and the central Volga region was soon up in arms too. Political entrepreneurs from Moscow exploited the situation – a nobleman called Molchanov actually impersonated 'Tsar Dmitrii', riding on the crest of yet another wave of rumours about his survival – and by October Moscow itself was under siege by rebels. As a result, food prices rose to famine heights inside the city. Tsar Vasilii Shuiskii was saved only by a rift in the rebels' ranks. The gentry among them were becoming increasingly uncomfortable with the levelling instincts of the lower orders, and soon went over to him. Thanks to them the siege of Moscow was broken, and the rebels were routed.

Nevertheless, huge swathes of the country were still under rebel control, and the government's tax income was falling steadily. Then a spurious 'Tsarevich Petr', arrived at the rebel base of Putivl with a large entourage of Cossacks and reinforced his claim to rule by executing dozens of gentry. Before long he moved on to take the town of Tula. But there his forces found themselves besieged by tsarist troops for four months. Then a second false Dmitrii made an appearance near the Polish frontier. Who he really was is still a mystery, but he and his 'retainers' were well rehearsed in a repertoire of theatrical tricks designed to convince onlookers that he really was the rightful tsar, and he soon boasted an army that included mercenaries from Lithuania and Zaporozhian Cossacks, as well as the usual motley array of angry peasants and slaves, other Cossacks, and would-be Cossacks.

Tsarist forces captured Tula, Bolotnikov and 'Petr' in October 1607, and this persuaded the second 'Dmitrii' to postpone the offensive he was planning. Instead he fell back to the Polish frontier, regrouped his forces, and waited for more to join him. Then, advancing on Moscow, he established his headquarters at Tushino, less than 10 miles to the north-west. A large force of Polish troops also came up, sent by King Sigismund to secure the return of Polish prisoners captured when the first false Dmitrii was killed; then another rebel army approached as the Tsar was trying to reach an agreement with the Poles. And the chaotic chain of events only became more tangled, aided by bad faith on all sides.

The Tsar was isolated in Moscow; then Marina, widow of the first false Dmitrii, decided to 'recognize' the second false Dmitrii at Tushino, which bolstered the pretender's credibility and his chances of establishing his rule over all Russia. But, although he now commanded the loyalty of more than half of the country, he lacked the funds to organize a proper government. He even lacked the wherewithal to supply and feed his own troops. They therefore had to live off the country and resort to forced confiscations and robbery in order to maintain themselves. The demands and depredations of the pretender soon seemed worse even than those of the Tsar, who had begun to confiscate Church plate.

Then the Tsar decided to cede territory to Sweden in return for the services of a force of mercenaries. The King of Poland now moved openly to capture the great frontier citadel of Smolensk. Russia's neighbours were beginning moving in like jackals on a dying beast to dismember the Empire. And still the chaotic civil war continued. The false Dmitrii and Marina moved to Kaluga, and some of the more prominent of their erstwhile supporters, including Filaret Romanov and others of his family, thought of backing King Sigismund's son Wladyslaw as candidate for the throne of Russia.

The damage to agriculture and the economy was as bad as the political damage. This was partly because of the disruption of the civil wars, but partly also the result of a renewal of vicious weather conditions. In 1607 there were serious floods in the Moscow region and deep frosts in western Russia, which prevented the germination of seedcorn and so precipitated yet another famine; in 1608 the crops in both central and western Russia were destroyed by a bitterly cold winter and heavy rainstorms in summer and autumn which washed out the harvest. There were epidemics and outbreaks of animal diseases that year too, and raging fires caused by lightning.

Bereft of support, the Tsar waited in the Kremlin for his fate to be decided. On 16 July 1610 the decision came. The power-brokers had decided to get rid of both him and 'Dmitrii' and to elect a new tsar. Vasilii Shuiskii was forced to become a monk, which emasculated him as a political actor. However, no agreement could be reached on who should succeed him, so a ministerial council of seven boyars assumed the task. In August they decided to elect Prince Wladyslaw, who had indicated his willingness to convert to Orthodoxy, as tsar. However, Wladyslaw himself now preferred to conquer Russia outright if he could, and other powerful Russians opposed his candidacy anyway. At last Zolkiewski, commander of the Polish forces which had managed to clear 'Dmitrii's' army from the Moscow area, decided on a *coup de main*. He persuaded the more important potential Russian candidates to form a delegation to King Sigismund at Smolensk to discuss Wladyslaw's election – and then had them arrested. So Vasilii Golitsyn, Filaret Romanov and others – including ex-tsar Vasilii Shuiskii – found themselves prisoners in Poland, where some of them were soon to die in mysterious circumstances.[27]

Curiously enough it was Poland's new role as the arbiter of Russia's fate that served as a catalyst for Russia's political recovery. Whatever Russians, including the rebels, thought of their rulers, the tsars were at least Orthodox Christians. People reacted strongly against Poland because it was Roman Catholic and predatory. As he made clear in a message to Pope Paul V, King Sigismund aimed to accomplish what his predecessor Stefan Bathory had failed to do: to gain dominion over Russia and return it 'from error and schism to obedience to the Holy See'. Sigismund revived the idea 'all the more ardently since in addition to all the other enormous benefits that would accrue to Christendom from the subjugation of Moscow' it would help him regain control of Sweden.[28] The old revulsion felt by Orthodox Russians at the prospect of 'Latinization' welled up again, and was given more force by the behaviour of Polish troops in Russia. These sentiments were exploited with energy by the Russian Church to form one plank of a springboard to recovery. Another came spontaneously from Russian servicemen and government functionaries.

Their movement had begun early in 1611 in efforts to depose Vasilii Shuiskii and eliminate the pretender Dmitrii. As a letter sent from Iaroslavl to Vologda in February of that year put it:

> The Poles have inflicted much oppression and outrage on the people of Moscow, and so the most holy Hermogen, Patriarch of Moscow and all Russia, and the people of Moscow had written to Prokofii Liapunov, leader of the gentry of Riazan province, and to the towns from the upper Oka to the lower Volga urging them to join together to march against the Poles . . . before they take Moscow . . . [This he had done and many soldiers had set out for Moscow] and you, gentlemen, should all stand firm in the Orthodox Christian faith, and not betray it for the Latin faith lest you destroy your souls.[29]

Letters were also sent from Iaroslavl to Kazan, from Solvychegodsk to Perm, and between many other cities, urging that men be sent without delay, whether on horseback or on skis, and all sorts of people besides gentry were soon involved in the enterprise. Townsmen and peasants, local officials, humble servicemen, blacksmiths were all urged to raise soldiers, equip them, and march them to Moscow, where they were organized by a triumvirate consisting of Liapunov, Prince Dmitrii Trubetskoi and the Cossack leader Ivan Zarutskii. Russian patriots were soon on the march.

But even now the agony did not end. Swedish forces invaded, laid siege to Novgorod, and eventually took it. The Poles captured Smolensk, and Polish troops were still in Moscow. Hordes of predatory Russians were still battening on large areas and sucking them dry. And now other foreigners began to think that they could gain from Russia's distress. The Pope wanted Russia for the access it would give his missionaries to reach all the heathens of Asia. King James I of England and Scotland wanted to gain control of Russia's oriental trade.[30] The Patriarch had been imprisoned by the Poles, yet a call to arms was issued in October 1611 by the abbot of the Trinity St Sergius Monastery at Zagorsk, and metropolitans, bishops and abbots across the land echoed his call. Even before that, scribes in towns throughout the realm wrote letters on behalf of the local governors and other notables, setting out the purpose of a mobilization, explaining the means, and trying to co-ordinate it: 'We should take oaths ourselves, and get the Tatars and Ostiaks to swear their Muslim oath, so that . . . we make common cause with them for our true and incorruptible Orthodox faith . . . against the enemies and destroyers of our Christian faith, against the Poles and Lithuanians.' They also made it clear that the next tsar must 'be chosen by the entire land of the Russian realm' rather than arbitrarily – in other words, that an Assembly of the Land must endorse the choice of sovereign.[31]

The movement's headquarters were in Iaroslavl on the Volga, and, though Prince Trubetskoi was still associated with it, Prince Dmitrii Pozharskii, commander of the local troops, now became its leading secular light, being elected by people of all ranks to command the army and the land. Also important was the elected representative of the great merchants (*gosti*) and other commercial interests, Kuzma Minin, a master butcher from Nizhnii-Novgorod. Pozharskii, in his appeals issued in the spring of 1612, blamed

> the Devil . . . [for] creating disunity among Orthodox Christians, seducing many to join corrupt and sinful company, and [causing] rogues of every rank to band together and introduce internecine strife and bloodshed into Moscovy [so that] son rose against father, father against son, and brother against brother . . . and there was much shedding of Christian blood . . .
>
> But now, gentlemen, we have exchanged messages with the entire land, vowed to God . . . and pledged our souls . . . to stand firmly . . . against the enemies and depredators of the Christian faith . . . We must choose a sovereign by common agreement, whomever God may grant us . . . lest the Muscovite state be utterly destroyed.[32]

Rousing appeals, a good religious cause and patriotism were not enough, however. There had to be sanctions to force the recalcitrant into line, and those who responded had to be fed and rewarded. Documents surviving from the first attempt at a national mobilization show how this was organized. Servicemen who failed to answer the call to arms and present themselves at the appointed place by the appointed date were to forfeit their service estates, though those who pleaded poverty could petition for their return. On the other hand, those who served well would be allotted estates and money pay.[33] These provisions had presupposed functioning state ministries – particularly the department of service estates and the financial departments, including the office that ran the crown estates – and as yet the movement had no control of these. Nevertheless, it did redistribute some land on this basis of its promises. But its first need must have been for money.

We know it commanded sizeable sums, because it was able to mint coins and pay the troops it recruited. Since the normal means of raising state income had broken down, one may assume that initially at least the Church was the chief source of funds. Very little is known about the finances of the Russian Church, but both the high profile of the Church in the revival and the fact that it commanded a major proportion of the country's resources, including approximately a third of all cultivated land, strongly suggest that the Church filled the critical financial gap.[34] And so in 1612 events at last moved towards a resolution.

In August 1612 the army – over 10,000 strong, but not particularly well equipped – arrived outside Moscow. It soon engaged the Polish forces of Hetman Chodkiewicz, forcing them into retreat. It also halted King Sigismund when he approached with an army to take control of the situation. Realizing that their prospects now seemed poor, in October the Russian power-brokers who had sponsored Prince Wladyslaw withdrew from the Kremlin, and on the following day the Polish garrison, now down to 1,500 hungry men, surrendered.

The call went out for delegates to come to Moscow to choose a tsar, and by January 1613 hundreds were arriving. Wladyslaw, the Polish candidate, was now ruled out, and the Swedish contender, Prince Karl Filip, had little more support. Trubetskoi's candidature was blocked by Pozharskii, and both of them opposed the sixteen-year-old Michael Romanov, who was hardly an impressive candidate and had been associated with the Polish occupiers. However, the Romanovs were rich, and they spent money to promote their man. The Cossack delegates were eventually won over – or bought – and on 21 February Michael was chosen.[35] His father, Filaret Romanov, was installed as patriarch, and Michael himself was crowned in July 1612. Though the Cossack leader Zarutskii, Marina and her four-year-old son (known as the 'little brigand') were not to be caught and dealt with until the summer of 1614, at last the work of reconstruction could get under way.

The Time of Troubles left in its wake both a damaged economy and damaged institutions. It also established a tradition by which governments were to be challenged by pretenders who denied the tsar's legitimacy. Such claimants sprang up from various parts of the country with increasing regularity over the next two centuries, threatening to destabilize government in Russia.[36] Yet there was a positive legacy too. The trauma impressed on most Russians a sense that even oppressive, autocratic government was preferable to the mayhem of anarchy, and the regime took care to remind them of it.

Events had also demonstrated that even in the early 1600s Russians were coming to share a common national consciousness. It has been argued that the imperial nature of the ethnically diverse Russian state inhibited the development of Russian nationalism, but a strong sense of patriotism – perhaps as strong as that manifested in Elizabethan England – was shared by Russians from the north and south, east and west. Russians knew who they were, and it was not only their Orthodox religion, contrasting with the Catholic, Protestant and Muslim faiths of their neighbours, that defined them; nor their language, which, except for the Old Church Slavonic used for religious purposes, was not yet a standard or literary one; nor their customs, which varied to some extent from region to region – though all these elements contributed. They shared a sense of community associated with the land, and, as the letters sent out to mobilize a national army demonstrate, even strangers among them, such as Muslim Tatars, were not excluded. They too were accepted as part of the Russian political community.[37]

And, though the Troubles had shorn Russia of much of its empire, there were some areas where the process of empire-building had hardly been interrupted.

7
Recovery

EARLY IN 1613 several groups of officials and clerks, with small retinues of servants carrying bales of sable-skins, live falcons and other valuables, were to be seen leaving Moscow by sledge or boat. These wise men bearing gifts were embassies bound for the courts of the Habsburg Emperor, the King of Poland, the Turkish Sultan, Denmark, England and several lesser powers. Later that year and the year that followed, others left – for Persia, France and Holland. Their purpose was to announce that Tsar Michael Romanov (together with his father, Patriarch Filaret) now guided Russia's destiny; that the Time of Troubles was over. But their brave show masked the sad condition of the country. The economy was shattered, the currency debased, the government bankrupt, administration in disarray, the population reduced and exhausted. And Russia was still pursuing unaffordable wars with Sweden and with Poland. The only foreign-policy options now were defensive; the only possible economic policy was retrenchment.

Despite its desperate need for revenue, the government had to suspend tax collection in some stricken regions for a time to allow them to recover, and the ambassadors were in effect sent out with begging bowls in hand. With Poland they were to negotiate a treaty of 'eternal peace', even at the cost of ceding rich tracts of territory and important towns including the great fortress city of Smolensk. Other powers were to be asked for military and financial aid.[1] But the brave show of formal ceremony which the ambassadors maintained, and their cautious, hard-headed, approach in negotiations, could hardly disguise the fact that Russia's aspirations to great-power status had become laughable.

Yet within forty years Russia's wasted muscles were bulging once again. By the 1670s roles had been reversed: proud Poland was much reduced; Russia had supplanted it as the strongest power in eastern Europe. How is the extraordinary turnaround to be explained? By what mysterious means was the pitiable Russia of 1613 transformed into a new Goliath? And how was it able to ward off a series of internal troubles that threatened to undermine its new stability: an open rift between tsar and patriarch; an irreparable split among Russian Christians; the appearance of yet more pretenders; and repeated rebellions, both urban and rural, some of massive scale?[2]

Imperial growth hinged on military power, but this in turn depended on size of population and the generation of wealth, both of which are difficult to measure for an age for which there are no census data, official statistics or economic indicators. Informed estimates suggest that the population grew from as little as 8 million in 1600 to 11 million or more by 1678,[3] but the increase was due to several factors other than natural increase: the acquisition of eastern Ukraine along with Smolensk in 1666 gave a big boost to population, and the conquest of Siberia added as many as half a million more. On the other hand the great plague of 1654 sharply reduced the population of Moscow, and war casualties – notably those sustained in the Polish war of 1654–67 – decimated the male population. These losses were offset to some extent by the government's practice of transporting civilians, especially those with skills, to Moscow from the western territories it occupied, and by the importation of foreign professional soldiers and technological experts. Even so the rate of natural increase must have been high, and the most obvious reason for this was improvement in diet since the Time of Troubles. There were fewer interruptions to the production and transportation of food; fewer famines, less disruption; and in the last three decades of the century Russia shared in the upsurge of prosperity and optimism enjoyed by most of Europe.

The economic recovery was quicker than the demographic. The leading American economic historian of Russia, Richard Hellie of Chicago, concludes that 'normal economic activity' had been restored by 1630. But Russia's ability to break through the ramparts that separated her from the West depended on more than this – indeed, on something like an economic miracle. Hellie argues that the absence of guilds, which had inhibited economic development in western Europe, was one advantage. The government created another in 1649, when it removed previously existing restrictions on urban craftsmen and traders, and limited the economic privileges of the Church. Furthermore, the state maintained a stable currency, enforced standard weights and measures, reduced the number of internal toll charges, and kept communications relatively safe from bandits for most of the time. All this helped to promote the economy. On the other hand the final imposition of serfdom, according to Hellie, was bad for the country's development, because it confined the peasant labour force to the

Volga–Oka region around Moscow, where soils were relatively poor, hampering agricultural development in the more productive Black Earth zones of the south and east.[4]

Yet the maintenance of a large labour force around Moscow was essential if the state, which protected the economy, was to function. A free labour market would not have guaranteed that. Nor would a free market necessarily have promoted faster economic development. The problem arose not so much from the state and the autocracy squeezing initiative out of society (as some historians argue) as from the conservatism of most Russian merchants, who showed much less initiative than their Western counterparts. They viewed their privileges merely as monopolies to be exploited.[5] At the same time wealthy magnates, so far from investing productively, tended to stockpile wealth and acquire luxuries, otherwise engaging with the market as little as possible. They continued to produce the bulk of their needs in their own households on their own estates, as in bygone times. Rather than the Russian state restricting economic growth through its interference in economic life, it could be argued that the taxes it imposed stimulated production and that it filled some of the gaps which unenterprising Russians of means had neglected.[6]

Siberia was to be a major factor in Russia's recovery. Ivan IV's backing for the Stroganov venture (see Chapter 5) continued to pay handsome dividends, but at the beginning of the seventeenth century the vast potential of Siberia had not yet been recognized. Its huge expanses remained almost entirely *terra incognita*, its population, chiefly native peoples, small. Although the disruption of the Time of Troubles had displaced many Russians and encouraged migration to the periphery of the Empire, most migrants preferred to move south rather than east; and although the laws required the return of runaway serfs to their landlords, those who benefited from their labour were reluctant to surrender them. So population movement into Siberia remained a trickle. Trappers and traders went there, but they lacked the resources, the capability and perhaps even the inclination to organize the exploitation of the territory in any thoroughgoing manner, and so the task fell to the state.[7]

Concern to secure the biggest possible tax income led it to build forts at distant trading stations and to devise settlement programmes. In 1601 the Godunov regime had mounted an expedition to a winter trading station called Mangazeia on the Yenisei river deep in the icy tundra at the very edge of the Arctic Circle. The purpose was to build a log fort and administration centre, where traders would gather and taxes could be collected. Although the dismal area was a hunting ground of the feared Samoyeds, who were reputed to eat their own children, they could be forced to pay tribute to the benefit of the state. Mangazeia was to become an important base for the penetration of Siberia as far as the Pacific.

At the same time, since all virgin land was regarded as crown property, the state was anxious to make cultivable parts of Siberia productive. It therefore encouraged peasants not already in the tax net to settle around new log forts, providing them with food and seedcorn, and sometimes much more, to get them started.[8] Such opportunities were to be announced in the market places of appropriate towns. 'Whoever is willing to go to the Taborinsk area . . .' ran one such proclamation, 'will be given a plot of arable land and money from our Treasury for horses and farm buildings . . . and tax exemption for one year or more depending on the condition of the land they settle, and one ruble or two for transportation depending on the size of the family.'[9]

The river Yenisei, Russia's eastern limit in 1601, also marked the eastern limit of cultivable land in Siberia, so the lure of free farms for would-be homesteaders did not work beyond that point. Nevertheless, within half a century Russians and the Russian state had reached the Pacific. Yakutsk, where there are frosts for nine months of the year, was founded in 1637; Lake Baikal was reached in 1647, the Bering Strait in 1648.

The quest had originally been for furs, then salt (the foundation of the Stroganovs' fortune), iron, fish and walrus tusks. Siberia's gold was as yet undiscovered, and its rich oilfields and natural gas and aluminium deposits – the bases of future wealth – were unknown and unneeded.

The pioneers were Cossacks, boatmen, trappers and traders. Their technology was simple, and they lacked navigational instruments. They sailed Arctic seas from estuary to estuary in boats they had built themselves; they traversed permafrost landscapes, and braved their ways across 4,000 miles of uncharted taiga to Chukhotka, Kamchatka and the frontiers of China. Many died in the process. Yet these Russian explorers found their way across the vast, inclement tracts of northern Asia amazingly quickly. Often they were oblivious of their achievement. One such was the Cossack Semeon Dezhnev, who found the straits separating Asia from America in 1648, eighty years before Vitus Bering.

Dezhnev was a Siberian serviceman who had been sent into the wilderness in search of 'new people' from whom the government could extract tribute. He set out with twenty-four other trappers, hunters and traders, most of them working on their own account. They went by sea and land –

whichever seemed more practical, given the topography and the season. Eventually they came to the river Anadyr. 'We could catch no fish,' he reported subsequently; 'there was no forest, and so, because of hunger we poor men went separate ways . . . [Half the party] went up the Anadyr [overland] and journeyed for twenty days but saw no people, traces of reindeer sleds, or native trails,' so they turned back.

Eventually the twelve survivors went by boat up the river, and at last came upon some Yukagirs.

> We captured two of them in a fight [in which] I was badly wounded. We took tribute from them by name, recording in the tribute books what we took from each and what for the Sovereign [Tsar]'s tribute. I wanted to take more . . . but they said 'We have no sables [for] we do not live in the forest. But the reindeer people visit us and when they come we shall buy sables from them and pay tribute to the Sovereign.'

The arrival of a rival tribute collector, however, sparked some violence and dried up the flow of tribute.

Dezhnev worked on in Siberia, and some fifteen years later we find him bombarding the Siberia Office with petitions:

> I, your slave, supported myself on your . . . service on the new rivers with my own money and my own equipment, and I . . . received no official pay in money, grain and salt from 1642 to 1661 . . . because of the shortage of money and grain . . . I risked my head [in your service,] was severely wounded, shed my blood, suffered great cold and hunger, and all but died of starvation . . . I was impoverished by shipwreck, incurred heavy debts, and was finally ruined . . . Sovereign, have mercy, please.[10]

Russian petitioners commonly expressed themselves in piteous as well as slavish terms, but Dezhnev's plea has the ring of truth, and in due course the government authorized reasonable compensation to be paid to him – though one may assume that it corroborated his claim with its records first.

The discovery of places and people continued apace, driven by the state's unassuagable appetite for more assets and more income, whether in coin or kind. But there were limits. One day venturers came across tribesmen who, when accosted for tribute, asked why they should pay the Tsar of Russia when they already paid tribute to the Emperor of China. By the 1680s the two countries were engaged in a border war. The Russians built forts – Albasin and Argunsk – on the lower reaches of the Amur river. The Chinese brought up a small army with artillery, and proceeded to destroy them. Hostilities were tempered by a mutual interest in trade, which, since the Manchu government banned the export of bullion, had to be carried on by barter, the Chinese paying in silk and tea for Russian furs and hides. A formal treaty between the two governments was concluded at Nerchinsk in 1689. The negotiation was conducted in Latin, Jesuits based in Beijing and a Romanian émigré to Moscow serving as interpreters, and, since at this point Chinese strength in the region was greater than Russia's, the deal was struck largely on China's terms.

The conquest of Siberia turned out to be a factor of critical importance to the development of a new Russian empire. It ensured a continuing supply of furs which soon accounted for as much as a quarter of the entire revenue of the tsar's exchequer.[11] In this way the ermine skins that trimmed the robes of English peers, the bearskins worn by European soldiers, and the sables prized by German burghers and by grandees at the imperial court of China contributed to Russia's rise to world power. Siberia furnished other assets too: rare falcons, prized by hunters in Europe as well as Arabia; oil and grease from the blubber of the seals that frequented the coasts; narwhal tusks, which some alchemists and physicians mistook for magic unicorns' horns; and the more common but still valuable walrus tusks. Siberia turned out to be rich in minerals, too – including gold – and its possession was to revolutionize Russia's strategic position, providing access to China, the Pacific and North America.

Some time was to pass before Moscow appreciated all this, however. Ironically, this generation of Russia's empire-builders found great difficulty in comprehending the geography of its possessions. In 1627 Tsar Michael did order a book to be compiled which described all the more significant settlements in his dominions and explained their accessibility to each other. The result was a great atlas in words, which was to be in almost constant use in the decades that followed, providing practical guidance for the tsar's messengers, who would take copies of the relevant sections before they set out on a mission.[12] The information was updated as new and better routes were reported, but the first conventional map of Siberia produced in Russia dates from 1667, and finding one's way to Siberia's extremities continued to depend very largely on directions given by old Siberia hands.

If geography was one problem, administration was another. The great distances involved (it took two years for a convoy to reach Moscow from Yakutsk), the very low density of population, and the harsh climate made supply, especially to remote outposts, a nightmare. The Russians in central and eastern Siberia needed regular supplies of rye flour and salt, besides fishing line, canvas, tools, clothing and other necessities, and beads and buttons for the natives. Merchants who provided such services risked life and limb as well as privation, though the rewards could be commensurate. The government often used them in fulfilling many of the state's functions. It had to enforce tribute and tax collection, and protect consignments of valuable furs and ivory from robbers; it was ultimately responsible for supply, especially of food, and for maintaining order and administering justice. All this had to be done with scarce resources. The officials who ran Siberia enjoyed greater freedom than most, but their responsibilities could be awesome.

Until 1637, when a separate department was set up exclusively to administer Siberian affairs, thirty or so clerks in the Kazan Department had to manage the logistics, finance and taxation, security and defence, justice and food provision for the entire south-east as well as Siberia. Since there was insufficient money to pay all its officials, the government allowed them to deduct their reward from the revenues they collected – usually in the form of furs, which in effect became currency in Siberia. Hostile natives were another problem. The state could not spare many troops to keep order, nor much equipment, and the natives' weaponry was not invariably Stone Age. One petition to Tsar Michael from a service outpost pleaded for 200 carbines and coats of armour, because Buriat tribesmen in the area 'have many mounted warriors who fight in armour and helmets . . . whereas we, your slaves, are ill-clothed, lack armour and our musket shot cannot pierce their armour'.[13] Taming Siberia was a shoestring operation.

Siberia's native peoples comprised a colourful variety of ethnological and linguistic types. They included Mongols, reindeer-herding Tungus (Evenki), Yakuts and Itelmens, in addition to smaller populations of Chukchis, Kets, seal-hunting Yugits and Eskimos, the great majority of them pagan animists.[14] If they suffered less from the colonial experience than did the peoples of Central and South America or Africa, it was largely due to very low population density. There could never have been more than a quarter of a million of them in the whole wide country in the seventeenth century. This limited the toll taken by epidemics, and increased opportunities to avoid danger, whether from Russians or from other tribes. Some clashes with the Russians were inevitable, especially since some of the first Russian venturers were desperate and violent men, but did the high profile of Russian officialdom make relations with native peoples any less bloody than they were in other empires being created at that time?

The state's policy of demanding native tribute provoked resistance and retaliation as well as compliance. Distance from Moscow encouraged some officials to collect more than was due and pocket the difference, to demand bribes, to sell justice, and to take natives as household slaves. But the natives sometimes retaliated. In 1634 Buriat tribesmen burned down Fort Bratsk, and ten years later, angered by the Russians, they mustered over 2,000 warriors to massacre them in their scattered settlements. The government understood at an early stage that ill-treatment of natives could lead to costly campaigns of pacification. As a result, it introduced a policy that took account of native fears and past experience. In 1644, for example, the governor of Irkutsk was told that

> The Sovereign Tsar . . . has ordered that [tribute-paying native people] always be treated with consideration, that they suffer no violence, losses, extortions or impositions, and that . . . they should live in peace without fear, pursuing their occupations, and serve the Sovereign Tsar . . . and wish him well . . . Servicemen are ordered to bring men of newly-discovered lands who do not yet pay tribute under the exalted arm of the Sovereign Tsar, but in a kindly, not a violent manner.

Furthermore, a governor receiving such an order was to announce the policy with formal ceremony to representatives of the natives concerned. Enforcement was sometimes difficult, but the government did take steps to enforce the rule and punish oppressive agents and officials.

Prejudice was confined to religion, but conversion was strictly a voluntary matter. Tributary people were to be baptized only 'after careful investigation to determine that they wish it of their own free will'.[15] Once baptized, however, a native was regarded as acceptable even to enter the tsar's service. Unlike most other colonizing peoples, the Russians were free of anti-native prejudices.

Two portraits of seventeenth-century Russian tsars reflect a massive change in vision and attitude that took place within a few decades. The first is of Michael, the first Romanov tsar, who was depicted in formal, almost symbolic, style as a passive, callow youth, albeit with crown and sceptre – a potential 'sufferer for Christ's sake'. The second, by a Dutch artist, portrays his son and successor, Alexis, realistically as a majestic and vigorous man of this world. The contrast is partially explained by caution. The new dynasty was vulnerable under Michael in the 1620s and '30s. It was therefore careful, acting well within the confines of tradition. By the 1660s, however, the dynasty was more strongly established. True, Alexis took care to claim descent from Ivan IV and, through him, the Roman emperors, but this was as much to justify an imperial role as to reinforce his legitimacy as a ruler. Although Alexis played the pious tsar as assiduously as Michael had done, in his reign Russia began to taste success again after a long interval. And, as confidence returned, the regime became more outward-looking, more open to the modern world.

Russia's first attempt, under Michael, to regain lost ground in the west proved premature. A two-year war with Poland ended in ignominious defeat in 1634. An even more shaming moment came a few years later. In 1637 the Cossacks of the Don stormed the Turkish citadel of Azov. Thanks to material aid from Moscow, they held it until 1641, when, after being bombarded by over a hundred heavy guns which the Turks had brought up to help them retake the place, they asked the Tsar to take it over. But this would have meant war with the Sultan. Could Russia afford it? The question was put to an Assembly of the Land. The answer, in effect, was 'No'. The chance of a break-through to the Black Sea was rejected.

At that juncture the security of the Volga–Caspian route was a greater priority. Robber bands up to 3,000 strong infested the lower reaches, and the Dagestan coast of the Caspian was the base of some of the most notorious robbers in the world in the 1630s.[16] A strong garrison had to be maintained at Astrakhan in order to protect the trade with Persia and beyond, and even then the city was occupied by robber Cossacks for a time in the later 1660s. The chief impediment to expansion in the south and west was no longer economic or demographic but lack of up-to-date military expertise and technology. It had long been Russian practice to engage foreign military advisers on an individual basis, but now, following the general European practice of the time, Moscow began to engage entire units of professional soldiers on the open market, and to use entrepreneurs to provide whatever military services and expertise it needed.

The Muscovite equivalent of the Habsburg Emperor's Wallenstein was a Scottish soldier of fortune, Alexander Leslie. Leslie's speciality, modern siege warfare, was particularly relevant now that Russia's military efforts had to be focused against Europeans and the Ottoman Turks rather than against Tatars. Expertise in steppe warfare was not enough to win wars on other fronts. The siege of Smolensk, at which Leslie served, demonstrated that. Well-drilled infantry units and improved artillery were the new priorities. At the beginning of the 1630s Leslie had been sent to western Europe to help raise ten infantry regiments trained on the Dutch and German model.[17] They fought in the Smolensk campaign, but were disbanded once it was over because of the expense. It was only under Alexis (r. 1645–76) that there was a sustained effort to modernize the army's weaponry and training.

One of the first signs was the publication by the state press in Moscow in the summer of 1647 of a translation into Russian of *The Art of Infantry*

Warfare, by Johann von Wallhausen. The book was generously illustrated with engravings of the tactics and drill described in the text,[18] which embodied the best European military practice. Its appearance suggests that the government intended to instruct Russian officers in how to modernize at least parts of its army. But when Russia next went to war with Poland, in 1654, the practice of engaging foreign troops was revived.

The scene is a tavern near the market place of Riga seven years later. Three Scots mercenary officers – Alexander Daniels, Walter Ert and Patrick Gordon – are sitting at a table, sharing a flagon of wine and discussing their employment prospects. Gordon, who recorded the scene, has quit the King of Poland's service. He has been contemplating a move to the service of the Habsburg Emperor, who might be engaging people for war against the Turks, but is also toying with the idea of Russia. His companions have served in the King of Sweden's army, but the King has run out of money and they have been paid off. The focus of the conversation moves to Russia. The Tsar is in the seventh year of a war with Poland, and they have heard that his agents are recruiting experienced officers like them. The pay is not much, but at least it is paid reasonably promptly, people say. Besides, there are good prospects of quick promotion to high rank in Russian service – and of good company to boot.

For Gordon the conversation was decisive. He signed up with Russia as a service officer, and his decision proved sound: he was to rise to the rank of general.[19] Many others had preceded him, and, since this tsar made a practice of inviting foreigners he had engaged to special levees at the Kremlin or at his summer palace at Kolomenskoe, many of their names are recorded in the court diaries. In June 1657, for example, a colonel of dragoons called Junkmann was graciously received by His Imperial Majesty, along with lieutenant-colonels Skyger, Serwin, van Strobel and Trauernich and many other officers. In October 1661 (to cite one of several other examples) the Austrian Colonel Gottlieb von Schalk was received, along with the thirty-seven officers, NCOs and trumpeters he had engaged for the Tsar's service, as was Colonel Henryk van Egerat, who had brought a contingent of 150 soldiers from Denmark. Most were sent to fight on the western front, but some went south to train the musketeer regiment at Astrakhan,[20] and from then on the policy priority was to train Russian conscripts in the new way, in 'regiments of new formation' under Russian officers.

At the same time, special military equipment (like trench telescopes) was imported, and efforts were made to modernize weaponry and expand

Russian arms production. The tax register for the long-established small-arms manufacturing centre of Tula, south of Moscow, which was to become the Russian Birmingham or Sheffield, shows that in 1625 the town boasted only 250 households liable to tax, besides 34 others and 21 empty workshops. Its inhabitants already included foreigners – presumably technical experts, musketeers and gunners to advise on and test-fire the guns produced.[21] But in 1632 the government commissioned a Dutchman, Andrew Vinius, to build a foundry using hydraulic power. Dozens of craftsmen were recruited abroad to teach Russians how to make guns, locks and swords to modern designs, and by the early eighteenth century Tula was to boast well over 1,000 gunsmiths producing 15,000 muskets a year as well as other weaponry. Nor was Tula the only arms-manufacturing centre, even in the mid seventeenth century. In 1648 a state musket factory was established near Moscow, and by 1653 26,000 flintlock muskets had been produced there, as well as numbers of the less efficient matchlocks. Even so, arms orders had to be placed abroad to bring Russia's small-arms stocks to a level for war.[22]

At the same time mineral-prospecting was encouraged, and specialist metallurgists were hired from abroad. Strategic materials like iron were also imported in increased quantities, for, although successful efforts were made to find and exploit deposits of copper, good-quality iron was not to be found west of the Urals, and the deposits in the Urals were too difficult of access. Even so it could be said that the origins of Russia's modern metallurgical industry as well as its arms industry date from this time. And the development of both the army and the arms industry was further stimulated by the Thirteen Years War, in which Russia at last gained the upper hand against its rival Poland.

The war was precipitated by developments in Ukraine. The Orthodox population there had long been resentful of the Catholic Church's campaign to drive them into the Catholic fold. Their discontent had reached new heights early in the century when Moscow, their only possible protector, had been preoccupied with its own troubles. The Ukrainian Orthodox were unable to combat the pressure on their own. They lacked organization and, though the merchant community formed confraternities and maintained some schools as well as churches, they could not compete with the Catholics in educational provision. They also lacked armed power – a resource commonly used to resolve spiritual differences in that era. The situation changed, however, when the Cossacks of Ukraine became restive, not only over the religious question, but also over land rights and registration for military service. Polish landlords had been intruding into the region, trying to establish great estates and introduce serfdom. This threatened the free farmer-warriors of the frontier zone. Furthermore, many of them were denied inclusion on the register of paid-service Cossacks, and this implied loss of their liberties as Cossacks. The coalescing of these different streams of discontent eventually triggered a huge rebellion against the Polish government. It began early in 1648.[23]

The leader, Bogdan Khmelnytsky, was a Cossack officer, and the rising was proclaimed as a 'crusade'. There being no Saracens or Turks within reach, the rebels' hatred was directed against Jews, who had been encouraged to settle in large numbers in Ukraine, as well as against the Poles themselves. This strategem pleased the Orthodox merchants, who were in competition with the Jews, as it did the Cossack rank-and-file and peasants, who tended to regard Jews as agents of the Polish lords, which many of them in fact were.[24] The irony of the situation was that Khmelnytsky, recognizing that the Cossacks could not resist the Poles alone, enlisted the help of the Muslim Khan of the Crimea, a subject of the Sultan, who joined the 'crusade' in the expectation of plunder and prisoners to ransom or sell into slavery. Cynicism was a feature of seventeenth-century politics, albeit less common than in today's.

The Cossacks defeated the divided and ill-led Polish army sent against them. This prompted a flood of support from the lower orders, and the biggest anti-Jewish pogroms before Nazi Germany's invasion of eastern Europe nearly three centuries later. The Polish government was slow to organize an effective response, but in June 1648 an apprehensive Khmelnytsky petitioned the Tsar: 'Our desire is to have a Sovereign Autocrat, an Orthodox Christian Tsar such as Your Majesty, to rule our land . . . If Your Majesty . . . will only attack [Poland] without delay, we shall be ready to serve your Tsarish Majesty, together with the entire Zaporozhian [Cossack] Host . . .'[25]

The Tsar, however, had troubles of his own. That same month a bloody taxation riot took place in Moscow, in which senior officials were lynched and the Tsar himself was confronted by the mob. The affair forced him to replace his chief minister and commit himself to a broad review of Russia's laws. This necessitated the calling of another Assembly of the Land. This much misunderstood institution, so far from being a parliament, possessed no powers. It was an assembly of representatives brought to Moscow, in this case to inform the government about local practices and to receive instructions as to what laws and rules they were to implement on their return. There were protracted consultations with interested parties inside and outside the Assembly before the issuing of a new code of laws, which was published in May 1649.

At that point another letter from Khmelnytsky was delivered in Moscow. It begged the Tsar to intervene against Poland and take Ukraine's Orthdox population under his protection. But the Tsar was still not ready. Claiming he was obliged by treaty to remain at peace with Poland, he confined himself to giving moral support and furnishing some supplies. The Ukrainian Cossacks would have to shed their own blood for their cause, while Russia conserved its strength and swelled its armoury.

In the event, political disarray in Poland allowed the Cossacks to sweep on as far as Lvov. It was to be 1651 before, deserted by the Tatars, they were beaten on the rain-drenched field of Berestechko. The struggle, however, continued, hostilities being punctuated from time to time by negotiations over a possible settlement. Meanwhile Khmelnytsky's offer to the Tsar remained open, and in 1653, perhaps fearing that the opportunity might disappear if he procrastinated too long, the cautious Tsar at last committed himself to war with Poland – though not before taking careful soundings on an individual basis of an Assembly of the Land. This time, Russia's treaty of 'eternal peace' with Poland was not regarded as an impediment. The Cossacks, it was argued, had already shaken off Polish rule and were an independent people. Besides, the Poles had committed such grave offences against Orthodox Christians in Ukraine as to cry out for retaliation. The following January the question of allegiance was put to a Cossack assembly (*Rada*) at Pereiaslav.

The summoning drums had sounded for an hour before Khmelnytsky appeared, and when the crowd fell silent he put the question. In essence, the Cossacks needed a protector. They could opt for the Sultan (who had already made overtures to them), the Khan of the Crimea, the King of Poland (who was willing to accept them back under his wing) or the Tsar of Russia. Whom did they choose? The cry went up for the Tsar. Khmelnytsky then led Cossack commanders into the church, where each in turn swore oaths of loyalty to the Tsar, and the Tsar's representative formally invested Khmelnytsky with a banner, mace, cloak and cap – his new insignia as hetman, or commander.

Some Ukrainian historians have tried to argue that a treaty was negotiated at Pereiaslav; that acceptance of Russian rule was conditional on the Tsar's honouring the terms; and that the Cossacks would be legally entitled to switch their allegiance if the Tsar reneged on any of his promises. But this misrepresents the evidence. The oaths that Khmelnytsky and the other Cossacks took were unconditional promises of allegiance. Colonel Bogun, the only notable who refused to swear, evidently understood this. Furthermore, even though the Cossack leadership had probably received intimations of what the Tsar was prepared to offer, the formal negotiations that defined what Cossack privileges were to be did not take place before the ceremony at Pereiaslav, but two months after.

The terms set out in the charter of privileges the Tsar then issued to his new subjects were better than could be got from Poland: an increase in the register of registered Cossacks (who were paid from state funds) from 40,000 to 60,000, confirmation of their previous privileges, freedom for the Orthodox Church, and the exclusion of Jews.[26] As expected, Poland contested the Cossacks' new allegiance and thereafter exploited differences within the ranks of the Cossack elite to promote rebellion. Securing Ukraine for Russia was to prove a long and costly business.

Though operations had to cover a wide front, the main thrust of Russia's efforts in the campaign of 1654 was against Smolensk. The Cossacks represented their war as a crusade; the Tsar referred to it as a 'blessed affair' whose purpose was 'to protect the true, Orthodox Christian faith', and the army reflected this religious purpose. Priests and holy icons accompanied the troops, and many of the military colours they carried were sewn or painted with coloured crosses, representations of Jesus, of cherubim with flaming swords, of the Archangel Michael and of St George. Furthermore, the soldiers were ordered to go into battle reciting the Jesus prayer.[27] That most of the foreign officers who marched with them were Catholics or Protestants rather than Orthodox Christians was of little concern, although a district of Moscow had recently been allotted for their exclusive use so that they could enjoy their own religious services without contaminating the civilian population.

The campaign succeeded. Smolensk surrendered in September after a three-month siege. A Cossack force provided material assistance, but the deciding factor was the artillery which the Russian commissariat had managed to bring up and which was deployed under the experienced eye of General Leslie in the presence of the Tsar himself. But, though matters at the front went well, there was bad news from Moscow. There had been a virulent outbreak of bubonic plague. This delayed the Tsar's triumphant return until the following February. He arrived to find that the losses had been grievous. Both the president of the ministerial committee left in charge of the capital and his deputy had died; so had all but fifteen servants left in the palace, half the translators in the Department of Foreign Affairs, and over 80 per cent of the city's monks – a particularly grievous blow, since monks cared for the sick and unfortunate. Many other cities suffered too. Three thousand died in Kostroma, half the population of Tver perished, and more than half in Kaluga. The Tsar helped raise morale, making a brave show parading war trophies before the surviving population. Then he returned to the front.

The campaign of 1655 was even more successful. Virtually every city of importance in Lithuania, including Vilna, was captured. Poland was helpless. Swedish forces had invaded in June, and the Polish court fled south to take uncertain shelter in the fortified monastery of Czestochowa. This prompted a radical rethinking of Russian strategy and a sudden switch of alignment. An accommodation was reached with the Polish king; Sweden now became the enemy, and the objective of the 1656 campaign was the famous port of Riga.

Once an independent Hansa city, Riga was now a Swedish possession. Russia had wanted such a trading outlet since the time of Ivan the Terrible (whom Tsar Alexis admired and on whom he modelled himself to some extent), and only five years earlier the Tsar's interest had been raised further by a project, presented by a Frenchman, to build ships for the international market. Gdansk was also considered. Only the previous year the Tsar had offered it his protection. But, with his sights now trained on Sweden, the army marched on Riga.

Its defences were strong and up to date, but the siege was methodical and the equipment strong. A learned work of the time published by Samuel Pufendorf, historiographer to the Swedish king and a pioneer of international law, contains a fascinating panoramic print of the action. It shows the Tsar, his back to the artist, on a hill overlooking the city, attended by his staff. They wear tall bearskin hats and are elegantly mounted as they discuss the situation and decide what is to be done. The Russian encampment is shown – the positions of the batteries, the placements of the infantry, the supply dumps and bivouacks, and, in between, messengers scurrying to deliver orders and reports. Mortar shells are lobbed in high trajectory over the walls; cannon shots smash into the fortifications, sending out sprays of splintered stone; a Russian powder store blows up. Through this scene of action flows the Western Dvina, which leads to the object of all these exertions: the estuary and the open sea.

The prize eluded Russia that year. It might well have been taken the next, had the Tsar only persevered, for Sweden was in financial straits and might not have been able to sustain its resistance. But the siege was not resumed. Troubles in Ukraine required a diversion of Russia's efforts.

When Khmelnytsky died, in 1657, deep fissures appeared within the Cossack ranks. Some, the more substantial sort who owned farms and hankered after the privileges and freedom of the Polish nobility (who were never freer than in that age), came to resent the high-handed way in which the Tsar's representatives dealt with them. They aligned behind the new hetman, Vygovsky. The poorer Cossacks, on the other hand, feared that their interests would be sacrificed, that they might lose their status as Cossacks, and even be reduced to serfdom. Their fears were soon justified. In September 1658 Vygovsky abandoned his allegiance to the Tsar and signed an agreement with Poland. This conceded rights to the Orthodox Church in Ukraine and to its burghers, but it also gave noble status to the top 300, predominately landed, Cossacks and reduced the number of registered Cossacks by half, which prompted an armed reaction by those dispossessed.

Regional divisions, between east and west Ukraine, the north and the Zaporozhian Sech in the south, which was self-governing but whose membership overlapped with the Cossack community beyond its borders, complicated the situation. Since the Cossack way was democratic,[28] these divisions and differences soon translated into anarchy, which in turn encouraged interference from outside powers – the Ottoman Empire as well as the Crimean Tatars; Sweden as well as Poland. Restoring order now became Moscow's priority. But how to do it in the most economical and effective way? In October 1659 the Tsar, who had backed Khmelnytsky's son, Iurii, as hetman and sent troops in to back up his authority, approved a new deal for the Cossacks – not a treaty, but articles granted in response to a petition. These allowed the Cossacks to apply their laws in the traditional way, and to exercise their rights without interference, but insisted that they present themselves for service as required. They were not to enter into negotiations with Poland or any other foreign power, nor to slander the state of Muscovy on pain of execution.[29] Little more than a year later, however, Ukraine was in anarchy again.

Poland had made peace with Sweden and once more turned against Russia. Worse, there was a crisis of confidence in the ruble. As war expenditure had soared, the government had succumbed to the temptation of devaluing the currency. More particularly it had been minting copper instead of silver coins. This eventually triggered the great Moscow 'copper riot' of 1662, when people realized that the new coins were worth less than their face value. In Ukraine they already understood this apparently because the copper coins were first used to pay the Russian soldiers serving there. The value of the coins they tendered in the local markets was discounted, and sometimes the coins were refused altogether. This not only created stresses between

Ukrainians and Russians, it encouraged mutiny. The soldiers had to be paid in real money. Within a year the minting of copper coins was discontinued and the offending copper kopeks were withdrawn from circulation. But the remedy was costly: rises in taxation, and the imposition on merchants of extraordinary levies on their capital wealth.

Meanwhile the situation in Ukraine went from bad to worse. Deserted by Bogdan's son and successor, Iurii Khmelnytsky, a Russian army found itself in an untenable position, surrounded by Polish forces, Crimean Tatars and dissident Cossacks. It surrendered. The Tatars began to massacre the disarmed troops before taking the rest into captivity. The commanders had to wait twenty years for their release.[30]

Gritting his teeth, the Tsar worked towards the election of another hetman, this time a shrewd illiterate called Briukhovetsky, who was favoured by the Cossacks of the Zaporozhian Sech and a hero to the Ukrainian poor. But the opposition was stiff. At last, in July 1663 at a chaotic and bloody Cossack assembly at Nezhin, Briukhovetsky was elected. But many Cossacks would not be reconciled to him. Opposition increased as Russian tax-collectors moved in, and a rival hetman with Turkish support, Doroshenko, took control of west Ukraine.

The major parties were exhausted by the time peace talks began in 1666, yet these were as hard-fought by the diplomats as the war was by the soldiers. It was finally agreed that Russia would keep Smolensk, Chernigov and part of Vitebsk province, and that Ukraine should be divided: the west for Poland; the east for Russia, which would also hold Kiev for two years (but in the event was able to hold it permanently). Both parties were to co-operate against the Turks. The Tsar's steadfastness had at least secured half of Ukraine.[31]

He was by no means the only hero of the hour, however. There were also peasant boys hectored by foreign officers until they learned how to slow march, handle a musket, fire it to order, and face the enemy (for to turn tail involved greater risks from the officers stationed at the rear); the poor gentry, who spent most of their income on maintaining their horses and equipment in a state of battle-readiness, and who fought for nothing except the free labour of a couple of serfs; and the ancient veterans who bore the scars of a dozen desperate fights on dangerous frontiers.

Artemii Shchigolev was an example – a professional serviceman who began to serve at Livny in his youth, helping to guard the steppe frontier. He was transferred to Bronnitsy just outside Moscow for a time, but was wounded and taken prisoner at Orel during the Time of Troubles and spent over two years as a prisoner in Poland. On his return he was enlisted as a mounted musketeer and sent to Ufa in the far south-east. He spent the next twenty-five years there, at first relatively quietly, but then in the 1630s the Kalmyks burst into the Ufa region, launching themselves into a ruthless campaign of plundering and burning. Shchigolev was among those who faced them in battle. He killed two men, but was wounded by an arrow which passed right through his chest. In another battle he rode in the van of an attacking force alongside his two sons. One of them was killed in the action, and he himself received another arrow in the chest. For 'his many services, the blood he had shed, his wounds and the blood shed by his sons' he was eventually rewarded with a small gift of money and a modest service estate.[32]

The Kalmyks were new and unwelcome arrivals, not only to the Russians but also to other peoples between the Urals and the Caucasus. They had come from Tibet via Central Asia and, though Buddhists, were as ruthless as any of the steppe predators who had preceded them – and contemptuous of the Russians when they attempted to come to terms. Yet before long the Kalmyks were to become allies. This achievement was due in part to Moscow's powers of diplomacy, and its deep understanding of the Kalmyks' wants and psychology; in part to its ability, in the old imperial tradition, to divide and rule, playing them off against neighbouring Nogais, Kabardinians and Crimean Tatars;[33] but chiefly to Russia's success towards the end of the century in capturing the Turkish citadel of Azov. And so the Kalmyks were finally persuaded to co-operate. That said, Moscow's diplomatic skills were as important as force in shoring up and extending Russia's new position in Eurasia.

Effective diplomacy depends on accurate intelligence and knowledge of an opponent's past as well as present condition, dealings and ambitions. Though Westerners often scorned Russians as barbarians, Moscow's external-affairs department was already proving itself to be more effective than some of its Western counterparts. This may seem surprising, since Russian diplomacy is often, and rightly, characterized as hidebound and slow rather than brilliant. But unlike Poland's diplomats, who were noble amateurs, Russia's were humble professionals, trained by endlessly copying diplomatic correspondence and by listening silently, and watching closely, when their betters engaged in the often tedious formalities of governmental exchange. They recorded everything, and they maintained their records for future reference.[34]

This was the basis of Russia's superior system of intelligence. But it was supplemented by the collection and transcription of news-sheets (*Flugschriften*), the forerunners of modern newspapers, which the Tsar ordered from his factors in western Europe. Summaries of their more important reports and digests of intelligence gathered from merchants and monks, diplomats and émigrés kept the Tsar and his top officials up to date on foreign military and political news, and apprised them of any unusual events. Occasionally the Tsar would ask for a report on something abroad which had sparked his curiosity, and so the department came to be as well informed about the topography of Venice and the Florentine theatre as about the hopes and fears of the Habsburg Emperor, the policies of Denmark's king, and the commercial pursuits of the English and the Dutch. And it was accurate intelligence about Polish politics that prompted the Tsar to send funds – through Benjamin Helmfeldt and the Marselis brothers, his agents in Germany – to support Prince Liubomirski's rebellion of 1666,[35] hoping it would help to soften the negotiating line of the Polish government at Andrusovo.

By the time Alexis died, early in 1676, Russia had made its mark as a European power. Denmark wanted it to join in a coalition against Sweden; Poland wanted its aid against the Tatars; the Emperor wanted it to join in coalition against the Turks. But in 1682 the unexpectedly early death without issue of his successor, his eldest son, Fedor, raised doubts about Russia's political stability once again. Of the two obvious candidates to succeed Fedor, Ivan, Alexis's surviving son by his first wife, was handicapped, and Peter, Alexis's son by his second wife, though healthy and intelligent, was only eight years old. This exacerbated the tensions which already existed at court between the old guard, including the last tsar's chief minister, Artamon Matveyev, and ambitious younger men like Vasilii Golitsyn and Ivan Khovanskii.[36] This might not have mattered if two domestic problems had not now come to a head.

Discontented elements came to the fore, each with its own agenda but united against innovation. Religious conservatives had been outraged by the confirmation in 1666 of changes to the liturgy. The 'Old Believers' would not be reconciled to them. At the same time there was widespread concern in the ranks of traditional army units, including the privileged musketeer corps, about modernization of the army. Many soldiers saw this as a threat; and many of them were also Old Believers, armed and stationed in the Kremlin. Their commander was the ambitious Ivan Khovanskii. The upshot was rebellion. On 15 May 1682 – the anniversary of the death of the Tsarevich Dmitrii at Uglich nearly a century before – false rumours spread that Ivan, the rightful tsar, had been murdered. Three days of bloodshed followed in the seat of government itself. Matveyev was butchered; so were the Kremlin's foreign doctors, along with other foreigners. The mob's attentions may seem to have been indiscriminate, but all the victims represented modernization in one or another of its forms. When order returned, Ivan and Peter reigned jointly, with Alexis's eldest daughter, Sofia, as regent. After an interval, Khovanskii and others involved in the rebellion were executed, and leading Old Believers were burned at the stake. The attempt to reverse the modernization policies was thwarted; the government's attention returned to foreign affairs.

The first priority was to establish a permanent peace with Poland. This was done in Moscow in the spring of 1686. The Poles ratified all the territorial transfers they had conceded at Andrusovo. They also ceded Kiev permanently to Russia in return for a payment of less than 150,000 rubles. Poland's king, Jan Sobieski, the 'hero of the siege of Vienna' only three years earlier, tried to avoid ratifying the treaty, but had to sign in the end. Russia's only concession apart from the money was a promise to attack the Crimea. Two campaigns in successive years were failures, but that did not alter the fact that Russia had replaced Poland as the predominant power in the region; and the success was due in no small measure to superior diplomatic methods, and to a succession of particularly able professional functionaries.

Although the political direction of foreign affairs in the later 1600s had been overseen by a succession of able ministers – Afanasii Ordyn-Nashchokin, Artamon Matveyev, Vasilii Golitsyn – their success was based largely on the strength of the support they received from those below. By the 1680s the Foreign Office had a staff of over forty translators and interpreters working in a variety of languages, chiefly Latin, Tatar, German and Polish, but also Persian, Swedish, Dutch, Greek, Mongol and English.[37] There was an even bigger cohort of clerks, and, above them were the senior officials. The permanent secretary at the time of the Andrusovo negotiations rejoiced in the name of 'Diamond Johnson' (Almaz Ivanov), 'Diamond' being his family name; his family were business people. He began his association with government in the 1620s, supervising the liquor outlets, and in the late 1630s he was in charge of customs and the liquor monopoly. He subsequently became Secretary in the state's main fiscal department before entering the Foreign Office in 1646. He served on embassies to Sweden and to Poland in the early 1650s, before being promoted to membership of the cabinet (*duma* – by now essentially a committee of the Tsar's chief ministers) as professional head of the Foreign Office. At the same time he was given responsibility for the State Printing Office. This was a particularly sensitive job in that it involved publishing translations of foreign books which contained essential expertise which Russia needed, but which were viewed with horror by most Russians, who, perhaps rightly, imagined that such learning threatened their faith.

Another top functionary, Dementy Bashmakov had a different sort of career. His early experience was as a scribe registering state lands in the north-west and as an under-secretary on the palace staff. On the outbreak of war, however, he was promoted to run the Tsar's campaign treasury, then to help administer the territory conquered in Lithuania. Soon afterwards he became secretary of the Tsar's new private office, and then 'Secretary in the Sovereign's Name', which gave him special powers to sign authorizations on the Tsar's behalf. He was given ministerial (*duma*) rank to run the Muster Office, before his appointment to the Foreign Office in 1671. He also served three spells in charge of the Printing Office, ran the Ukraine Office for a time in the 1670s, and, as an experienced trouble-shooter, continued to serve spells in various financial ministries, in the Petitions Office, and on commissions of inquiry – notably that into monetary problems after the copper riots.

The official most concerned in achieving the 1686 treaty with Poland, Emelian Ukraintsev, had a more conventional career in foreign relations. Nevertheless, he served a seven-year apprenticeship in a financial department before taking up post in the Foreign Office. His rise was meteoric. Sent on a low-grade mission to Sweden and Denmark in 1672, he became senior under-secretary in the department the same year, was promoted to the rank of full secretary in 1675, and joined the *duma* in 1681. A specialist in the affairs of the north-west, he had served in the department administering the most north-westerly province of Novgorod, and also in that administering Ustiug in the far north – where he watched the Swedish border provinces closely, as well as Sweden's court. But after his triumph of 1686 (for which he was awarded estates, hereditary as well as service-obligated) he carried major responsibilities for Ukraine and its neighbours. He accompanied the expeditionary forces to Crimea in the late 1680s. His last recorded service was as ambassador extraordinary to Turkey in 1699.[38]

Outsiders were also given diplomatic missions from time to time. Robert Menzies, a Catholic Scot by birth, was sent to the Pope; the Romanian known as Spafarius (who at least was Orthodox) advised Regent Sofia's Foreign Minister, Prince Golitsyn. But the backbone of the service was Russians like Ivanov, Bashmakov and Ukraintsev. Though senior Foreign Office functionaries, they were all experienced in domestic affairs too, not least in financial matters. They had been trained to see things in the round and to understand the implications, broad as well as narrow, of the moves they and others made. In addition to guiding Russia's relations with foreign powers from Spain to China, their knowledge of the outside world – so rare among Russians of that period – meant that they were in demand to handle any matter involving foreigners or foreign things. They were therefore concerned not only with diplomatic dealings, but also with the foreign doctors who served the tsars – indeed, with all the many foreigners who served Russia. They advised on foreign books, helped procure foreign armaments, negotiated foreign trade, and administered territories with sensitive frontiers. And, since so much of the work involved the West, they played a crucial role in the country's modernization, in laying the foundations of Russia's 'Westernizing' policies that became increasingly evident from the 1650s.

By 1700 Russia had not only recovered from the collapse at the beginning of the century, but was poised for two centuries of almost uninterrupted empire-building. That story begins in the eighteenth century, but the launch pad for the brilliant series of advances had been constructed in the 1600s.

8

Peter the Great and the Breakthrough to the West

On 22 October 1721, at a ceremony in the new but unfinished city of St Petersburg which he had founded, Tsar Peter I, son of Alexis, was offered a new title by the Senate which he had created: 'Father of the Fatherland, Emperor of All Russia, Peter the Great'. In explaining the award, the Chancellor, Peter's long-standing confidant and sometimes bawdy correspondent Gavrilii Golovkin announced that Peter had 'brought us out of the darkness of ignorance on to the world stage of glory; from non-existence, as it were, to existence, and on to terms of equality with the political nations'.[1] Ever since, not only most of the outside world but many Russians themselves have believed that Peter created Russia. The myth was at least in part a deliberate construction, the work of Peter's acolytes and successors, not least of Catherine the Great, Voltaire, Daniel Defoe (albeit anonymously) and a dozen other hired publicists. As a result, no other European ruler before Napoleon was to be branded more deeply into the consciousness of future generations.

Peter's size (he was over six and a half feet tall) and his immense energy, curiosity and informality all contributed to his mythic status. Even so, and discounting Golovkin's hyperbole, the Petrine legend has a core of truth. It was in his reign that Russia came to be universally regarded as a great power. He won famous victories, including one which most military experts count as one of the ten most decisive battles in European history. He founded new institutions, including an Academy of Sciences. He Westernized the dress of the elite, developed industries, and Europeanized institutions and manners to some extent. He also served in the ranks of one of his own regiments, always regarded himself as the servant of the Russian state, and has a genuine claim to be regarded as an enlightened monarch *avant la lettre*.

Yet, far from inventing Russia, he built on foundations laid by others. He suffered crushing defeats as well as winning famous victories. He opened a window on the West, and advanced down the shores of the Caspian Sea, but was ultimately thwarted in his attempts to break through to the Black Sea and into Central Asia. And Russia's advance to the Pacific, completed in his reign, would have happened anyway.

For Russians, Peter remains the most popular of historical heroes, but in the West his image is tarnished by the massive wastefulness which was the by-product of his imperial ambitions. Quite apart from casualties in his wars and in his suppression of rebellions, tens of thousands of labourers, prisoners of war, convicts and servicemen – Russians and non-Russians – perished in the building of St Petersburg and his ambitious canal-cutting projects to link the Neva to the Volga and the Volga to the Don, the latter begun in 1701, but never finished. And Peter could be as cruel as any of his predecessors. He participated in the investigation under torture of his son and heir for treason, and was present when the young man died of his injuries. No one could say that the Emperor shirked his responsibilities.

In formal terms Peter's reign began in 1682, when he became tsar jointly with his older but less able and less energetic half-brother Ivan. The mutiny which followed was directed against members of Peter's mother's family, the Naryshkins, and against Westernizing ministers and foreigners, some of whom were lynched. Though Peter and Ivan reigned, power was now in the hands of Peter's half-sister Sofia and her ministers. Chief among these was Vasilii Golitsyn, who directed two major campaigns against the Crimea. Both failed, and the failure precipitated another regime change and yet more violence. When calm returned and Sofia had departed, the seventeen-year-old Peter was at last free to exercise his autocratic powers. Yet he preferred instead to prolong his adolescence.

His childhood games came to be played on an ever larger scale, and more realistically. They involved bigger and bigger boats – even the building of seagoing ships – and real soldiers rather than toy ones, with live ammunition and real casualties. So when the twenty-two-year-old Peter eventually went to war in 1694, marching as a bombardier with his own artillery train, he was no stranger to military pursuits.

Peter's target in the campaigns of 1695 and 1696 was Azov, the formidable Turkish citadel which blocked Russia off from the Black Sea and the western flank of the Caucasus. The attempt of 1695 was not successful, but Peter was as yet a strong, young Sisyphus and he cheerfully resolved to try again next year, encouraged by his now being a member of an anti-Turkish coalition that included the Habsburg Emperor, who promised to help with engineering and explosives expertise, the King of Poland and the Doge of Venice, one of whose subjects, an expert in building and handling galleys,

Peter was soon to commission as vice-admiral in his service. Intelligent as well as persistent, Peter already understood that battles and storms were the lesser part of war: that thorough preparation, careful planning and good logistics were the bases of success. And so we find him inspecting the arms-manufacturing base at Tula at the conclusion of the campaign, and early the following year he was at Voronezh, upriver from Azov, building a fleet of galleys and barges which was to neutralize the Turkish fleet. He also planned to build frigates in the yards there to exploit victory when it came.

And this time the operation did succeed. The pasha commanding Azov surrendered it in July. Since Ivan had died two months before this, Peter returned to Moscow as sole tsar and autocrat. Yet Moscow was not to detain him long. In March 1697 he began his famous, and in part notorious, tour of Europe, sometimes presenting himself as the young ruler of the new power of the north, sometimes travelling incognito. He visited states in central Germany, England, Venice and Vienna, but his particular goal was Holland, where he set out to master all the secrets of modern shipbuilding. He was already intent on making Russia not only a great European power but a great sea power, and to do this he had to achieve what Ivan IV and Alexis had both failed to achieve: a breakthrough to the Baltic.

Arriving in Moscow in October 1696 he found that another revolt of musketeers had been suppressed in his absence. He felt obliged to supervise the interrogation of those involved, and, following his principle that no subordinate should be ordered to do anything that the Tsar himself was not prepared to do, whether in carpentry, battle, hammering sheet iron, or execution, he himself took part in the proceedings, which involved torture and killing. High treason was not, after all, a crime for which it was politic to show clemency. The proceedings were not to be concluded until 1705. Meanwhile, once a long-term truce with the Turks was in the offing, Peter turned impatiently to drive Sweden, the strongest power of the north, away from the eastern shoreline of the Baltic.

He did so in coalition with the kings of Denmark and Poland, and with the promised support of a fifth column of Swedish subjects in Livonia, headed by a local baron called Patkul, who, like others of his class, was enraged by recent and extensive transfers of land and peasants from the private domain to the Swedish crown. Tens of thousands of Russian troops were prepared for the campaign, ready to march as soon as news should arrive of the signing of an agreement with the Turks. It came in August 1700, but by that time Peter's coalition had fallen to pieces. Denmark, which had begun aggressively by invading Swedish Holstein, had been forced to seek peace and withdraw from the war. The Polish king had begun well, sending his Saxon troops in against Riga, but the attack failed. The Russians had therefore to fend for themselves.

Still, their prospects looked reasonably good. Peter had over 60,000 troops ready to descend on Narva, which, if he could take it, would give him the access he needed to the Baltic Sea. Its walls were strong but its garrison was relatively small, and so the siege began – and with it a trial of strength between the two rival monarchs. Peter was twenty-eight years old and fresh from victory against the Turks. His opponent, Charles XII, was ten years his junior and virtually untried. On the other hand Sweden had long been recognized as a power to be reckoned with, while Russia was still regarded as a neophyte. The struggle between them would decide the supremacy of northern Europe.

The first clash of arms came in November, when Charles led a Swedish force to the relief of Narva. Though outnumbered three to one, he immediately took the initiative, launching an attack which wrong-footed the Russians. The day ended with a stinging rout for Peter's forces, although the Tsar was not present in person, having returned to Moscow for Christmas. The Russian losses were serious: 8,000 men and nearly 150 guns. That encounter and the long struggle which followed reflected the two monarchs' quite disparate military talents. Charles, by far the superior field commander, was master of the unexpected. Peter, having no talent as a tactician, depended on his generals (in the case of du Croy, whom he left in command at Narva, a rather careless one). In fact, given his reliance on councils of war, it could be said that this Russian autocrat governed military operations by committee. Peter's strength lay as an organiser and energiser. The virtual destruction of his northern army galvanized him into raising another. Fortunately for him, Russia was able to meet all his demands for men and resources. And fortunately, too, he and his generals developed a talent for exploiting the adversary's difficulties.[2]

Charles had wanted to follow up his victory at Narva by advancing immediately against Pskov and from there into the heart of Russia. He was thwarted, however, by the need to secure his lines of communication against the Poles and Saxons. So he decided to occupy Courland and develop it as a base for his army. Eventually (in 1706) he forced Poland to abandon its alliance with Russia, but meanwhile Peter was able to capture Narva and send forces down the river Neva to snatch the unpromising marshes near its mouth. It was there, in 1703, that he began to build a fort which was to become the nodal point of a new city he called St Petersburg.[3]

The decision to develop St Petersburg rather than expand Narva was taken in the light of long experience going back to Ivan IV and with an eye to long-term strategic advantage. The new settlement was less exposed than Narva or any other point along the southern Baltic. Moreover, it gave access to Russia's river system, so that, with the development of relatively few canals, it could become an organic part of a single communications system. It also gave access to Western merchantmen, and Peter lost no time in selling them the idea of the makeshift settlement (as it remained for several years) as a profitable new trading port in the making.

Once set on his radical strategy to solve Russia's Baltic problem, Peter would not contemplate abandoning it, even though the great maw of this infant St Petersburg swallowed resources on a gargantuan scale. Indeed, he would happily have surrendered Narva and his other gains around the Gulf of Bothnia, and made other concessions, had Charles only been prepared to cede that small piece of uncertain ground. But Sweden was not content for Russia to have any outlet to the Baltic at all, and so the struggle had to be played out to a violent finish. In terms of resources, Russia had the advantage, though greater difficulties in mobilizing its forces, but Sweden had the better military machine. In 1707 matters moved towards a climax.

The Russian staff expected a Swedish offensive, but not in the direction from which it came – across the Masurian Marshes, to establish a new forward base at Mogilev in Belarus. However, a defeat in Estonia led the Swedes to abandon plans for an amphibious operation against St Petersburg. So far the Russians had suffered more damage than the Swedes in action, but neither side had gained a decisive advantage. Then the weather intervened. Heavy rains turned the roads along the Swedish line of supply into a quagmire, and with the Russians burning crops in the dry areas Charles was soon facing a problem of feeding his army. If the Swedish general Lewenhaupt had arrived earlier, according to plan, bringing supplies, all would have been well for the Swedish offensive into west Russia. But Lewenhaupt was delayed too long, and the Russians used the time to fire the villages and crops along what would have been the Swedes' line of march eastward. In September the thwarted Charles led his army south towards Ukraine. Soon afterwards the news came that Lewenhaupt had been defeated. The die had been cast.

The outcome of the war was turning not on the size and the leadership of armies, but on logistics. The Swedish had the better army, but had to feed it. The Russians understood their enemy's difficulty, and exploited it to their own advantage. This forced the Swedes to change their strategy. Rather than taking a direct approach against St Petersburg or Moscow, they decided to move south to Ukraine to secure supplies and join forces with Russia's enemies.

Charles had good reason to hope that the Turks, Tatars, Poles and Ukrainian Cossacks – though subject to the Russian crown – would all join him in the fight against Peter. In the event only Hetman Ivan Mazepa of Ukraine did so, and even he could not bring all his Cossacks over with him. Soon after he had declared for Sweden, a Russian force descended on his base at Baturin, sacking the place and massacring many of its inhabitants. Still, the Swedes had the prospect of wintering in food-rich country with some local support and a less inclement climate. But then the weather intervened again. Winter came early that year, and some Swedish soldiers froze in the saddle that Christmas. The Russians may have sustained many more casualties from exposure to the elements, but they could be replaced. The Swedes could not make good their losses. Spring came, and the Russians destroyed the Zaporozhian Sech, eliminating any chance of a widespread popular movement in support of Mazepa. Then, in June 1709, having for so long avoided a major battle, they offered it. But, true to form, it was Charles who attacked.

The rout of the once all-victorious Swedish army has often been attributed to bad luck – not least by Charles's chief apologist, his chamberlain Gustavus Adlerfelt. But the Russian strategy of attrition had served to wear the Swedish troops down. True, the co-ordination of the Swedish battle would have been better had not Charles been *hors de combat* having received a stray bullet in the leg two days earlier. On the other hand the Russian command, having analysed their initial failure at Narva and their other encounters with the Swedes, had set the scene to suit themselves. They had built redoubts to block certain approaches to the enemy and divert them from their main objective, the Russian encampment at Poltava. And this time when the Swedes attacked the shock was absorbed. Charles's troops were slowed, then stopped, and finally turned. That day Charles lost nearly 10,000 men dead or taken prisoner. Of the prisoners, the rank and file were put to work on useful projects, and several of the officers, educated men, were to find useful employment in the Russian service, in Siberia and elsewhere.

Charles had set out with high hopes and twenty regiments. According to Adlerfelt, 'Sweden never saw so considerable a force, nor could . . . [it] have been conducted with more prudence good council and wisdom.' There was never a braver leader, claimed Adlerfelt, nor more loyal and disciplined troops. Defeat when it came was unbelievable, and Adlerfelt tried to deny it: 'If the Muscovites had gained so complete a victory as they pretended, why did they not immediately follow the remains of the army?'[4]

The answer was that there was no point. What remained of that famous army, 17,000 strong, had had its sting drawn, and most of its troops soon capitulated. Only Charles and Mazepa with their staffs and some close retainers fled into Ottoman territory, where they were accorded political asylum.

The victory at Poltava raised Russia's profile in the consciousness of Western powers, though even before this England had begun trying to lure Russia into an alliance. It also seems to have marked shifts in Russia's military policy, both to more open forms of warfare and to preferring Russian over foreign generals in appointments to top commands. Furthermore, since Charles, even in exile, refused to make peace, Sweden had to be forced to come to terms. This required a build-up of Russian naval power in the north, involving the expansion of shipyards at Onega and Ladoga to give them a capacity to build both frigates for deep waters and galleys to negotiate the shallow Baltic. The fruit was Russia's first significant victory at sea, when, off Hango in 1714, a flotilla of Russian galleys defeated a Swedish force, capturing a frigate and over 100 guns.

This feat was enough to give Peter command of the shallow seas off Finland, and made even the Swedish heartland vulnerable to attack. Since Russian forces had by then occupied Livonia and Estonia – taking Riga, Pernau, Reval, Viborg, Kexholm and most other Swedish holdings on the southern and eastern shorelines of the Baltic – Sweden had virtually no negotiating cards left to play. But Charles was as obstinate as he had been headstrong. He rejected further overtures in 1718, when he was offered the return of Finland, Estonia and Livonia if only he would cede Ingria, Narva and Viborg. He was even offered help to conquer Norway. His death later that year allowed negotiations to proceed, but it was only under pressure of further military operations in the Baltic and Russia's threat to support the pretensions of the Duke of Holstein to the throne of Sweden that peace was eventually concluded at Nystad in 1721.[5] At last the fireworks could be fired over the Neva and Peter could accept a new title.

Sweden had been the chief focus of Peter's attentions for the preceding twenty years and more, but it had not been the only one. There was intense diplomatic activity in central Europe, where a policy of dynastic imperialism was promoted. A series of political liaisons marked the progress of this policy. He married his half-cousin Anna to the Duke of Courland, her sister to the Duke of Mecklenberg-Schwerin, and her daughter to the Prince of Brunswick-Bevern. His son Alexis was married to a princess of

Brunswick-Wolfenbuttel, his daughter by his second wife, Catherine, to the Duke of Holstein-Gottorp. In this fashion Peter's kin and progeny came to be included in that talisman of aristocratic respectability the *Almanach de Gotha*, family ties were created with several strategically placed territories in central Europe, and precedents were laid for the intermarriage of Romanovs and some of the grandest crowned heads of Europe.[6]

The defeat of Sweden, with its breakthrough to the Baltic, was Peter's most famous achievement. It was associated with his creation of St Petersburg, which he made his capital in 1713, despite the fact that (or perhaps because) the plague, introduced by Swedish troops, had taken a heavy toll of life among the urban population and of the Russian forces in the Baltic area. This step, designed to entrench his hold on the Baltic, served to reorient the Empire towards the West, distancing decision-making from Russia's other frontiers.

Yet, paradoxically, the successes in the Baltic region had the effect of promping new Russian lunges in other directions. Russian observers had noted that Holland, Britain, even Portugal had been growing immensely rich thanks to their colonies and trade in India and south-east Asia. The Russians had long since secured access to Persian silks and the gemstones of India. The acquisition of Baltic ports was, as expected, a stimulus to trade. Projects to establish colonies in Madagascar and the Molucca Islands were mooted before being sensibly rejected.[7] Finally it was decided that commerce with the West could be made much more profitable if Russia exploited its central position in the Eurasian land mass by establishing itself as the intermediary for trade with the East.

But access to the Mediterranean would be better. The Turks blocked the way. However, with the help of an uprising by the Orthodox population of the Balkans, who were sympathetic to Russia, an expeditionary force might force a way through. A campaign into the Ottoman Balkans with this purpose in view had been mounted in 1711, and it marks the origin of the 'Eastern Question' over which British statesmen were to agonize in the nineteenth and early twentieth centuries. The Turks were at war with Russia – hoping to regain Azov and to shore up their position in south-eastern Europe – when prominent Romanians, Serbs and other Orthdox peoples subject to the Turks became excited at the prospect of a Russian victory. In a Romanian parallel to Mazepa's fatal switch of allegiance from Russia to Sweden (and for similar reasons of personal advancement), the hospodar of Moldavia, Dmitrie Cantemir, only recently installed by the Turks, declared for Russia.

The Russians responded by trying to rouse the Orthodox population in other parts of the Balkans too, but for formal and diplomatic reasons the call went out from the Patriarch of Moscow rather than from the Tsar himself:

> To all faithful Metropolitans, Governors, Sirdars, Haiduk, Captains, Palikaris and all Christians [whether] Romanians, Serbs, Croats, Albanians, Bosnians, Montenegrins, and to all [others] who love God and are friendly to Christians:
>
> You know how the Turks have trodden our faith into the mud, seized all [our] holy places by treachery, ravaged and destroyed many churches and monasteries . . . and what misery they have caused and how many widows and orphans they have seized . . . as wolves seize on sheep. But now I am coming to your aid . . . Shake off fear, and let us fight for the faith and for the Church to the last drop of our blood.[8]

In effect, Peter had revived the Orthodox version of the crusader tradition which had died in the fifteenth century. But though this generated some excitement among the Balkan Christian elite, there was a disastrous failure to co-ordinate operations with the invading force. As a result, Peter was trapped by Turkish and Tatar forces on the river Pruth, and was forced to conclude a humiliating peace. Among the concessions he was called upon to make were to return Azov, Russia's gateway into the Black Sea, to the Turks and to withdraw his troops from Poland (though on this he dragged his feet).

This latest failure against the Turks turned Peter's attention further east. On the Central Asian front ambition was also to exceed capability in the short term. The chief impediment was not the opposition of rival powers, because Russia had a monopoly of access from the north, and was minded to keep it, but distance and keeping communications secure from local predators. It took a caravan about forty-five days to journey from Astrakhan to Bukhara, and another two weeks to reach Tashkent. In 1717 Peter ordered a reconnaissance in strength to be mounted along the famous Silk Road to Khiva. A force of 2,000 cavalry, including many Cossacks from the Terek, set out under the command of a Kabardinian prince who had been Russianized, Aleksandr Bekovich-Cherkasskii. But having survived a long and perilous journey across the desert, they were inveigled into a trap by the Khan of Khiva, and the entire force was slaughtered or taken as slaves.[9] And if the Central Asia khans were wily, the steppe nomads were as ravenous as ever, both for booty and for slaves.

In 1720 a group of over 100 Yaik Cossacks and Russians taking salt and fish to market on the Volga was intercepted by a much larger raiding party.

A Cossack called Mikhail Andreyev was among those taken. He managed to escape, taking two horses with him, but then fell foul of a small group of rampaging Bashkirs, who kept him for two months trying to sell him. Fortunately for him a Russian tribute-collector came to his rescue, ransoming him for a silver-trimmed bridle, a pair of boots and a fur hat.[10] The ever lurking presence of such steppe bandits, who sometimes rode in large parties, constituted a serious deterrent to commercial investment in the oriental trade overland.

The arrival of the Jungarian Kalmyks posed a problem, for they mounted raids into the province of Kazan. So did the Kazakhs, who blocked Russian approaches to Sinkiang and Mongolia. The fact that the Bashkirs, despite their nominal subjection to Russia, threw off their traces from time to time and went on wild, destructive rampages compounded the problem of order on the steppe. It was to contain the threat of the Kazakhs and Kalmyks in particular that Peter ordered the construction of a defensive line in southern Siberia east of the Iaik (Ural) river. This so-called Orenburg Line, begun in 1716, consisted of forts interspersed with redoubts, with beacons at regular intervals which were to be lit to give warning of approaching raiders.[11] These forts became information gathering points concerned with the movement and mood of steppe peoples not only locally but over all inner Asia. The security of the caravan route to China became important from 1719, after a splendid embassy led by Lev Izmailov with attendant gentlemen and secretaries and a cohort of interpreters, clerks, valets and footmen, besides an escort of smart dragoons, a military band and a Scottish doctor,[12] made its way to Beijing to gain some valuable commercial concessions. These advantages were to be reinforced eight years later when China agreed to accept triennial Russian caravans of up to 200 traders and to pay their expenses during their stay.[13] Yet Peter seems to have been more interested in trade with Persia and India than with China.

Peter's instructions to Artamon Volynskii, whom he had appointed envoy to Persia in 1715, suggest as much. They focused particularly on Persia's trade and its communications with India. At the same time, watchful Russian eyes were trained on the Caucasus. Peter had in mind the creation of an emporium somewhere in this mountainous and treacherous region to serve as Russia's base for trade with Persia, India and beyond. And in 1721 an opportunity arose when the chief of the Lezghians asked for Russian support against Persia. Peter decided not to let the opportunity slip, and ordered substantial forces to muster at Astrakhan the following spring. At that point it was learned that the Afghans had also rebelled against the

Shah. When the Safavid dynasty crumbled, Russian intervention became urgent, since the crisis in Persia would certainly bring the Turks in to exploit it. Peter himself travelled with the expedition to the Caspian.

The coastal town of Derbent surrendered without a fight, but Baku resisted and Peter turned back. At one point on this expedition an officer suggested to him that it would be much easier, and cheaper, to get to India via the river system of Siberia and the Pacific. Peter replied that the distance was too great. Then, pointing south towards Astrabad in the south-eastern corner of the Caspian, he remarked that from Astrabad 'to Balkh and Badakshan with pack camels takes only twelve days. On that road to India no one can interfere with us.'[14] In this Peter revealed his chief motive in going to war with Persia – a war which would continue until 1735.

Meanwhile Russia involved itself in the politics of the Central Asian steppe. In 1723 the Kalmyks began to move into the valley of the Syr-Darya and towards Tashkent, forcing the Kazakhs west and north, and in 1725 some Kazakhs approached the Russian government with a request to be taken under its protection. The Russians set out to gain control of the northern part of the desert steppe, in order both to protect west Siberia and to trade with the Kazakhs. Mutual need promoted co-operation, but Russia soon became the dominant partner – thanks to its trading position rather than force. Thereafter it was to be a matter of negotiating and re-negotiating terms as the local situation and the aims of Russian strategy changed. Before long Kazakhs were helping to guard the Orenburg area, which soon became a focus for Kazakh trade. Thenceforth St Petersburg was able to control the Kazakhs by offering economic incentives and controlling the prices of the goods they needed and wanted to sell.[15] On the Central Asian front ambition might have exceeded capability in the short term, but Peter's aims were to be pursued with vigour in the two decades following his death in 1725.

Peter's preference for a Persian road to India and his preoccupation with the Swedish war had led to his neglecting Siberian affairs. In 1708 Siberia had become a province (*guberniia*), one of eight into which Peter divided his realm, but it was so vast and had such difficulties of communication that it had to be divided into five only slightly more manageable districts. Three years later all Siberia was put in the charge of the experienced Prince Matvei Gagarin, who had headed the central government's Siberian Department and was now allowed to continue in that office. The arrangement left lines of responsibility unclear, and gave him far too much power.

The door to corruption was left open, and Gagarin strode happily through it. In particular he defrauded the government by breaching its China trade monopoly, selling permits to merchants and his own goods to the Chinese, representing them as the state's. So far from being exclusive, the princely title in Russia was heritable by all descendants, not only the eldest of each generation, and it did not save Gagarin from retribution. He was hanged publicly in St Petersburg in 1714, as a warning to others. The warning was repeated in the edict (*ukaz*) on the Preservation of Civil Rights issued eight year later: 'Anyone . . . behaving like Gagarin contrary to this decree shall be put to death as a law breaker and an enemy of the state . . . [without being given] mercy on account of his former merits.'[16]

Meanwhile the frontier in Siberia was being pushed further out, the limits of the unknown receding. In 1696 a handful of Cossacks sent to subdue local Koriak tribesmen had found their way to the river Kamchatka and back to their base fort on the Anadyr. It took until 1711 to bring all of the great Kamchatka peninsula under control. Of its inhabitants, the Kamchadales were to be described as 'timorous, slavish, and deceitful', but in 1706 they had rebelled, attacked a Russian fort, and slaughtered many Cossacks. As for the Koriaks themselves, they spoke loudly 'with a screeching tone' and, according to Stepan Krashennikov, who was sent to study Kamchatka and its peoples later in the century, were 'rude, passionate, resentful . . . cruel' and ridden with lice, which they ate. They 'never wash[ed] their hands nor face, nor cut their nails . . . [ate] out of the same dish with the dogs . . . [and] everything about them stinks of fish.'[17]

This was not a simple case of better-armed colonizers coming to exploit and oppress innocent but backward natives. These natives could be bellicose (they rebelled in 1710 and again in 1713), and the Kamchadales treated enemies who fell into their hands barbarously – burning them, hanging them by their feet, tearing out their entrails, lopping their limbs off while they were still alive.

In 1714 Peter sent shipwrights to Okhotsk, on the mainland coast opposite Kamchatka in order to bypass Koriak territory. If there were assets to be had there the colonizers might have found the risks posed by natives worthwhile, but in this region there were few resources except for fish and reindeer, and Russia had no shortage of either. Hence the development of Okhotsk to the north of Sakhalin, westward from Kamchatka across the Sea of Okhotsk. However, the Russian population of eastern Siberia was small (66,000 in 1710), and it grew little for some time thereafter.[18]

At the time of Peter's death it was still not certain whether Siberia was contiguous to North America or separated by the ocean, but in that year steps were taken towards finding the answer. Peter's widow and successor, Catherine I (a former serving girl captured in Livonia), commissioned Vitus Bering, a Danish sailor in the Russian service, to go east to Okhotsk and Kamchatka, build two ships, and sail them east.

> You shall endeavour to discover, by coasting with these vessels, whether the country towards the north, of which at present we have no distinct knowledge, is part of America or not.
>
> If it joins the continent of America, you shall endeavour, if possible, to reach some colony belonging to some European power; or in case you meet with any European ship, you shall diligently enquire the name of the coasts, and such other circumstances as it is in your power to learn . . .

It was to take Bering two years to reach Okhotsk overland, and another year to build the boats, but at last, on 14 July 1728, he set sail in the *St Gabriel* with two officers and a crew of forty. On 8 August he met a Chukchi in a boat, and soon some islands, but spied no other land.[19] Thus Bering discovered the strait that was to be named after him, returning to base that same September. The islands, which we now know as the Aleutians, and the surrounding waters turned out to be rich in sea otter and other animals yielding valuable furs, but this was incidental. Russia was already feeling its way to becoming a Pacific power.[20]

There is a widespread assumption that the reasonable, co-operative face which Russian imperialism sometimes showed to newly associated or subject peoples had the purpose of lulling suspicions and masked an intention to dominate as soon as circumstances permitted. This interpretation is largely the work of latter-day nationalists, for whom the imperialist power is ever the villain against which the virtuous oppressed have to struggle for their freedom. Such a telling of the story does not always conform with the historical record. It does not in the case of Central Asia, where the security and development of commerce was the spur, negotiation and the manipulation of interests the means, and political domination only incidental – a means to secure other objectives. Nor does it in the case of Ukraine.

Peter undoubtedly imposed a harsher regime on Ukraine in the wake of Mazepa's betrayal. Nevertheless, the tale told by nationalists misrepresents the truth.[21] Peter had been given reason to distrust the Ukrainian elite. Associates of Mazepa and those suspected of association with him were therefore examined and tortured, and, if local legend can be believed, nearly a thousand of them were executed. On the other hand the new hetman and other loyalists were rewarded. The Zaporozhian Sech was destroyed (though it was subsequently to be revived). Some Russians and others benefited from a great share-out of land in Ukraine, but the chief beneficiaries were members of the indigenous Ukrainian elite. Ukrainian regiments were marched to Ladoga and other points to labour on Peter's projects. However, these consequences were not part of any long-standing plan for domination. Rather they were a response to what had happened, the outcome not of Russia's nefarious intentions but of betrayal by Mazepa and by Ataman Hordienko of the Zaporozhian Sech. And the rebels and their supporters were motivated not by nationalism, which belonged to a later age, but by a desire to be on the winning side and the hope of accreting more property and personal privileges.

However, although the original contract of 1654 between the Tsar and Ukraine had been broken by subsequent rebellions, the Russian government was not eager to create trouble for itself by alienating subjects who might be loyal, or at least politically inert. The subsequent shifts in policy stemmed largely from changing circumstances and pragmatic attention to Russian interests.

The situation in the Baltic territories of Livland and Estland (corresponding with part of today's Latvia and Estonia) was quite different. After conquest in 1710, the existing rights and privileges of their landholding nobility and inhabitants were immediately confirmed, though their nobility were, as it were, effectively obliged to serve on the same terms as their Russian counterparts. As it was expressed in pompous, careful legal language, all former 'privileges . . . statutes, rights of nobility, immunities, entitlements, freedoms . . . and lawfully held estates are hereby confirmed and endorsed by Us and by our rightful successors'. The Lutheran Evangelical religion was permitted without any let or hindrance,[22] and German was allowed as the language of the courts and administration.

True, the conditions were only for 'the present government and times', which left the way open for Peter's successors to withdraw them at some future date. But these two new provinces were accorded, and continued to receive, extraordinarily privileged treatment. In 1725 a separate College of Justice and a financial office were set up for them, staffed by Germans and allowed to deal with other parts of the central administration in German. Concessions by the imperial authorities were commonly prompted by fear of rebellion or administrative convenience, but in this case they were informed by a wish to reform Russian institutions along more efficient Germanic lines. Peter had been deeply impressed with the ideas of the early

Enlightenment, including the concept of 'the well-ordered police state' that was being introduced into some of the states of central Europe, and the more educated, German-speaking population of his new possessions were in touch with that world of *Mitteleuropa*. Furthermore, he had a high regard for their legal system and institutions of local government, which derived from both German and Swedish practice and which he thought might serve as models for Russia.

It was recognized, too, that in taking over these territories the Empire had acquired an important human asset which was badly needed – a large number of highly educated men skilled in many useful professions, from navigation to pharmacy, and from economics to engineering, administration and the law. The Baltic German elite and Russia found a commonality of interest, and from that point on these Germans were to play a prominent part in both Russia's cultural life and the running of the Empire.[23]

Yet, despite the extent and strategic value of Peter's gains, on the Baltic, the Caspian and the Pacific, the Empire remained overwhelmingly Russian in character. It has been calculated that in 1719 over 70 per cent of its population were ethnic Russians, and at least another 15 per cent were Ukrainians or Belarussians, whose languages were very similar, though there were significant differences related to culture, primarily religion. Of the remaining minorities, the largest groups were Estonians and Tatars (1.9 per cent each), Chuvash (1.4 per cent), Kalmyks (1.3 per cent), Bashkirs (1.1 per cent), and Finns and Latvians (1 per cent each).[24]

Great resources had been expended on the Empire's expansion, though by modern standards they were modest. Peter left an army little more than 200,000 strong, yet that represented an almost three-fold increase. He also left Russia's first fleet of significance: 48 ships of the line, as well as 800 smaller vessels.[25] In the northern war alone Russia lost 100,000 men killed, died of wounds and of disease, and a total of over 365,000 were drafted into the armed services during Peter's reign – but this was little more than 15,000 a year out of a male population of nearly 7.8 million.[26] The costs were proportionate. However, between 1710 and 1725 the state's revenues increased threefold – or by some 250 per cent allowing for inflation.[27] This proved sufficient to feed, clothe, arm and equip the army and navy, and to build the core of St Petersburg, together with all its related infrastructure, and dozens of forts and settlements besides. Funds were to prove insufficient to prevent most of the navy going to rot after Peter's death. On the other hand his military priorities produced some useful by-products: expanded woollen cloth and arms industries, and an expansion in iron production sufficient not only to meet the demands of the armed services, but to roof half the buildings of the new capital, and to export sufficient quantities in pig form to help get the heavy-industry sector of Britain's Industrial Revolution under way.

Despite the immense cost in terms of money, people and material, Peter's projects turned out to be affordable. In the later seventeenth and early eighteenth centuries Russia's assets had grown significantly, thanks to conquest and to more peaceful conditions in the productive Black Earth zone of the south. Furthermore, along with other parts of Europe, the Empire profited from a marked economic upswing that stemmed from a beneficent global warming. As harvests became more abundant, diet improved and so did fecundity. Epidemics were somewhat fewer, and their death toll less severe. With population increasing, the economic tempo quickened – and the demands of government accentuated the trend. In this context Peter's huge expenditure on war and on building projects (shipyards, mines and factories as well as a new capital city) was in the end to yield dividends – notwithstanding the claims by some economic historians that the country's economic development would have been even better without it.[28]

And there was a moral dimension besides. More than a century later Russia's greatest poet, Aleksandr Pushkin, who well understood the suffering involved in the creation of St Petersburg, wrote a poem, *The Bronze Horseman*, which celebrates the city and its creator. Pushkin demonstrated nothing less than love for the imperialism and militarism the city represented:

I love you, O military capital,
Love your acrid smoke and the thunder of the guns
That announce the birth of a son in the imperial palace
Or a victory over the enemy.
Russia triumphs again . . .

To this day many Russians share Pushkin's sentiments, even though they know about the costs. And the moral dividend was also to help sustain the imperial momentum, and even quicken it.

It is said that Peter the Great left a testament encapsulating his advice to his successors on how to enlarge the Empire. Indeed, France's Ministry of Foreign Affairs contains a copy of this plan for the domination of Europe. It begins with exhortations to Europeanize Russia and to keep it in a perpetual state of war 'in order to harden the soldier and militarize the nation'.

All possible means were to be used to expand in both the Baltic and the Black Sea regions. More particularly, Sweden was to be softened up for subjugation by stirring up England, Brandenburg and Denmark against her. Similar indirect means were recommended to assist Russia's advance in other directions.

In this document an alliance with Habsburg Austria against the Turks was advised in order to 'facilitate Russia's expansion to Constantinople', and, while the Habsburgs were being sapped of strength by war in the Balkans, their German neighbours were to be stirred up against them. To this end and others, Russia should 'contract marriage alliances in Germany in order to gain influence there', and use every opportunity to become involved in the quarrels of Germany and indeed of all Europe. 'Encourage anarchy in Poland with the object of subjugating it,' and 'use religious dissent to disrupt Poland and Turkey.'

Commercial imperialism was central to the plan. The English should be courted and brought into a 'close commercial alliance', because it was through them that Russia could acquire the necessary commercial and naval skills to acquire a world empire. Outside Europe the objective should be the Levant, because by controlling the eastern Mediterranean Russia could monopolize 'the commerce of the Indies and thus become the true sovereign of Europe'.

The final step would be to make secret proposals to both Habsburg Austria and Bourbon France, offering each a half share, with Russia, in the domination of the world, while getting them embroiled in an exhausting war with each other. Then, at an appropriate moment, Russia would join Austria and march its troops to the Rhine. At the same time two large fleets would sail from Archangel and Azov and head for the Mediterranean, there to disgorge swarms of 'nomadic and greedy' Asiatic peoples who would overrun Italy, Spain and France, carry off much of the population to settle in Siberia, and subjugate the remainder.[29]

As we have seen, several strategies recommended in the document had already been implemented by Peter. Others were to become evident in Russian policies later in the eighteenth century. All this gives the testament the ring of truth. Yet it is spurious. Its vision of a European Armageddon is imaginative rather than practical, and the mindset that created the document is quite un-Russian. Indeed, the document turns out to have been composed later in the century, using ideas deriving from Ukrainian exiles, Poles, Hungarians and Turks, probably by the notorious diplomat the Chevalier d'Eon. Its purpose was to arouse fear of Russian expansionism in Europe, and France had ample motive to use it.

France was in a state of accelerating decline since the grand reign of Louis XIV. It had been Sweden's ally and had seen it defeated. It had worked closely with the Turks, but feared their powers were waning. It was Britain's rival at sea, but increasingly apprehensive of its competitiveness, especially since Britain had drawn close to Austria, France's rival on land. And now upstart Russia was empire-building at a dangerous rate. Just as Polish diplomats and German publicists had whipped up fear of Ivan the Terrible's Russia, so France now encouraged fears of an insatiable Russia swallowing all Europe. It contributed to the pervasive fears of later ages too. The growth of an empire reflects power; it may bring wealth, and it certainly attracts enemies.

9
Glorious Expansion

IT HAS BEEN argued that empires, like companies, must grow or die, that an expanding empire generates costs that can only be met with more resources, and that these resources can only be found by further conquests.[1] The principle may only apply to continental empires based on agriculture, like that of the Aztecs of Mexico, the Incas of Peru or the empire of Kievan Rus – though China seems to be a doubtful case – but the second Russian Empire seems to conform to it. Governments have a chronic disposition to outspend their incomes, of course, but Russia's financial plight after Peter's death (to the extent that it can be established from the record) seems to have been serious. As the British minister to the Russian court, Claudius Rondeau, remarked in 1730, with only a little exaggeration, 'They have not a shilling in the treasury, and, of course, nobody is paid.'[2]

Certainly the decades that followed Peter's death were to see brilliant advances on almost every front. Russia's armies and fleets were to win astonishing victories over militaristic Prussia in the Seven Years War and over the underestimated Ottoman Turks in two subsequent wars. Russia was to prevail in yet another war with Sweden, and, besides fighting a series of lesser engagements with steppe nomads, Persia and wild tribes of the Caucasus, was to be largely instrumental in sweeping the armies of revolutionary France out of northern Italy in 1799. Russia's generals and admirals were showered with gem-encrusted orders, diamond-studded swords, and exquisite gold or enamel snuffboxes by their generous monarchs as tokens of their appreciation – and, not surprisingly, because they had made huge strategic gains for the Empire.

By 1800 Poland was erased from the map of Europe, the greatest part of it swallowed by her age-long antagonist, and Russia had also pushed out her frontiers in Central Asia, acquired a bridgehead in North America, taken the Crimea, established itself on the Danube estuary, and become a power in the Mediterranean as well as the Black Sea, the Baltic and the Pacific.

And, despite Peter's efforts, all this was accomplished by a state which was regarded as institutionally ramshackle as well as financially weak. As Edward Finch, Britain's envoy in St Petersburg, reported in 1741,

> After all the pains which have been taken to bring this country into its present shape . . . I must confess that I can yet see it in no other light, than as a rough model of something meant to be perfected hereafter, in which the several parts do neither fit nor join, nor are well glewed [*sic*] together, but have been only kept so first by one great peg and now by another driven though the whole, which peg pulled out, the whole machine immediately falls to pieces.[3]

Peter himself had served as the first peg. But who now could keep the Empire from crumbling?

Eighteenth-century Russia was dominated by women. Of Peter's immediate successors, his widow, Catherine I, his half-niece Anna and his daughter Elizabeth together ruled Russia for more than thirty-two of the thirty-six years following his death, and Catherine II, known as 'the Great', reigned for more than thirty years thereafter. Peter II (1727–30), Ivan VI (1740–41) and Peter III (1761–2) interrupted the sequence, but had little impact on events.

The fact that most of these rulers were women did not diminish their authority, though there was some muted grumbling among the lower orders. However, none of them had received an education to fit them for supreme office, and apart from Catherine II they tended to be rather more dependent on one or two trusted advisers than most rulers. Cronyism and factionalism do seem to have increased at the Russian court, though this may be an impression given by observers who expected it to be so. The eighteenth century was a heyday for gossips. Empress Anna's favourite, Biron (Bühren), was the dominant figure in the government, yet not – in Finch's view at least – the linchpin that was needed. That function, he thought, was fulfilled by Count Andrei [Heinrich] Ostermann.

Ostermann, Russia's ambassador to Sweden, was given charge of the Foreign Office after Peter's death, and soon undertook a thorough reassessment of Russia's foreign relations in the light of current circumstances. The findings of this complex exercise led him to conclude that, although Peter's policy of alliance with Denmark and Prussia had helped to keep a usually complaisant Poland in tow, it involved risk and yielded insufficient dividends. Prussia had proved an unreliable ally, and the orientation towards the Baltic region was too narrow to serve the Empire's interests in the new era. Ostermann wanted to extend Russia's influence in Europe as a whole, and, at the same time, to promote imperial growth. He was to achieve both these aims with brilliant economy, through one revolutionary turn of the diplomatic rudder.

The means was an alliance with Habsburg Austria, which was signed in August 1726. The two powers had a number of interests in common. They wanted to preserve the independence of their mutual neighbour Poland, the 'sick man' of Europe for the previous half century (its brilliant showing at the siege of Vienna in 1686 had been deceptive). They also wished to contain the Ottoman Empire, and to deter their other enemies – in particular France. But expansion to the south also figured in Ostermann's strategy. His instructions to Ambassador Nemirov, Russia's representative at peace talks with Turkey in 1735, included claims to the Crimea and the Kuban. As yet they were only negotiating points to be conceded, but they were not forgotten. Indeed, two years later Ostermann drew up a plan for the dismemberment of the Ottoman Empire. Strategists tend to plan for contingencies of course, but the Ottoman Empire was nowhere near collapse, as Ostermann well knew. These aims were for the longer term. A generation later they were to be pursued by Catherine the Great. Meanwhile the immediate thrust of Ostermann's policy was directed further west.[4]

One fruit of Ostermann's policy of co-operation with Austria had ripened in the early 1730s, when the allies succeeded in getting their candidate, rather than France's, elected as king of Poland – though not before a Russian army had advanced to France's frontier on the Rhine. Russia had at last become a member of Europe's major league. But the allies' first war against the Turks ended in disappointment in 1739: Austria lost Belgrade, and although Russia regained Azov it was forbidden to harbour warships there.[5] In 1741, when Peter's daughter Elizabeth was brought to the throne by a *coup d'état* carried out by the guards regiments, Ostermann was arrested and purged. But the alliance with Austria continued to hold firm, and was to serve as the launch pad for brilliant advances late in the century. Where, then, did the cause of failure in 1739 lie?

Peter had left an army of 200,000 men – seven battalions of crack infantry guards, fifty regiments of infantry, and thirty of dragoons. Apart from a few hussars, the remainder were mostly garrison troops. By 1730 the complement of the guards had increased – by five squadrons of cavalry guards and three battalions of infantry. Three regiments of cuirassiers had been added to the establishment, and fourteen militia regiments to defend Ukraine. By 1740 Russia had 240,000 men under arms, and by 1750 270,000 – not counting over 50,000 irregular troops, mostly Cossacks and

Kalmyks. Although the range of Russia's military commitments meant that few more than 120,000 regulars could be fielded in a campaign, the army was growing in size.

Nor was it deficient in equipment. There were formidable magazines at Briansk, for operations in the west, and at Novo-Pavlovsk, for operations in the south, aside from the great arsenals in St Petersburg and Moscow. There were six cannon foundries, and two small-arms manufactories, one at Tula, the other outside St Petersburg, in which 'everything is so well ordered that the *connoisseurs*, who have seen them, agree, that they are masterpieces of their kind'.

There was also provision now for specialist troops: an engineering school for the army; a navigation school for the navy. There were even some successful operations. In the Crimean campaign of 1736 Tatars had swarmed round the invading force as soon as it crossed the Perekop, but the regiments formed into square formation and marched on to the capital, Bakhchiserai. They captured it and sacked it, but they could not hold it. A third of the army had fallen sick, and the rest were exhausted from the great heat. However, in the following year the great Turkish citadel of Ochakov on the Dnieper estuary was taken, and its fortifications were demolished. Eighty-two brass cannon fell into Russian hands on that occasion, along with nine horsetail banners – the Ottoman emblems of senior rank. Those who had participated received a gratuity of four months' pay from a grateful government. Four years later Swedish Finland was invaded and the well-defended strong-point of Wilmanstrand was stormed, taken, and 'razed to the ground'.[6]

Yet these successes were both hard-won and expensive. The root of the problem, according to an experienced officer, was not the enemy, however. 'The Turks and Tatars . . . were what [the army] had least to dread; hunger, thirst, penury, continual fatigue, the marches in the intensest [*sic*] heat of the season, were much more fatal to it.'[7] And then there was the plague which broke out among the troops at Ochakov in 1738 and spread quickly into Ukraine.[8] No wonder that by the end of a campaign regiments were seriously under strength, some by as much as 50 per cent.

The great empires of the age depended on sea power, and both France and Britain had considerable navies. Russia's, on the other hand was outclassed even by those of Spain and Holland. The navy had been neglected under Peter's immediate successors. The proud Baltic fleet of thirty ships of the line with their attendant frigates, sloops and cutters had mostly been allowed to rot. Empress Anna made some attempt to halt the decline after 1730, but in 1734 when the city of Gdansk had to be besieged the

Admiralty found difficulty in fitting out even fifteen ships of the line, and some of those proved barely seaworthy.[9] A serious programme of naval construction finally got under way again in 1766. But three years later, when the government attempted to send a fleet to the eastern Mediterranean to support a Greek insurrection against the Turks, operational difficulties soon became apparent. Since the enemy commanded the Black Sea, ships had to be sent from the naval base of Kronstadt near St Petersburg. The long lines of communication were as problematic as the army's logistical problems had been on the long marches to the Crimea. Without help from Britain the voyage might never have been managed.

Admiral Spiridonov set sail from Kronstadt with many troops on board in the summer of 1769. The flotilla under his command was bound for Hull, where Admiral Elphinston was fitting out another force of three ships of the line and two frigates. Things did not go well from the start. One of Spiridonov's 66-gunners had to turn back almost at once, and a frigate was lost in the Gulf of Finland. The rest proceeded to Copenhagen, there to be joined by an 80-gun ship; but bad weather in the North Sea caused the flotilla to disperse. They eventually put into Portsmouth, some of the ships in poor condition and their crews tired. But the British Admiralty had instructed the authorities there to be helpful, and by the spring of 1770 they were repaired, refreshed and ready to sail for the Mediterranean, Admiral Elphinston carrying his flag in the 84-gun *Sviatoslav*. This tidy force of nine ships of the line, three frigates and three sloops sailed on to engage a superior Turkish fleet of fourteen bigger-gunned ships off the coast of Greece in the Bay of Chesme. A Scots officer in Russia's service, Captain Samuel Greig, led the attack in the *Ratislav*, and fire-ships proved the decisive factor. As many as 200 Turkish sail were set ablaze. It was a famous victory.[10]

Greig was only one of many foreigners who were to influence the development of Russia's armed services and its traditions. Scots, Greeks, Irishmen, Germans, Danes and Italians all served in them, as did a future American hero, John-Paul Jones. The best remembered are mostly those who held high rank: marshals Münnich and Lacy, generals Keith and Lowendal and a brother of Jeremy Bentham in the army; admirals Greig, Arf and Elphinston in the navy. However, the chequered career of a little-known naval captain, John Elton, draws attention to lesser men who served as instruments of Russian imperialism, and in less well-known areas of operation – in this case the territory of the lower Volga, Central Asia and Persia.

★

Elton was not a conventional sort of eighteenth-century hero. He won no brilliant victories, was not an enlightened reformer, had no political importance, and was unknown in the *haute monde*, though he was for a time a serious nuisance to officials, businessmen and diplomats. Venturesome, entrepreneurial and courageous, he was also choleric and unstable in his loyalties. At times, indeed, he appears as an anti-hero rather than a hero. Entering Russia's service in the early 1730s, he was employed as an explorer and cartographer on land rather than being given a command with the fleet. He served with the so-called Orenburg expedition, set up in 1734 to secure the area round the confluence of the rivers Or and Ural, to explore the region's potential for agriculture, mining and trade, to navigate the river Syr-Darya, and to investigate the suitability of the Aral Sea for navigation. Elton was involved with all these projects. He was also sent to Tashkent, disguised as a merchant. He surveyed the coast of the Aral Sea, which had been thought to be connected with the Caspian, looking for a possible site for a dock to build ships; he helped construct the citadel of Orenburg itself, and sounded the upper reaches of the Ural river to determine its possibilities for navigation.

It was while exploring the low-lying steppe beyond the east bank of the lower Volga that he mapped the great salt lake which still bears his name. His find soon proved very useful to the state, which maintained stocks of salt in order to guarantee the supply of this essential commodity and control its price. When the Stroganovs began to demand higher prices for Perm salt, Moscow was able to resist the demand thanks to Elton, and an ecological problem was also avoided, for the salt-boilers used a great deal of wood and the government now had a policy of forest conservation. Lake salt could be panned from the brine; it did not need boiling. Production at Lake Elton was expanded, and by the late 1750s it became by far the biggest source of salt in Russia.[11] Long before then, however, Elton, piqued at failing to receive the promotion he thought his due, had resigned the service and had immediately become involved in other ventures.

He set out to pioneer a new trade route from England, across Russia to Khiva, Bukhara and Tashkent. If such a route were found, he knew fortunes could be made by selling English woollen cloth there and bringing back valuable silks. While working with the Orenburg expedition he had questioned people who had crossed the Central Asian steppe, including Cossacks who had been taken as slaves on Bekovich-Cherkasskii's ill-fated expedition of 1717. Concluding that the plundering Kyrgyz, Khivans and Karakalpaks made that approach too dangerous, he now set out to promote a new and safer route that went down the Volga, across the Caspian Sea to

Rasht, and thence by camel caravan across the desert to Meshed and points east. Having negotiated the approval of the Persian authorities, he took his proposal to the British minister at St Petersburg and the Russia Company in London. Recognizing that the route would give it an advantage over its rivals, the Levant and East India companies, the Russia Company seized the opportunity and appointed Elton its agent.[12]

But Elton soon fell foul of the Russian authorities, who suspected him of being in the pay of the Persians and of building a fleet for them to contest Russian mastery of the Caspian. Following diplomatic representations by the Russian minister in London, the Russia Company tried to recall Elton, promising him the handsome sum of £400 a year from the company's profits and to use its influence with the British Admiralty to obtain a naval command for him. Elton, however, preferred to stay. He was distrusted now by both the Russians and the British. A political revolution following the death of his protector, Nadir Shah of Persia, made his position untenable, and he was eventually shot dead by his Persian enemies.[13] His contributions to Russian imperialism survived, however.

The Orenburg project which Elton had served had been planned in the 1720s but was implemented only in the early 1730s. The submission of a group of Kazakhs under Abdulkhayir of the Little Horde in 1731 had given impetus to the scheme. They had wanted Russia's protection against the Jungarians further east, and they had held out the prospect of helping Russia to subdue the Karakalpaks, Turkmens and Khivans. But most Kazakhs would not submit, and, realizing that diplomacy alone would not resolve the problem, the Russian government proceeded to develop a new fortress city of Orenburg at the point where the river Or flowed into the Ural river, between the Bashkirs to the north, the Kyrgyz-kaisaks and the Volga Kalmyks.

Two primary purposes were to exploit mineral deposits in the south-east and to find the most convenient routes to access the silks of Persia and the rubies, gold and lapis lazuli of India. A third priority, on which the others depended, was to protect the south-east frontier from the steppe nomads, and to insulate them from restless groups within the Empire, notably the Bashkirs of the southern Urals and the Volga Kalmyks. Furthermore, if these peoples could be brought into submission, not only would the region become safe for settlement, and hence more productive, but the tribute or taxes they paid would help the needy exchequer.

A range of persuasive means was used to encourage the steppe peoples to submit to Russian rule. The Kalmyks were allowed to trade at the frontier free of customs duties, and Muslim Kazakhs were allowed to build mosques in Orenburg. Chiefs were persuaded to send a son into Russian care to receive an education, and to serve as surety for the group's good behaviour; they were also promised protection against their enemies, and sometimes an attempt was made to awe an important subject chief and prospective client or subject by showing him the sights of St Petersburg, including the collection of wonders in its new Academy of Sciences.

A key figure in the dealings with the Kazakhs was a former Tatar *mirza* who was employed by the Foreign Office as a translator. He was used in negotiations in 1734, later converted from Islam to Russian Orthodoxy, and was promoted a major-general based at Orenburg. His efforts paid dividends. In 1740 the Middle Kazakh Horde at last paid allegiance to Empress Anna, and the relationship proved to be mutually profitable. The Kazakhs were encouraged to divert their trade to Orenburg, where, so long as they met the Russians' requirements of good behaviour, they were offered good prices for their wares and advantageous terms for Russian goods. By 1747 they were bringing 7,000 horses and 28,000 sheep a year to Orenburg.[14]

But, although some Bashkirs had continued to serve the state, many opposed the Orenburg project. They had ambushed one of the first columns bringing labourers, building materials and supplies from Ufa, killing its commander and more than sixty dragoons and labourers. They also rode off with over forty carts carrying supplies. The building of Orenburg proceeded, but other Bashkir raids followed. Fearing that the Bashkirs' attitude might be contagious, St Petersburg ordered up strong reinforcements from Kazan and put a new commander in charge of operations in Bashkiria. A bitter colonial war was soon under way there. The raids continued, some of them on a large scale. In retaliation, villages were torched and such leading rebels as could be caught were hanged.

Eventually a cordon of Cossack villages was established and stable administration followed, to a large extent using the Bashkirs' own elders. But the pacification had been as cruel as such operations tend to be. 'Seize their wives and children, their property, horses and livestock . . .' ran an order from Kirillov, the Russian commander at Orenburg. 'Destroy their homes and punish the main instigators as an example to the others.' Minor offenders and male children were sent to the Baltic as conscripts for the army or the fleet. The women and girls were given to 'whoever wants to take them . . . in order that their roots will be completely torn out', for Kirillov reckoned that rebellion in Bashkiria tended to run in families. In 1740, after five years of rebellion and suppression, 17,000 Bashkirs had lost their lives, over 3,000 had been sent to the Baltic, and nearly 700 villages destroyed.[15]

These operations had also been costly to the Russians, but the rewards were great. Rich new deposits of copper and iron had been found in that part of the Urals which was Bashkir country, and no time was lost in exploiting them. By 1750 the area accounted for 90 per cent of Russia's considerable iron production and 70 per cent of its copper.[16] Furthermore, the Bashkir threat to Russian communications with Central Asia had been eliminated. Both Bashkiria and Kazakhstan could now be counted among the Russian Empire's permanent possessions.

On New Year's Day 1740 St Petersburg was treated to an exotic spectacle. Representative couples of various native peoples in the Empire, including Bashkirs, went in procession to an ice palace, constructed on the ice of the river Neva, where the wedding of a courtier, Prince Mikhail Golitsyn, was celebrated. Charivari had long been a feature of the Russian court at this season, but the like of this had not been seen before. Pairs of Lapps and Finns from the far north, Tatars, Kyrgyz from Central Asia and Tungus from furthest Siberia, as well as the Bashkirs, rode on sleds drawn by dogs, reindeer, camels or whatever their native beasts of burden were deemed to be; each couple contributed to the festivities by dancing their native dance, and ate a celebratory dinner of their native foods. It was an exotic show, but also a live, if incomplete, demonstration of the Empire's ethnic variety, which by that date included peoples even more exotic than these.[17] In the far north, beyond the river Lena, for example, lived the Yukagirs and Nganasans, who were totally dependent on the seasonal migrations of wild deer for their food, housing and clothing; and in Chukhotka, in the far north-east (which involved a considerable journey not only in space but back in time) were the settlements of the Yugits, who hunted walrus and Greenland whales and wintered in dug-out igloos framed with giant whale bones.[18]

The native Siberian population was soon to be severely reduced, however – not so much by war, for many of them had fought each other before the Russians came, but because of influenza and smallpox, which the colonizers inadvertently introduced, and syphilis, which became endemic because of their crowded living quarters. Nor was Russia the only power that wanted to impose its order on the natives. The Chinese, Russia's competitors in Dzungara, slaughtered many Mongol- and Turkic-speaking natives in the 1750s. Yet the Russian government's policies were enlightened, and even in furthest Siberia its administrators and explorers often exemplified the civilized values of the age. Some, indeed, were almost touchingly earnest in trying to persuade the native population to abandon their primitive ways. As one of them told the natives in the far north-east as he doled out a gift of beads and showed them portraits of Empress Catherine II and her son, the future Emperor Paul, 'The Russian monarch and her successor are extremely gracious and diffuse their blessings among innumerable people. They also pay indefatigable attention to the welfare of all these nations who border on the Russian empire and have no protector; employing all possible means to preserve them in content, peace and security.'[19] One gets the impression that the speaker believed what he was saying. Another conscientious representative of enlightened imperialism

> laboured to persuade [the natives he encountered] to quit their savage life . . . which was a perpetual scene of massacre and warfare, for a better and more happy state. I showed them the comforts of our houses, clothes and provisions; I explained to them the method of digging, sowing and planting gardens, and I distributed fruit and vegetables and some of our provisions amongst them, with which they were highly delighted.

All in all, Russian colonization in this period was kind rather than cruel, and if the smallpox the explorers introduced took its toll among the native peoples, so it did in St Petersburg. The population of Siberia as a whole grew at roughly the same rate as the rest of the world from the eighteenth century.[20]

Chappe d'Auteroche, a member of the French Academy, who visited Russia in the early 1760s, published an account of it in 1768 which enraged Empress Catherine II. In his book he denigrated the condition of Russia, and even poured scorn on its armed services. The army might be a quarter of a million strong, but it could field no more than 70,000 effective regulars. Moreover, the infantry was effective only in defence, and the cavalry was 'the worst in Europe'. Russia's artillery might be good, but 'the corps of engineers . . . [was] incapable of conducting a siege.' As for the navy, it had few ships and 'the sea officers have as little knowledge as those on land.' 'In the present state of population and wealth in Russia, an army cannot be sent beyond the confines of the empire without being ruined even by the victories it may gain; a Russian army in such a situation must be almost entirely destroyed.'[21]

Chappe was to be confounded on every point of his assessment. During the Seven Years War (1756–63) Russian troops had not only raided Berlin, they defeated the army of Frederick the Great at Gross Jägersdorf and at Künersdorf. And they were to triumph, almost without interruption, on every European front for the remainder of the century. The upshot was a considerable expansion of the Empire, much of it at the expense of Poland. Yet Russia did not initiate the first partition of Poland, in 1772. It had no interest in doing so. Poland was already a client state. Its king, Stanislaus Poniatowski, had been the Empress's lover, and Russian garrisons were already quartered there. It had been Poland's weak government, derived from its lopsided constitution ('anarchy tempered by civil war' was what one wit termed it), which had invited intervention. Russia did not want instability on its frontier. Furthermore, there was the question of the treatment of Orthodox Christians in Poland. Russia's use of this issue is often regarded as a cynical excuse to intervene. So it may have been, but the Polish Church had a long record of persecuting Orthodox Christians, and Empress Catherine, who had been born a Protestant and was herself a convert to Orthodoxy, could hardly overlook it.

In fact the first partition was precipitated not by Catherine but by Frederick of Prussia. The port city of Gdansk and the Vistula estuary on which it stood divided his realm, and he wanted to unite it. He chose his moment to propose a partition carefully. Both Russia and Prussia had their hands full fighting the Turks. In other circumstances Catherine and Maria Theresa of Austria would have combined to warn Frederick off. However, as things were, they agreed to territorial compensation at Poland's expense. So Russia gained a swathe of territory between Riga and Chernigov, whose inhabitants were predominately Orthodox and ethnically Ukrainian or Belorussian. It was soon to make more gains as a result of the Turkish war: the western shore of the Black Sea, the coast between the rivers Bug and Dnieper, and the Kerch Strait between the Crimea and the north-east shore of the Black Sea. And Ottoman troops were to quit the Crimea itself.[22]

The Crimea was nominally independent, but since pro-Turkish sentiments were rife among its predominately Muslim population, and since the neighbouring Kuban region was as unstable as Poland, in November 1776 Russian troops crossed the Perekop again, and installed a Russian puppet, Shahin Girey, as khan. But this device did not work well enough for long, and so on 8 April 1783 Catherine annexed the Crimea, accusing the Turks of bad faith in order to justify her own breach of the treaty terms. The new imperial property was doubly valuable. It not only yielded a range of exotic crops – from wine, silk and olives to sesame seeds, dyes and cotton[23] – it offered command of the Black Sea. Before long the old Tatar towns of Akht-mechet and Akhtiar began their transformations into the city of Simferopol and the naval base of Sevastopol.

It had been the birth of a second grandson, in 1779, that had served to crystallize Catherine's ambition for the Empire's advance to the south. She had him christened Constantine, after the founder of Constantinople, engaged Greek nurses, and later tutors, for him, and asked her secretary, Count Bezborodko, to sketch out a plan which was to achieve notoriety as 'the Greek Project'. This contemplated the division of the Ottoman Balkans, the creation of an independent Romanian state of 'Dacia', even the replacement of the Ottoman Empire by a revived Byzantine Empire, to be ruled by the infant Constantine. In due course the plan, which drew on the earlier ideas of Andrei Ostermann, was shown to her ally Emperor Joseph II. This is somewhat surprising, since Austria might well have been expected to object to it as potentially detrimental to its interests. But, though Joseph demurred, he did so only on grounds of feasibility. Nikita Panin, president of Catherine's College of Foreign Affairs, was soon dismissed and replaced by Ostermann's son, Ivan. Thenceforth Russia's policy in the south became more aggressive, as did its economic exploitation of conquered territory. But it did not go uncontested.

A substantial number of Nogai Tatars – nomads who had roamed the north Caucasian steppe since the Mongols had arrived centuries earlier – raised a revolt in the north-western foothills of Caucasus. Ottoman agents and Muslim religious had probably helped to stir them up, as they did other Muslim groups deeper into the mountains. In 1782 Aleksandr Suvorov, the general who had performed so brilliantly in several battles of the First Turkish War of 1768–74, was sent in to sort the problem out. His objective was to secure the eastern flank of the operation, which was to bring under direct Russian administration not only the north Caucasian plain and the north-eastern shores of the Black Sea, but also the Crimea and the Black Sea littoral as far as the river Bug to the west of it.

Suvorov employed a whole armoury of means to persuade the Nogais to accept Russian rule. He staged demonstrations of force; he used diplomacy; he offered bribes; and, inviting them to swear oaths of loyalty to the Empress, he laid on a feast to celebrate the occasion – 100 roast oxen and 800 sheep, to be washed down with dozens of barrels of brandy. The results, however, were disappointing. Only 6,000 Nogais turned up to the ceremony, and at least as many took up arms against the invading Russian troops. Three thousand were killed in one battle; many more fled towards the mountains, but pursuing Russian units caught up with them as they retreated northward up the river Laba, and its banks were soon littered with their bodies. The establishment of a new line of Cossack settlements along the banks of the river Kuban now went forward, and the Greben and Terek Cossack lines to the east were strengthened. Before long the rolling plains to the north and west of the Caucasus were being marked out for settlement. But country further south was also brought within Russia's sphere. In 1783 Catherine had agreed to a request for protection from King Erekle of Kartlo-Kakheti in Georgia. Some authorities have seen in these episodes the real origins of the Eastern Question.[24]

However, the fate of the Nogais had sounded alarms among the Muslim Chechens of the northern Caucasus, and by 1785 Sheikh Mansur Usherma had succeeded in bringing together most of the diverse mountain peoples, from Dagestan to the Kuban, in an anti-Russian jihad. That year Sheikh Mansur's warriors trapped a sizeable force of Russian troops on the river Sunzha, and massacred most of them. The Russian command reacted systematically as well as strongly. By 1791 Mansur had been taken and imprisoned. Those followers who survived were subdued. Officials in the region remained watchful, but decades of relative peace were to follow, with no obvious sign that Mansur's victory on the Sunzha was to be a harbinger of things to come.[25]

A few months later the Sultan finally accepted the loss of the Crimea, at which Russia quickly put the new property to use. A primary aim was to establish naval bases, but increasing its population was also a matter of strategic concern: census-takers counted only 160,000 inhabitants in 1793. The troubles prior to the occupation had taken their toll of casualties; so had the disturbances which followed it, and the plague. But the chief factor was an exodus of population, including most of the Tatar elite, once the Treaty of Jassy confirmed the Crimea's transfer to Russia, removing all hope that the Tatar state would ever be resurrected. However, those elements of the old Tatar establishment who stayed on – Muslim clerics as well as secular notables – were prepared to co-operate with the Russians, and the transition was further eased in the first instance by having Tatars versed in the old ways of doing things administer Russian rule. Furthermore, the demands imposed on the remaining inhabitants were at first very light. Until the end of the century they were even exempted from taxation and the standard recruitment laws. However, the kid gloves were slowly drawn off and a regime more consistent with practice in the Empire as a whole was gradually imposed, including an obligation to furnish sufficient recruits to man two regiments.[26]

The repopulation of the Crimea was doubly advantageous for Russia.

Not only had the country been rid of hostile elements, now there was space for new settlers and new projects. But the ambitious colonization programme for the south – of which Prince Grigorii Potemkin, the Empress's one-eyed lover, had charge – involved far more than the Crimea itself. All the new territory between the lower Bug and Donets, along with the Zaporozhian Sech, which had been broken up in 1775, was placed under his administration as part of a new province called New Russia (*Novorossiia*). Its economic potential matched its strategic significance, but first new foundations had to be laid. Potemkin's far-reaching plans for his new satrapy were based, according the Empress's wishes, upon the most rational and enlightened ideas of the time. The policies he implemented as viceroy derived in part from legislation of the early 1760s which aimed to encourage foreigners to settle in Russia. However, the approach now concerned not only individuals, but entire communities. The purpose was to make underpopulated areas more productive.

Orthodox Christian settlers–including 20,000 Greeks, some Armenians who knew how to raise silkworms, and others – were recruited from Ottoman territory to help make the land fruitful. Some Georgians also arrived, responding to the offer of protection and financial inducements,[27] and soon a major colonization programme was being implemented. Romanians who understood viticulture and Albanians also came. Poles were allowed to settle there too – and even Jews, who for the most part were confined to the-so-called 'Pale of Settlement' in the Polish provinces. These Jews, generally excluded from Russia proper, were valued here for their skills as artisans and, like the Greeks, for promoting trade. The policy was to result in a healthy development of commerce as the immigrants exploited connections with their places of origins and former trading partners. Greeks had long been important in the Levant; Jews were responsible for the growth of overland trade with western Ukraine, especially through Austrian Lemberg (Lvov), though many of them later became free farmer settlers. They were also prominent, alongside Italians and other immigrants, in the development of the port city of Odessa, which by 1802 was receiving an average of over 300 merchant ships a year.[28]

Substantial numbers of Germans were also attracted to the Russian south. Indeed they were reckoned at a premium on account of their industry, orderliness and farming skills.[29] The terms offered them were tempting indeed: freedom to choose their occupation, cash subsidies or an allocation of up to 70 acres if they wished to farm, seed for the first winter and spring sowings, two horses per family, and either free equipment or money in lieu of it. They would also enjoy freedom from taxation for up to thirty years, be exempt from recruitment into the services, and receive the costs of passage if they needed it. Some settlers were even told that they would be under a form of administration based on the Swiss cantonal model. Recruiting contractors were engaged and were offered appointment to a military rank (which brought some privilege and prestige) if they produced a large enough number of settlers.

The prospects for German migrants were painted rosily by the recruiting agents. A prospectus for the Saratov area of the Volga issued in 1765 informed the public in the targeted area that the climate of their potential new habitat was 'similar to that of Lyons in France . . . The soil . . . is extraordinarily fertile . . . There are the most magnificent meadows . . . also a great quantity of stock . . . The horses are . . . swift . . . can travel up to fifteen German miles a day and cost no more than six rubles . . . A milch cow [costs] not above three to four' and the best of meat cost only a kopek a pound. In some areas grapes could be cultivated, yielding wine of 'a splendid flavour', and the soil was also suitable for tobacco. Fruit and flowers grew in abundance, and there was a profusion of game to be shot. The prospects, in short, were altogether excellent. But in case there should be any residual doubt, an assurance was offered: 'The director of the colony . . . will make [every effort] to ensure that each new settler . . . shall be able to enjoy a peaceful and plentiful life.'[30]

Not all the colonists found the Volga to be quite the promised Eldorado, but the strategy as a whole proved productive. This scheme, like many associated with the Empress, bore the hallmarks of the Enlightenment. Indeed, some of the leading luminaries of the Enlightenment, including Diderot and Voltaire, longing for a country to receive their progressive ideas, and judging Bourbon France to be a hopeless case, now looked to Russia as the great hope for the future. This was not simply because Catherine was powerful and subscribed to many of their ideas, but because Russia was so backward and possessed so few institutions. This meant that the Empire could accept the imprint of their ideas and be moulded by them.

But if the government's policy towards immigrants bore the stamp of the Enlightenment, what was it in regard to its other subject peoples?

In Poland, which presented such contrasts to Russia institutionally and culturally, sentiment was not totally hostile to Russian rule. Indeed, as a German traveller observed, 'the Poles, particularly the nobility and gentry, are better affected to the Russians than the Prussian, as was . . . manifest [at the partition crisis] . . . when they made no scruple of openly declaring their intention to receive the Russians with open arms.'[31] The vast majority of the population, of course, were politically inert peasants.

Although some nobles were fiercely hostile to the new regime, a number of prominent aristocrats, notably those of the Czartoryski family, had been inclined towards Russia before the partition, and served their new masters willingly. What reconciled the more important Polish nobles to Russian rule, even though they were Catholics, was not simply the preservation of their noble status, with all the rights that in Russia went with it (Kazakh chiefs who did military service enjoyed the same privileges), but the preservation of serfdom. Its abolition in neighbouring Prussia threatened to undermine many of their compatriots across the frontier economically and destroy their local power. Even though, in conformity with Catherine's provincial reforms, Russian laws and the Russian language were introduced to eastern Poland, the nobility was left in control of local government, and the Catholic Church was not interefered with.[32] In fact most peasants and many townspeople in Russian Poland were Orthodox. The second and third partitions of Poland, in 1793 and 1795, brought 1.7 million of these under the Russian crown, and when the Uniate Church was brought into the Orthodox fold and under the administration of Russia's Holy Synod it seems that as many of its communicants were relieved as were offended.

The partitions, however, created another religious problem by bringing well over a million Jews as well as several million Catholics into the Empire. This was the chief source of Russia's reputation for anti-Semitism. Hostility to Jews had been imported into Russia, as into every other Christian country, with the writings of the Church Fathers. Yet Russians themselves were no more anti-Semitic than other European peoples, and less so than many. Before the partitions few Jews had been allowed to enter Russia proper except by express command of the tsar – a policy most probably due to the state's care to avoid antagonizing the privileged merchant class, on which it was long dependent for financial advice and tax collection, as well as the Church, which had been an important economic support for the state before the eighteenth century. Anti-Semitism in the Empire was for the most part characteristic of certain subject peoples rather than the Russians themselves, having been entrenched for centuries among Ukrainians, Balts and Poles – in short, among the people who inhabited the frontierlands of the Catholic Church where it confronted Protestants or Orthodox Christians.

Although what had been eastern Poland was now subject to Russia militarily, the occupying power did not wish to alienate the Polish ruling class and so delayed the imposition of Russian norms on the Polish territories. But in the 1790s the Polish elite as well as the Russian authorities became increasingly concerned about how to counter the influence of revolutionary France. Polish landowners were terrified by the Jacobinism which had infected some of the budding intelligentsia in the towns, and Russian rule became more popular. But Russian concern resulted in the Polish elite retaining their social, cultural and legal distinctiveness. This helped to embed them as a 'foreign body' within the Russian *imperium*, creating a problem for the future.[33]

Russian Ukraine west of the Dnieper was administered as part of Russian Poland, but eastern Ukraine was subject to policies that would help absorb it, indeed Russify it. This was not the consequence of any master plan to extinguish Ukrainian independence and distinctiveness, however. Since nationalist sentiment did not develop there until well into the nineteenth century, there was no need no counter it in the eighteenth. Nevertheless, some Ukrainians valued their autonomy as well as their traditions, and the Russians were to eliminate Ukrainian autonomy. They did so partly to improve security and prevent disorder. This is why the Zaporozhian Sech had been destroyed and its inhabitants dispersed in 1775, although some of its Cossacks had promptly gone over to the Turks, who allowed them to form a similar community on the lower Danube under their protection. The removal of obstacles to an enlightened monarch's power was in itself an enlightened idea. So was the abolition of regional, sectoral and any other rights regarded as antiquated and irrational.

The occasion for implementing this principle of uniform centralism had come long before, in 1763, soon after the Empress's accession. The Ukrainian elite, numbering about 2,200 out of a population of a million, had petitioned for their Council of Officers to be converted into a constitutional Diet of the Nobility. They had also wanted parity of rank and privilege with Russia's nobility. At the same time Hetman Razumovsky of Ukraine, who had been the favoured lover of Empress Elizabeth, asked for his appointment to be made hereditary. This had angered the enlightened Catherine, who had just acceded to the throne. She not only denied the petitions, but abolished the post of hetman, appointed a governor-general for Ukraine, and looked forward to the time when, as she put it, even the memory of hetmans would be obliterated. There was strong resistance from those who demanded a new appointment, but the Russian authorities reacted with severity. Thirty-six of the objectors were sentenced to death, though they were subsequently reprieved.

Russia's new system of regional administration, proclaimed in 1775, was applied to Ukraine. However, this obliged the government to recognize the Cossack elite as nobles on a par with the Russian nobility, and in 1783 serfdom was introduced into Ukraine. These measures mollified the Ukrainian elite, who were landowners as well as Cossack officers, so that when Ukraine's own indigenous institutions were abolished, as they were in the 1780s, protest was muted. Indeed it was Ukrainians on the Russian governor-general's staff who installed and administered the new regime. Although the Ukrainian elite continued to take pride in their Cossack past, most of them accepted the new order, and in time many of them were to become Russian patriots.[34]

The processes by which differences in wealth within a community increased, and the officer class was accorded both the privileges of noblemen and the right to keep serfs, took place in other Cossack communities which had previously been rebelliously inclined. In 1773 the Don Cossacks had produced in Pugachev the most terrifying rebel of all, but another development also helped to break them in. This was the emergence of an ethos of pride in loyal service which the state helped to shape. The ethos related conveniently both to a sense of social privilege and to pride in military glory.

The later eighteenth century saw an almost uninterrupted series of campaigns in which Cossacks were involved. The imperial citations, awards of decorations for bravery and donations of colours combined to create a patriotism that was gradually to blot out any will to assert a collective independence. Indeed, when the government needed to establish a new Cossack community to build and guard the Kuban river line, former Zaporozhian veterans who had served as marines in the Second Turkish War of 1787–92 were allowed, as a reward for their valued service, to kneel down before the Empress and petition for a grant of land in the area on which they could settle. The petition was, of course, granted, the purpose of the ceremony having been achieved. In an age when glory could inspire both pride and awe, the state now possessed a means other than suppression to fend off thoughts of protest and manipulate its subjects. That is how the Cossacks came to be psychologically enslaved.[35]

The Baltic provinces constituted a quite different case. The great majority of the population there were peasant serfs whose horizons extended very little further than their village and who spoke local Baltic dialects (the modern literary languages had not yet been constructed). Russian rule made little difference to such people, except that men in Russian rather than Swedish uniforms garrisoned the towns and when necessary patrolled the countryside. Authority was represented by the same lord that they had

had before. The lords themselves were predominately German-speaking, and, as we have seen, they had been co-opted into the Russian elite. Every governor-general in the eighteenth century was a Baltic German except one, and he, George Browne, was an Irishman married to a Baltic German.

The dependence of government on educated Germans became so pervasive from the 1730s that many a provincial governor would put his signatures to reports that were actually written in German.[36] So long as the Baltic Germans preserved their right to use German in the local courts and in correspondence with the imperial government they had little incentive to learn Russian unless they aspired to very high office. Indeed, until the middle of the century German was the principal language of the imperial court, as subsequently French would become the favoured medium. Furthermore, in the later eighteenth century Baltic Germans held a far higher number of senior positions than their numbers warranted in the imperial administration, the judicial service and the military. They were content with Russian rule. The honeymoon ended only when, in August 1796, the terms of Catherine's Charter of the Nobility of 1785 were applied to them. The charter deliberately ignored the noble traditions and institutions of the Baltic Germans. Its introduction prompted polite remonstrance, and then protest. But Catherine – a German herself – was adamant. The protestors, she said, did 'not appreciate the advantages offered to them, but [clung] to traditional habits . . . The disposition of rulers', she warned, 'should at all times be accepted with respect and obeyed without demur.'[37] The sword of the enlightened improver cut evenly against ancient constitutions and the habits of savages alike.

As ever, there was less restlessness among the peoples of the north and west than in the southern provinces of the Empire. In part this was due to rising affluence, in part to a measured combination of firmness and concession. Indifference and inertia also counted. But, if there was little opposition to Russian rule, there was little inclination to assimilate either. Religious toleration – another principle of enlightened government – helped reinforce the distinctiveness of Catholic Poles, German Protestants and Jews. So did the preservation of serfdom and the persistence of private law. The state was beginning to encroach on privilege and localism, though decades were to pass before the effects were very visible. Had these reforms been implemented earlier and been more widespread, a far higher proportion of the population would have been Russified and there would have been less scope for the nationalism of an age yet to come.

Yet no thoroughgoing Russification policy was applied consistently, even in the mid-Volga region, one of the earlier scenes of Russian empire-building. If Russians came to predominate in that region, this was because of demographic expansion rather than policies of absorption. Russians had formed the majority of the population at least from Peter I's time. In the 1790s the Chuvash in the region numbered 310,000, the Cheremis 140,000 and the Votiaks only 127,000, but there were more than 250,000 Mordvs and 400,000 Tatars. Some of these minorities, as well as Russians, moved into the Bashkir areas of the southern Urals. The Kalmyks, about 200,000 strong, found they had to share their part of the steppe with Ukrainian, Tatar, Mordv and German as well as Russian colonists. Again, no great effort was made to Russify these elements, although between 1740 and 1755 the Church did mount a missionary campaign directed at animists, and groups whose co-operation the government particularly valued were offered inducements to convert to Christianity. Kazakhs and, later, Crimean Tatars and others who did so were granted three years' remission of taxes and allowed to own Christian serfs. Yet no attempt was made to make even the patriarchate of Moscow a Russian preserve. Of the 127 Orthodox bishops installed in the Empire between 1700 and 1762, no fewer than 75 were Ukrainians and only 38 Russians.[38] And there was no policy to promote ethnic homogenization.

Russia's laws, policies and institutions – including Catherine's 'enlightened' rationalizing measures – came to apply to the new provinces as well as to the old, to the Crimea as well as to Livonia and Ukraine and Moscow Province. Not only did they arouse understandable resentment, however, they sometimes resulted in anomaly rather than standardization. In 1795, thanks to the partitions and the age-old policy of co-opting elites, there were some 600,000 registered noblemen (*szlachta*) in Russia's Polish provinces – four times as many as in Russia proper. Many of them, however, were devoid of resources – in effect they were the servants of noblemen with means.[39] And, although the local-government reforms of 1775 were applied throughout the Empire, their norms regarding the administration of justice in particular remained a dead letter in Siberia, because the new laws had allotted various administrative functions to members of the nobility, and the Siberians had no noble class.[40]

The Second Turkish War, which formed the backdrop to these developments, confirmed Russia's superiority over Ottoman Turkey, and established its power in the Black Sea and the northern Caucasus. Success in that war was achieved through a succession of brilliant victories in hard-fought battles – the defence of Kinburn, the battle of the Rymnik, the storming of Ismail. At the same time Russia was able to sustain successful operations, chiefly by sea, against a hostile Sweden. The gains resulting from this triumphant progress were only half digested when another southern project got under way. In 1796, 30,000 troops moved down the Caspian coast to take Derbent and Baku and to prepare for an advance into the heartland of Persia. The ultimate objective of this 'Oriental Project', led by the brother of the last of Catherine's lovers, Platon Zubov, was to seize Tibet and the roads into India.

Already alarmed by the build-up of Russian sea power in the Black Sea and the eastern Mediterranean, Britain was spared further concern by Catherine's death later the same year. But, although the Oriental Project was called off and British interests in India became safe for the moment, the progress of Russian arms was not to end there. Suddenly, in November 1798, the Knights of St John – based on Malta, the pivotal point in the Mediterranean – elected Catherine's son and successor, the Emperor Paul, grand master of the order, so Malta in effect became a Russian protectorate.[41] Yet there was to be no clash between the Russian fleet and the British who had helped to create it. Indeed, they were soon united by a common enemy: revolutionary France. Thanks to Russia's alliance with Britain, Napoleon Bonaparte was to be denied Malta and Egypt, but Russia's Mediterranean plans were also to come to nothing.

By the end of the century the Empire covered well over 2 million square miles, more than a fifth of them in Europe. Just before the turn of the century a Russian–American Company was founded to exploit the trading possibilities in the north-eastern Pacific and to administer territories on the eastern side of the Bering straits 'belonging to Russia by right of discovery'. Russian explorers had already been burying inscribed copper plates in new-found lands and erecting crosses over them declaring them to be 'imperial Russian territory'. The company was empowered to make new discoveries south as well as north of the 55th Parallel, and to exploit them.[42]

This had all been achieved with relatively modest military resources, given how great a power Russia had become. Of a total military establishment of 435,000 in 1782, more than half were garrison troops, labour battalions (of convicts, rebel tribesmen and the like) and frontier troops such as the Cossacks. There were only 118,000 regular infantry, 52,000 regular cavalry and 29,000 artillerymen. The cost, according to the reliable Le Clerc, was 5,173,000 rubles a year. The navy cost a further 1,226,999 a year, compared with 1,588,747 for the court and a mere 73,000 for the Academy of Sciences.[43] Richard Hellie has estimated that the army cost one-eighth of all Russia's productive resources in the eighteenth century.[44] Russia lost

653,000 men in its eighteenth-century wars, nearly a third of them in the Turkish wars. High as these costs were, they were not an excessive price to pay for the immense assets gained – territorial and human – and it has been calculated that between 1719 and 1795 the male population had grown by almost 7 million, not counting the population of the new territories.[45]

Russia was incontestably a world power now, and, as powers do, it attracted opposition. Not only traditional rivals like the Ottoman Turks and France, but former allies now harboured misgivings. Britain was concerned at possible Russian threats to its interests in the Mediterranean and India; Habsburg Austria, long Russia's closest ally, was now worried that a collapse of the Turkish Empire, previously unimaginable, might precipitate serious problems for it in the Balkans. In the natural way of things, these powers would have been expected to club together with France against Russia in order to restore a balance of power in Europe – but this did not happen. A new factor had intruded itself: the rise of revolutionary ideology. Concern about France's radically new form of imperialism with its weapons of mass mobilization, democratic populism and subversion was ultimately to mobilize a new, nationalist, form of opposition to it. But in the meantime the disruption of Europe in the Napoleonic Wars was to facilitate the further expansion of Russia's traditional empire.

10

The Romantic Age of Empire

THE LATE EIGHTEENTH and early nineteenth centuries were not a propitious age for empires. It was the age when Britain lost most of North America, Spain her vast possessions in Latin America, and Portugal Brazil. France's empire shrank too, and by then the Dutch were already out of the reckoning as an imperial power of world scale. Yet, against the current, Russia's empire grew, and, as if to symbolize its world role and continuing ambitions, in 1803–4 a Russian ship circumnavigated the globe for the first time.

The prospects had not seemed so bright even a short while before. In 1800 Russian forces had to make a difficult withdrawal from Italy through Switzerland. The Malta project was abandoned, and Russian ships were forced out of the Mediterranean altogether. Finally, in 1812, Russia lost not only Poland but western Russia and indeed Moscow itself to Napoleon's army. Despite these dramatic reverses, however, the nineteenth century then saw Russia bound back to become master of half of Europe and a third of Asia again and to make significant additional imperial gains.[1] Paradoxically, both the reverses and the advances were precipitated by the same factor: the impact of revolutionary France.

Napoleon destroyed the strategic balance in Europe, and persuaded powers which might otherwise have been hostile to Russia to co-operate with it, against France. When Napoleon crushed the allied armies in a series of brilliant campaigns in central Europe, the Emperor Alexander, who met him on a raft near Tilsit, reluctantly contrived a deal with him in 1807. This effectively divided Europe into French and Russian spheres, though it was not to hold beyond 1811. France's embargo on Britain hurt Russia's trading interests, its threat of reviving an independent Poland threatened to destabilize Russia's western frontier again, and Alexander would not be treated as a satellite. In the meantime, however, he made the most of the opportunities which Tilsit had presented to him. In 1808–9 Finland was annexed from Sweden and in 1811 Bessarabia was taken from the Turks. Meanwhile the advance in the Caucasus had been resumed.

The figure who symbolized this, the most romantic, phase in the conquest of the Caucasus was General Pavel Tsitsianov, commander of the entire Caucasian front from the Cossack lines of the Terek and Kuban in the north to Georgia in the south. Although middle-aged, Tsitsianov was a romantic sort of hero: proud, brave and cruel, a dashing man of action, subservient to no one – not even the Tsar. Arguing that St Petersburg was too far away to dictate policy and approve decisions, he insisted on wide discretionary powers – and got them. Young Tsar Alexander agreed that central-government policies should be submitted to the general for approval, and that Tsitsianov need report significant actions only once they had been taken.

Tsitsianov strengthened Russia's hold on Georgia, and set out to push the frontiers south through Azerbaydzhan to Persia – and as far as Tabriz if he could. With this in mind, he decided to upgrade the rough road that Potemkin had built over the mountains to Tiflis (Tbilisi), the so-called Georgian Military Highway. This strategic link between southern Russian and Georgia cut across Europe's highest mountains and past the homes of some of Europe's most troublesome peoples. Tsitsianov's policy towards them was uncompromising, especially if they were Muslims (treacherous, he called them, and some of them were). Though many resented his rule, he was largely successful. He conquered Ganjeh, subdued Shirvan, and then tried to take Yerevan, the chief city of Armenia, but was diverted by rebellions in Georgia, the Kabarda and Ossetia as well as Chechnya. He answered resistance with firmness, blood with blood, opposition with retribution. 'I tremble with eagerness to water your land with your criminal blood,' he declared. He would impose order, he warned, 'with bayonets and grapeshot until your blood flows in rivers'.[2] He burned villages and took hostages, and his punitive measures succeeded in quietening the Ossetians and the Kabardinians. Even the Chechens lay low for a time. Before he could complete his programme, however, the feisty, arrogant satrap met his nemesis.

The Khan of Baku was affronted by Tsitsianov's high-handedness, but nevertheless tried to strike a deal. No doubt regarding the Khan as another untrustworthy Asiatic, the general refused to treat, and demanded the city's submission. With characteristic bravado, he rode up to the walls attended only by an aide-de-camp and a solitary Cossack. The Khan's men shot him dead together with his aide, then cut off his head and both his hands. The Cossack got away to deliver his gruesome report.[3]

★

Tsitsianov's proconsular style was by no means typical of Russian imperialism. In the less turbulent countries of Finland and Bessarabia, which also came under the imperial wing in the first decade of the nineteenth century, the government's approach was markedly different. Thanks to a Finnish officer in its service, the Russian government was briefed and prepared to cope with the Finns. Colonel G. M. Sprengtporten had drafted rules for an autonomous Finland under Russia's protection twenty years before the provinces were seized from Sweden in the war of 1808. When Russian troops invaded that February, care was taken to reassure the population: 'We do not come to you as enemies, but as your friends and protectors, and to render you more prosperous and happy . . . [Affairs will be conducted] according to your ancient laws and customs . . . [and] prompt payment shall be made for all provisions and refreshments required for the troops.' The caring Tsar Alexander had even arranged to set up storehouses to feed indigent Finns.[4]

In March 1809, when a Finnish Diet was summoned for the first time ever and its members' freely gave oaths of allegiance, the Tsar confirmed 'the preservation of their [Protestant] religion and fundamental law, together with the liberties and rights enjoyed by each individual estate and by the inhabitants of Finland collectively'. In effect, his edict gave the Finns greater autonomy than they had enjoyed under Sweden. They were exempted from military obligations, given control of their own currency, and administered by their own officials. Indeed, their only link with Russia was to be the person of the Tsar, their grand duke. Most Finns had no problem dedicating their loyalty to him on those terms.[5]

The acquisition of Bessarabia occurred in the context of another war with the Ottoman Turks. In fact Russia had been minded to acquire not only Bessarabia but the other Romanian-speaking Ottoman properties, Moldavia and Wallachia, too, and sentiment in the Balkans was favourable to the Russian cause. As a young man had explained to the French consul in Moldavia's capital, Iasi, in 1806, 'Russia has been good to us. It is to her that we owe our political emancipation [from the Turks], our limited duties and our part in the country's administration . . . Russia protects us. Her armies are here.' The consul felt that, were the French in occupation, the young man's loyalty might readily be transferred to them. However, though young people with some education were beginning to embrace revolutionary ideas alongside their traditional Orthodox religion, Napoleonic France still supported their Ottoman overlords, whose enemy was Russia. Most, therefore, continued to look on Russia as their potential saviour. It became a question of how far its forces could advance in the Balkans before

Napoleonic France, having paused for breath after its devastating victories over Austria and Prussia, would resume its advance eastward. As soon as Napoleon struck – which everyone knew could not be long – all Russia's strength would have to be concentrated on the defence of the fatherland.

The man entrusted with the difficult Balkan mission was General of Infantry Prince M. I. Kutuzov, a wise, hard-headed veteran of Turkish wars, remarkable for his acute strategic judgement and strong sense of timing. Knowing that his army was likely to be recalled at any moment, in 1811 Kutuzov managed to make enough ground militarily to force the Turks to the peace table. Kutuzov himself led the Russian side in the negotiations; the outcome was the annexation of Bessarabia. This might seem but a modest triumph judged against the scale of Russia's earlier gains in the two great Turkish wars of the later eighteenth century, and given that the Romanian elite of Moldavia and Wallachia would at that time gladly have accepted Russian rule. In the fraught context, however, it was a signal success. The fact that the Ottoman negotiators were subsequently executed confirms this view.

Since the new territories were seriously underpopulated, the mandarins in St Peterburg immediately extended the Empire's enlightened settlement policies, previously applied in New Russia, to Bessarabia.[6] But Napoleon was already leading his great army eastward across the Russian frontier. At the end of May 1812 Kutuzov and his troops were ordered home at once to help meet the threat.

Napoleon's invading *Grand Armée* was massive by the standards of the age – more than 350,000 men. It was also international, including Spaniards, Dutch, Swiss and citizens from many states in Germany and Italy, in addition to Frenchmen. The Russians could muster barely half that number to confront them.[7] Moreover, Napoleon was at the height of his powers and supported by a formidable array of talented, battle-hardened generals who knew his mind – Davoust, Ney, Saint-Cyr, Murat and Mortier among them. They marched directly into the Empire's heartland. Towards the end of August the ageing, portly Kutuzov was given command of the Russian forces on the western front, and early in September he tried to do what was expected of him: stop the invaders before they reached Moscow. The ensuing battle of Borodino was fiercely fought but indecisive. Kutuzov's next actions confounded amateur strategists: he gave orders to withdraw, and continued to fall back beyond Moscow, abandoning the ancient capital to the invader.

Kutuzov's reasoning was sound, however. Napoleon had sent out columns to threaten his lines of communication, and the move had to be countered. The abandonment of Moscow, for all its religious and symbolic importance, mattered less than the desperate need to frustrate the enemy. As Kutuzov explained in a letter to Tsar Alexander, 'So long as Your Imperial Majesty's army is intact . . . the loss of Moscow is not the loss of our fatherland.' He had had no hesitation in choosing to preserve the army rather than risk it in the defence of Moscow. But, as he hastened to assure his commander-in-chief, his strategy was by no means passive. Indeed, he was already launching an operation of which he had high hopes. He had ordered a new order of battle, 'with all our forces in a line extending from the Tula and Kaluga roads. From these positions units will be able to break into the enemy's line of communications which stretch from Smolensk to Moscow. This would stop all support the enemy army might receive from its rear, and at the same time draw its attention. By these means I hope to compel him to leave Moscow.'[8]

The effect on morale might have been expected to be catastrophic, however, and much of Russia's elite was indeed terrified – not only of the invaders, but also that their peasant serfs might seize the opportunity to rise against them. Yet the morale of the Russian troops held up rather better than that of the French and their allies, and it soon transpired that the peasantry hated the invaders more than their own masters. By the time Napoleon had been in Moscow a week or two he must have suspected that he was lost. He had confidently expected emissaries to arrive from Alexander, begging for peace and the return of the city. Yet no one came. Alexander had set his face against any dealings with the upstart intruder. As day after day passed without word from St Petersburg, Napoleon's suspicion hardened into the sombre realization that he was doomed.

It was not the intervention of the Russian winter that had decided the matter, however. As a contemporary pointed out, 'People still talk of "General Frost", forgetting that the autumn of that year was warmer than in France . . . [and that as early as October] entire brigades and divisions had already begun to disappear from the enemy army.'[9] Confirmation comes from the great military theorist Clausewitz, who was serving with the Russian staff. The French army, he wrote in an assessment of the campaign, had lost no less than a third of its strength even before it reached Smolensk, and another third before it got to Moscow, chiefly through desertions. By that time it was 'already too much weakened for the attainment of the end of its enterprise.'[10] Kutuzov also knew this, and that, by cleverly withdrawing to the south-west in order to keep his own lines of supply open while threatening to intercept the enemy's, he had placed Napoleon in an untenable position. At last, on 19 October, five weeks after he had arrived in Moscow, Napoleon decided to abandon the city. By then, however, it was too late to save what was left of his *Grande Armée*.

What, then, had eroded the invader's strength? In part it was the time-honoured Russian strategy of denying the enemy food and provender and stretching his lines of communication; in part the Russian army's reluctance after Borodino to offer battle, its sharp surprise attacks, its blocking movements and harrying tactics. These methods combined to wear the invaders down, though what broke Napoleon's own morale was Alexander's unexpected and adamant refusal to come to terms after the occupation of Moscow. Kutuzov's contribution was significant too – his brilliant manoeuvring, his strategy of pursuit without engaging in set-piece battles, his patience. And the enterprise was also aided by a surge of patriotism which embraced the peasant serfs, who might well have rebelled had Napoleon proclaimed their emancipation. As it was, when groups of the enemy seemed vulnerable, peasants often proceeded to slaughter them. Some 40,000 Poles, including émigrés from the 1790s, had joined Napoleon, but for the most part the subject peoples had remained loyal to Russia or inert.

Yet, when all these factors have been taken into account, it is difficult to escape the conclusion that Napoleon himself was primarily responsible for the disaster. His preparations for the invasion had been inadequate. His maps were inferior, his logistical support poor, his intelligence inferior, his horses inappropriately shod, his assumptions about Russia's resilience and the Tsar's firmness of purpose mistaken. In brief, his hubris doomed him.

The cost of victory was heavy enough. Kutuzov's army, 120,000 strong when it began the pursuit, had shrunk to a mere 35,000 by the time it crossed into the Duchy of Poland,[11] and the campaign as a whole had cost Russia 250,000 men. Yet in long-term perspective the loss seems small. Russia's population was soon to recover; the demographic cost to France was more serious. The Russian campaign heralded the decline of France as a great power, while Russia now became the strongest power in continental Europe. Wellington and Blücher won what the former called the 'close-run thing' against France at Waterloo in 1815, but, with a powerful Russian army marching towards him, Napoleon was doomed even had he won at Waterloo.

While Europe's statesmen gathered in Paris and then Vienna to redraw the political map, Russian soldiers bivouacked in the Champs-Elysées and gave a Russian word, *bistro*, to French dictionaries to denote fast food service.

Since both Castlereagh, who represented Britain, and Metternich for Austria feared Russia's power in Europe, they tried to limit it by co-opting France into the ranks of respectability in order to provide a counterweight. Although Russia did not gain all it had hoped for in the peace settlement, it nevertheless got most of it – the lion's share of Poland as well as Bessarabia and Finland.

Russia's rule over Poland could hardly be characterized as oppressive. Tsar Alexander and his brother Constantine, whom he appointed his viceroy in Warsaw, were children of the Enlightenment and had both been reared on advanced ideas.[12] Some of these were reflected in Russia's new regime for Poland. The constitution, largely the work of the Polish magnate Adam Czartoryski, provided for a parliament that included elected representatives of the respectable classes of both countryside and town. Poland was to have its own army of 35,000 men, and would be united with Russia only through the person of the Tsar in his capacity as hereditary king of Poland. The Catholic religion was guaranteed, and Polish was established as the official language of government, the courts and education. Furthermore the viceroy, Grand Duke Constantine, was liberal by disposition and married to a Polish lady.

The Polish political classes as a whole would not be reconciled, however. Traditionalists still hankered after the greater Poland of a former age, while many of the educated young were fired by revolutionary ideas. But there were some prominent Poles who believed in working with the Russians for the good of their country. It was a policy that soon bore fruit. Largely due to their reforms of the 1820s, for example, the foundations of a modern economy were laid in Poland.[13]

The prospects darkened, however, with the Warsaw uprising of 1830–31. Led by a group of young intellectuals, including army officers, it did not gather much of a popular following, and was put down with relative ease. But it raised the spectre of Jacobinism again. Fear of radicalism ran very deep in governments across Europe, including Russia's. Thenceforth Russian policy in Poland became much harsher. Strangely perhaps, this failed to elicit any protest from Russia's own radicals, the so-called Decembrists, who had themselves attempted to overturn the autocracy in 1825, when Tsar Alexander died and was unexpectedly succeeded, not by the elder of his surviving brothers, Constantine, but by the younger, Nicholas. On the contrary, Aleksandr Pushkin, who had sympathized with the Decembrists, was outraged by 'demagogues' in the French Assembly who protested about the crushing of the Polish rebels. In an angry poem, he dismissed the protest as unbased and unjustified. The repression in

Poland was merely a phase in the longstanding 'domestic quarrel' between two Slav peoples, which foreigners should stay out of. Had Westerners protested when Polish forces occupied Moscow? Why did they hate Russia, rather than being grateful for its saving Europe from the Turks and from Napoleon? Russians had spilled their blood for Europe's freedom. If the West dared back its rhetoric with action it would find

a shield of flashing steel raised
Over the Russian land from Finland's cold rocks to flaming Colchis,
From the shimmering Kremlin to the walls of impassive China.
So, you demagogues, send us your sons indoctrinated in hate.
There's room enough for them in Russia's fields
Alongside the graves of their compatriots.[14]

Pushkin's poetic diatribe reflected not only patriotism but a pride in empire which most educated Russians seemed to share. And the sense of estrangement from the West and the possibility of war conveyed by the poem were prophetic. Russia's imperialism was indeed to provoke a war with the West – though not in Pushkin's lifetime, and not over Poland, but over Russia's expansion to the south.

The besetting imperial dilemma of St Petersburg's bureaucrats at that time was whether to devolve power in the Empire or to centralize it. Should governors be accorded the freedom to act as local circumstances demanded, which would impede centralization and the enforcement of legal rights? Or should the government insist that all regions comply with the law laid down by St Petersburg, which would promote officialism and insensitivity to local conditions and sentiment?

In Finland and in Russia's other Baltic territories imperial rule continued to be marked by a certain complaisance, although when Alexander had confirmed the rights and privileges of Estland and Livland he had taken care to add the proviso 'insofar as they are consistent with the general decrees and laws of our State.'[15] But trying to draft laws that would be equally appropriate to the educated populations of the western territories, the Russians of the heartlands, and the tribesmen of the Caucasus, Central Asia and Siberia turned out to be much like attempting to square the circle.

Alexander had grappled with ideas of constitutional reform since the beginning of the century. He had corresponded with Thomas Jefferson about them, consulted John Quincy Adams, and discussed them with his inner circle of able advisers. These included Novosiltsov, who wanted to redesign the Empire as a federation of twelve huge provinces, each with a bicameral ruling council (*duma*); Czartoryski, architect of the well-intentioned but unappreciated arrangement for Poland; and Mikhail Speranskii, who was to be looked back on as the most visionary reformer of all.

One solution to the problem of running so vast and variegated an empire equitably was federalism. But the desperate war against Napoleonic France and the threat of revolution that loomed over Europe afterwards discouraged the idea of dismantling the autocracy, so the proposed federalist solution had been diluted, reduced to the creation of a few super-provinces, in central Russia, the north-west (including the Baltic) and the south (where New Russia, Bessarabia and the Caucasus were brought together). There was also some tinkering with provincial institutions, but Speranskii himself was sent away to be governor of Penza province, and then to Siberia as governor-general.

Nowhere was the fundamental problem of empire more intractable than there. Much has been made of the memoirist Vigel's comparison of Siberia with a remote estate of a wealthy landowner who appreciates it for the extra income it brings and the interesting objects it yields but otherwise pays it no attention. That the centre interfered so little is hardly surprising given the difficulty of communication. The furthest point on land was nearly 9,000 miles from St Petersburg. Seaborne communications were quicker, but as late as the 1840s it was to take eighteen months for a reply to a query sent from New Archangel on Sitka Island in the Gulf of Alaska to arrive from St Petersburg.[16]

However, it did not seem reasonable to devolve responsibilities on to the indigenous leadership of a society which, as in Yakutia, respected shamans who worked their curative spells by hopping about to the accompaniment of a doleful chant, and 'making the most hideous distortions of face and body' before pretending to plunge a knife into their belly.[17] And if the natives were insufficiently modern to be allowed to share in government, the local Russians, aside from the administrators, were little better – chiefly merchants who were as rapacious, ignorant, oppressive and insensitive as those portrayed by the novelist Leskov (and later by the composer Shostakovich) in his 'Lady Macbeth of the Mtsensk District'.

Speranskii introduced the rule of law into Siberia with his statutes of 1822, but it did not take him long to realize that the people had 'less of a conception of legality than elsewhere', and that the population – many of whom were migratory by habit – could not be treated like Russians. Their officials would have to be appointed rather than elected. However some members of the Yakut and Kamchadal elite appointed to office proved to be at least as oppressive as any Russians. Speranskii decreed that, apart from criminal offences, the people were to be ruled by their own tribal laws. He recognized the rights of nomads, assigned them land, protected it from encroachment, and left it to them to decide its distribution. He even inspired the setting-up of a council for the nomads, though the new institution survived for only ten years.[18] Speranskii's more lasting reforms were administrative and organizational rather than institutional. For the rest, he could only pray that the natives would be Russified, as for the most part the Tatars had been, and as soon as possible.

In the south, Russia continued to press forward at Persia's expense. A war between them ended in 1828 with the annexation of Yerevan and the plains of Ararat, whereupon tens of thousands of Armenian Christians from further south flocked there seeking Tsar Nicholas's protection, although many Muslims moved in the opposite direction. Nicholas approved the creation of a new, Armenian, province for them, though it was to be merged into a Caucasian super-province twelve years later.[19] If Armenians welcomed Russian rule, however, many Muslims of the Caucasus continued to resist it.

Not that Russian policy had been anti-Muslim in principle. On the contrary, the state had often sponsored Islamic institutions. When Russia had occupied the Crimea it had confirmed Muslim clergy in office, and it left both their spiritual authority and their control of religious education intact. It had also allowed them to retain properties that yielded untaxed revenues to support their mosques, schools and charities. It even paid their salaries. But it insisted that the civil law take priority over Islamic law, defined the clergy's responsibilities, and, from 1834, obliged them to register births, marriages and deaths.[20] This gentle approach would not work in the Caucasus, however. Certainly the army command was sceptical about it.

The new governor-general in the south, General Yermolov, was an established war hero before he arrived in the Caucasus. A proconsul in the Tsitsianov mould, he had no doubt about Russia's cultural superiority to the peoples with whom he now had to deal, and in his forthright way he sometimes did what he thought best, notwithstanding the Tsar's milder views. 'I want my name to be associated with terror,' he declared. 'This will protect our frontier territories more effectively than . . . fortresses. For the natives my word should be a law more inevitable than death.' On another occasion he wrote that 'Asiatics see condescension as a sign of weakness. I shall be unswervingly severe simply out of humanity – because an execution saves hundreds of Russians from destruction and thousands of Muslims from treason.'[21]

Yermolov was lionized by society, and admired by radical youth – not least by the poets Lermontov and Pushkin. It has been fashionable lately to castigate the likes of Yermolov for excessive cruelty, bred of prejudice. It is also argued that his methods were counter-productive – that they provoked opposition unnecessarily.[22] However, as Baddeley points out, the Russians hardly differed from the British and other imperial powers in their behaviour when their will was contested by peoples they regarded as uncivilized, and it is difficult to imagine that some of the peoples they encountered would have been any more tractable whatever Russia's actions. It is here that we encounter the origins of the Chechen problem, which stretch back long before 1800.

As the multiplicity of languages recorded in its valleys testifies, the Caucasus had attracted refugees since ancient times. As with the Basques in the Pyrenees or the Romansh-speakers of Switzerland, isolation aided survival. So did belligerence, and the peoples of the Caucasus included some, the Chechens among them, who were more belligerent than most. This tendency was accentuated by the difficulty of winning a living from the stony mountain soil, and by the need to carry arms to defend one's sheep and goats from wild beasts.

Violence, moreover, could be productive for the mountain people. Trade routes crossed the Caucasus, and so the local population not only sold their services as guides, like the Swiss, but turned to robbery – for money, goods and slaves. (Unsold slaves were set to work in the household or with the animals.) From the sixteenth century at least, reports by travellers make frequent reference to robbers infesting the western shores of the Caspian Sea and its hinterland. Chechen Island, situated at a hazardous but strategic point in the Caspian opposite the estuary of the river Terek, takes its name from the Chechen pirates who used it as a base. Stepan Razin, Cossack leader of a great insurrection in the 1660s which incorporated a robber expedition, is also said to have used it.[23] Nearly two centuries later a French traveller in the Caucasus remarked that mountain settlements (*auls*) in the eastern Caucasus were prosperous because of the booty their inhabitants had accumulated.

Since no state could impose its law on them, these mountain societies tended to be regulated by the blood feud, which they had come to apply collectively to intruders like the Russians. The German scholar Pallas noticed the same tendency among the spirited, but disorderly, Circassians to the west, a decade and more before Tsitsianov first arrived in the Caucasus. 'Among the Circassians', he wrote, 'the spirit of resentment is so great that all the relations of the murderer are considered as guilty. The customary infatuation to avenge the blood of relatives generates most of the feuds, and occasions great bloodshed among the nations of the Caucasus; for unless pardon be purchased or obtained by intermarriage between the two families, the principle of revenge is propagated.' The customary law of family vengeance was already being applied to communal retribution, however, and 'the hatred which the mountainous nations evince against the Russians, in a great measure arises from the same source.' Moreover, when a member of the Circassian elite was killed, blood money was not acceptable in compensation: 'They demand blood for blood.'[24]

In time, some Circassians, like the Tatars and Bashkirs before them, were recruited into the Russian army and were even shown off in the capital like a particularly exotic, colourful imperial trophy. Martha Wilmont, later Lady Londonderry, who lived in St Petersburg with the Princess Dashkova, who had been an intimate of Catherine the Great, for five years from 1803, described 'a small group of Circassians, wild looking people with mail caps, scarlet shirts, armour and long spears, looking like warriors of old' leading a St Petersburg parade, displacing even contingents of the elite Chevalier Guards.[25] However, their feuding passions did not diminish. 'Revenge . . .' wrote a visitor to the western Caucasus in the 1830s, 'is with them paramount to every other consideration; no wealth can purchase forbearance, no entreaty for mercy can avert the blow; blood must be requited alone by blood; for when a Caucasian falls, hundreds of his comrades vow to avenge his death, and until that vow is accomplished, their hearts are steeled to every pleading of pity or humanity.'

The Chechens were an even harder case than the Circassians. Their upright bearing, handsome looks and eagle-beak noses fitted a Romantic image of the noble savage and was to help them win friends in mid-nineteenth-century England, but back in the 1790s the naturalist Peter Pallas had thought them to be 'the most turbulent, hostile, and predatory inhabitants of the mountains . . . [and] without exception the worst of neighbours on the lines of the Caucasus'.[26] Even more savage than their neighbours, they were little inclined to work, and fanatical.[27] Their elite (there was also an underclass of captive slaves) was carefully schooled in the martial arts from infancy. Entrusted to a tutor-cum-guardian (*usden*) from outside the family, a boy would be taught how to ride, use arms, steal and to conceal his thefts. 'He is afterwards led to more considerable and dangerous robberies, and does not return to his father's home until his cunning, his address, and his strength are supposed to be perfect.' Until then his tutor received nine-tenths of his loot.

Lacking other occupation or income apart from what meagre crops their slaves could grow for them, it is hardly surprising that the Chechens should have become professional robbers. As they lived close to the main artery connecting Russia with Georgia and the rest of Transcaucasia, the Russian government, whose trade and communications they threatened, had no choice but to deal with them. War with the Chechens could therefore be regarded as inevitable. Nevertheless, the threat the Russians posed to their traditional way of life – the introduction of laws which reduced the power of the mountain princes; the ban of the slave trade, from which the mountain peoples had profited since times beyond memory – deepened the Chechens' hostility. They could not remember a time when they had not exported girls to Istanbul, took pride whenever one was taken into the harem of some potentate, and always hoped that one might be taken for the Sultan himself. The mountain men were of the stuff that myths are made. In their white, shaggy sheepskin hats they seemed to be 'of gigantic height'; their expression was wild, and each was armed to the teeth with gun, axe, dagger and steel-barbed 'club that might have served Hercules'.[28] For Circassians and Chechens alike the laws of feud were extreme, and hard as iron. And they applied them ruthlessly to their struggle with the Russians.

On the mountaineers' side the war was total, fought to the death. Baddeley described an encounter relatively early in the war, when the Chechen village of Dadi-Yurt was attacked. Since every house was guarded by a high stone wall, it had to be to be pounded by artillery and kept under relentless small-arms fire. Once a breach was made, soldiers rushed in, but were met in the dark by Chechens wielding daggers. 'Some of the natives, seeing defeat to be inevitable, slaughtered their wives and children . . . Many of the women threw themselves onto . . . [the soldiers] knife in hand, or in despair leaped into the burning buildings and perished in the flames.' The Russian commander proposed a parley, but the answer, given by a half-naked Chechen, black with smoke, was 'We want no quarter.' 'Orders were now given to fire the houses from all sides. The sun had set, and the picture of destruction and ruin was lighted only by the red glow of the flames. The Chechens, firmly resolved to die, set up their death-song, loud at first, but sinking lower and lower as their numbers diminished.' Eventually some broke out, preferring to die from bullets or the bayonet rather than burn to death. Some Dagestanis who were with them were captured, but 'not one Chechen was taken alive.' Seventy-two men 'ended their lives in the flames.'[29]

Casualty rates in such a war are inevitably high, and on the Chechen side they included women. The demographic effect on the Chechens – who numbered about 150,000, of whom 60,000 were adult males[30] – was manifest, and the wars eventually reduced the mountain population sufficiently to allow the survivors to subsist without robbery. So resistance abated. Yermolov's methods had apparently worked, and his successor, General Rosen, managed to quell the Chechens and quieten Dagestan. But the lull proved only temporary.

The great Chechen leader Shamyl had recognized the demographic problem, and set out to counter it by encouraging younger marriages. As the population recovered, the fundamentalist Murid creed, which had arisen in Dagestan but had spread to Chechnya in the 1820s, gained adherents. Governed by their imam, they saw it as their overriding purpose to die in battle against the infidel, and the war flared up again. The Russian state had long experience of accommodating Islam, but Muridism – puritanical and fiercely anti-Western – was a new force to contend with.

The Russian advance through the Caucasus and into Persia threatened to restrict the operation of Muslim law and led to some mosques being appropriated and converted to other uses. The Russian advance was therefore perceived as a threat to Islam, and this intensified the conflict. So did the conversion of those among the mountain peoples who had hitherto remained heathens.

In 1830 mountain men, fired by Muridism, began to raid the Cossack lines along the Terek, and even threatened Vladikavkaz at the southern approach to the main pass across the central Caucasus. But steps were already being taken to shore up the south's defences for the longer as well as the shorter term. From 1829 free peasants were allowed to move south and enlist as Terek Cossacks. Runaway serfs under the age of thirty-five apprehended in the southern provinces were transported to the Terek to work for them and to build the necessary infrastructure for projected settlements. Eighteen months later, for a limited period, townsmen were also allowed to enlist as Cossacks, either on the Terek or in the adjacent Astrakhan Cossack Host. Thanks to these and other measures General Veliaminov eventually succeeded in quietening the Caucasus for the remainder of the 1830s[31], but in the early 1840s the region caught fire yet again.

Some time before that, the British had begun to exploit the situation. They were prompted by the threat to their imperial interests posed by Russia's recent expansion in Asia following the defeat of the Persian army by General Ivan Paskevich, who had succeeded Yermolov, in December 1826. The following summer Paskevich had taken Nakhichevan and advanced on Tabriz. Under the terms of the subsequent Russo-Persian peace treaty, Russia annexed Yerevan, Nakhichevan and the territory north of the river Aras. This territorial gain put the Russians within striking distance of Tabriz, then the Persian capital. Beyond Tabriz lay the road to Baghdad. The treaty also guaranteed Russia a monopoly of trade and shipping on the Caspian, ensured Persian neutrality in any Russian war with Turkey and secured the famous Ardebil Library, with its precious Persian and Islamic manuscripts, for St Petersburg, Tsar Nicholas having professed an interest in Islam. London and Paris, as well as Istanbul, found the treaty's provisions disturbing.

Russia's victory over the Turks in the war of 1828–9 deepened their disquiet. Although most of territory occupied during the hostilities was returned, according to the Treaty of Edirne the frontier was moved south to include the entire Danube delta and Akhalkalaki, which rounded out the frontier of southern Georgia. The fact that Russia's troops had actually taken both Tabriz and Erzurum during the war suggests forbearance in concluding the peace, but Russia's non-territorial gains were considerable: open access to Danube and to the Mediterranean through the Straits, the right to trade throughout the Ottoman Empire, and reparations which helped retrospectively to finance the wars – 10 million ducats from the Turks, and the equivalent of £3 million from the Persians.[32]

Russia's strategic position was improved even beyond that. In Europe Russia gained the lasting goodwill of the Greeks for having made the largest military contribution to securing an independent Greek state, and of Serbs for gaining autonomy for the pashalic of Belgrade, core of the infant state of Serbia; and its troops remained in the Romanian principalities, where the elite and the Orthodox Church looked to the Tsar for protection. With access to the Mediterranean, influence in the Balkans, and command of most of the high ground on the frontiers with Turkey and Persia, Russia's southern provinces seemed secure and set for prosperity.

By the early 1830s Odessa, with its capacious harbour, was fast becoming the dynamic, cosmopolitan emporium of the south. Populated by 'Russians, French, Italians, Greeks, Armenians, Jews, Germans, Poles, Turks, Tatars, Americans, English, etc. – all eagerly prosecuting their commercial concerns in this free city', it was already a handsome town of some 25,000 inhabitants with stone buildings lining spacious, if as yet unpaved, streets, fashionable shops, French restaurants and 'a public garden, laid out in the English style . . . [which was] a favourite resort of the citizens in fair weather'. Rational plans for its enlargement and improvement had been devised by no less a figure than the émigré duc de Richelieu.[33]

Another of the Empire's cities, Tiflis, capital of Georgia, presented contrasts of a different kind.

> The quarter inhabited by Russians . . . [wrote an earnest German visitor in the middle of the century] has a perfectly European look: straight streets, rows of modern houses, elegant shops, milliners and apothecaries, even a bookseller, with cafés, public buildings, a Government palace, churches with cupolas and towers, the various Russian military uniforms with French palitots and frock-coats, quite transported us back to Europe. But where this European town ends, one of a perfectly Asian character begins, with bazaars, caravanserais, and long streets, in which the various trades are carried on in open shops . . . A row of smithies, the men hammering away at their anvils . . . Another row . . . where tailors are seated at work . . . After these . . . shoemakers, furriers, etc. . . .
>
> The population is no less varied and interesting: here Tatars . . . in another part, thin, sunburnt Persians with loose, flowing dresses. Koords, with a bold and enterprising look; Lezghis and Circassians engaged in their traffic of horses; lastly the beautiful Georgian women, with long flowing veils and high-heeled slippers; nearly all the population displaying a beauty of varied character, which no other country can exhibit – an effect heightened by the parti-coloured, picturesque, and beautiful costumes. In no place are both the contrasts and the connecting links between Europe and Asia found in the same immediate juxtaposition as in Tiflis.[34]

However Russia's imperialist rivals, Britain and France, were uneasy about Russia's new ascendancy at the gates to Asia, and the threat it posed to Ottoman Turkey. If Russia should succeed in unblocking the roads to the Levant and India, as seemed quite possible, they would be the losers. Hence Whitehall's change of policy from one of friendship towards Russia following the Napoleonic Wars, to watchfulness in the 1820s and '30s, and finally to open hostility by the early 1850s. But the Crimean War was heralded in the 1830s by a proxy conflict in the Caucasus.

David Urquhart, part-time diplomat and anti-Russian publicist, was active from an early stage in this secret war. In 1834, unnoticed by the Russians, he landed at the Black Sea harbour of Anapa not far from the entrance to the Sea of Azov. His purpose was to make contact with Circassian chiefs of the western Caucasian highlands, known to be hostile to Russia, and to encourage them to create a national independence movement. The outcome was a

'Declaration of Circassian Independence Addressed to the Courts of Europe'. The appeal went straight to the hearts of Westerners of romantic disposition – as it was calculated to do, with its child-like assertion of outraged innocence, its hyperbole, its heroic assertiveness against the odds.

These Circassians represented themselves as fundamentally

> honest and peaceable . . . but we hate the Russians with good cause, and almost always beat them [despite the fact that] we have no artillery, generals, ships or riches. Russia tells the West that the Circassians are her slaves, or wild bandits and savages whom . . . no laws can restrain . . . [But] we most solemnly protest in the face of heaven against such womanish arts and falsehood . . .
>
> We are four millions [they declared], having unfortunately been divided into many tribes, languages and creeds . . . We have hitherto never had one purpose . . . But we are now at last united all as one man in hatred to Russia.[35]

Two years later, thanks to Urquhart's intervention a British schooner, the *Vixen*, belonging to George Bell & Son, slipped into a little port further down the coast. The idea was to connect the Circassians with the Danube and Turkish territory, which was their source of gunpowder and their market for slaves. But in 1837 a Russian gunboat, the *Ajax*, intercepted it and impounded it at Sevastopol. Urquhart evidently hoped that Palmerston, the British prime minister of the day, might use the incident as a *casus belli*, but Palmerston would not rise to the bait.

The Circassians fought on nevertheless. The howl of the jackal echoed more frequently across the valleys. This was the sinister war cry that heralded the descent of the Circassian warriors to ambush Russian soldiers. Urquhart and his friends J. A. Longworth and James Stanislaus Bell, a connection of the *Vixen's* owners, who had arrived in the western Caucasus in 1836, persisted in their efforts. Both were to publish accounts of their experiences in Circassia.[36] The Turks, too, sent in their agents and preachers, and presented the insurgents with a handsome banner (twelve stars surmounting three crossed arrows on a blue ground), representing them as 'sheriffs' of an Ottoman province (*sanjak*). Bell and Longworth ran guns in, and encouraged the Circassians to translate their claim to national independence into a formal bid for sovereignty.

A moment propitious for the enterprise soon offered itself. In the same year Circassian chiefs warned the Russian command that they would make trouble if the Russians proceeded with their plan to build a new fortified line across their territory. The warning was disregarded, and in the fol-

Saints Boris and Gleb: their martyrdom in 1015 was used to legitimate the Grand Princes of Kiev. Fourteenth-century icon of the Suzdal School

Emperor Constantine VII receives Princess Olga at his palace during her visit to Constantinople, *c.* 955–7. Reconstruction of a fresco in Kiev's St Sophia Cathedral

Model of the St Sophia Cathedral, Kiev, as it would have looked in the eleventh century

The construction of Moscow's Kremlin (1491): miniature from the Shumilov Chronicle. Litsevo Manuscript Codex

Left: Portrait of Ivan III. Sixteenth-century woodcut by Hirschvogel

Below: Russian cavalryman of the sixteenth century. Woodcut by Hirschvogel

ight: Punishments for
:calcitrant natives. From
ıe Remezov Chronicle
Mirovich version)

:low: Reindeer-power in
khotsk. After a drawing
W. Alexander in
. Sauer, *An Account*
a Geographical and
tronomical Expedition
the Northern Parts of
ıssia (London, 1802)

A ceremonial show of force to greet the submission of an important chief.
From a drawing by Juan van Halen in his *Memoirs* (London, 1830)

Tiflis, one of the Romanov Empire's multicultural cities.
Lithograph from the Chevalier Gamba's *Voyage dans la Russie Meridionale* (Paris, 1826)

The Darial Pass: Russia's gateway to Georgia and the Near East. From an 1837 drawing by Captain R. Wilbraham, in his *Travels in the Transcaucasian Provinces of Russia* (London, 1839)

A Tatar encampment. Soft-ground etching from John Atkinson and James Walker, *A Picturesque Representation of the Manners, Customs and Amusements of the Russian[s]* (London, 1803)

Yakut shaman treating a patient. Engraving from G. Sarychev's *Account of a Voyage of iscovery to the North-East of Siberia* (London, 1806)

lmyks. From E. Ysbrants Ides, *Three Years Travels from Moscow Over-land to China* ondon, 1706)

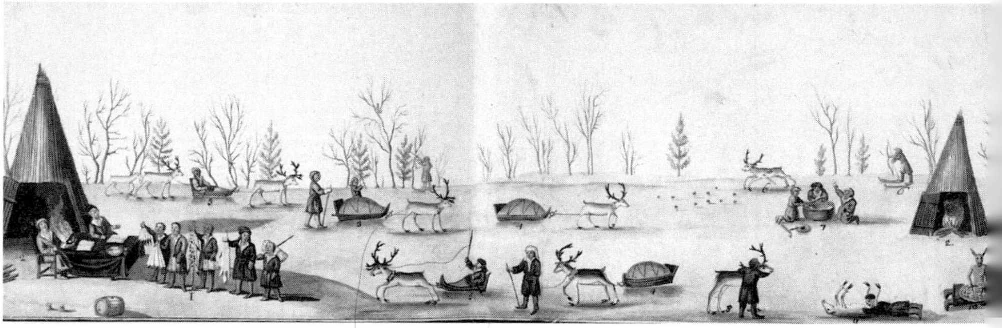

Woodcut showing a Lapp shaman's view of the world

Access to Japan, Alaska and the Pacific: SS *Peter and Paul*, Kamchatka, in the late 1770s
Engraved drawing by John Webber, RA, artist with Captain Cook on his last voyage

Russian embassy approaches the Great Wall of China, 1693. From E. Ysbrants Ides, *ree Years Travels from Moscow Over-land to China* (London, 1706)

shkirs. Soft-ground etching from John Atkinson and James Walker, *A Picturesque presentation of the Manners, Customs and Amusements of the Russians* (London, 1803)

An Estonian girl

An Ostiak ermine-hunter

A Chukchi in armour with his family

A Mordvinian woman

Engravings from W. Miller, *Costume of the Russian Empire* (London, 1803)

ırcassian princes arriving for a conference, 1836. Stone lithograph from E. Spencer, *avels in Circassia, Krim Tartary* (London, 1837)

ɔerial diplomacy: Persians paying Russian representatives an indemnity in bullion ler the terms of the Treaty of Turkmanchai, 1828. Engraving by K. Beggrov, after Moshkov

Barracks for Gulag prisoners cutting the White Sea–Baltic Canal, 1933. Photograph from W. Chamberlin, *Russia's Iron Age* (London, 1935)

Poster celebrating the completion of the Dnieper Dam (early 1930s). From W. Chamber *Russia's Iron Age* (London, 1935)

mpleting the furnaces for the Soviet Union's largest steel plant at Magnitogorsk
rly 1930s). Photograph from W. Chamberlin, *Russia's Iron Age* (London, 1935)

Not to be trifled with: President Putin in uniform brandishing a model of the *Molnia* spacecraft

lowing year more Russian troops were landed, more Circassian villages were laid waste. The building went ahead.

By this point a forty-year-old bushy-bearded imam called Shamyl had assumed the leadership of the Muridist movement. He was based in Dagestan, but he succeeded in uniting the opposition in the western as well as the eastern Caucasus. Chechens, Circassians and Dagestanis all joined forces. Shamyl's name soon reached the ears of the Tsar, who was on a tour of the Caucasus. He immediately invited Shamyl to meet him, but after some hesitation the invitation was refused and the imam's followers were soon offering more resistance to the Russians than ever before.

In 1842 a Russian task force of 10,000 men with 24 guns, closely supervised by the War Minister himself, was forced to retreat with a loss of nearly a fifth of its strength. An entire army corps had to be ordered down to the Caucasus to restore the position. Yet two years later a force of 20,000 men under M. S. Vorontsov, the new commander-in chief, Caucasus, was trapped in the mountains and lost 4,000 men and his war chest before he could be extricated.

These were significant losses for the military establishment of the northern Caucasus, which numbered about 80,000 men. And combat was not the only scourge. In the winter of 1841–2 fever took a toll of one man in six. But the unrecorded losses of the enemy were serious too. Several Caucasian communities which Shamyl had hoped would join him responded to his call without enthusiasm or not at all. Even the ardour of some of the Chechens had cooled. Again the demographic factor seems to have governed events. An ecological balance between the population and resources of the northern Caucasus had evidently been regained. Even so, it was only after the Crimean War that the Chechens were subdued. Shamyl was to be captured in 1859, and his movement was broken.[37]

Success had been bought at a high financial cost, however. 'Never was the state so oppressed with debt as it is at this day,' wrote a French engineer who spent five years in southern Russia. 'The war in the Caucasus, the grand military parades, and the payment of a countless host of diplomatic agents, avowed and secret, all absorb immense sums.' In 1841, the Finance Minister, Kankrin, had annoyed the Tsar by telling him the proposed military expenditures were unaffordable. Stamp duties were quadrupled and countless public works were halted in consequence.[38] The crisis was hardly to be wondered at given the size of the military establishment, and the costs were not to diminish. In 1848, when it was put on a war footing, the army could field no fewer than 368 infantry battalions, 460 cavalry squadrons and 996 guns in European Russia alone.

In this same area the Empire's population had risen from 36 million in 1800 to 60 million by 1850. This implied a huge increase of both taxpayers and young men liable for military service. This strong demographic growth helped to make the huge army more affordable. So did the immensity of the Empire's natural assets. By 1843 Siberia was producing twice as much gold as all other gold mines in the world, and the state was collecting over 20 tons of it a year for its own purposes. But, though the Empire survived the immediate financial alarms, the seemingly insatiable demands for military and naval expenditures was soon to lead to an effective devaluation of the ruble, which Kankrin had gone to great pains to stabilize.[39] This, however, was not the only cost.

The immensity of Russia's armaments now thoroughly alarmed other powers – Britain in particular. It could be argued that Russia needed these arms to defend at least half a dozen vulnerable points along its far-flung frontiers as well as the long Polish border. On the other hand they seemed a looming threat to Britain's vital interests in the Middle East, India and the Pacific. A growing imperial power makes enemies, and the enemies were already combining to halt Russia's progress.

Europe's 'Year of Revolutions', 1848, hardly touched the Empire. Not even Poland saw an insurrection. An attempt two years earlier had been scotched by the authorities simply by turning the serfs (many of them Ukrainian) against their hated Polish landlords. Nationalist ardour had remained cool ever since. But other powers were promoting it elsewhere. Partly in response to liberal opinion, partly to enlarge their markets, France and America as well as Britain were, albeit unofficially, encouraging national risings in the name of democracy. This tendency strengthened the anti-revolutionary stance not only of Russia, but of Prussia and Austria too. Together they had agreed, by the Convention of Berlin of 1833, to go to each other's aid if threatened by external or internal enemies. In 1849, in accordance with the convention and at the request of the Emperor of Austria, Russian troops marched west to help suppress insurgent Hungary. Their actions prompted cries of protest from French and British liberals, though no action by their governments. Nevertheless, relations grew increasingly strained.

It was not only Russia's southward advance at the expense of Turkey and Persia that gave rise to Western concern: its progress in central Asia and the Far East was also worrying. By 1847 a Russian base had been established on the Aral Sea, and army units were soon probing the frontiers of China beyond. Russia's trading connection with China had recently become more important than ever. The Opium Wars had cut off Britain's East India Company's supply of tea, and Russia was well placed to fill the gap in the market, its supplies coming by caravan through Kyakhta.

In 1851 a new Cossack Host, which included some Buriat and Tungus tribesmen as well as Russian peasants, was to be set up on the far side of Lake Baikal, demonstrating that Russia intended to extend its presence along the Chinese frontier, and two years later an expedition was sent nearly 500 miles up the river Syr-Darya, towards Tashkent. Other imperialist methods were manifested further east. As early as 1836 there were already over 30,000 colonists on Russian territory in North America;[40] in 1853 the island of Sakhalin was taken over by the Russia–America Company,[41] and a Russian squadron visited Japan. Russia's continuing advance on almost all fronts at last brought confrontation.

When it came, the prime target was the Russian port of Sevastopol, chief base for the Black Sea fleet. (By some irony, the fleet's commander a few years earlier had been Admiral Lazarev, who in his youth had served as a midshipman on Lord Nelson's flagship *Victory* at Trafalgar.) The British and the French were both well informed about Sevastopol. Travellers like H. D. Seymour provided good accounts of its defences. Nevertheless, it was no mean undertaking to attack it. Russia could now field nearly a million men, at a cost of 84.2 million silver rubles a year. Though half the size of the Baltic fleet, by 1854 the Black Sea fleet nonetheless boasted 16 first-rate warships fit for service, 7 frigates and 30 steam-boats. Its first-class armament and ordnance included incendiary shells delivered by the deadly Paixhans gun,[42] although the ships were mostly built of pine and fir rather than oak, and were vulnerable to the local woodworm.

Money had been lavished to make Sevastapol a fitting base for the southern fleet, observed another traveller, Laurence Oliphant, but he noticed a weakness: many of the 1,200 guns which guarded the approaches to the harbour had been poorly sited. He stressed another disadvantage for the Russians too: 'Notwithstanding the large numerical force which occupies the south of Russia, the greatest difficulty must attend the concentration of the army upon any one point, until railroads intersect the empire, and its water communication is improved.'[43] It remained to be seen if his prognostication would be borne out.

The occasion for war arose in 1853, when Russia insisted that Turkey revoke the right it had recently granted to the Catholic Church to protect the holy places in Jerusalem, and also recognize Russia as protector of the Orthodox population of the Ottoman Empire. The Turks, with French backing, rejected the demand, whereupon Russian troops marched south into the Romanian principalities. In response, British and French fleets sailed for the Black Sea in readiness for combat; the Turks declared war on Russia, and fighting began. The Russian Black Sea fleet destroyed the Turkish fleet at Sinope, but then the Western powers joined in – and on several fronts.

Operations in the Crimean War were not confined to the Crimea and the Black Sea. British and French ships made a brief foray into the Baltic; they destroyed the Arctic settlement of Kola, and attacked Petropavlovsk in faraway Kamchatka, where a landing party was repulsed by Russian guns and a bayonet charge. The Russian army was defeated on the river Alma in the Crimea by a superior force, and also lost the battle of Inkerman. In a diversionary move, British naval units and Circassian insurgents together took the little Black Sea naval station of Novorossiisk. The key port of Sevastopol, doggedly defended by General Totleben, held out, and then the main Russian land force, under General Paskevich, advanced to take the strategic Turkish citadel of Kars. However, in September 1855 Sevastopol and the fleet which sheltered there capitulated after very heavy fighting. Negotiations, which had hardly ceased throughout the period of hostilities, were concluded soon afterwards. But the decisive factor which led the Russian government to come to terms was an ultimatum from Austria.

For the first time in a century Russia had failed at arms, and it paid the price in the ensuing settlement. Its frontier was moved away from the Danube, and it was barred from the Black Sea, as were Turkish warships. Russia's advance in the west had been halted, its primacy as a European land power ended, and it sustained a grievous blow to its prestige. It paused to take stock.

In fact the war had been fought inefficiently by both sides. However, it was recognized in St Petersburg that the roots of the Empire's problem lay in an inadequate transportation system, underdeveloped industry, and an antiquated social system based on serfdom. Yet the realization that these problems must be addressed was not quite new. In 1842 Tsar Nicholas had 'decreed the construction of a railroad from St Petersburg to Moscow, to be built according to the example of other powers at the treasury's expense, for the general good'.[44] The state would keep control of it, but it was expected to be of great importance to industry and, generally, to stimulate activity. Only the financial deficit had delayed implementation.

Nicholas had also made it clear in a speech to the State Council the same year that he was contemplating radical change to the social system. He did not want to alarm the nobility, who were descended from the service class that had built the state, and who depended on their serfs, so he did not talk of emancipation. Nevertheless, he explained in a cautious, convoluted way that 'it is essential at least to prepare the way for a gradual transition to a different order . . . A way must be opened up to a transitional order combining emancipation with the inviolable preservation of hereditary land ownership.'[45]

In 1846 he had gone further. Serfs should not be emancipated, as they had been in the Baltic provinces at the beginning of the century, without land on which they could support themselves. The following year he told a delegation of nobles that serfs should not be considered as chattels. Fundamental changes were on the way. It remained to be seen whether they would come in time to save the Empire – or whether the disruption that reform would involve would undermine it.

11

Descent to Destruction

A FAMOUS NINETEENTH-CENTURY novel, less well-known in the West than in Russia, pictures a lethargic hero who is reluctant to confront the world, or, indeed, to leave his bed. Ivan Goncharov's Oblomov is a good-natured, well-to-do young gentleman full of excellent intentions. Only he cannot stir himself to take any necessary action – whether to save his fortune or to keep the girl who loves him. His friend, a German who embodies the dynamism that Oblomov lacks, tells him what he needs to do, encourages him, cajoles him; but in vain – Oblomov cannot find the will to transform intention into action. He dissipates his fortune, sinks slowly into penury, marries a peasant woman, and ends his days on a country smallholding surrounded by clucking chickens.

Oblomov[1] is, of course, a metaphor for Russia at a point of crisis, facing – or rather avoiding – the challenges of the modern world. Powerful forces of inertia encouraged Russia to go Oblomov's way. They were contested by the advocates of progress in government, and, on the whole, the new tsar, Alexander II (r. 1855–82), inclined towards progress. He was well educated, literate in French and German, dutiful and decent, and he disliked serfdom. Well informed about civil as well as military affairs, he had already served on bodies concerned with the problem of serfdom and with railway-building. He became tsar at the age of thirty-seven, at the moment of decision.

Defeat in the Crimean War gave the country the jolt it needed to shake off complacency and move the government to action. It was a reverse for Russian imperialism, of course, and delivered a heavy blow to Russia's prestige, but otherwise it was hardly a disaster. Few assets of much value were lost; the financial cost of war, though serious, was not serious enough to cause political disruption; and the deep structural faults in the economy and society, which underlay the glittering outward show of power, had at least been revealed and were to be quickly and conscientiously addressed.

The defeat did not even halt the Empire's expansion for long. The peace settlement blocked an advance to the south, but the Empire was making significant gains in Asia, edging its frontiers out towards India and Japan. It also contrived to enlarge its sphere of influence in the Balkans, and created a new one in Korea.

By the 1850s, senior figures in government had understood that serfdom was no longer compatible with Russia's status as a great power, and that if the Empire did not industrialize it would soon be overtaken by other powers. Serfdom trapped a major part of the population in the relatively unprofitable agricultural sector, threatening to starve emergent industries of labour. It supported a noble class which had ceased to be liable for service to the state a century earlier and had therefore lost its *raison d'être*. And, since it was deeply unpopular with the peasants, it nurtured a permanent threat of rural rebellion. Yet to free the serfs without land, as had been done in the Baltic provinces early in the century, would lead to massive impoverishment and further inflame peasant tempers, while to give them land without compensating the nobles would alienate a large part of the literate class, on which the state relied.

Reforming the system was not only politically dangerous; it required solutions to a tangle of problems, immense in scale and hair-raising in their administrative complexity. Millions of acres of land had to be surveyed, the quality of their soil assessed, woods and common lands assigned to village communes, and fields apportioned fairly between all the peasant households. The powers of the village commune, which operated collectively and was to be given responsibilities for the peasants that were formerly the lord's, also had to be defined. Organs of local government had to be set up, their membership – representative of both lords and peasants – laid down, and their responsibilities and mode of operation, which was to be largely democratic, specified. Local magistrates' courts with elected justices had to be set up too, their powers defined in relation to the existing regional judicial system, with separate provision made for native peoples, priests, the military and commercial cases. There were also the financial aspects. Money had to be found to compensate the erstwhile serf-owners, arrangements made eventually to recoup the cost from the peasant beneficiaries in the form of redemption payments, banks founded to lend money at reasonable rates to peasants . . . At every stage the process was plagued by political differences and bureaucratic infighting, yet, albeit imperfectly, the task was accomplished, the challenge answered.[2]

While this revolution was taking place in the countryside, modernization in the form of the railway was beginning to break down rural isolation, to enliven commerce and, with its increasing demand for coal and steel, to stimulate industry. The creation of a rail network had been mooted for some time, but the St Petersburg–Moscow line was the only important link that had been completed before the Crimean War demonstrated the military cost of an obsolescent communications system. The opponents of the railway at last gave way, and in 1857 the Tsar felt able to order action as soon as hostilities should cease. The construction of a rail network in European Russia was opened up to tender from private enterprise, and the Tsar himself attended the ministerial meeting that decided to let the contract. It was granted to a consortium of Russian and foreign capitalists. The consortium undertook 'to build at its own expense within ten years . . . [a] rail network extending some 2,500 miles, the government guaranteeing interest of five per cent on the construction costs'. The system would be run by the consortium for eighty-five years, after which it would become the property of the state.

The scheme succeeded in extending the railways from a total of 600 miles to 11,000 in less than twenty years, and to nearly 15,000 by 1882. By that time St Petersburg and Moscow had been connected with Warsaw and the Prussian frontier to the west, and with Nizhnii-Novgorod, New Russia and the Crimea to the south. The network had been expected to boost Russian grain exports, and it did so. Indeed, by 1914 southern Russia and Ukraine had become the grain basket of Europe. The new railways also facilitated a huge expansion of the textile industry, and encouraged the growth of banks, a big expansion in joint-stock-company flotations, and the introduction of new technology and organizational methods. But in 1871 Imperial Germany had come into existence, and it proceeded to forge further and further ahead of Russia in both industrial production and capacity. Another shot in the arm was needed if Russia were to stay in the race.

Since the Empire lacked sufficient capital, efforts were made to raise investment for further railway-building from local authorities, and to encourage foreign investment. But all these sources combined proved inadequate. The stimulus eventually had to come from the state.[3] Most continental powers had the same experience. On the other hand, demographic data promised strong future economic growth and even larger armed services. The Empire's population was teeming. Between 1850 and 1875 it grew by 25 per cent in Europe and by almost 45 per cent in Asia.[4] Commensurate territorial growth, through exploration, colonization and conquest, might have been expected. Indeed, it was already on the way.

In 1864 the Russian government informed other powers quite openly of its intention to expand. The minister for foreign affairs, A. M. Gorchakov, also provided a disarming explanation. Expansion was 'the fate of all states placed in a similar situation. The United States of America, France in Africa, Holland in its colonies, England in the East Indies were all driven to choose the path of onward movement, not so much out of ambition as of dire necessity. The greatest difficulty lies in being able to stop.' The problem stemmed from the fact that, once it had

> come into contact with half-savage nomadic tribes which lack firm social organization . . . the interests of border security and commerce demand that the more civilized state exercise a certain authority over its neighbours, whose . . . unruly ways make them very troublesome. It begins by curbing raids and pillaging, which . . . often requires the subjection of neighbouring tribes to some degree of control. But . . . once this has been done and they become more peacable, they in turn are exposed to attacks from tribes farther away . . . So the state has the choice of giving up this . . . effort and dooming its frontiers to constant unrest, making prosperity, safety and cultural progress impossible, or else of advancing ever farther into . . . the wild country.[5]

This was not quite the 'civilizing mission' justification for empire, but it made a valid point, exemplified repeatedly in Russia's past.

But by the 1860s educated Russians had caught the spirit of the time. Ideas of empire were reflected in plays and poetry and in animated conversations at soirées. Some Russians were concerned about the costs of territorial expansion, but for most such expansion was a source of pride, and they justified it in a variety of ways. For the poet Tiutchev the connections with Imperial Rome and the Eastern Orthodox Church were all-important. For him, Imperial Russia was

> The legitimate, direct descendant of the authority of the Caesars . . .
> [It] knows no historical equal.
> It represents two entities: the fate of an entire race, and the better, and
> Most sacred, half of the Christian Church.[6]

The historian of Asia Vasilii Grigorev, however, did invoke the idea of Russia's civilizing mission, especially in Asia:

> We are called on to protect these peoples from the destructive influence of Nature itself, hunger, cold and sickness . . . to put these people's lives in order, having taught these rude children of the forests and deserts to acknowledge the beneficent power of [civilizing] laws. We are called on to enlighten these peoples with religion and science.

And Russia had a specific mission because it was

> closer to Asia . . . [and had] preserved in itself more of the Asiatic element . . . If the science and civic life of Europe must speak to Asia through the mouth

> of one of its own people, then it will of course be us . . . Is it not obvious that Providence preserved the peoples of Asia as if intentionally from all foreign influences so that we would find them in an entirely undisturbed condition and therefore . . . more inclined to accept the gifts we bring?[7]

A third proponent of empire was at once more practical and more traditional. N. Ilminskii was an oriental-languages expert who taught at the Orthodox seminary at Kazan and then at Kazan University. An ideological crusader, he saw himself in the vanguard of Russia's cultural advance against Islam, and the objects of his particular attentions were the Tatars, Bashkirs, Kazakhs and Turkmens of the old frontier lands along the Volga. In 1863 he founded a school for baptized Tatars, intended to serve as a model for others. Tatar was the language of instruction; the school was equipped with appropriate dictionaries and grammars as well as school books, and the curriculum was infused with Christian content. A few years later he also established a teacher-training college for non-Russians. By 1904 it was attended by Korean as well as Tatar, Chuvash, Votiak and Cheremis teachers and priests, and even a Yakut. One of his students, N. Ostroumov, introduced Ilminskii's system into the Far Eastern and Central Asian provinces. It proved highly successful in insulating animists and new Christians against Islam, but had only limited impact in areas where the rival religion was already entrenched.

The government assumed that the indigenous peoples of the middle Volga and Urals were already integrated into the Empire. They were subject to military service on the same terms as Russians, and their nobility were co-opted into the imperial nobility. Reforms introduced around the turn of the century restricted the autonomy of some other native peoples, but imperial administrators treated the Buriats, for example, in the same way as Russian peasants, even though most still clung to Buddhism.[8] Russian imperialists made very limited progress in converting the peoples in their Central Asian possessions.

British officials in India became increasingly concerned as they observed Russia's advance into the continental heartland. In 1864 (on the initiative of a local commander) Russian forces entered Chimkent and occupied Turkestan, a useful producer of cotton. The next year they took Tashkent, and in 1868 Samarkand on the ancient silk road to China. Five years later the khanate of Khiva followed, and in 1876 Kokand. Most of these new acquisitions became Russian protectorates, like Bukhara, the Russians assuming responsibility for their foreign relations but otherwise leaving government in the hands of their respective khans. However, a rising staged against the Khan of unstable Kokand called for a full-scale intervention. An Uzbek tribe had recently appropriated the most fertile area, the Fergana valley, the Persian Tajiks were at daggers drawn with the inward-migrating Turkic Sarts; and the Sarts and Kipchaks tried to exterminate each other. These troubles had preceded Russian occupation. Most of the population came to accept Russian rule, but the Sufi Muslims of Fergana continued to give problems. In 1898 they mounted an armed attack on Russian barracks. Kokand had to be administered directly.[9]

In general, Russian colonial administration was closer to the French than to the British model, in that the territories were regarded as part of Russia. They were governed by a military hierarchy down to district level, although local courts, taxation, irrigation and other functions were usually delegated to elected officials. In this fashion Russian norms were adapted to local realities. The Muslim population lacked the rights prevalent in Russia proper, but were not subject to military service or Russian taxation. The problem in Central Asia, however, was not the regime as such but the administrators on the ground. Some Russian colonial governors, such as Muravev-Amurskii in the Far East, combined humanity with efficiency and were first-rate by any standard, but the dross of the service tended to be posted to Central Asia. Many officials in Turkestan in particular had been sent there as a punishment. They were overworked, and rarely bothered to learn the local language; and their low pay encouraged many to take bribes.[10]

The acquisition of Central Asia added a further million and a half subjects to the Empire's population, not counting another 3.5 million in the khanates of Khiva and Bukhara. Apart from the enlargement of its domestic market, Russia also acquired some commercial assets and strategic advantages. As Gorchakov had claimed, Russia was only rounding out its frontiers and ensuring their stability. Nevertheless, though Bukhara, north of the Amu-Darya, might be a Russian protectorate, Afghanistan to the south was a British one.[11] As yet there was no confrontation between the two powers, but it was to come before long.

Russian imperialism, which had always differed in the European provinces, took a new turn in the later nineteenth century, following the Polish insurrection of 1863. Trouble there had been expected for some time before it actually erupted, prompting the government to announce reforms that would have given the population more self-government. Most Poles seem to have been content with this, but extremists – hitherto a comparatively rare breed – were determined to scupper any reconciliation. They organized demonstrations to mark past rebellions, the death of an archbishop, and anniversaries of significant events in Polish history and of martyred Polish revolutionaries. The temperature rose. When the authorities reacted it rose even higher. The Tsar's brother Constantine, who served as his viceroy in Warsaw, was still inclined to conciliation, but an alliance was emerging between the radical nationalists and the Catholic Church that made a negotiated settlement virtually impossible. Attempts on the lives of the viceroy and his chief adviser, Marquis Bielopolski, were answered with executions. The moderates on both sides had lost out. Conscription was ordered to take young men, regarded as the most susceptible recruits to the nationalist cause, out of circulation, and this sparked an armed insurrection.

It turned out to be a messy business. The revolutionaries were disunited and poorly organized; the suppression was often severe. The attempted revolution degenerated into a sporadic guerrilla war. Most Polish nobles, though sympathetic to the rebels, stayed aloof from the action. Both sides used terror tactics, and the Polish peasants sometimes reacted violently against both sides. Britain, France and Austria demanded that Russia make concessions to the Poles, but the chance of that disappeared with the departure of Grand Duke Constantine. Eighteen months passed before order was fully restored.[12] St Petersburg then changed its strategy in Poland. It had switched its favour from the Polish nobility to the Polish peasants by going ahead with a land reform even before the rebellion had been fully suppressed. In this way the elite were punished for their lack of loyalty and the peasants were rewarded for their 'good sense' in resisting the lures of the rebels and 'standing fast under all manner of threats and violence'.[13] It also began a policy of Russification in its Polish provinces. Russian, not Polish, was to be the language of the courts and the chief language of instruction in schools. Since the vast majority of Polish peasants were illiterate, a race ensued for their hearts and minds between the state-controlled schools, which encouraged loyalty to the Empire, and the informal Church schools, where increasingly nationalist priests taught Polish and preached the idea of Polish independence.

Victory eventually went to the priests and the Church schools, but it was a close-run contest and the outcome was in doubt until the turn of the century. Russia had been slow to appreciate the possibilities of education as a force capable of winning the young and thereby promoting imperial integration.[14] Partly because of this, but partly also because Russia lacked the resources to implement it sooner, Russification eventually turned out to be counter-productive. On the other hand, in Poland as elsewhere, the disunity of the opposition allowed the occupying power to 'divide and rule' in the great imperial tradition.

St Petersburg soon had to cope with a rising tide of nationalism in its other provinces too. In Estonia and in the Latvian-speaking hinterland of Riga, where in the late eighteenth century modern nationalism had been 'discovered' by Gottfried von Herder, the German elite had been co-opted by the government and it took some time before the peasants were to become aware of their distinct linguistic and cultural identity. It took even longer for them to realize that it might entitle them to claim political rights and even autonomy. In rural Lithuania, where the elite were Polish and the city population largely Jewish, the case was somewhat different. So it was in Finland, where nationalism took root in reaction against the dominant Swedes, not the Russians. A semi-autonomous grand duchy, Finland had its own parliament, which in 1863 decided that Finnish should be used as the language of public business within twenty years. The growth of elementary education in the 1870s ensured the triumph of the Finnish language and, eventually, of Finnish nationalism, but for the moment the Finns were loyal, and, to signal his appreciation, in 1863 the Tsar personally opened the Diet at Helsingfors (Helsinki).

Meanwhile the use of Romanian in schools and churches was being restricted in Bessarabia; integrationist policies were reinforced in the Crimea and in Transcaucasia, while in Ukraine what remained of independent institutions disappeared and Russian became the sole language of administration. From the 1880s measures were also taken to stifle any cultural assertion by Armenians, and particularly oppressive language policies – including a ban on printing in the vernacular – were introduced into Georgia, and succeeded in damping down the nationalist movement. But Russification policies were doomed to failure in many areas not only because the multifarious peoples of the Empire varied so much in cultural level, but because the state had been so slow to introduce universal education. In particular, the peasants were overlooked until too late, and they were eventually to embrace the rising creed of nationalism most strongly. Nevertheless, Russification was not entirely without success. Nikolai Gogol, though Ukrainian, wrote in Russian and always saw himself as Russian. So did the historian George Vernadsky a century later. Many Tatars and members of other minorities preferred Russian to their own vernacular because Russian was associated with a stronger culture, and because it gave access to greater opportunities.

But outside the government there were Russians who tried to exploit language issues to promote imperial expansion though pan-Slavism, an idea which used the common origin of the Slavonic languages as a basis for constructing a movement that advocated the common interests of the Slavonic-speaking peoples. The original pan-Slavists were not Russians but Czechs, Slovenes, Serbs and others in the German-dominated Austrian Empire who had gathered in Prague in 1848 to assert their rights against the dominance of German. The movement, though influential culturally, was based on a romantic idea, and too impractical to have much political effect. However, Russian nationalists – particularly proponents of Orthodox unity – took up the idea and shaped it into an instrument of Russian imperialism.

The regime itself did not favour pan-Slavism, although in 1858 the Tsar endorsed the setting up of a Slavonic Benevolent Committee, whose purpose was to promote the Orthodox religion, education and national development among the south Slavs. In 1867 this body organized an ethnographic exhibition in Moscow to stimulate interest in the idea, but it raised more concern about Russian expansionism abroad than it drew interest from the Russian public.[15] Of more account was a poem called *The Eagle*, written as early as 1835 by A. S. Khomiakov, a former cavalry officer and religious enthusiast who believed that God had chosen Orthodox Russia to serve as his instrument. The eagle, of course, represented Imperial Russia, and the other, emerging, Slavonic nationalities were represented as eaglets in need of the older bird's protection.

You have built your nest high,
O eagle of the North.
You have spread your wings wide
To fly deep into the sky.
Fly on . . .
. . . but do not forget
Your younger brothers!

There are many of them there,
There, where the Danube rages,
Where clouds gather round the Alps,
In the creviced cliffs of the dark Carpathians,
In the dales and forests of the Balkans . . .
Your enslaved brothers await your call.

When will your wings spread out
To protect their vulnerable heads?
Remember them, O eagle of the North.
Let them hear your piercing screech in greeting.
It will comfort them in the darkness of their slavery.
Show them your bright light of freedom . . .

Their time will come. Their wings will stiffen,
Their young talons spread.
The eaglets will cry out – and your iron beak will shatter
The cruel chains which holds them captive.[16]

The poem may not have gained wide popularity immediately, but it was to be read, declaimed and savoured by the literate classes over the years. The message certainly reached the officials and army officers who made and implemented policy. And it gained particular resonance in 1875, when a crisis flared up in the Balkans.

The chain of events that was to lead to war began in the hard land of Hercegovina. The harvest had been particularly bad, and the peasants rose against Turkish tax-collectors and landowners. The rebellion spread to Bosnia, and received support from independent Serbia and the tiny principality of Montenegro. The rebels also had Russian sympathy. In this way a peasant revolt developed into a war between Orthodox states and Ottoman Turkey. The Russian consul-general in Dubrovnik had done nothing to foment the insurgency, but he was a keen pan-Slavist, and did his best to help the rebels by channelling money to them once it started. Since he was also Russia's agent in Cetinje, Montenegro's capital, he was well placed to do so, and he was aided by a deputy and two Russian colonels, one representing the Slavonic Benevolent Committee, the other from the Ministry for War.[17] The insurgency spread further.

Then articles appeared in St Petersburg and Moscow journals proclaiming a modern crusade. Excited intellectuals explained why Russians had a duty to liberate the poor Balkan Slavs from material want and spiritual oppression, and the public was stirred to action. Money and consignments of humanitarian aid were soon on their way to Serbia and to Bulgarians in the Ottoman Empire, as well as to Bosnia and Montenegro. Though the authorities kept quiet about it, arms and volunteers – some released from the army for the purpose – went too. In the spring of 1876 a rebellion duly broke out in Bulgaria. It was suppressed, occasioning protests in Russia and in England, where W. E. Gladstone fulminated about Turkish atrocities – although atrocities had been perpetrated by both sides. Then Russia joined in to help the beleaguered Serbs, making common cause with Austria for the last time, and in the spring of 1877 a Russian army marched south to the Danube. It was joined by troops from Romania (which, though not Slav, was Orthodox). The key Turkish fortifications at

Pleven were eventually taken after heavy fighting. The Turks organized anti-Russian uprisings in the Caucasus and landed troops there, but early in the following January Russian forces took Sofia and Plovdiv and, in conjunction with Austrian forces, seized the Shipka Pass. Edirne fell without resistance. The road to Constantinople was open – and by 31 January 1878 an armistice brought the fighting to an end.

By the Treaty of San Stefano, signed in March 1878, a new state, Bulgaria, which included most of Macedonia, came into existence. Russia, to which it owed its existence, had made another friend and gained another client, to join Romania, Serbia and Greece. But the Powers, especially Britain, thought the new Bulgaria too large, as was Russia's power in the Balkans. Bismarck agreed to host an international congress in Berlin, at which, by agreement, Bulgaria was much reduced, the rest being returned to the Turks, although eastern Rumelia was to have some autonomy under a Christian governor. This reduced Russia's sphere of influence in the Balkans, but in return it was allowed to add Kars and Batum to its empire in the Caucasus. Russian statesmen were satisfied, though popular opinion, by now committed to pan-Slavism, was outraged.

The shame of defeat in the Crimean War had been exorcised; but Russia was no longer the predominant power in Europe. That place now belonged to Germany, conqueror of Austria and France. In the wake of the Congress of Berlin, Austria allied itself with Germany. So did Romania, and eventually even Serbia and Bulgaria. Thwarted in the Balkans, Russia turned its attentions back towards Asia.

The spotlight fell first on Central Asia, and on railway-building. The first Russian railway boom had petered out, but in 1879 army engineers started work on a strategic line from Krasnovodsk on the eastern coast of the Caspian Sea, opposite Baku, along the Persian frontier, and into Central Asia. By 1886 it had gone through Ashkhabad to reach the oasis of Merv. Two years later it had been extended to Bukhara and Samarkand. From Tashkent the line diverged, one branch going north, the other to Kokand and Andijan in the shadow of the Tien Shan mountains. It brought rail transportation within range of the Irkeshtan Pass and, beyond it, Kashgar in Chinese Xinjiang. In 1885 Russian troops defeated Afghan forces at Pendjeh on the Afghan border. Russia was established on the road to Kabul and the Khyber Pass. Within ten years its forces were confronting the British in the Pamirs. This prompted Anglo-Russian negotiations which resulted in the demarcation of spheres of influence. By 1898 the Russians had pushed a branch line from the Trans-Siberian Railway up to Kushk on the Afghan frontier.[18]

But the simultaneous extension of Russia's influence into Persia was hardly less impressive. In 1879 the Shah asked Russia to organize a Persian Cossack brigade and send in officers and NCOs. They were to provide the only disciplined troops in the country, and were to be used early in the twentieth century to suppress the Shah's own obstreperous Majlis. By that time Britain had agreed that Russia should exercise a dominant influence in northern Persia, and have a commercial outlet on the Persian Gulf, where Russian warships were soon to appear.[19]

Meanwhile on the western side of the Caspian a railway was constructed to connect Baku with the new possession of Batum and with Tiflis. The network locked newly acquired territories into the Empire, and enabled forces to be quickly switched between the Caucasus, Central Asia and the imperial heartlands. Only communications across Siberia remained as slow as ever. It was obvious that if Russia was to have a successful future as a Pacific power this needed to be rectified. The American Civil War had demonstrated that success in war was now a product of barbed wire, steam power and mass production as much as of the dash of cavalrymen and the endurance of foot soldiers. Efficient transport for mass armies, vastly expanded output of iron, coal and steel, and the production of the tools of war were now prerequisites for any great power. In 1891 the Russian government took a decisive step towards meeting these demands by starting construction on a railway to the Pacific.

For a vast developing country with little native capital, the decision to build by far the longest railway in the world over its most difficult terrain was certainly ambitious. But, though the trans-Siberian project was risky, its completion promised alluring rewards. Linking Moscow with the Pacific would enable the Empire to build up its power on the Pacific and on the frontiers with China and Korea. The massive orders it would generate for rails and engines would stimulate industry. And, together with the construction of new lines linking the industrial regions with each other and with the ports, it would provide an even bigger stimulus to the economy as a whole than the first railway boom had done. On the other hand the cost of borrowing the necessary capital would impose an immense burden of debt which would take many years to pay off; the projected maintenance costs were also alarming, and the technical difficulties in, for example, cutting over thirty tunnels to find a way round Lake Baikal and establishing a stable bed for rails over deserts and morasses would pose formidable problems for the engineers. Moreover, 1891 was a famine year in Russia, so the project had to be justified in social terms.

The project's mastermind, Sergei Vitte, had headed the railway department of the Ministry of Finance since 1889. His background was in state railway administration in southern Russia, but he had also worked in the private sector. He knew that, since the Empire could not generate sufficient capital, this had to come from the West – chiefly from France, Germany, Belgium and Britain. He also knew that the costs of servicing the loans and borrowings would constitute a serious burden on the budget, but that the price had to be paid. He was soon presented with the responsibility for finding the means of paying it: in 1892 he was promoted, in quick succession, to be minister of communications and then minister of finance.

Aside from its military and economic potential, the great project would help to answer looming social problems, permitting the rapid transportation of food to famine areas, argued Vitte. Once bureaucratic reluctance to encourage large-scale settlement in Siberia had been overcome, it would also help to relieve the rising rural-population pressure in European Russia. Vitte's promotion of Russian industry was also to absorb some of this excess rural population. Even so, the capitalist-minded Vitte himself remained conscious of the Empire's fundamental problem. In a secret memorandum to the Tsar dated March 1899, he was to compare

> Russia's economic relationship to western Europe . . . [with] that of colonies to their mother countries. The latter see their colonies as convenient markets from which they can sell their . . . industrial products advantageously and from which they can extract the raw materials they need . . . To a large extent Russia . . . is such a . . . colony for the industrially-developed states. It provides them with the products . . . at low prices, and buys . . . their products at high ones.

There was one saving grace: Russia was a powerful independent state able to break out from dependency and create 'a fully independent national industry'.[20] The Trans-Siberian Railway project was the first major step towards this goal, and, overall, the achievements were brilliant.

Within ten years the extent of the Empire's rail network grew by over 73 per cent, from little over 19,000 in 1890 to over 33,000 miles in 1900. By 1904 the lines extended over 38,000 miles. Thanks to the demand the project generated, pig-iron output rose three times over in the 1890s; steel production expanded tenfold.[21] There were huge expansions in coal-mining, especially in southern Russia and Ukraine, and of iron in western Siberia, though textiles remained the Empire's biggest industry of all. And, thanks to Vitte, the Empire's finances remained stable throughout this period of disruptive change. Only, as he realized, a spirit of enterprise as well as capital and technical expertise were needed. Until they were found, Russia would still be in a position of dependence on more developed powers. Meanwhile, Vitte aimed to exploit the railway to promote further imperial expansion.

Three new provinces – Transbaikalia, the Amur and the Maritime Province – were created to organize these distant possessions. Further expansion in North America and the acquisition of California had been mooted in the 1820s and again in the 1830s, but Nicholas I had rejected the idea. The matter had been raised yet again in the 1850s. However, Count Muravev, governor of the furthest territories, who had himself annexed the lower Amur, understood that geography imposed limits to the growth of empires. Railway development reinforced him in the view. The wise men of St Petersburg concurred, and decided to limit the Empire to Europe and Asia. The strategic island of Sakhalin was occupied, but in 1867 Alaska, which had been acquired almost by default as a natural continuation of the exploration policy launched in the eighteenth century, was sold to the United States.[22] It was, after all, half a world away from St Petersburg, and boasted few obvious assets, yet funds had to be found for its administration and defence. It was a burden better disposed of.

Nevertheless, Vitte was minded to expand further into Asia, not only through territorial acquisition and direct rule, but, as great powers like Britain and America were now doing, through economic concessions and dominating influence. As he recalled in his memoirs, by May 1896, when royalty and statesmen gathered in St Petersburg for the coronation of Nicholas II,

> Our great Trans-Siberian railway had almost reached Trans-Baikalia, and it became imperative to decide what route it should follow beyond that. It was quite natural that I should think of continuing it straight to Vladivostock, cutting through Mongolia and northern Manchuria [for] this would speed up its construction considerably. In this way the Trans-Siberian would become . . . an artery of world-wide importance, connecting Japan and the . . . Far East with Russia and Europe.[23]

Vitte immediately sought out China's chief minister, and struck a deal. Vladivostok duly became the terminus of the Trans-Siberian, and Manchuria opened up to Russian development. The price involved a commitment to defend China against attack from Japan.

Thanks to Vitte, Russia was also able to penetrate China economically, masterminding the foundation of the Russo-China Bank and negotiating controlling rights over the construction and running of the East China Railway. Military planning went hand in hand with economic penetration and diplomacy, and the military build-up in Transbaikalia and the Maritime Province on the Pacific played a part in China's agreement two years later to cede the warm-water port of Lüshun (Port Arthur) on the peninsula dividing the Bay of Korea from the Gulf of Liautong to Russia for twenty-five years, and grant a concession to build a railway through southern Manchuria, which the Japanese had wanted to do. The achievement was the culmination of adroit Russian diplomacy over many months.

The encounters between Russians and Chinese which became much more frequent as a result were unusual in the history of imperialism. The Russian soldiers may have been under instruction not to antagonize the Chinese they encountered, and punishment for mistreating them was draconian (a soldier convicted twice for stealing was hanged). Even so, a visiting Englishman was astounded to find that 'the Russians have no racial antipathy for the yellow race . . . The Russian soldiers and the Chinese fraternise as people belonging to the same race and the same class, and not only the soldiers but the officers treat the Chinese lower classes, and let themselves be treated, with great and good-natured familiarity.'[24] These soldiers presented a face of Russian imperialism that contrasted with the Cossack Khabarov's bloody excursions through Dauria centuries earlier, and with the behaviour of Russian merchants in the region. China, of course, was a friendly power, but similarly humane and easygoing manners were to characterize Russians' treatment of the Japanese, who were soon to be enemies.

Russia had prevailed on the Japanese to share some of their influence in Korea, but the two Powers were already on a collision course. Britain's nose, too, was put out of joint. The prospect of Russia gaining a predominant influence in Manchuria as well as in Korea was not widely popular.[25] Only Germany encouraged Russia to satisfy its expansionist ambitions in the Orient rather than looking to the West, which would impede Germany's own imperialist ambitions. As for the United States, Russia's sale of Alaska to it in 1867 had sweetened their relations, although they were to cool somewhat after the Mexican War of 1898, the American acquisition of the Philippines, and the extension of US economic influence in the Pacific.[26] But while the Great Powers manoeuvred on the world stage, their domestic problems began to loom larger – and nowhere more so than in Russia.

By emancipating the peasants in the 1860s the government unwittingly contributed to an even greater problem: a population explosion. Between

1850 and 1900 the population of the Russian Empire is calculated to have almost doubled, rising from 70 to 133 million. For an underpopulated country this would not have constituted a problem, but, although much of the Empire was underpopulated, European Russia was not, and there the population grew from 60 to 100 million in the same period.

The problem had not been foreseen, and the reasons for it are still the subject of discussion among scholars. A better diet, leading to improved female fecundity, was one factor; a lower death rate from diseases of malnutrition was another. Earlier marriages and fewer wars and epidemics in the later nineteenth century also counted. So did less onerous terms of compulsory military service after 1874, and improving public health provision. But the emancipation of the serfs also contributed – not simply by engendering excessive optimism among the peasantry, but by abolishing their labour-service obligations to landowners. This reduced both the incentive for peasants to treat their sons as labourers and their resistance to their marrying and setting up on their own earlier in life.[27]

Earlier marriages, the earlier division of household property, and entitlement to shares in the communal land led to a problem of which Malthus had warned: that the population could outgrow its land resources and hence its capacity to feed itself. The government could implement plans for famine relief, as it did in 1891. It also began to encourage peasants to migrate to Siberia, and booming industry created a healthy demand for labour which led to a rising tide of migration from countryside to city. But the structures of village life were such as to precipitate a crisis beyond the power of such measures to prevent.

By the turn of the century, with village lands having to be shared between an ever increasing number of households, the average size of family farms was shrinking and increasing numbers of them became marginal. Even the Cossack communities, a privileged part of the population, were affected. Between 1861 and 1914 the Don Cossack population increased by 80 per cent, while changes in conditions of service introduced in 1875 had quadrupled the costs of service. As a result, by the turn of the century one Don Cossack out of every four called to the colours had to be excused on account of family poverty.[28] In many parts of European Russia the countryside began to grow restive again. At the same time, rural conditions were driving more and more young people to the cities, creating social problems there.

The government was careful to monitor conditions in the spawning mills and factories, and recognized that it had a duty of social care to the employees. Legislation to protect workers was no worse than in most other industrializing countries and better than in many. Nevertheless, as everywhere else at this stage of an industrial revolution, conditions in the slums of Moscow and in the working-class suburbs of St Petersburg and many other cities deteriorated. Most of the inward migrants, women as well as men, were young people uprooted from quiet rural Russia, Poland and Ukraine, where the pace of life was sloth-like, and plunged into a disturbingly noisy, crowded, stressful scene. The consequence was a sharp rise in the political temperature of urban Russia.

The big factories of Russia's late industrial revolution facilitated unionization, while the crowded tenements became hothouses for strong and simple political ideas. In this environment Marxism soon gained appeal. Its ideas – purveyed by educated, idealistic, sometimes resentful young people – came to be interpreted at pie stalls and factory gates, and were debated enthusiastically in bookshops. In the process of transfer to a poorly educated following, Marx's ideas were sometimes oversimplified and often misunderstood, but the vocabulary of Marxism conjured up believable icons of oppressed workers and an exploitative, unproductive bourgeoisie, together with the promise of an inevitable 'crisis of capitalism' and the ultimate triumph of communism. Marxist iconography presented a congruent parallel to Christian iconography, and, since the Church failed to keep effectively in touch with them, many of the young immigrants to the cities took to the new ideology as to a religious belief. Organization, whether in unions or movements, also offered a sense of purpose and comradeship, while the conspiratorial nature of the enterprise lent a sense of adventure. The only problem was the intellectuals' tendency to differ in their analyses of conditions and their interpretations of the awesome literature. Divergencies and splits became common, and the drift to violence quickened.

However, the bomb-throwings and assassinations which became almost commonplace in the Empire around the turn of the century were not born of the peasant problem, nor of industrialization. They stemmed from a fundamentally middle-class intellectual tradition and from a pervasive, though far from universal, sense of guilt about the peasantry. The terrorism also reflected a romantic compulsion to act, and frustration with an exclusionary and seemingly unresponsive autocratic governmental system. In this context, to shoot a functionary or throw a bomb at the Emperor seemed to some a constructive thing to do. In 1881 Sofia Perovskaia arranged to blow up the Tsar Alexander as he passed by one of the lovelier St Petersburg canals.

The attempt succeeded – and did nothing to change the system in the direction that Perovskaia desired. On the contrary, it killed the 'Tsar-

Liberator' at the point when he was considering the introduction of democracy, and prompted increased security precautions and police activity. It may have given the perpetrators a sense of achievement, but it did nothing to destabilize the regime. Terrorism was irrelevant. Marxism, however, helped the regime by offering malcontents an alternative to nationalism, giving the government another means by which to divide and rule.

Vitte had been concerned about Russians' peasantish understanding of property and economics in an age when banking and commerce were becoming a vital adjunct to empire-building. Some attempt was made to address this problem by the founding of commercial schools which increased from eight in 1896 to sixty-eight in 1904.[29] Russia's particular strength in this period was the calibre, though not the number, of its emerging professionals, whether soldiers, engineers, bankers, doctors or soldiers. Able, and often innovative, many of them gained responsible posts while still young and their work reflected mental vigour as well as youth. Some had received their training in the technical schools that Kankrin had founded earlier in the century, and Vitte saw to it that some, at least, of the financial skills required were furnished in commercial schools, though many professionals, especially the engineers, were army-trained. Indeed, the army was to be regularly called upon to repair the technological deficiencies of civil society.

Many of the railway engineers were army men. So were the creators of another, commonly overlooked, achievement of the period: the drainage of wetlands. A special project had been set up in 1873 to reclaim swamps in European Russia and Belarus. Serving as a model for other such projects, it was headed by an army engineer and funded chiefly by the state. By 1900 it had cut nearly 3,000 miles of drainage canals, built 550 bridges, and sharply reduced the incidence of anthrax and other vile diseases damaging to animals as well as humankind.[30] Meanwhile canal-building for communications had gained a significance almost comparable to that of railways. A canal-cutting project to join tributaries of the rivers Ob and Yenisei in Siberia, begun in 1882 and completed ten years later, created over 3,000 miles of navigable waterway connecting Tiumen with Irkutsk.[31]

Technological changes also inspired innovations in the army, particularly in the structure and operations of its general staff. Whatever his qualities as a commander in the field, Nikolai Obruchev was a hero as an administrator and, in effect, the formulator of imperial strategy from 1865 until 1898. He and the able group of young colonels who worked under him drew up mobilization plans for wars on the many fronts that had to be defended. They collected intelligence, topographical and statistical data of many kinds, and engaged in some thorough social research to underpin decisions; they also maintained an up-to-date base of technological knowledge relevant to warfare, and promoted military education. It was not by chance that many of the most energetic and innovative of these 'action officers' were from the guards regiments. This was a reflection not so much of snobbery as of the fact that the guards had a system of accelerated promotion. This allowed Obruchev to recruit a number of able senior officers who were young, mentally energetic and open to ideas. Together they applied scientific methods and ways of thinking to military planning and training. They aimed at professionalizing the army staff, and to a large extent they succeeded. Such developments promoted the Empire's efficiency, but not all the efforts were sustained.

Obruchev's ability was to be measured by the consequences of his departure. This, according to a military historian, coincided with 'deepening strategic anarchy at the highest levels of the government'. War planning was disrupted by the repeated reorganization of the department; the operation lost direction, and became less dynamic, more complacent. Soon even the army's ability to convince the government of its financial needs faltered.[32] The consequences were to be seen in the impending war with Japan. And misdirection of the army staff was only one ground for concern. The vigour of the young commanders (civil as well as military) and all the inventiveness of the technical intelligentsia were outweighed by the underproductive, restive rural population. The proportion of peasants to total population actually increased in the late nineteenth century.[33] This fundamental problem, and the regime's inability to cope with it, effectively helped to drive Russia towards the disaster of 1905.

There is a monument on the banks of the Neva in St Petersburg on which sailors' brides throw their bouquets on the evening of their wedding day. It commemorates those lost at the disastrous battle of Tsushima. Beset by a rising tide of domestic unrest, some government ministers had sought war as a diversion; and the Tsar, with his ill-advised sponsorship of dubious speculators active in the Far East, had helped provide the occasion for it. The Japanese had sounder reasons for engagement: to recover from the effects of Vitte's démarche in having outwitted them to gain influence over China and Manchuria and a voice in Korea. Soon after Russia went to war with Japan in 1904, its hopes vanished. Port Arthur surrendered after a long siege in January 1905; the army was forced to abandon Mukden, and when the great Baltic fleet which had sailed majestically round Europe, Africa and Asia finally gave battle in May 1905 it lost a dozen battleships along with most of its smaller warships. But an even worse disaster had occurred in St Petersburg in January.

Troops had fired on a large but peaceful demonstration of workers passing the Winter Palace, killing over a hundred of them. Members of all classes throughout the Empire raised a chorus of protest. They also made a variety of demands. The working class called vociferously for better pay and conditions, the educated classes cried out for representative government, while Poles, Finns and others demanded national independence. Crowds clogged the streets of major cities; strikes became frequent and widespread; there was a mutiny in the Black Sea fleet; high-ranking officials were assassinated. Then the peasants rose. The disorders, especially in the countryside, were to take many months to suppress, but suppressed they were.

The departure for the front of so many military units that were normally available near the biggest population centres had encouraged the insurgents, and when the Tsar recalled Vitte and, with American help, peace was arranged with Japan, the tide soon turned. Soldiers dislike crowd-control and suppression duties, but these operations were on the whole well-managed, and casualties were comparatively few. A total of 2,691 people died as a result of terrorism; 2,390 people were executed for terrorist acts.[34] Meanwhile the Tsar's promise of democratic elections to a parliament or Duma served further to quieten the middle-class opposition.

In terms of the territorial extent of the Empire, the peace with Japan cost Russia relatively little: the Lüshun Peninsula, half of Sakhalin, and recognition that Japanese interests should predominate in Korea. However, Russia retained the East China Railway and its dominant position in northern Manchuria. Vitte had deftly extricated the Empire from what had promised to be a much greater disaster. Furthermore, as sometimes happens in the complex affairs of great empires, inertia decreed that there would be some successes even in the wake of cataclysmic defeat. The Orenburg–Tashkent line started after the turn of the century was finished in 1906; the Tiflis–Julfa railway opened for traffic the following year.[35] And in 1907 Britain was persuaded to concede the division of Persia into Russian and British spheres of influence.

To the west, the threat of Germany and Austria was countered by Russia's alliance with France and Britain, while at home attempts were made not only to accommodate the regime to democracy, but to solve the peasant problem. This task fell to an experienced provincial governor, Petr

Stolypin, and the solution which he applied was radical. His strategy was to turn the more substantial peasants into private farmers, break up the peasant commune, and force those who could not survive to sell their plots and move either on to the labour market (which was short of manpower) or to underpopulated Siberia. Between 1906 and 1914 2 million people did so.[36] The destruction of a traditional way of life invariably involves cruelty, but there seemed to be no workable alternative. Stolypin claimed that, given twenty years of peace, his reforms would transform Russia, creating a solid, prosperous farmer class which would benefit the economy and stabilize politics. But while attending a performance in Kiev's handsome cream, red and gilded opera house in 1911 he was killed by an assassin's bullet. His reforms might have succeeded but they were to be overtaken by the First World War only three years later.

Nor was the experiment with parliamentary democracy successful, though the fault did not lie entirely with the regime. Stolypin's offer to the majority liberal opposition of seats in a coalition government was rejected. As one liberal was himself to recall, the politicians saw in 'compromises and gradualism "a lowering of the flag". They wanted *everything*, and wanted it *immediately* . . . A "constitutional democracy" was certainly attainable, but it could not be realized at once . . . The intolerance of the doctrinaires . . . was sharpest in questions involving "theoretical . . . principles". A concession in *this* area was regarded as treason.'[37] The result was an unrealistic attitude to the monarchy. The democrats wanted to form the government, even though they had no experience in office, and in effect they forced the government to change the electoral process in the hope of getting a Duma with which it could work. But it proved impossible to reach an accommodation even with a slightly more tractable Duma. The problem was partly constitutional, partly the intransigence of the democratic leaders, but partly, too, the Tsar's.

Experienced statesmen had noticed a problem in Nicholas II some time before. In July 1901 A. Polovtsev, Chief Secretary of the State Council and a senator – a loyal official in a central position – noted in his diary that

> Things are done piecemeal . . . on momentary impulse, through the intrigues of one person or another, or through the importunities of various fortune seekers . . . The young Tsar is becoming increasingly contemptuous of the organs of his own authority and is beginning to believe in the beneficial effect of his own autocratic power. [Yet] he exercises it sporadically, without prior deliberation and without reference to the general course of affairs.[38]

The Tsar's ill-judged patronage of the adventurer Captain Bezobrazov and his Korean Timber Company had helped to lead Russia into confrontation with Japan;[39] his support for the dissolute hypnotist Grigorii Rasputin was to help discredit the monarchy itself. This is not to suggest that all members of the imperial family shared Nicholas's faults. Grand Duke Mikhail proved to be more open-minded and in touch, and it was thanks to Grand Duke Aleksei that an air ministry was formed and 77 aircraft were in service by 1913.[40] It is true that the problems of governing the Empire in Nicholas's reign were more complex than before, and the pressures greater. But it is also true that, partly because of deficiencies in his private chancery, Nicholas was out of touch with all but a very small stratum of his subjects and yet under the illusion that he understood them. Moreover, he was temperamentally unsuited to running the Empire, unwilling to delegate authority to those who were, and often unwilling to take their advice. Although fundamentally decent and well-meaning, he was a poor judge of men, and intellectually limited. Uxorious to a fault, he was much influenced by a wife whose judgement was even worse than his. He obstinately played the part of autocrat, but erratically, and he evidently failed to understand many of the issues on which he took decisions. 'A fish', it is said, 'begins to rot from the head,' and the proverb applies to Imperial Russia.

Some of the consequences had already been noted. They had been seen in the war with Japan, when, although the armed services performed with their usual steadiness and courage, command had been poorly co-ordinated and the logistics inadequate. They had been seen in 1905, when, due to confusion or misjudgement, troops fired on peaceful demonstrators passing near the Winter Palace, precipitating a revolution. They were seen in a series of questionable appointments and decisions; and when Russia went to war in 1914 they were seen in ever sharper form. The decision to go to war may have been virtually impossible to avoid, but clear warning of the consequences had been given.

Six months before the war began, Petr Durnovo, a member of the State Council and a former police chief and minister of the interior, wrote a long memorandum to the Tsar. It reflected a thorough grasp of the relevant facts, and the analysis was acute. There were two power blocs in Europe, he argued, and Russia was allied to the wrong one. Russia's vital interests did not conflict with Germany's. Furthermore, if Russia fought Germany and won it could gain nothing useful as a result, whereas 'those territorial and economic acquisitions which might prove really useful to us are only located in places where our ambitions may meet opposition from

England.' War with Germany, he warned, would bring disaster. 'The main burden of the war will . . . fall on us,' and Russia was unprepared for this. Its war industries were 'embryonic', so that its arms and munitions supplies were insufficient. Its strategic railway system was still inadequate, and there was insufficient rolling stock to cope with 'the colossal demands that will be made upon it in the event of a European war'. Then there was the question of cost:

> There can be no doubt that the war will require expenditures that exceed Russia's limited financial resources. We shall have to turn to allied and neutral countries for credit, but this will not be advanced for nothing. The financial and economic consequences of defeat . . . will unquestionably involve the total disintegration of our economy. But even victory promises us extremely unfavourable financial prospects.

The social and political consequences of war (and here the expert on subversion spoke) would be 'mortally dangerous for Russia . . . no matter who wins'. A social revolution would break out in the defeated country, which would 'spread to the country of the victor', and 'any revolutionary movement will inevitably degenerate into a socialist movement'. The liberal democrats in the Duma had no support among the people, who 'do not seek political rights, which they neither need nor comprehend. The peasant dreams of obtaining a free share of somebody else's land; the worker of taking over all the capital and profits of the manufacturer. Beyond this, they have no aspirations.' Defeats and disasters would be blamed on the government; the army would be too demoralized to maintain law and order. In brief, Russia would probably be defeated, and defeat would bring anarchy. But so too would victory, albeit by another route.[41]

Events were to follow his first alternative scenario, and it proved accurate in every particular.

When war was declared in August 1914 a surge of patriotism swept over the Empire. Vast crowds turned out to cheer, and virtually everyone called to the colours responded promptly. Representatives of the most disaffected of the Tsar's subjects, the Poles, declared their readiness to fight for the Empire, and when the fighting began many Poles showed a readiness to speak Russian which they had not done before. The war against Germany started badly with the rout of an invading Russian army at Tannenberg, though Russian arms were more successful against the Austrians. Yet the outcome was to depend on capacity to withstand attrition and, as Durnovo had foreseen, Russia's stamina would prove limited. Over 6.5 million men were mobilized by the end of the year, but nearly 2 million of them lacked rifles[42] and, though this shortfall was eventually made up, logistical problems were to persist.

From the beginning, the main burden of fighting the war fell on Russia, as Durnovo had foretold. The first ill-fated Russian offensive had been launched to relieve the French. In terms of grand strategy it succeeded, drawing sufficient German forces to allow a Franco-British victory on the Marne. But the costs of answering subsequent calls, notably in 1916 to take pressure off the French armies at Verdun – at a time when Russia, in addition to maintaining its war efforts on two fronts, had to cope with a serious Kazakh uprising against conscription and requisitions – were not easy to sustain, even though the Allies were to return the compliment: the terrible British assault on Passchendaele in 1917 was mounted partly to help Russia. It won a diplomatic victory when the Allies agreed to Russia's controlling the Straits after the war, but meanwhile the Turks continued to block the route to much needed shipments from the West. Since the Baltic was also blocked, supplies of strategic materials had to go by the hazardous northern route to Archangel or, even less conveniently, to Vladivostok. The industrial sector was energized by the participation of civil agencies in the war effort, but, as in other countries at war, this led to calls for political participation, which the Tsar was not prepared to concede. Instead, he took to replacing ministers. The changes were not usually for the better, and were both disruptive and demoralizing.

Defeats in the spring of 1915 led to xenophobic riots in Russian cities and raucous calls for a change in the army command. Despite a chorus of advice from ministers and advisers, Nicholas responded by assuming the command himself, and departing for headquarters at the front. It was a disastrous decision. By his own admission he was not equipped for the job (in effect a general deputized as Chief of Staff). It would associate him personally with future defeats, and leave ministers without access to him at a time when conflicting demands of the military and civilian authorities needed to be resolved – for instance over the army's control of the railway system. Officers had the power to commandeer trains to meet the needs of their commands but this led to the disruption of production and food supplies. In 1916 General Brusilov's offensive broke the Austrian front, and this brought Romania into the war on the Allied side. But the success only delayed the reckoning.

By the end of 1916 Russia had lost well over a million war dead and over 3 million wounded. Calls for a government that would command public confidence continued to grow; inflation was soaring, making life almost impossible for the mass of city-dwellers, and, though food production was adequate, its distribution to the cities had become uncertain and working-class families were becoming increasingly angry and distressed. Afraid of diluting the autocratic powers he retained under the constitution, the Tsar stood obstinately against concession. Only the murder of the Tsarina's ill-chosen favourite Rasputin in December 1916 prompted him to return to St Petersburg at last. But, rather than addressing the political crisis, he simply dismissed the premier, Trepov, who had held office for barely a month, and gave the post to someone even less qualified. The new government commanded no credence.

Insisting on powers which he did not know how to use sensibly, Nicholas allowed the monarchy's legitimacy to waste away. Foreign observers expected revolution, and when the British ambassador was received by Nicholas he suggested that, in order to avoid disaster, the Tsar should appoint a credible premier who commanded public confidence and allow him to choose his ministerial colleagues. At this Nicholas stiffened: 'Do you mean that *I* am to regain the confidence of my people or that they are to regain *my* confidence?'[43] There was no functional fault with the governmental system. Nor was there any shortage of ministerial talent and experience. Only the Tsar fell short.

The reckoning came a few weeks later. Soldiers in the capital began to refuse to obey orders. Even Cossacks, hitherto the most loyal of servicemen, began to side with the St Petersburg crowd against the police. The Tsar procrastinated, so the Duma formed a provisional government with the support of the self-proclaimed St Petersburg Council (in Russian, *Soviet*) of Workers' and Soldiers' Deputies. Power had slipped entirely from the Tsar's hands, and he abdicated in favour of his brother Mikhail. However, Mikhail refused to accept the crown unless it were to be offered by popular decision.

The Provisional Government announced a general amnesty, abolished distinctions based on class, religion and nationality, and proclaimed freedom of speech, assembly and the press. It also began preparing for elections to a Constituent Assembly which was to decide the Empire's future. But the Provisional Government itself had not been elected, and felt that its chief claim to legitimacy was the recognition of other states, notably Russia's allies, the Western democracies. Pending elections and the establishment of a popular legitimacy, therefore, it continued the war.

Now people began to whisper that there was to be a distribution of land to peasants, and soldiers began to desert their stations and drift home to make sure they got a share. The rate of desertion grew steadily in the months that followed. Meanwhile, disruptions and dislocations behind the lines continued to sap morale and increase worker militancy. The Provisional Government reconstituted itself more than once in order to reflect what it sensed to be the increasingly radical popular mood; and then the state administration began to crumble. The ministers in St Petersburg became increasingly isolated and ineffectual. Such were the circumstances in which Lenin's small group of Bolsheviks[44] took over power with the help of elements in the St Petersburg garrison and railway and telegraph workers, who prevented troops from the front arriving to establish a military dictatorship.

Hostilities with Germany, Austria and Turkey were ended by an armistice signed in December 1917 – but too late to save the Empire. Nicholas II had been the last, flawed, keystone of the autocratic system, and without it the edifice collapsed. Elections to the Constituent Assembly held soon afterwards showed that the liberal and democratic elements in the political spectrum had lost popular credibility and that the Bolsheviks – thanks to Lenin's promises of bread for the cities, land for the peasants, and an end to the war – were fast gaining popularity. However, the hands-down electoral victors were the Social Revolutionaries, another Marxism-influenced party oriented towards the peasants. In any case the Constituent Assembly was not to decide the Empire's future. Soon after it assembled, Lenin closed it down. By then, however, it was not a question of who would govern Russia, but whether there would be anything to govern.

12

The Construction of a Juggernaut

THE RUSSIAN REVOLUTION has become a traditional dividing line for historians, but its use in this way can be misleading, because it divorces the history of the new regime from its context in war. It was the war, and the costs and dislocations the war created, which allowed Lenin to take over and which helped to mould the culture of the new Soviet state with its coercive, military methods. Too rigid a distinction between the old regime and the new also leads to important continuities being glossed over or ignored. Though it tried to shrug them off, the new Soviet Russia was forced to carry many of the burdens that had weighed its predecessor down, and despite desperate attempts to make over everything as new – abolishing the imperial army and the police, the courts and much of the bureaucracy – it was soon cannibalizing what remained of the old imperial machine to build a new one. It employed thousands of officers and officials who had served the tsars to help run the new army and the new bureaucracy. Experts on trade, banking and other capitalist arts, and even police officials, were also engaged – for even revolutionary regimes need such skills. Historical inertia sometimes exerts more influence than the power of revolution.

There was no clean dividing line between war and peace. Hostilities between the new Russia and Germany, Austria and Turkey were formally ended in December 1917 by the armistice of Brest-Litovsk and that of Erzincan, but German forces stayed on to occupy Ukraine. Then, when Germany and its allies themselves capitulated late in 1918, Allied troops occupied Murmansk in the far north, and set up camps in southern Russia, the Caucasus, Central Asia and the Far East, where a large Japanese force operated until 1922. A bitter, chaotic civil war between Bolshevik 'Reds' and anti-Bolshevik 'Whites' had been waged since 1918 and was to continue into 1920, while, in a desperate attempt to link up with Marxist insurgents in Germany, the new regime also fought a losing war with the reconstituted state of Poland. Russia was engaged in total war for six years, not three, and when hostilities eventually petered out the country was bankrupt and ravaged, its people exhausted. No other power in modern times except, perhaps, for Germany in 1945 has presented so many scenes of desolation.

When Lenin and his supporters replaced the Provisional Government in the old imperial capital and occupied governmental posts, they found them to be only the shell of an imperial system in an advanced state of decomposition. These circumstances, as well as his innate distrust – a characteristic of conspirators – persuaded the new leader to use his small but disciplined Bolshevik Party to monitor government agencies at every level and to undertake executive tasks. The Party also enforced his ideas of the politically correct, for Lenin set the highest value on ideology. Lenin had never imagined that his Bolsheviks could survive in power except as part of an international Marxist revolution, or at least without a revolution in Germany which would then come to his aid. Events were eventually to show that even this hope was futile. Not until December 1924 was the doctrine of 'Socialism in One Country' to be proclaimed and the Empire reconstituted in the guise of a free association of socialist states, though by then Lenin was dead.

Hard experience and practical necessity slowly eroded parts of the theoretical Marxist model with which the Bolsheviks had set out. Indeed, in some respects the new regime came to bear a startling resemblance to its tsarist predecessor. As the American correspondent of the *Christian Science Monitor* in Russia was to observe in the 1930s, though 'the masks are new . . . the technique of government' was strikingly similar to that of the Empress Anna two centuries before, when 'espionage became the most encouraged state service; everyone who seemed dangerous or inconvenient was eliminated from society [and] masses were banished.'[1] However, the empress had been primarily concerned to supervise the morals of her courtiers. The call now was for security which was comprehensive and severe.

The process had begun with the need for the new regime to secure itself against its competitors, as any regime must do. Recognizing this, Lenin created a new security agency to guard the Revolution, appointing a Pole, Felix Dzerzhinskii, to run it. Known as the Cheka, this was the forerunner of the KGB. It maintained a surveillance system which kept every foreigner and suspected 'class enemy' in its sights and set up detention camps, interrogation centres and all the other apparatus needed by an efficient secret police service. Given the war conditions that prevailed when it was established and the regime's vulnerability in its early years, the Cheka's zeal and cruelties were hardly surprising, but the characteristics became ingrained.

In March 1921 a serious armed rising was mounted by sailors at the naval base of Kronstadt, who were more radical even than the Bolsheviks. As under the old regime, there were recurring peasant disturbances, in particular a huge one in the province of Tambov, a regular scene of large-scale rural protests in tsarist times. It was in suppressing these efficiently that a former lieutenant in the imperial army, Mikhail Tukhachevskii, commended himself to the new regime. A massive emigration of the old elite was still in progress; most of the officer corps gravitated to the anti-Bolshevik Whites, but a surprising number of them stayed on to serve the Reds. In fact the new Red Army employed no fewer than 75,000 former tsarist officers, including 800 of general rank.

Inertia was the principal reason. Many opted to keep their jobs rather than concern themselves too much with the regime. Others felt that any firm government, even a Bolshevik one, was preferable to anarchy; and straightforward patriotism was a factor too. As the celebrated General Brusilov, hero of the successful offensive against Austria-Hungary in 1916, confessed:

> I thought it the duty of every citizen to stand by the country and live in it whatever the cost. At one moment under the stress of family troubles . . . I was tempted to retire to the Ukraine, and then to leave Russia. But my doubts did not last, and I returned to my heartfelt convictions. It is not every nation that has had to pass through so vast and so distressing an upheaval as the agony of Russia. The path may be hard, but I can choose no other, even if it should cost me my life.[2]

But once enrolled in the Red Army many officers stayed on out of fear, for the Bolsheviks were terrified of subversion and – especially in times of danger, as when the White commander General Yudenich moved his troops on St Petersburg in 1919 – they would shoot their ex-imperial officers on mere suspicion of betrayal.

The transition was distressing, the suffering widespread. In the countryside, food requisitioning became a scourge of the peasantry. Used as an emergency wartime measure to ensure food supplies to the cities, it was adopted by the Bolshevik regime, which sent teams of young Party men into the countryside to requisition grain, confiscate hidden stores of it, or simply steal it. The practice caused anger and distress, and it had been an issue in both the Kronstadt and the Tambov rebellions. But the root cause of the food shortage lay in a shattered economy. Cities faced starvation because peasants did not market enough grain, and the peasants did not market enough grain because there was nothing to buy with the proceeds. Industry could not be rebuilt without capital, and Russia was devoid of capital. Nor could capital be raised abroad as it had been before the war.

The first three years of war had cost the Empire 16.5 billion gold rubles – four times the internal debt of 1914 – not counting the massive issues of paper money which had fed inflation. On the eve of the World War, thanks largely to railway-building, the Russian economy had already been dependent on foreign credits, but by 1918 its foreign debt had grown from under 4 billion to nearly 14 billion gold rubles. About half this enormous sum consisted of war loans. The major creditors were Britain and France, its erstwhile allies and new-found enemies. Russia was in no position to repay, and Lenin had no intention of doing so. In January 1918 he annulled 'all foreign debts without any exception or condition'. Four years later, in 1922, an international conference held in Genoa tried to resolve the problem. Russia's creditors recognized that loans were needed for reconstruction, but insisted that the debt, which the country could not repay, be recognized. However, Moscow (the capital again from March 1918) was obdurate, and so Soviet Russia was isolated by the international community – until in March 1922 at Rapallo Russia made common cause with the other outcast European state, debt-ridden Germany.[3]

The country's economic rebuilding had to proceed without benefit of foreign investment. Foreign trade surpluses might have contributed, but as late as 1926–7 they were only a third of what they had been before the war. World demand for grain had slumped in the aftermath of war. Somehow the economy had to be lifted, but it was clear that the Bolsheviks' original ideas would not work. They had started out by nationalizing the banks and business. They had even abolished money. With industrial production in 1920 down to a fifth of what it had been in 1913,[4] theory was soon sacrificed to necessity. In the spring of 1921 an attempt was made to stimulate activity by means of a 'New Economic Policy'. This permitted small-scale private enterprise, including private shops, and commercial middlemen. Farmers were now allowed to rent land and hire labour; state subsidies for raw materials and wages were abolished, and taxation reduced somewhat,[5] though large enterprises remained firmly under central control and subjected to strict central planning and discipline. In October 1921 a state bank was set up, run by a Constitutional Democrat who had served as a minister before the war. It proceeded to issue paper banknotes, of apologetically tiny dimensions, and even a gold coin.

These concessions to reality eased the situation. Enough food and consumer goods appeared to avert immediate catastrophe. Nevertheless, the country's economic problems were so great that only central direction could get the country moving. In the judgement of the historian best acquainted with the early Soviet period, planning was a product of national emergency rather than doctrine.[6] Even so, serious economic problems were to recur. Meanwhile the Party was alternately mounting campaigns to recruit enough members to enforce its line in every outpost factory and farm and being 'cleansed' or 'purged' of 'opportunists' and 'adventurers' who rushed in when the ranks were opened.

And despite all these pressing concerns, the new regime set about building an empire – albeit an empire of a different kind to that of the tsars.

In November 1917 Lenin and Stalin, his commissioner for nationalities, published a *Declaration of Rights of the Peoples of Russia.* It proclaimed them to be equal and sovereign, and asserted their 'right to free self-determination, up to the point of secession and the formation of independent states'. It also pledged the 'free development of national minorities and national groups inhabiting the territory of Russia'.[7] On 24 January 1918 the situation was clarified by a *Declaration of the Rights of Oppressed Nationalities.* This transformed Russia, and by implication the Empire – or what could be salvaged of it – into 'The Republic of the Soviets [Councils] of Workers', Soldiers' and Peasants' Deputies. The Soviet Republic', it continued, 'is constituted on the basis of a free union of free nationalities as a Federation of Soviet National Republics.' The declared aim was to create a genuinely 'free and voluntary union of the working classes of all the nationalities of Russia'.[8] The fact that the term 'Russia' itself denoted both a nationality and an empire was not addressed. The policy, based on the idea that nationalities could realize themselves while happily coexisting with one another, could be traced back to the earliest followers of Herder. Yet, as we now know, nations will compete and even fight unless restrained by some higher authority or greater force. How the new regime would be able to square the circle of nationalism remained to be seen, but the declaration conveyed the message that nationalism was consistent with socialism.

In the short term the policy enjoyed some success, but it was military power rather than political ideology that often decided outcomes on the ground. Indeed, the policy was founded on interest as well as principle. The new regime wanted to win over the non-Russian nationalities in its struggle against the anti-Communist White forces. That was why, in the words of one historian, 'the Russian Communist Party bent over backwards to appease non-Russians', even to the extent of ejecting Terek Cossacks from their farms and handing the land over to Chechens, with whose Sufi leader, Ali Mitaev, it was in momentary alliance.[9] It was therefore thanks to the Soviet regime that Chechens were able to claim a moment of sovereignty in 1921, though Mitaev was to meet his death at Soviet hands only a few years later.

In the wake of the German withdrawal from the Baltic provinces in 1918, Bolshevik forces moved into Estonia, Latvia and Lithuania to help establish Soviet republics. There was some indigenous support for these regimes, but in the end they could not hold out against opposing forces, and the three Baltic entities became independent states. Lenin had already launched Finland into independent statehood and abrogated any claim to Poland, but he was not prepared to write off the idea of a zone of nations around the Russian Republic which would cohere with it.

The first success was Ukraine, which fell into the throes of civil war and chaos following the departure of the Germans. Local Bolsheviks fought supporters of Ukrainian independence. Polish forces occupied a substantial part, including all Galicia; anti-revolutionary White Russian forces under General Denikin also entered the fray, while independent gangs of robbers, 'Cossacks' and anarchists caused mayhem in many districts. Serious famine added to Ukraine's woes, as did outbreaks of black typhus, massacres and pogroms. Humanitarian aid sent in from the West, as it was into Russia, barely touched the problem, and the proximity of French troops did not help. At last, with the help of Ukrainian groups which decided to throw their lot in with the Bolsheviks, but mainly thanks to the disintegration of the White forces, most of the country emerged as the 'Ukrainian Soviet Republic'. Since a Belorussian Soviet Socialist Republic had come into existence at the beginning of 1919, the new Soviet Russia could be said to have achieved a second 'ingathering of the Russian lands', first achieved by Ivan III (see Chapter 4).

How much freedom nationalistic Ukrainians would be allowed soon became apparent. Ukrainian, recognized as a distinct language by the former imperial government only in 1913, became the official language, though Russian was soon given the status of second official language. Mikhail Hrushevsky, doyen of Ukrainian historians and a notable patriot, became president of the new Ukrainian Academy of Sciences. Newspapers were published in Ukrainian; theatres, museums and libraries were Ukrainianized, and Ukrainians were given prominent posts in Ukraine's government and Party. Agreements with Russia were sometimes dignified by the status of international treaties, but key decisions were taken by Moscow. There was freedom for cultural nationalism, not for political nationalism. The new Soviet Union could be a federation of independent nations provided a central Communist Party supervised them all from Moscow.[10]

Though Stalin was a Georgian, as well as being a former trainee for the Orthodox priesthood, he did not at first support the idea of Georgian independence. Instead he lumped Georgia together with Armenia and Azerbaydzhan in an attempt to create a Transcaucasian Federation. Such a federation had been formed in the wake of the Revolution, only to split up into three ephemeral independent states, and it was force, as represented by a victorious Red Army, which eventually decided the matter. So it was that in the spring of 1921 the Georgian Soviet Socialist Republic came to replace the Georgian Democratic Republic. Azerbaydzhan was brought into the union in September 1920, and Armenia a year later. In 1922 representatives of a 'Transcaucasian Republic', which subsumed all these, signed a union treaty with the Russian, Ukrainian and Belorussian republics, but Transcaucasia proved too fissile to survive.

Further east, most Kazakhs seem to have favoured autonomy and, like the local Cossacks, sided with Admiral Kolchak's White army against the Reds. The fighting was heavy, widespread and prolonged, but by the end of 1919 the Reds had prevailed in eastern Siberia, Orenburg and the northern Kazakh territories. By the spring the Seven Rivers territory was also in their hands. Famine followed. Although the Soviet regime had established political dominance, it discovered that it could not administer an economy based largely on semi-nomadic livestock-herding.[11] In both the Kazakh areas and the rest of what had become Soviet Central Asia officials had to cope with societies seriously different from those to the west. These societies were largely Muslim and poorly educated. Some regarded the new regime as liberating, but rather more disliked their new rulers much as they had the old. Still further east Bolshevik rule took longer to establish. Eighty thousand Japanese troops had occupied the Amur region in 1918, and, though the Communists had soon set up a 'Far Eastern Republic' in Siberia east of Lake Baikal, it was 1922 before the Soviet Union secured that region. The United States had put 7,000 troops into Vladivostok, and the British a further 800.[12] Only in 1923 did Chukhotka and Yakutia become Communist.

In 1924 a constitution for the Union of Soviet Socialist Republics was promulgated. The Union was to be a 'federal multinational socialist federation' based on the principle of self-determination. It consisted of three Republics of the Union – Russia, Ukraine and Belarus – and eleven Autonomous Republics – including Kazakhstan, Karelia and the Crimea, and others for Buriat-Mongols, Volga Germans, Tatars and others. There were also thirteen Autonomous Provinces designed to accommodate, *inter alia*, the Udmurts of western Siberia, the Koni, the Chechens and the Maris. Jews were allotted Birobijan in the Amur region of the Far East as a national home; the Ulch and other small peoples were given 'national districts'. However, Kazakhstan and Ukraine contained large minorities of ethnic Russians, and not a little ethnic-Russian territory was parcelled off to Estonia and Latvia, which were outside the Soviet Union.[13] Political and ethnic frontiers were not congruent in the Soviet Union, but, given the propensity of peoples to reproduce at different rates, to acculturate and to migrate, they never could be. How genuinely the values earnestly proclaimed in the Constitution were reflected in the Union is open to question, but if it really was an empire that had taken shape it was a new kind of empire.

The system aimed to accommodate the aspirations of the 'nationalities', and to a large extent it succeeded. It ensured that a larger proportion of each group would get official jobs and that most of the subject population would be administered by people of their own kind. It also provided a stimulus to national self-expression in most forms of art. Furthermore, the loyalty of the provincial nationality elites was fostered by a series of institutional links which strengthened personal connections with Moscow. Not only the Party itself but professional, academic and artistic associations networked across the Union, promoting links between the great metropolis, Moscow, and the peripheries. Recognition by the centre became a point of pride, and access to the Union's capital, where privilege shops gave access to goods unobtainable elsewhere, was much sought after.

Aspects of the nationalities policy showed that, though the Soviet regime, shaped in the crucible of pitiless warfare, had inflicted great cruelties and that dogmatism, dragooning and repression were fast becoming entrenched in its culture, the infant Union also possessed a kindlier and more constructive face. This was largely because the Bolsheviks had been constrained to co-opt proponents of the progressive agenda. Hence the government's enlightened attitudes to women and minorities, its enthusiasm for literacy and education, and, in part, its campaigns against the obscurantism of the Church and all religions. It also encouraged talent – and never more so than when it found someone who conformed to a Soviet ideal and had been neglected by the old regime.

Konstantin Tsiolkovskii, for example, had good proletarian credentials. He came from mixed Russian, Polish and Tatar stock, was a modest schoolteacher in Kaluga, and was handicapped by deafness. He was also a genius in the field of aerodynamics and a visionary who helped make space travel possible. Ignored by the scientific establishment, he had built Russia's first wind tunnel at his own expense, and in 1899 he had published a key paper on atmospheric pressure on surfaces, also at his own expense. Once the Soviet regime was in power, however, his research was funded, he was elected a member of the Academy of Sciences, and allotted a life pension. The physicist Kapitsa, the economist Kondratev, the writer Maxim Gorky and the composer Sergei Prokofiev were among other luminaries who shone in this early Soviet period.

The New Economic Policy stabilized a country careening out of control, and the basic indicators of demographic strength and economic growth flickered and began to rise. Indeed, the population in the period 1922–7 grew at the phenomenal rate of 2 per cent a year. This was chiefly due to a decline in the death rate. Winnowed by the hardships of the tragic years, the population had been growing hardier.[14] National income was also creeping up. In 1925–6 it reached 75.7 rubles per head of population – 75 per cent of what it had been in 1913. Yet, of a total population of 150 millions, almost 82 per cent lived and worked in the countryside. A brilliant future, Communist or not, could not be built on such a basis. In proportion to population, Russia's national income was less than a fifth of Britain's and less than an eighth of that of the United States.[15] And by 1928 a serious economic and social crisis was looming. It led the Party to resort to military methods again, and worse.

The crisis was linked to the onset of the world depression but stemmed from serious inadequacies in Soviet economic arrangements. Industry was failing to produce goods the peasants were interested in buying. The peasants therefore saved themselves the labour of sowing so much land for the next harvest. The result was a dearth of grain not only for export, but also for the cities and hence industry. The state reacted with what since the war had become a traditional remedy: requisitioning grain from the peasants. The recurring problem arose from a failure to match supply and demand, but there were more fundamental inadequacies in the management of the economy, the approach to which was often too simplistic for so complex an undertaking. As Kondratev himself explained in a paper requested by one of the new leader's, Stalin's, closest associates, Viacheslav Molotov:

> The planned management of our national economy is one of the main aims. But planned management . . . requires good plans. In practice, when we draw up the plans we very often misunderstand the problems and opportuni-

> ties involved. This is why our planning is so full of enthusiasm, why it wastes too much energy, why it is so isolated from economic policy in practice, and why it produces [unpleasant] surprises.[16]

Idealism and enthusiasm by themselves could not direct the economy efficiently. Indeed, they sometimes combined to undermine it. Meanwhile the urban labour force needed for industry, though increasing, was still less than it had been in 1916.[17]

In 1926 agricultural production showed a welcome increase, but in 1927 it declined quite sharply.[18] The recurring problem of peasant production undermined Stalin's faith in the free-market prescription of the New Economic Policy and, together with problems experienced in getting industry launched, built up momentum for a root-and-branch solution. This took shape in 1928–9. It involved the forced collectivization of peasant farming. Huge collective farms were the closest the Communists would go to replicating the highly productive great estates of the pre-revolutionary era without compromising their ideology. Peasants, including the richer ones, known as kulaks, whom Stolypin had encouraged, would no doubt object, but they would have to be suppressed. Collectives, with their economies of scale, would release a mass of surplus rural labour for industry, especially if industry could equip them with tractors and other farming machinery. The workless peasants would be directed to urban centres to serve as grist to the wheels of industry. Capital was essential, of course, and this was scarcer in Russia than it had ever been. What little surplus the budget could scrape up would have go to foreign companies willing to provide essential technical expertise in turbine construction and the like. The bulk of the capital would have to be found by squeezing resources out of the population at large, by forcing them to produce significantly more value than they consumed. They would be paid largely in promises.

Propaganda would stoke up enthusiasm, especially among the young, and raise peoples' eyes above the bleak immediate prospects to a rosy future in which all needs would be met and grand projects realized. Force would also be needed, not only to coerce the peasants, but also to find labour for essential projects in unpleasant places – but opponents of the governments' schemes and social misfits could be put to useful work for nothing.

As the programme was climbing into top gear, in February 1931, Stalin made a powerful speech invoking Russian patriotism. The old Russia, he said, had been beaten by the Mongols, defeated by the Turks and Swedes, occupied by the gentlemen of Poland-Lithuania, worsted by French and

British capitalists and by the Japanese. They had done down Russia because Russia had been afflicted by backwardness –

> military backwardness, cultural backwardness, political, industrial and agricultural backwardness. They beat . . . [us] because it was profitable and could be done with impunity. Such is the law of the exploiter – to beat the backward and the weak. It is the jungle law of capitalism . . .
>
> We are fifty or a hundred years behind the developed countries. We must catch up that distance in ten years . . . Or we shall be crushed.[19]

Retrospect credits Stalin with prescience. The Soviet Union was indeed to face a life-and-death crisis ten years later, but he had in mind the hostility of the world in general. He could hardly have foreseen the triumph of Hitler so early in 1931. Other, gentler, means to the desired end might well have worked, but force was quicker. Stalin was in a hurry.

Both the achievements and the costs of Stalin's revolution are reflected in the census data. Painstaking research into the demographic history of Russia in the 1930s concludes that by 1937 the urban population had increased by 70 per cent, and by substantially more than that in the industrializing areas of Siberia. This reflected a strategic plan to shift the centre of economic gravity towards the east. On the other hand the rural population had shrunk by 3.4 million souls.[20] The number of ethnic Russians rose, although even their numbers fell in 1933, as did the Tatar, Azerbaydzhani and Circassian populations. The Ukrainian and Kazakh populations fell more sharply. By 1937 there were 29 per cent fewer Kazakhs than there had been in 1926, and 15 per cent fewer Ukrainians. The Kazakh losses are attributed to collectivization and cross-frontier migration; the loss of 5 million Ukrainians is also blamed on collectivization, and to a dreadful famine of 1931–2 which was associated with it.[21]

The massive mortality has been ascribed to genocide, but the charge is unfounded.[22] True, the regime disliked political nationalists, and in 1931 it shot a former premier of the puppet regime set up by the Germans in 1917 and then some Ukrainian Communists suspected of nationalist leanings.[23] But Ukrainians were by no means the only nationality to suffer, and it was not Ukrainians but kulaks and anyone who stood in its way whom the regime targeted. Nor was the famine as such man-made, as has been alleged. The regime had no interest in dead peasants and starving subjects. It wanted live and active workers. Rather than being deliberately induced, the famine was the consequence of mistaken policy, ruthlessly implemented.

Kulak opposition to collectivization had been anticipated, and was confronted by force. Peasants – by no means all of them kulaks – slaughtered their livestock rather than let the collectives have them, precipitating a meat shortage that was to last for decades. They and anyone else who impeded the imposition of the programme were carted off in droves to detention camps. Worse still were the grain-procurement quotas and the punitive ways in which they were enforced. Peasants had long been used to hiding grain from requisitioning squads, but things had reached such a point where there was virtually nothing left to hide; and the quotas demanded were set unrealistically high. The impetus to what turned out to be a major human disaster was the regime's attitude.

It was interested in industry-building, in infrastructural development and in resettlement. It was not interested in agriculture except as a means of dredging up resources to realize its ambitions. Peasants not prepared to work under direction in a collective should find jobs in towns. If they opposed the new system in any way they should be arrested and forced to work on government projects. But the combination of ideology, bureaucracy and enthusiasm created havoc in Ukraine. The Communist agronomist who had initiated the tractor-station programme described the consequences of the policy to create gigantic collective farms:

> The policy . . . was implemented in an exceptionally bureaucratic and senseless manner. Collective farms of 55 to 100 hectares were suddenly transformed, without adequate technical preparation, into collectives covering tens of thousands of hectares . . . In some cases, 'to simplify matters', a whole region containing hundreds of villages was to declared to be a single collective. All boundaries between village lands were eliminated; and the entire expanse . . . [was] divided into farms of several thousand hectares each – without any regard to where the villages were actually situated. [Hence] cattle and agricultural machinery were scattered about over scores of kilometres.[24]

Many of the planners, as well as those charged with implementation, were raw recruits to their allotted specialisms. Furthermore, behind them loomed authority demanding results. In these circumstances, what enthusiasm could not achieve desperation often did. Inevitably things went wrong, but scapegoats were readily found to take the blame. Hundreds of thousands of peasant families were uprooted from their ancestral villages along with various others who had run foul of authority. Many of them were transported to distant and unpleasant places which were short of labour. As chaos mounted, reports arrived in the Kremlin of a growing death toll, and of crowds of destitute and starving peasants clogging the roads. In 1932 the cities were also on the brink of starvation. The worst year of all was 1933, when it has been calculated that deaths exceeded births by almost 6 million.[25] Then the crisis turned. The chaos subsided; conditions began to ease. Meanwhile a combination of censorship, propaganda and clever public relations muted concern about what had happened and diverted attention from where responsibility lay.

The mood of urban Russia in the 1930s was surprisingly optimistic. The focus was on youth and hope and the building of a socialist paradise. Living conditions verged on the impossible. There were huge shortages and lengthy waiting-lines outside the shops. Many goods that were obtainable were shoddy. Only the black market, patronage networks and *protektsiia*, the deployment of friendships and favours, made life tolerable for many people. But for the young migrants there was hope and a sense of purpose. Mundane labour suddenly became heroic. A burly miner called Stakhanov, who cut more coal in a shift than others, was lauded like an heroic knight of old. It became possible for young people to rise, to exercise authority, to wield power. They were building a new and better world. As in Mussolini's Italy, there was a sense of creating a new kind of man – in this case *Homo sovieticus*.[26]

The results were visible, tangible. Impressive new buildings were rising, new cities in process of creation, new infrastructure under construction. In Moscow, new brick-and-concrete blocks of worker housing replaced ramshackle wooden building in the suburbs, overshadowing neglected monasteries and churches. A handsome underground-railway system was excavated beneath the city, equipped with deep, fast escalators and stations like palaces with their marble halls and striking statuary – palaces for the people. Across the continent new cities rose up with vast industrial plants. New canals were being cut, dams constructed, rivers diverted, and 'palaces of culture' erected in towns and even villages for the entertainment and instruction of the people. On dozens of different sites across the vast terrain, virgin lands were turned into swarming ants'-nests of activity as the regime mobilized the population to meet the overambitious targets that would at last realize the country's immense potential. On one site just east of the Urals the whole amazing process could be observed in little –

> a strange combination of soaring ambition, driving energy, faltering and sometimes highly defective execution, large-scale building, hard and primitive living conditions, idealism and ruthlessness.

> Magnitogorsk at first conveys a confused series of impressions: heaps of bricks, timber, sand, earth and other building material, thrown about in characteristically Russian disorderly fashion; long lines of low wooden barracks for the construction labourers; towering new industrial structures, with belching smokestacks . . . The town is a product of ultramodern industrialization, yet . . . one's first impression is that of an Asiatic city.[27]

Never before had so many resources and so much human energy been concentrated to realize impossibly ambitious plans in so short a time. The achievement was great; so was the human cost. The labour for big projects in the wilderness was found from the twin offspring of revolution: the enthusiastic believers and the sullen hordes of the oppressed. The cheerleaders of the enthusiasts were the Young Communists, who, in the words of an American observer at Magnitogorsk, were

> always ready to fling themselves into the breach if some part of the building were lagging, willing to work under the hardest material conditions without reckoning hours . . . [But] at the other end of the scale were the unfortunate kulaks . . . who, after being stripped of their possessions, were sent here, sometimes with their families, to work for the success of a system that is based on their ruin.

The working day was long, wages low, rations minimal, the barrack-type housing primitive and sometimes miles away from the site. It was 'the same story at the Cheliabinsk tractor plant, at the Berezniki chemical works, at the Dnieprostroi hydroelectric power plant' and, for that matter at the heavy-machine-building plant at Sverdlovsk, the iron and coal complex at Kuznetsk in central Siberia, the agricultural-machine factory at Rostov-on-Don, the motor-vehicle plant at Nizhnii-Novgorod.[28]

At the same time an 80-mile canal was being cut to link Moscow directly to the Volga; others were cut across the Kola Peninsula to Murmansk in the far north, and to connect Lake Onega (and hence Moscow) with the White Sea. This last project, where conditions were among the harshest, was built by political prisoners, enemies of the regime. The Gulag system, which had its origins in the penal colonies of tsarist Russia, was much expanded; the camps were more rigorously run than their forerunners, and the death rate in the worst of them was very high. The largest lay north and east of Yakutsk, near the Kolyma goldfields.[29]

The first Five Year Plan, introduced in 1929, did not quite meet its ambitious targets, but its purpose was ultimately achieved. Modern industries were built. Moreover, the new factories and steel plants could be used to make tanks and various other types of military hardware – and much of this capability was well out of reach of potential enemies to the east as well as the west. Even though consultants had occasionally been hired from the West, and some contracts were even let to Western companies, the operation was inefficient by Western standards – sometimes highly inefficient – but the regime could use media manipulation to assign blame for these failings and encourage improvement.

In the last months of 1930 the newspapers announced the execution of dozens of economists, engineers and other specialists. Arraigning real or supposed opponents of Stalin's rule on trumped-up charges of 'wrecking' was found to be an effective way of explaining failures and attributing blame to others than the leadership. Such travesties of justice also served a psychological need of the public – that of identifying 'the sinful', the supposed authors of all their woes. As the pace of construction heated up and more shortcomings came to light the 'show trial' was used more frequently, along with the Party purge.

In a series of trials in the later 1930s, prominent Party men including economic planners were tried publicly and executed, some for transparently false economic as well as political 'crimes' such as plotting to market butter containing broken glass. A public ever eager to see those in authority diminished was heartened by the spectacle, but the victims included scapegoats for the failures of industrialization. Ukrainians were not disappointed to see most of the provincial Party leaders fall. And as the purges cut wider they created huge possibilities for promotion. In 1938 the armed services were purged. Perhaps because of his long-standing acquaintance with German generals under military co-operation agreements, Tukhachevskii, the Chief of Staff, was shot, along with most of the senior commanders. Their replacements were raw and, on the whole, less able.

The new commanders were rushed through staff college and other training schemes in the hope of equipping them for command in time. But the critical juncture was only months away and, though the feared security agency itself was also purged, the leadership of the Soviet Union's defences had been much weakened.

Stalin, the controlling genius of Russia's fortunes, no doubt had his moments of paranoia, confusion, even panic, when confronting situations of which he was not the master. He also had the destructive capacities of a believer. He was, however, aware of the costs of his action. He subsequently confessed that the protracted struggle with the peasants over collectivization was the fiercest he had known: 'It was terrible,' he told

Churchill. 'Four years it lasted.'[30] The economic transformation cost the Soviet Union heavily in lives, although manipulation of the census figures for the late 1930s distorted the truth for some time. The scale of the deception has been calculated to have been as high as 2.9 million deaths, and it was most pronounced for provinces like Komi and Karelia, where GPU hard-labour camps had been sited. Such camps had been used 'on a gigantic scale.'[31] Furthermore, what Stalin saw as political stabilization achieved by the purges of the later 1930s was highly destructive of talent and expertise in every imaginable field. Such was the price. What had it bought?

The chief benefit was in large quantities of military hardware and capacity. By 1941 the Red Army could field more than half of all the tanks in the world, including a thousand excellent T-34 tanks. A further forty T-34s were rolling off the production lines every week. There were almost 2,000 fighter aircraft in service, including numbers of the MiG-3.[32] At its best, the standard of weapon design was excellent. Nevertheless, there were serious problems. Production of the better models was too slow, and the equipment was not distributed to best advantage. The ideas of the Red Army's leading tanks specialist, D. Pavlov, had prevailed over those of Tukhachevskii.[33] And after the purges there were problems of leadership, personified by the incompetent Marshal Voroshilov, who was responsible for a series of organizational mistakes which were to show up when hostilities began.

The Second World War was preceded by two curtain-raisers. The first clash to involve the Soviet Union came in August 1939, over the territory of Khalkhin-Gol in the Far East, which was in dispute with Japan.[34] The second, in the autumn and winter of 1940, was with Finland. In the first, Soviet troops, deploying several hundred of the new tanks under General Zhukov, were successful in heavy fighting. In the second, Soviet forces were out-manoeuvred and badly mauled by Finnish troops who were seriously outnumbered. Although the Finns were eventually ground down by overwhelming force,[35] the encounter did not bode well for the Soviet Union when Hitler ordered his surprise invasion in 1941.

After the Munich Agreement of 1938, France and Britain decided that they must make no more concessions to Hitler's Germany and began to entertain the possibility of co-operating with the Soviet Union in defence of Poland and Romania. Eventually military talks were held in Moscow. However, the threatened states were reluctant to allow Soviet troops to cross into their territory before hostilities actually began, which was understandable but impractical given the nature of mid-twentieth-century warfare. For their part, the Soviets were at least as worried about Japan as about Germany, and were disinclined to make sacrifices for powers which had been adamantly hostile to them until now. Irritated by the sluggish pace of negotiations, the Soviet diplomats became more and more ambivalent. Then the German government, with uncannily good timing, made an offer of attractive terms. A deal with Germany would remove the spectre of having to fight a war on two fronts. Besides, the Soviet Union had been ostracized for decades, and now a major Power was offering to treat with it on equal terms. Stalin was flattered,[36] and decided it would be better to sup with the German devil than with the stand-offish French and British.

Under the secret terms of the Nazi–Soviet Pact which was then drawn up, Stalin connived at a German invasion of Poland in return for territory on his western frontier – eastern Poland as far as the river Bug, and a sphere of influence that included the Baltic states. But Stalin did not move when German forces invaded Poland on 1 August 1939. Only when it became obvious that the Poles had been decisively defeated did he order Soviet troops in, and call in the promises under the Pact.

Much as Alexander I had done with Napoleon at Tilsit in 1807, Stalin had delayed a major war by concluding a spheres-of-influence agreement with Hitler. Not only had he delayed invasion, he had thrust out the Soviet Union's western frontiers to create a useful screen against attack, and had regained old imperial territories lost in the aftermath of the Revolution. Estonia, Latvia and Lithuania became constituent republics within the Soviet Union. Finland remained independent, but after the winter war which followed it was forced to cede a strategically important area in Karelia, south of Murmansk and the northern shores of Lake Ladoga. For good measure Stalin also took the opportunity to take back Bessarabia. He did not expect to remain permanently at peace with capitalist powers – either Germany or, more particularly, Japan. But he now felt secure against any imminent attack from the West. He deceived himself.

There were intimations that Hitler might order an invasion. Army intelligence warned of the possibility in April; other disturbing rumours came through diplomatic channels. The Kremlin's response was sluggish. Construction work was started on defensive positions, a few more units were moved into the Baltic region, but Stalin was sceptical of the warnings, suspecting that the Western Powers were trying to trick him into war with Germany. When the blow fell, on 22 June 1941, it caught him by surprise and most of the Red Army unprepared.[37]

*

The invading German armies were joined by substantial contingents of Romanian, Hungarian, Italian and Croatian formations, so that, as with Napeolon's invasion, the operation took on the appearance of a crusade. As the crack panzer divisions rolled forward there were prospects of their being joined by a 'Fifth Column' of the disaffected, not least among the subject nationalities, particularly in the newly Sovietized Baltic states, in Ukraine and elsewhere.

The next four months saw a series of unmitigated military disasters for the Soviet regime.[38] Enemy forces advanced on every front, Moscow was threatened, and Stalin fell out with his own Chief of Staff, Zhukov. The issue concerned high strategy. Zhukov advised the transfer of units from the Far East to stiffen the defences of Moscow. Stalin would not have it and made the ailing Shaposhnikov Chief of Staff while assuming direction of the war himself. Yet he was soon to contemplate having to abandon Russia and seeking asylum with his new-found Western ally Britain. Soviet losses were already enormous in terms of both men and material. By September Leningrad (as St Petersburg was now called) was under siege, Moscow itself was in danger, and in the south German forces were racing towards the lower Volga. Survivors of the army purges were quickly released, fed a meal or two, and pressed back into service.

This war was not like the others, and Marshal Tukhachevskii, executed nearly three years earlier, had foreseen what form it would take:

> Operations will be inestimably more intensive and severe than in the First World War. Then, frontier battles in France lasted for two or three days. Now, such an offensive operation can last for weeks. As for the Blitzkrieg which is so propagandized by the Germans, this is directed towards an enemy who doesn't want . . . to fight it out. If the Germans meet an opponent who stands up and fights and takes the offensive himself . . . [the] struggle would be bitter and protracted . . . In the final resort it would depend on who had the greater moral fibre and who at the close of operations disposed of operational reserves in depth.[39]

Already Tukhachevskii's prognostications were being borne out, and the outlook seemed increasingly bleak. Yet, despite the losses and the panic, there were some more hopeful indications of the moral fibre which Tukhachevskii had thought might be decisive. Some desperate counter-attacks were somehow organized; some units had continued to fight doggedly on although surrounded; others operated as partisans in the invader's rear. All this slowed the tempo of the invader's progress. At the same time a vital operation finally got under way – to evacuate such war industry as had not already fallen into enemy hands out of the line of the enemy's advance into the safety of Central Asia and Siberia. The scale of the effort is reflected in statistics:

> In the first three months of the war . . . [the railways] moved two and a half million troops up to the front lines, and shifted 1,360 heavy plants . . . 455 to the Urals, 210 to Western Siberia, 200 to the Volga and more than 250 to Kazakhstan and central Asia . . . The evacuation had used 1,500,000 trucks, and by mid-November 914,380 waggons had shifted 38,514 loads for the aviation industry, 20,046 for ammunition plants, 18,823 for weapons factories, 27,426 for steel plants, 15,440 for the tank industry . . .
>
> In Saratov, machinery began operating and the walls of a new factory went up around it; fourteen days after the last train-load of machines were unloaded, the first MiG fighter rolled out. On 8 December, the Kharkov Tank Works turned out its first twenty-five T-34 tanks, just short of ten weeks after the last engineers left Kharkov, trudging along the rail tracks.[40]

Over the winter of 1941–2 the industrial plants in the Urals were to produce about 4,500 tanks, 3,000 aircraft and 14,000 pieces of artillery. Supplies were also shipped from Britain and, under Lend-Lease arrangements, from the United States – especially lorries, jeeps, machinery, munitions and corned meat. But these had to take perilous routes to Murmansk or the Far East through seas infested with enemy submarines.

Once again a Russian migration was in progress. Troops and factories were not the only items on the move. The transportation of entire peoples was soon under way. Its Canadian and American allies may have interned citizens who were ethnic Japanese, the British detained German and Italian citizens, but the Soviet Union deported Chechens, Kalmyks, Balkars, Karachais, Crimean Tatars and even the Volga Germans, who had been domiciled there since the eighteenth century, to put them beyond reach of the invaders. These measures may have reflected Stalin's suspicious nature or perhaps his caution, for there is little evidence that the regime was popular among these peoples.

Moscow's defences held despite the battering, and a carefully timed counter-offensive was launched on 5 December. Within two weeks it succeeded in breaking the German front and relieving the pressure on the capital. Attention turned north to Leningrad, which, though surrounded and subjected to unremitting pounding, still held out. A fresh German offensive against it, launched in January, achieved only limited success and soon ran out of steam. Meanwhile, under cover of the dark days, something very like a revolution was taking place in the senior command. Generals like Pavlov, who had been found wanting, were replaced, Mekhlis was demoted, Voroshilov (who was said never to have opened a book on his trade) was sidelined. The new men – Vasilevskii, Sokolovskii, Vatutin, Malinovskii, Koniev, Rokossovskii, Chuikov – were more competent, and had proved themselves in the crucible of battle. Yet Stalin, like Hitler, still kept command in his own hands, and his most brilliant general, Zhukov, though involved in the high command, was still excluded from the top post that would have given him the direction of operations.

Meanwhile, in December 1941 the Japanese had attacked Pearl Harbor, bringing the United States into the war on the Allied side, and in February 1942 they had struck south against Singapore. This finally diminished fears of a Japanese attack on the Soviet Union, allowing more troops to be transferred from the Pacific to the European front. Even so it was to be a close call.

In May 1942 a Soviet offensive at Kharkov failed, and over twenty divisions guarding the Crimean front were routed. This reverse finally convinced Stalin of the incompetence of the commander, Mekhlis. Sevastopol was cut off except for perilous submarine runs, and was subjected to pulverizing attacks. When the defending guns finally ran out of ammunition, the surviving gunners blew them up; Sevastopol succumbed. Voronezh fell, and in July Rostov-on-Don. Enemy units crossed the Don and threatened to wheel south into the Caucasus. Had they succeeded, the prospects for the Soviets would have been grim. Not only would the Baku oilwells be at Hitler's disposal, but he would be able to call on the help of local peoples who would be as grateful as many Ukrainians had been at first for liberation from Communism. But General von Manstein's thrust was stopped on the river Terek. He had run out of fuel.

Attention now centred on Stalingrad, and it was a measure of the importance Stalin attached to this battle that Zhukov was brought in as his deputy. The fighting was as grim as any battle fought in this war or any other. The German command fully expected the city to fall before long; attempt after attempt to relieve it failed, and Soviet security troops are said to have executed as many as 14,000 Soviet soldiers for cowardice in order to stop flight and prevent desertion.[41] The two sides fought building by building through late September and early October – and still the terrible struggle was not ended. At this point preparations, supervised by Zhukov personally, were made for an offensive to start in November 1942. Reserves were brought in, and what remained of shattered units were re-formed into new ones and re-equipped; wounded soldiers released from hospital were posted in to provide a leavening of battle-hardened men.

In the Stalingrad operations Soviet artillery loosed off as much ammunition as in the rest of the war.[42] Five million German troops were deployed over the front – with dive-bomber support at crucial times. The Soviet forces lacked air support – but the Soviet command mustered over 6 million men against the invader.

The eventual Soviet assault was heralded by salvos of rockets. Then 3,500 guns and mortars roared and thundered out their bombardment along a 14-mile front. After an interval, tanks bearing sharpshooters began to trundle forward through the freezing fog. The Germans counter-attacked, sending in the Romanian Third Army, which quickly met its doom. The Soviet tanks moved forward. The most convenient point for crossing the river Don was seized, and at 2 p.m. on 26 November units of the Stalingrad front joined up with tanks of South-Western Command to surround between 80,000 and 90,000 men of the German Sixth Army under Friedrich von Paulus. He thought of breaking out. Hitler ordered him to stay firm. In the end he was forced to surrender.

By the end of January 1943 it was clear that the invader's southern front had been shattered and preparations went forward for an offensive to break its backbone. The triumph at Stalingrad had given a huge fillip to morale, and the fresh troops rushed up to front-line positions were no longer merely dour and determined but eager for battle. The elation, however, led to overconfidence on Stalin's part. Rather than concentrating resources on the achievement of one objective and against one of the three enemy army groups, he ordered a series of offensives along the entire front.[43]

This onslaught, which began in late January and early February, was overambitious and soon ground to a halt. The Germans regained some territory; the scales of war tipped one way, then the other, until eventually a state of equilibrium was reached. In August the city of Kharkov was finally retaken, and then a battle which was to take its name from the Kursk salient began to take shape. It covered a vast area of the steppe, lasted from August to the beginning of October, involved multiple armies, and was directed on the Soviet side by Zhukov and on the German by Field Marshal von Manstein. It is regarded by some specialists as the decisive battle of the Second World War, and it ended in complete Soviet victory. The German general staff itself concluded that from that point on Soviet Russia would surpass Germany in the mobilization of men and the production of equipment, and in the field of propaganda.[44] It was not long before yet another mass offensive was started and Soviet troops were crossing the Dnieper and racing towards the western frontier. The tide of war had changed decisively.

*

This awesome result, which had seemed so unlikely less than two years earlier, was the product of many factors. Chief, perhaps, was what Tukhachevskii had termed 'moral fibre' – the grit and determination not only of the Soviet forces, but of the civilian population, not least the women. But for the patience and fortitude of its people in the face of many months of bombardment and privation, the ruined city of Leningrad could not have withstood the siege; but for the unremitting efforts of workers, even in the hardest circumstances, the front-line soldiers would never have been supplied. As the danger had increased, the Soviet population – including most of the national minorities, peasant kulaks, and even victims of the purges – seemed to acquire a commitment which had not existed in the beginning. As in 1812, the war had become a genuinely patriotic struggle. The invaders, it seems, had themselves generated the antibodies which would smother them.

Yet in retrospect it also seems that the Soviet regime was aided by some strokes of good fortune. One was Japan's refusal to co-ordinate its war plan with Germany's. Another was Hitler's faulty direction of strategy, especially in the case of Stalingrad. Another self-imposed handicap was his racial doctrine. Many Ukrainians had welcomed the invaders, greeting them with bread and salt. Yet Nazi racial theory classified Slavs as inferior, and barred their acceptance on equal terms as some army officers had advised. Ukraine had at first proved a good recruiting ground for the invaders, but the punitive actions taken in response to partisan activity alienated the bulk of the population who had initially seemed so well disposed.

Some Chechens joined the invaders, though some were decorated for gallantry in fighting against them. Perhaps because they had easier access to the Germans, numbers of Cossacks collaborated – and in April 1942 Hitler did sanction the formation of Cossack volunteer units. Some served in police detachments on the Don, but there were several requests to form a Cossack army to fight the Communists, and eventually the request was granted, though the Germans set their face against Cossack independence. An army major of Cossack origins who joined the Germans was allowed to form a squadron from Cossack prisoners and deserters and was employed in front-line propaganda, encouraging desertion with promises that collective farming would be abolished. And a Russian major-general, Vlasov, who had been taken prisoner, opted for the Germans. He set about recruiting an 'All-Russian Army of Liberation' from prisoners of war, hoping to raise a million men. Fewer than 200,000 joined him.[45] It was 1943, and the tide of war had changed. Few factors are as efficient as success in shoring up loyalties.

The scale of the victory came as a surprise to the world, and even to Stalin's allies. But once the message sank into consciousness that the neophyte, half-ruined, economically crippled Soviet Union had thrashed the hitherto invincible war machine of Europe's strongest economic power, together with its satellites, attitudes were revolutionized. The erstwhile pariah suddenly acquired immense prestige, even legitimacy. At the same time a genuinely Soviet patriotism had emerged. Participation in the most total of total wars to date also resulted in a liberation of sorts. Realizing that the circumstance demanded compromise, Stalin restrained his ruthless security forces, for there was now a general commitment to the cause against the common enemy.

13
The High Tide of Soviet Imperialism

Although their cause was already doomed, Hitler's armies fought on with fierce desperation for almost two years more. By the time they were overwhelmed and Hitler himself had committed suicide in the ruins of Berlin, Stalin's armies controlled the larger part of Europe. The Soviet Union now regained all the territories it had claimed under the Nazi–Soviet Pact (though Britain and the United States would not recognize its rule in the former Baltic states as legitimate). It also acquired the ancient German city of Konigsberg, renaming it Kaliningrad. Albeit tacitly, the Western Powers also recognized the Soviet Union's right to a sphere of influence in eastern Europe beyond its own frontiers, and with the advent of the 'Cold War' two years later – though not before – the construction of a new kind of Russian empire consisting of nominally independent dominions got under way.

In the Far East, the Soviet Union's belated participation in the war with Japan enabled it to add southern Sakhalin and the Kurile Islands to its possessions. China turned Communist, and for a moment even France and Italy seemed likely to do so. Marxist internationalism proved to be a far more potent lure than pan-Slavism had ever been. Furthermore, since the Soviet regime offered both a model for overcoming backwardness and help for peoples oppressed by other imperial powers, many more countries, including Egypt, Afghanistan and Cuba, were to become Soviet clients. For a time only the Western monopoly of nuclear weapons seemed to prevent a stampede to enter Stalin's corral, and, thanks to its espionage service, the Soviet Union soon broke that monopoly. Just as the Soviet leaders came to poach Western technology and suborn useful citizens, they learned to exploit discontent in capitalist countries and cut a dash in the Third World.

Soviet prestige and world influence now exceeded those of any former Russian empire, and they continued to grow. In 1961, to general astonishment, the Soviet Union sent the first astronaut to orbit planet Earth, and when the ebullient new Party Secretary, Nikita Khrushchev, boasted that it would be able to match the United States in terms of economic output in a decade or even less, his claim did not seem entirely ridiculous. Within the short span of twenty years Soviet Russia had moved from the position of an embattled pariah to become a great power with a strong claim to world pre-eminence.

Once the German offensive at Kursk in the summer of 1943 had been broken, Soviet military operations read like a triumphant progress. But the successes were not won easily. Attention focused first on a stretch of the front along river Dnieper near Kiev, where Russian longboats had once gathered for the voyage to Constantinople. The first Russian imperial capital was defended by battered, but still formidable, divisions under the command of the able Field Marshal von Manstein, and by the great and treacherous river itself. The man in charge of the Soviet forces in the sector of intended breakthough to Kiev was General Vatutin. The carefully planned operation was heralded by a terrible barrage of more than 2 ,000 guns, mortars and rocket-launchers concentrated on to a front only 4 miles wide. A few days later guns in Moscow firing blank charges roared out a salute to greet the news that Kiev had been cleared of enemy troops. Czech troops under a Colonel Svoboda had taken part in the operation. They had been told that in fighting for Kiev they would be fighting for Prague. Events were to justify the claim.[1]

From this point on the story of the war can be reduced to a series of pincer movements which snapped shut to trap enemy armies; and a list of battles to cross great European rivers – the Bug, the Vistula and the Danube, the Oder and the Elbe. Prague was one of the very last cities to be taken: the Germans held it even after the fall of Berlin. But the war was fought on many levels. Aside from the military operations, there were diplomatic wars between the Allies over grand strategy and struggles between political leaders and military commanders. Moreover the war helped to shape the peace which followed. The victory over Nazi Germany was comprehensive and, as the Allies recognized, due largely to Soviet sacrifice. The shape of the new Europe was determined partly by the position of forces on the ground when the fighting stopped, and partly by agreements made between the Allies while the war was still in progress.

Peace arrangements, like military operations, were the subject of careful planning. The partition of post-war Germany, for example, had been proposed at an early stage by the Americans, though on the basis of a north–south rather than an east–west division, and the Soviet government was engaged in strategic preparation for the peace many months before the war ended. At Tehran in 1943 it was agreed that Poland's frontiers should be moved westward, leaving the Soviet Union in possession of Polish territory it had occupied in 1939 (the predominately Orthodox areas) but compensating the Poles in the west at Germany's expense. In November 1944 Maxim Litvinov, who had been Soviet Foreign Minister before the war and was now engaged in foreign-policy planning, sent his successor, Viacheslav Molotov, a position paper based on the premiss that the United States might revert to isolationism or even fall out with Britain (and they did indeed disagree over important questions such as the future of the British Empire). In such an event, he argued, Anglo-Soviet co-operation would bring advantages. With this end in view, Litvinov suggested that the British be accommodated over Iran (Persia), Afghanistan and Sinkiang in return for control of the Straits and hence free access from the Black Sea to the Mediterranean (which had been offered to Russia during the First World War).

> Such an agreement [he added] can only be brought about on the basis of an amiable delineation of spheres of interest in Europe . . . The Soviet Union can consider Finland, Sweden, Poland, Hungary, Romania, the Slavic countries of the Balkan peninsula, and also Turkey as [constituting] its maximum sphere of interests. Holland, Belgium, France, Spain, Portugal and Greece [on the other hand] can certainly be included in the English sphere.[2]

When Churchill met Stalin in Moscow in 1944 they agreed a division of the Balkans into spheres of influence, subsequently known as the 'percentages agreement'. According to this, Romania and Bulgaria would be in the Soviet sphere, Greece in the British, while Soviet and British influence in Hungary and Yugoslavia would be split fifty-fifty. It was also agreed that the three Allied Powers, plus France, would occupy Germany at least until it was de-Nazified. It seemed unlikely that the Western Powers would yield the Straits, however, so in June 1945 Moscow proposed joint Soviet–Turkish responsibility for their control, and pressed the Turkish government to allow Soviet troops to be stationed on the Bosphorus and at the Dardanelles. It even proposed that part of Trabzon and Karasund be transferred to Soviet control – but Turkey stood firm. So did Iran when it was pressed to cede some territory on the frontier with Azerbaydzhan.[3] At Potsdam in July–August 1945 the Allies called on Japan to surrender unconditionally, and agreed that the Soviet Union should receive southern Sakhalin and the Kurile Islands, and reparations from all those countries that had fought against it. It also made provision for continuing co-operation between the Allies after the war. Not everything had turned out as expected, however.

Stalin had undertaken to declare war against Japan within three months of Germany's defeat, but when the time came the United States no longer needed Soviet participation and did not want it – but Stalin insisted on joining in for fear that the Americans would otherwise dictate peace terms and so threaten Soviet interests in the Far East. Britain and the United States refused to recognize Soviet retention of the Baltic countries, yet did not dispute it. It transpired that, while most Romanians and Hungarians would have preferred their countries to have been included in the West's sphere of influence, most Greeks – and for a time most Frenchmen and Italians too – were sympathetic to Communism and would have preferred inclusion in the Soviet sphere.

Contrary to popular belief, Stalin stuck to the letter of his agreements with the Western Powers. Rather than being ideologically motivated, he believed that 'whoever occupies at territory also imposes his own social system on it.'[4] Not only did he sacrifice the Communists in Greece and allow those of France and Italy to be thwarted, he conceded rather more in Hungary than he need have done. In brief, he was a cautious empire-builder of the old Russian type – a realist, intent on achieving concrete objectives. To this end he used the Communist Party as an Established Church, as a means of controlling his own followers, like Russian grand princes of a former age; and he adapted Communist ideology quite freely to direct the faithful at home and around the world in the directions he desired. Until the Soviet Union acquired its own atomic bomb in August 1949 , however, his posture to the West remained defensive. Both Russia and its Western allies were subject to similar pressures, economic and popular, to demobilize quickly and most of the victorious Soviet troops who had first occupied central Europe were soon ordered home.

High though the German casualty rate had been, Soviet casualties were higher.[5] Certainly the Soviet command had been less careful with lives, and when the war ended it was just as careless in demobilizing soldiers. In the summer of 1945 an Italian Jew recently released from a concentration camp in Germany observed squads of recently demobilized soldiers on their way home, singing songs. They

> had been demobbed in the crudest, simplest fashion; their commanders had said to them: 'You have finished fighting the war, now go home'; and home they went, on foot. Now anyone with any idea of the size, the distance along parallels within the Soviet Union, will realize what sort of a repatriation this was. There were squads on foot, some even barefoot, carrying their boots over their shoulders so as not to wear them out. Others had found the most incredible means of transport, clambering up onto lorries, onto Berlin buses

> towed along like trains. We saw one motor unit towing two or three Berlin city buses still with the Berlin signs as they travelled east, homeward with still another thousand, two thousand, three thousand kilometres to go, perhaps into the heart of Siberia; and they sang [the popular song] '*Kalinka Kala*' as they passed by in front of us, this and other songs, waving to us all, survivors and the rest.[6]

But sufficient troops remained to keep order. The surviving German population received the occupiers with fear and sullenness, and many Hungarians and Romanians were hardly joyful. The newly liberated Czechs, Slovaks and Yugoslavs, by contrast – even most Poles – had greeted them with relief. Although the Ukrainian (Ruthenian) tail of Czechoslovakia was immediately annexed along with eastern Poland, these countries were compensated with territories at Germany's expense, and at the request of President Benes over 3 million Germans and nearly half a million Hungarians were expelled from the Czech Sudetenland and Slovakia with the assistance of Soviet troops. All this added to the chaos on what remained of eastern Europe's roads.

Yet, as UNESCO reported in 1945 , some form of Soviet occupation was inevitable for the immediate future since eastern Europe was almost entirely dependent on the Soviet army for the transportation of food, medical supplies and other necessities, and in many areas for the restoration of basic services too.[7] Furthermore, Britain and the United States had agreed that the new governments should be friendly to the Soviet Union and purged of Nazi influences. These factors called for Soviet troops to remain in these countries for some time. There was an air of inevitability about the Soviet takeover of eastern Europe.

The region was for the most part poorer than western Europe, and boasted little industry. Its nobility belonged to another age, its clergy were largely reactionary, but the mass of peasantry and the small, alienated middle class, including those few Jews who had survived the Nazi period and other social outsiders, including intellectuals, were ready for a revolution of some kind. Soviet forces removed regimes most of which had become unpopular and there were hopes that the new order would bring a better kind of life. The situation had been foreseen even before the war. As early as 1935 a Hungarian economist and former centrist minister who had migrated to New York published an article which turned out to be prophetic. Analysing the effects of the Great Depression on Hungary and the Balkan countries, he concluded that the experience had trapped them in a hopeless economic situation which encouraged militant nationalism. The consequence, he forecast, would be war or revolution. In fact it had led to both. He had also forecast likely trends in the aftermath of the cataclysm:

> After a bloody chaos mass misery may find its solution. This will come, however, not through a peaceful reform of the agricultural production on the basis of independent peasant holdings and cooperation but . . . in the form of the bread factories of Russia with dictatorial methods [i.e. collectivization]. This might also lead to a new political union but . . . [it] would not be . . . [a] federation of the free . . . countries [but] Slav unity under Russian dictatorship.[8]

In short, he was suggesting that the Soviet way and Russian rule would seem the only practical way by which poor countries could avoid mass poverty and political instability. Whatever the perceptions of a shrewd political economist, the experience of fascism and the extreme clericalism of the Catholic Church in eastern Europe had given Communism broad appeal, especially to younger people. The older generation was not so attracted – except, ironically, in the most developed of all the eastern-European countries, Czechoslovakia, and there a Communist-dominated left-wing government was freely voted into office.

For two or three years after the war the priority in eastern Europe was to clear the debris and re-establish a working economy. Fascists and those who had collaborated with the Nazis were harshly dealt with, as they were, at first, in the West, though there were no general restrictions on individual freedom. But as soon as it became possible to look towards the longer term, the Soviet model seemed promising not so much for ideological reasons but because it seemed to be the most effective way of quickly rebuilding something better on the ruins of a discredited system.

The taproot of the Cold War, however, went back to the mistrust between the Powers which had increased from 1944. When Truman informed Stalin at Potsdam that the United States possessed an atomic bomb, which it was soon to drop on Japan, Stalin thanked him. But his intelligence service had already informed him of the fact some time before. America's reticence did not inspire trust and the United States' subsequent refusal to entertain requests for credits further undermined the close wartime relationship. Yet the Cold War could have been avoided even after Churchill's 'Iron Curtain' speech of March 1946.

The curtain fell only over a year later, when the Marshall Aid programme was introduced to help Western European countries to recover from the war. Its terms had been designed to be unacceptable to the Soviet Union and its followers. We have this on the authority of George Kennan, the architect of American post-war foreign policy.[9] So, when the Soviet Union and Czechoslovakia applied for Marshall Aid, and learned that as beneficiaries they would be subject to public American scrutiny on a collective basis, like all other beneficiaries, they withdrew. It was, after all, unthinkable that the Power which had done most to defeat the common enemy should be exposed to what was tantamount to public humiliation. That was what Washington had been counting on.

From that point in 1947 tendencies in Eastern Europe hardened into firm trends. The coalition governments which had been the norm there, as in most of continental Europe, were transformed into obedient satellites following policies of planned production, collectivization of farming, and obedience to Moscow's political line. Five-year, even six-year, plans were introduced; agriculture was collectivized; the Communist Party, sometimes with a more agreeable local name, assumed authority in almost every institution; and the secret police thrust out their tentacles in all directions. With these systems in place Moscow had no fewer than three channels through which to control its new European empire: diplomatic relations, the Communist Party of the Soviet Union, to which all satellite parties were expected to defer, and the security services which shared intelligence and took their cues from NKVD headquarters. Those who fell under suspicion were purged. In time other institutions would be established to knit the region together for purposes of defence and economic co-operation, but Stalin always preferred bilateral to multinational dealing.

The fiat of the Soviet Party ran far wider than Europe, however, and in 1948, when the Chinese Communist Party took power from the Nationalists under Chiang Kai-shek, its leader, Mao Zedong, publicly accepted Stalin's line. The new state of Israel, however, to which the Soviet Union had been the first power to extend *de facto* recognition and which, with Moscow's blessing, had been supplied by Czechoslovakia with arms for its war of independence against the Arabs, disappointed Stalin's hopes and aligned with the West (which may help to explain the subsequent purges in Czechoslovakia and the execution of its Jewish Party Secretary Rudolf Slansky). The Yugoslav Communist Party was excommunicated because its leader, Josef Tito, fell foul of Stalin by trying to form a Balkan confederation. Another purge – of Titoists, Zionists and other 'deviants' – was expected in the Soviet Union itself, but at the beginning of March 1953 Stalin collapsed and died.

The news was greeted with relief by many, but the predominant reaction was sorrow. This was only partly a result of deliberate image-building, which presented him as a great war leader with an affinity to Ivan IV in his youthful, conquering phase. Stalin was genuinely popular, despite – even because of – the blood he had shed. As a British historian writes, 'Unpalatable as it may be . . . for liberals both East and West to admit that tyranny and terror can have a certain popular appeal, to pretend otherwise does not help us understand these phenomena'.[10] But with Stalin gone the atmosphere slowly changed.

The telephone rang in a flat overlooking Suvorov Avenue in Leningrad. A young woman answered. A harsh voice, sounding like a demon from Hades, asked rudely who had answered the call. She gave her name. Then the voiced rasped out her father's name. Her father had been arrested in the 1930s; there had been no news of him since. He would arrive within the hour, barked the caller, and hung up. Minutes later there was a knock at the door. Her father, long feared dead, had returned.[11] There were many such reunions in this period – and many sadder resolutions too.

Fears of another period of terror, which had grown again with the alleged 'Doctors' Plot' of 1952, slowly cleared. It was three years after Stalin's death, in February 1956, that a new Party Secretary, Nikita Khrushchev, addressed a secret session of the Twentieth Congress of the Communist Party of the Soviet Union. His text was soon leaked, no doubt deliberately, through a fraternal Polish delegate. And so the shattering news reached the Soviet people and the world: Khrushchev had denounced Stalin for making costly mistakes and ordering unnecessary killings. From then on changes came faster.

The Party line began to ease both in domestic affairs and in foreign policy. The strict controls favoured by Stalin could not be sustained indefinitely. In the Soviet Union itself economic plans were soon altered to provide more consumer goods, and Stalin's demise excited greater expectations. But not all satellite leaders followed the new line, and a few weeks later workers in East Germany rebelled against excessive work norms imposed by Walter Ulbricht, the Party leader. Three years later a major revolt in Poland was narrowly averted by bringing the popular Wladyslaw Gomulka to power and raising living standards, but later that year, 1956 , the forces of protest in Hungary produced a full-scale revolution which was suppressed only by the application of considerable force.

It was noted, however, that although the American-run Radio Free Europe had encouraged the rising in Hungary, Western forces did not intervene to help the insurgents. In the longer term it also became clear that, although collectivization was reimposed in Hungary (though not in

Poland), it was done in a way that won acceptance. And if the Soviet regime was learning how to keep power through the judicious use of concession as well as repression, it was also proving adept at extending its influence abroad by the careful dispensation of aid. India, in particular, was courted. In 1953 a five-year trade agreement was signed with it, and two years later the Soviets undertook to build a steel plant there.[12] They also provided oil-prospecting equipment and a million tons of steel to assist India's industrialization at a crucial stage, helped with mineral prospecting, and provided other technical aid. Economic help was paralleled by high-profile gestures of political co-operation. India's leader Pandit Nehru was feted in Moscow; Khrushchev was festooned with garlands in Delhi.[13]

Burma, Cambodia, Afghanistan and several African and Arab countries, especially Egypt, were also targeted as recipients of Soviet largesse and influence. Competition with the West for influence in non-aligned countries could be fierce, however, and it was expensive. In 1954 Moscow agreed to buy Burma's entire rice crop when it was unable to sell it elsewhere; it also bought Iceland's fish surplus at the time of the 'cod war' with Britain. But great powers were expected to act thus, and aid was an important element in a bigger, worldwide, struggle.

The West made a concerted effort to confine the Soviet Union to its sphere by building a series of military alliances: NATO to protect Western Europe and the Mediterranean; the Baghdad Pact which set up CENTO (an alliance which included Iran and Pakistan) for western Asia; and the South-East Asia Treaty Organization, which also included Pakistan. Moscow reacted sharply: Marshal Zhukov, now Soviet defence minister, warned the United States against interfering on the Soviet Union's southern frontier. Russia had possessed a hydrogen bomb since 1953, but in 1957 NATO, led by the United States, raised the stakes still higher by introducing nuclear warheads and building bases for ballistic missiles of intermediate range. The Soviet reaction seemed intended to wrong-foot its rival: it suspended nuclear tests, undertook not to use nuclear weapons under any circumstances, and dropped plans to deploy them in East Germany, Poland and Czechoslovakia. It also undertook to scale down its conventional forces to a level that would maintain the existing balance between East and West.[14] This non-belligerent stance made for good public relations, but was deceptive. The Soviets proceeded with the development of their own inter-continental ballistic missiles, and test-fired one later that year. Then, in October, to the astonishment of much of the world, they launched the first space rocket to orbit the earth.

Soviet influence in the world now grew at a tremendous rate. Following a *coup d'état*, Iraq was persuaded to leave the Baghdad Pact and legalize a Communist Party. In 1959 Soviet engineers arrived in Egypt, which would not permit a Communist Party, to start work on a huge hydroelectric and irrigation project, the Aswan Dam. This scheme, intended to revolutionize Egyptian agriculture, soon came to symbolize Soviet prestige in Africa and the Middle East. The same year Fidel Castro took control of Cuba and, encountering difficulties with the United States, offered himself to Moscow as a protégé. At the beginning of that year, in the course of announcing a new Seven Year Plan, Khrushchev boasted that by 1970 the Soviet Union would have caught up with the United States in industrial production. 'By that time, or perhaps even sooner, the Soviet Union will advance to the first place . . . both in absolute volume of production and production per head.'[15]

If the claim was credible, the implications were awesome. In 1961 Iurii Gagarin orbited the Earth, becoming the world's first traveller in space. Given the technological competence demonstrated in the Soviet space and nuclear programmes, the economic pre-eminence that Khrushchev forecast implied military pre-eminence, and promised pre-eminent political influence in the world too. Furthermore, the Soviet Union had what the United States lacked: a working model of empire with a directly controlled inner sphere; a sphere of indirect but nonetheless effective control, as in Mongolia, North Korea and Eastern Europe; and, beyond that, a sphere of influence including such diverse states as Cuba, the United Arab Republic, North Vietnam and Ghana. Its arsenal of influence also included channels for cultural, scientific and professional exchange as well as responsive Party organizations round the globe. And in the shorter term, at least, Khrushchev's claim showed every sign of proving justified. Six years later gross national product of the Soviet Union had increased by nearly 60 per cent and industrial output by 84 per cent.[16]

These were heady days for Khrushchev. He participated in an impromptu televised debate with Vice-President Nixon, publicly upbraided President Eisenhower for ordering US spy-planes to overfly the Soviet Union, and put the captured pilot of one which had been shot down on public display. In fact the United States and the Soviet Union were already on the way to convergence. This development, had its costs, however. Mao did not favour rapprochement, and denounced it. This fractured Communist solidarity. It also lost the Soviets their submarine base at Valona on the Adriatic, for Albania sided with China. Distant Beijing seemed preferable to Moscow as a protector of so small and vulnerable a state. Then Kennedy was elected president of the United States and Khrushchev had to face a double standoff with him over Berlin and Cuba.

In Berlin the East German authorities had felt constrained to counter the steady flight of population – including an ever increasing proportion of young, technically trained people – to the West. In 1961, in desperation, they had erected a wall between the eastern and western sectors of the city. This action reflected badly on the Soviet Bloc's image, but the West felt unable to contest it. In the following year Kennedy did contest the movement of Soviet missiles to Cuba, however, and Khrushchev responded by withdrawing them – though not before eliciting an undertaking from Kennedy to remove US missiles from Turkey, which were as uncomfortably close to the Soviet heartlands as Soviet missile sites in Cuba were to the United States. The Cuban missile crisis removed that problem, but the Soviet Union had suffered an unnecessary public humiliation and Khrushchev was soon sacked for 'adventurism'.

The fact that German forces had come so close to penetrating the Caucasus in 1942–3 had prompted Moscow to order the immediate deportation of over 3 million native people – including Crimean Tatars, Volga Germans and nearly half a million Chechens and Ingush[17] – to less hospitable regions far behind the lines. Their status as suspected traitors led to gratuitous ill-treatment, and barely half the number that were moved out were ever to return. After Stalin's death, however, the repressive line towards the nationalities eased somewhat. A degree of decentralization was introduced, more Party members belonging to minorities were promoted to posts in central government, and tolerant policies on language and culture were reintroduced. Nevertheless, it was recognized that the 'national question' would not disappear as quickly as Marxist theory had suggested and so, while the Chechens, Ingush and Kalmyks deported in 1943 were allowed to return to their former homes with an apology from Khrushchev himself for the 'abuses' they had undergone, Volga Germans, Crimean Tatars and Meskhetian Turks remained unrehabilitated, in exile.

Soviet attempts to manage a multinational, multi-ethnic empire recalled tsarist preoccupations, and the policies followed embraced both old and new methods. The Baltic republics were favoured, as in tsarist times, as a testing ground for innovation, which helped to soothe feelings hurt by their loss of independence in 1939 and their reabsorption into the Soviet Union at the end of the war. However, Central Asia, despite considerable investments to establish cotton-growing, remained backward economically and its peoples largely unacculturated. On the other hand, economic and social development, as well as Soviet policies of positive discrimination, led to previously neglected minorities, including Kazakhs, Buriats, Kabardinians and Yakuts, overtaking ethnic Russians in the proportion of their population receiving a higher education.

Some issues, it turned out, were beyond the power of both theory and governmental action to control. There were some unexpected outcomes from deliberate changes, and secular developments were creating changes of their own. Members of minorities, no longer educationally disadvantaged, began to expect more in terms of privilege and status, and became impatient if opportunities were slow to open up to them.[18] From the 1960s the proportion of ethnic Russians in the total Soviet population began to decline rapidly from its high point of almost 55 per cent, and living standards showed less improvement in Russia than among other ethnicities in the periphery.[19]

Khrushchev's boast that the Soviet Union would catch up and even surpass the United States was not to be justified. Yet in the forty years that had passed since the inception of the first Five Year Plan in 1928 immense strides had been taken economically. Gross national product had expanded seven or even eight times over. This represented an average growth rate of 6 to 7 per cent a year – better than that attained during the second period of industrialization under Stolypin. Fixed investment had grown thirty times over, and as much as 30 per cent of the economy was being reinvested in the early 1960s, although productivity was less impressive.[20]

Agricultural production increased too, though hardly enough to justify the huge investments that had been poured into it. The acreage under the plough in Kazakhstan more than tripled between 1953 and 1958 yet yields fluctuated wildly year by year. The dairy industry and sheep-rearing there also saw impressive expansion; and the Kazakh economy as a whole, primitive at the outset, came to be well integrated into the Soviet Union's.[21] The output of consumer goods also grew encouragingly, but their quality was poor; and, although the cities saw the erection of vast housing estates, the housing was cramped and shoddy by Western standards. Shostakovich's hilarious musical *Cheriomushki*, named after a real Moscow surburban tower-block development, is a monument both to the popular hopes invested in such projects and to the inefficiencies and corruption involved in them. It was taken off after one brief season, and not repeated.

Nevertheless, by the 1970s the population of the Soviet Union was better fed, better housed and enjoyed a higher real standard of living than it had ever done. Contentment spread, especially among the generations old enough to have experienced the privations of the Stalin period, and it extended to the nationalities. At the same time, Communism had wrought great changes in the ethnic map since tsarist days. This was partly a consequence of industrialization and urbanization. In Siberia some of the smaller ethnic groups, like the Khanty (Ostiaks) and Mansi (Voguls), had become outnumbered in their own lands by as much as five to one as ethnic Russians and others poured in to work on various projects.[22] The ethnic and linguistic configuration of many parts of the Soviet Union was altered, sometimes significantly. So it was that Russians came to form almost three-quarters of the population of Karelia, 61 per cent of Buriatia's and around half of the populations of Yakutia and Tatary.

This was the result of migrations, both forced and spontaneous. Aside from the deportations, the government directed labour through job postings and used incentives to tempt workers to places where they were needed. In particular, ethnic Russians, Ukrainians and Belorussians were encouraged to settle in sensitive strategic areas where the authorities wanted to dilute strong ethnic concentrations of native peoples. In Chechnya-Ingushetia almost a quarter of the population came to be Russian, in Circassia 40 per cent; and substantial Russian-speaking populations were also planted in the Baltic republics and in the frontier areas of Transcaucasia and southern Kazakhstan.[23] Population growth in Russia proper slowed considerably. So did that of ethnic Russians. These phenomena may have been related to settlement policies, but they were irrelevant to the policy-makers. They hoped that the population as a whole, but particularly its elites, would develop a distinctive Soviet character, reflecting similar educational standards, sharing the same values, and enjoying the same privileges. A Soviet nationality composed of Party members of all ethnicities and others who took pride in Soviet achievements was indeed being formed, and it suggested a better fate for the Soviet Empire than that of its tsarist predecessor. Yet after a time nationalist sentiments began to grow despite these policies.

The Crimean Tatars, frustrated at their failure to recover the land of their birth, began to organize and eventually delivered a petition signed by most of them. It was rejected, but this did not end their efforts. Jews were also energized, but by Israel, which had developed into a far more attractive 'national home' than Birobijan, which Stalin had allotted for the purpose. Thanks to American representations, some 200,000 Jews were allowed to leave for Israel by 1981[24] – a fact which encouraged more Jews and half-Jews, and even non-Jews, to put in applications to migrate, and roused some interest, and resentment, among other sections of the population. The populations of the Baltic provinces were quiescent at this time, as were those of Belarus and Ukraine, though by the later 1960s the KGB had become concerned about underground activity by supporters of the Uniate Church, which had been suppressed after the Second World War but which was believed to be receiving support from Rome. The KGB infiltrated, or suborned, agents in order to monitor the situation.[25] At this stage Soviet security was more concerned about religious than nationalist subversion, but, as events were in due course to demonstrate, the two were connected.

In the satellite countries of Eastern Europe improving living standards became more effective than secret-police activity and repression in maintaining stability through the 1960s and '70s. In Hungary the Kadar regime produced an apparent miracle in the early 1960s, transforming a population seething with resentment after the suppression of the 1956 rising with the offer of a social truce under the slogan 'Whoever is not against us is with us.' Collectivization was reintroduced, but more sensitively than on the first occasion, and in a practical rather than doctrinaire fashion. In time, many of the collectives became profitable, set up shops and restaurants in nearby cities, and began to resemble Western-type companies. Traditional industries like food-processing came into their own along with high-technology industries like the manufacture of optical instruments, which were favoured for investment. The 'black economy' was partly legalized, workers were encouraged to use factory equipment to make products outside working hours to sell for their personal profit, and moonlighting became common. The economy grew; so did people's incomes. Television sets and washing machines, which had once been very scarce, became almost commonplace.

In East Germany, where a Communist substitute for Hitler's Volkswagen came into mass production, people were encouraged by the prospect of owning a Trabant car, or a boat to sail on the Baltic, or a cottage by the sea or in the country, the equivalent of the Russian dacha, which had remained its owner's private property even under Stalin. This was a twentieth-century reflection of Russia's chronic condition of plentiful space and relatively sparse population, and it applied in some measure to other parts of Eastern Europe too. Bulgarians were less consumer-oriented, but their long-standing reputation as market gardeners was reflected in large collectives specializing in grapes and growing roses for perfume, as well as in vegetables. In Romania the old oppressive peasant economy had disappeared, but the mentalities it had bred remained evident, and many Romanians were still disoriented by the novel experience of city or factory. The

Hungarian and German minorities there had long provided the only modernizing leaven, and they suffered most from the transition, for in backward states like Romania the modernizing force of Communism adopted nationalism as its partner.

In Poland the sense of common purpose between the leadership and the masses was lowest of all. Poles had lost nothing of their nationalist pride and became the most demanding of the satellite populations. After an unsuccessful attempt to impose collectivization in 1948, the policy was abandoned. So deep an emotional issue had it become that even Stalin dared not insist on it. Shortages of consumer goods and meat, particularly pork, could provoke serious protests, and so Poland was eventually allowed to run up substantial foreign debts and thereafter the Soviet worker in effect subsidized Polish living standards.[26] But though Moscow indulged the Poles, it could act harshly if others overstepped the line.

It did so in August 1968, when Leonid Brezhnev, who now presided in the Kremlin, reluctantly authorized Soviet forces to suppress the 'Prague Spring'. Liberalization in Czechoslovakia had produced a ferment there which, it was feared, might lead to disturbances and, given the country's geographical position, pointing as it were to the heart of the Soviet Bloc, invite Western military interference. Albeit by the narrowest of votes in the Politburo, pre-emptive action was taken. No matter that the operation was designed to avoid casualties and was implemented reluctantly, alongside contingents from other members of the Bloc (but not Romania), it seemed shocking that the Soviet Union should have used violence against an ally of such long standing, the only country in Eastern Europe, apart from Yugoslavia, which had freely voted the Communists into power. Leonid Brezhnev took care to explain the action to the world, proclaiming a Soviet equivalent to America's Monroe Doctrine. But, rather than straightforwardly delineating a sphere into which other powers must not intrude, he chose to dress the message up in the awkward language of Party principle:

> The Communist Party of the Soviet Union has always advocated that each socialist country determine the concrete forms of its development . . . but when deviation from common laws of socialist construction and a threat to the cause of socialism in that country arises . . . it is no longer just a problem for that country's people but a common problem for all socialist countries.[27]

Washington reacted by assuring Moscow that American ideological objections to the action would not be allowed to interfere with negotiations between the two nuclear superpowers. And the Czechs themselves – more pragmatic and less romantic than the Poles – soon diverted their energies from the public to the domestic sphere.

In the Soviet Union itself, Party membership offered a promising career path to aspiring youth and the Party not only served to co-ordinate policy, it offered means of social interaction through mutual visits and conferences, and provided a kind of social glue. Party functionaries, like ministers and senior police officials, got to know each other, to take each other's measure, to share a sense of common purpose. Other Soviet Bloc organizations served similar social as well as political ends. The Warsaw Treaty Organization was formed in May 1955 in response to the rearming of West Germany and its inclusion in NATO, and came to mirror NATO to a great extent. The supreme commander was invariably a Russian general, as NATO's was an American, and the equipment followed the standards set by the alliance's leading partner. Meetings not only thrashed out differences and provided a forum for the statement of national wishes, they were also occasions for the exercise of charm and persuasion and encouraged a spirit of comradeship in arms. The Poles, whose army was second only in size to the Red Army, found the WTO somewhat reassuring because it constituted a guarantee against a German resurgence, for many Poles felt that they had suffered even more at German than at Russian hands. Yet when Khrushchev had proposed integrating most of the member forces under Soviet command with standardized uniforms and ranks as well as arms, Romania baulked. Such conformities denied Romania's distinctiveness.

COMECON, which promoted economic co-operation within the Bloc, pre-dated the WTO. In 1954 it was given the task of co-ordinating the national plans of the member countries, and it soon assumed other roles, developing a common electricity grid and sharing a pipeline which gave members access to Soviet oil. It seemed to be imitating the West's European Economic Community (now the European Union): the design of its Moscow headquarters seemed to have been inspired by the EU building in Brussels. But its philosophy was different. Its strategic aim, agreed in 1962, was to 'eliminate technical and economic backwardness . . . [chiefly by means of] socialist industrialization with the principal emphasis . . . on heavy industry and its core, engineering'.[28]

It also tried to encourage specialization and a division of labour within the Soviet Bloc, but to this Romania objected. Its leaders objected to being split between two great regional zones as had been suggested. The economic planners had classified Transilvania, the northern third of the country, as semi-industrial, along with Hungary and Poland, but zoned the southern regions of Moldavia and Wallachia as agricultural, along with

Bulgaria. This seemed to threaten the country's national integrity. True, Romania was a backward Balkan country, predominately peasant both in social structure and in outlook, but its leaders were economic Stalinists whose Communism was intertwined with nationalism. For them the development of heavy industry was more than an element in economic modernization (one which even at that stage was beginning to seem outdated): it was a measure of Romanian achievement.

Soviet leaders had long since abjured Stalinist methods, so Romania was given sufficient latitude to thwart COMECON plans for economic integration. However another – voluntary – approach was to achieve limited success. By 1976 COMECON had promoted specialization in machine-building, created a large pool of railway rolling stock, and built a gas pipeline through the Bloc. It had also founded a joint nuclear research institute, a Bank for Economic Co-operation and had set up organizations to modernize the region's steel industries and to co-ordinate the manufacture of ball-bearings and chemicals. The fact that the headquarters of these new organizations were allotted to Budapest, Warsaw and East Berlin, rather than being retained in Moscow, mirrored EU practice and suggested that the dirigiste character of the Bloc had given way to a freer form of cooperation.

As for Romania, it continued to find occasion to defy Moscow. It was an effective way for leaders to advertise their patriotism to a population most of whom either resented Communists or were politically innocent. Unlike Czechoslovakia, Romania escaped punishment for stepping over Moscow's line, but then it did not border a NATO state and it remained stable internally under the oppressive Ceausescu. It is curious, however, that after thirty years of Communism the economic pecking order of the East European countries was the same as it had been half a century, and indeed a century, earlier. The richest countries, in terms of average income per head, were still Czechoslovakia and East Germany; and the poorest were still Albania, Romania and Russia itself.

By 1970 the Soviet Union matched the United States in the number of intercontinental ballistic missiles deployed. The balance of nuclear power had reached the point of perfection. In these circumstances neither side wished to risk their use for fear of reprisal, and both now moved towards détente and to limiting the spread of nuclear weapons to other states. Anticipating this change in strategic circumstances, in 1969 both sides signed a Nuclear Non-Proliferation Treaty, and talks began on Strategic Arms Limitation.[29] Only China, jockeying for a better position in the race for world power and trying to seize leadership of the Communist movement from the Soviet Union, objected vehemently both to détente and to the Brezhnev Doctrine, viewing them as breaches of Marxist principle. Ideological purity had only ever had brief tenure in the Kremlin. Indeed, reasons of state had long since tended to shape the ideological line that Moscow laid down.

Despite détente, however, competition between the Soviet Union and the USA continued. During the 1960s Moscow's influence in Africa had waned. The ousting of Kwame Nkrumah in 1966 meant the loss of Ghana as a client; Soviet influence in the Middle East diminished sharply after Egypt's defeat in the Six-Day War with Israel in 1967; and after Nasser died in 1970, Egypt ceased to be an ally. Yet Soviet influence in other regions grew. Concern about Washington's courtship of Pakistan and fear of China prompted an intensification of relations with India. This culminated in a treaty of considerable strategic significance signed in 1971. It made port facilities available to Russian ships at Bombay, Goa, Cochin and the Andaman Islands, and opened up an air corridor for Soviet aircraft from Tajikistan in Central Asia down to the Bay of Bengal.[30] The Soviet Union thus became a power in south Asia and the Indian Ocean.

At the same time Moscow was securing new allies on the very doorstep of its Marxist rival, China: North Korea and North Vietnam. It gave the latter significant economic and diplomatic support for its fight against the US-backed regime in South Vietnam, but gauged it carefully so as not to disrupt détente with Washington. But economic aid and a model of development that seemed more effective than market forces were not the only attractions that won new allies and friends. The Soviet Union represented an opposite ideological pole to the United States and, as such, exerted an attractive force around the world. So it was that not only Ethiopia, Angola and Mozambique aligned with Moscow, but close ties were developed with the Chile of Salvador Allende.

Competition in some parts of the globe contrasted with détente in Germany, however. In 1970 Moscow granted recognition to the Federal Republic of Germany in response to friendly overtures from its leader, Willy Brandt – a development which helped to change the tone of East–West relations in central Europe from confrontation to co-operation. In Asia, however, as in Africa, competition remained the norm, and it was to become particularly fierce over Afghanistan. Russia had been anxious to secure a position there since the later nineteenth century, in order to insulate and secure her territories in Central Asia against attack and gain a lever in southern Asia. This interest was to be maintained. As early as 1927

Soviet engineers had begun work on a road through the Salang Pass over the high Panjshir range to link Samarkand and Dushanbe with Kabul, but the project had been thwarted by the Afghani revolt in the following year. Progress was resumed in the 1950s, when Moscow provided aid to develop the country's communications infrastructure by building bridges, roads and an airport at Baghram in the east of the country, on the route to Kandahar.

In this fashion the Soviet Union had built a dominant influence in Afghanistan and a strong position in the heights of Asia, with access to both friends and potential enemies to the south. The position was not yet impregnable, however. In September 1979 Hafizullah Amin was to stage a bloody coup in Kabul and prepared to switch sponsors. This prompted the Kremlin to order intervention. Soviet special forces stormed the presidential palace and, after heavy fighting took it, killing Amin in the process. A Communist, Babrak Karmal, became president, and Afghanistan changed its status from protégé to satellite.[31]

The Kremlin had been helped in the immediate post-war era by the prestige it had won in the Second World War, by the worldwide ramifications of the Communist Party, and by the effectiveness of its intelligence service. The Soviet spy network had succeeded in penetrating the secrets of the 'Manhattan Project' at an early stage, thanks to agents like Klaus Fuchs and Alan Nunn May in Britain and Theodore Hall and David Greenglass in the United States. At the same time the celebrated and notorious 'Cambridge Five' (Philby, Maclean, Burgess, Blunt and Cairncross) had penetrated the British Foreign Office and security agencies, including MI5, SIS and SOE. This had allowed them to convey essential information not only about the atom bomb, but about other weapons, codes and ciphers, and top-level political and military intelligence.[32] The idealism which led so many brilliant young people to serve what they took to be the cause of Communism rather than their own countries was a major asset to Soviet intelligence. It gave the Kremlin significant advantages from the later 1940s, and was probably decisive in eliminating the scientific and technological gap between the Soviet Union and the Western Powers so quickly. Yet the Soviet Union was not devoid of native dynamism in these areas.

Apart from the occasional quack, like Stalin's protégé the geneticist Lysenko, it made use of many scientists who were leaders in their fields. They included the famous biochemist Aleksei Bakh, the ground-breaking physicist Petr Kapitsa, the aircraft designer Andrei Tupolev, and the inventor of the best small arms in the world, Mikhail Kalashnikov. The roots of the first-rate Soviet scientific establishment stretched back through two centuries of Academy of Science traditions to the Enlightenment, and its fruits were to include the development not only of the first space ships and astronauts but of the first safe heart drug. But for a strange accident at a Paris air show, when another aircraft on an unauthorized flight crossed the flight path of a prototype Tupolev supersonic airliner, causing it to crash, the Soviet Union might also have led the world in commercial supersonic intercontinental flight services. Yet the great sophistication in science and technology coexisted with simple forms of collective human life which had changed little with the passage of centuries, and the Soviet regime's concern to 'civilize' native peoples stemmed from the same burning sense of mission that had fired missionaries everywhere.

All these contrasts were represented in Siberia. On the banks of the great river Ob, upriver from the ancient city of Tomsk, lies Akademgorodok – as its name suggests, a town founded for the specific purpose of serving the most sophisticated scientific research. Siberia was a land of great riches as well as tundra desolation: of diamonds, gold and oil, and great hydroelectric schemes, as on the Yenisei and Angara rivers, models for famous 'Third World' projects like the Aswan Dam. But Siberia was also home to peoples who, for all the ministrations of tsarist missionaries and earnest Communist educators, had hardly advanced from the Stone Age in material culture or understanding of the modern world. Although the processes of adjustment and absorption usually proceeded quietly, there were occasions when the two worlds clashed. There was the occasional squalid fight in dreary Siberian towns between drunken natives and Russian louts yelling racist abuse, and one fracas in Yakutsk was serious enough to bring troops out on to the streets. Nor were well-meaning attempts to inform native peoples always welcomed by them. '"What is the October Revolution?" Evenk reindeer-herders had plaintively enquired, "Who are the bourgeois elements? What is technology? What is industry?"' When a community of Chukchi were invited to elect a committee they resisted on the reasonable ground that 'if they elected one, the number of walrus would not increase.'[33] It was native practicality rather than innocence which spoke. Soviet values did not resonate with Chukchi mentality.

Despite rumblings of discontent in one or two COMECON countries, the Soviet Empire in 1980 seemed stable and reasonably successful. The Soviet Union itself had not caught up with the United States in terms of economic output as Khrushchev had boasted, but it was incontestably a world power, its peoples more prosperous and freer than in the 1950s. True, the Communist movement was no longer a dynamic force in the world, but Moscow was still a beacon of hope for poorer countries, and also for some less poor that wished to distance themselves from American culture and the embraces of capitalism. Even though the system had not yet quite succeeded in replacing nationalism with a supranational Marxist faith, no informed observer seriously expected the vast and powerful Soviet fortress, with its huge outworks of control and influence spreading halfway round the world, to suffer any marked decline in the foreseeable future. Yet within a dozen years, as if subjected to some potent combination of strange chemical forces, it simply evaporated. The fourth, and greatest, Russian Empire was gone, never to be resurrected.

14
Autopsy on a Deceased Empire

At midnight on 31 December 1991 the Soviet Union ceased to exist. The satellite states had gone their separate ways two years earlier, but now the Baltic states regained their independence and Ukraine, Belarus, Kazakhstan and all the other constituent republics started out on a new existence as sovereign states. The red flag with the hammer and sickle was run down the Kremlin flagstaff, and a blue, red and white tricolour was run up instead. Russia had again been shorn of empire.

The reasons why the Soviet Empire collapsed have been disputed ever since. Many believed that dissident activity and popular protest had brought the regime down. Others argued that President Reagan's Strategic Defense Initiative – otherwise known as 'Star Wars' – had established an unchallengeable American superiority in the arms race, and that this had forced the Kremlin to admit defeat and wind its empire down. Some who resented the passing of the old regime explained its fall in terms of conspiracy theories; economists attributed it to industrial obsolescence, political scientists to advances in computer technology which made it impossible for the regime to control the dissemination of information. Other theorists ascribed the collapse to the rigidity of Soviet institutions and their inability adapt to new conditions. (However, it seemed odd that none of the experts who explained the inevitability of Communism's collapse had actually predicted it.)

Then there were those who said that it was the reform of the Soviet system itself which had precipitated the trouble. They held Mikhail Gorbachev, the last General Secretary of the Communist Party of the Soviet Union, responsible for a situation that a less reckless leader would have avoided. And there were some who attributed the collapse simply to ill-fortune (or act of God), to a remarkable series of unforeseeable, uncontrollable and damaging events. Each of these explanations contains some truth. None has so far gained universal acceptance among the ranks of the informed. To gain a fuller understanding of the processes involved we should retrace our steps to the mid-1970s, the high point of Soviet fortunes.

★

As late as the 1970s and even in the 1980s there was no obvious indication of impending disaster. Indeed, the auguries read well. The Soviet Union was as mighty in weaponry as its only rival; surprising as it may seem, its population was as contented as that of the United States; and there was hardly a ripple of dissidence or nationalism anywhere in the Empire. Its policy on nationalities since the 1920s had provided institutional recognition of ethnic nationalism, and since the Second World War a credible 'Soviet nationalism' had emerged. The sense of solidarity had been reinforced by millions of marriages between partners of different nationality. Furthermore, since Brezhnev had given non-Russian nationalities primacy in the constituent republics,[1] it could no longer be argued that one had to be Russian to have a good career.

A survey carried out in 1976 found that most Russians rated their material life at as high as four points on a scale of one to five. There was, after all, no hunger, unemployment or homelessness. Standards of medical care and public order were high, and of education very high. There were shortages, and goods were often shoddy – but that had always been the case. There was a virtual absence of luxury as it was known in the West, but there was welfare at public expense for the young, the old, the sick and the disabled. Rather more Russians than Americans were satisfied with the amount of free time their work allowed them, and more Russians than Americans enjoyed both their work and their leisure. Russians might hate their local bureaucrats, but, as a leading opinion researcher (who was no friend of the regime) has concluded, most people 'accepted the political, economic and social order, including official values such as patriotism, collectivism, respect for the Army, the Soviet empire, national solidarity and the Communist Party. Russians steadfastly supported Soviet foreign policy, including the invasions of Hungary, Czechoslovakia and Afghanistan.'[2] Dissidents existed, but they were few, and their voices were muted by media control, warnings, imprisonment or, as in the case of the novelist Solzhenitsyn, exile in the West. Nationalists hardly stirred, and there was no sign of serious discontent.

Nor was there much restiveness in the countries of the Soviet Bloc. In 1976 a dissident playwright called Vaclav Havel was among a number of Czech intellectuals who issued 'Charter 77' in January that year. This petition invoked the new International Covenant of Rights to protest against the prosecution of a pop group called Plastic People of the Universe, which had infringed the government's canons of decency. In retrospect this might seem a significant blow for freedom, but it was no threat to the regime. Nor were some violent strikes by miners in Romania. Even the election of the Cardinal Archbishop of Cracow, a long-standing thorn in the side of the Polish government, to the papal throne in October 1978 caused hardly a ruffle in the Kremlin dovecotes. Rome would be less of a restraining influence on the Polish Church, reported the Soviet ambassador to Warsaw somewhat blandly, but the election would deprive 'the reactionary part of the episcopate . . . of its leader'.[3]

Two years later the Solidarity movement emerged in Poland. It began as an unofficial strike in support of a dismissed woman crane operator in a Gdansk shipyard. Pope John Paul II had never feared confrontation with the government when he had been a mere archbishop, and he now lent Solidarity, whose followers were overwhelmingly Catholic, his moral support. This gave the movement an aura of religious and patriotic legitimacy in many Polish eyes. Of more practical importance, however, was the fact that militant trade unionists, primarily concerned about standards of living, and intellectuals, concerned about rights and freedoms, were united for the first time. An association known as KOR, made up of lawyers and other professionals who helped and advised the strikers, had been important in promoting this unity. So powerful was the combination that a weak government agreed to negotiate with it – live, on television. The result was a public triumph for the opposition and a series of agreements, some of them unaffordable and impractical. Even so, the complaisant government managed to hold on for many months amid rising fears of a Soviet invasion.

At last in December 1981 a new premier, General Jaruszelski, imposed martial law. Jaruszelski, however, was regarded as a patriot, and the army was Poland's most popular secular institution. Calm was restored, and thereafter Poland remained quiet. Moreover the excitements there proved not to be contagious: there was no significant reaction elsewhere in the Soviet Bloc. The Pope's pastoral visit to neighbouring Slovakia in 1986 did generate some excitement, notably among the young, but the effect was transient. The papacy as a factor in the collapse of the Soviet Empire has been exaggerated.

The war in Afghanistan, where the insurgents were sustained by covert US aid, had continued to soak up resources. However, since the Soviet economy was buoyant, the expense was affordable. In 1983 industrial output was 5 per cent higher than in 1982, agricultural output 7 per cent higher. Two Party secretaries, the able Iurii Andropov and the despised and ailing Konstantin Chernenko, died in quick succession, but in 1985 – the year Soviet intelligence recruited a senior CIA officer, Aldrich Ames – the Soviet Empire gained a new leader.

Mikhail Gorbachev had been Andropov's protégé. He was youthful, engaging and reform-minded. He started his reign as General Secretary by reviving some of Andropov's policies. He launched campaigns against corruption and excessive drinking. He also called for production to be speeded up. The Russian word for this, *uskorenie*, became the new regime's first policy principle. Others were to follow. Gorbachev was a new kind of Soviet leader. As outgoing as Khrushchev, though less crude and excitable, he was ready to engage with the public and made a point of encouraging debate. Openness, or *glasnost*, became his second watchword. The third was *perestroika*, reconstruction. This signalled his intent to reform Soviet institutions, and was to prove the most radical, and fateful.

The notion that basic reforms were necessary had been canvassed as early as Brezhnev's time, but actions had been allowed to peter out when difficulties were encountered. Andropov, however, realized that, although there was no immediate crisis, continuing success must be based on more radical economic and administrative reforms than had been attempted in the past. Among the reports Andropov commissioned was one from an academic think-tank which recommended far-reaching changes to the central planning system.[4]

It was also recognized that Russia's rich reserves of oil and natural gas were being wasted. Government had developed a tendency to buy off trouble simply by pumping them out at a greater rate. Energy was being exported at below world market prices to members of the Bloc, and was used wastefully in the Soviet Union itself. Nor were these the only problems. With the easing of East–West tensions, the Kremlin had allowed its European satellites a latitude they had not previously enjoyed, including the right to borrow money from Western banks. As a result, when interest rates rose, interest payments became a significant factor in the budgets of several Soviet Bloc countries. At the same time Poland in particular had been piling up arrears of interest and repayments to the Soviet Union as well as to the West. Moscow did not insist on payment, however, for fear of triggering a rash of cost-of-living riots, to which Poland had become prone, and precipitating a political crisis. The Kremlin was learning that imperial status could be costly.

Gorbachev soon began to look more and more like a Western politician in the run-up to an election. He promised incentives and benefits to win over any Soviet group or sector that seemed discontented. This further increased pressure on the budget. Moreover, since the range of available goods was limited and their quality variable, many people tended to save their money rather than spend it, and this stored up obligations to provide goods to satisfy consumers in the future. The conservative fiscal principles that had characterized the Kremlin's economic policies for decades were being eroded. Then bad luck struck – not once, but serially.

In 1984 Ronald Reagan was re-elected president of the United States and proceeded with the 'Star Wars' project he had announced the year before; a nuclear reactor in a Ukrainian power station overheated, precipitating the Chernobyl disaster of April 1986; and there was a resurgence of nationalism. Early in 1988 there were violent clashes between Azeris and Armenians over Nagorno-Karabakh, an area in Azerbaydzhan where the majority of the population were Armenians. An independence movement began to emerge in Lithuania, and there were problems between Abkhazians and the government of Soviet Georgia. These problems required massive additional expenditures which added to Gorbachev's existing budgetary problems and created an unpropitious setting for his radical reforms.[5]

The chief aim of the 'Star Wars' programme was to create an anti-missile screen which would render the United States, and those that the USA chose to include under it, impervious to nuclear attack. The project was ostensibly defensive, but its success would enable a protected power to launch a nuclear attack on another without fear of retaliation. The programme would take years to complete, and its success was by no means certain, but the Soviet leadership was not inclined to take chances, and the maintenance of nuclear parity at this new level required an appreciable increase in expenditure.[6]

The men in the Kremlin looked for savings. By October 1985 they were beginning to contemplate troop withdrawals from Afghanistan; by February of the following year, at the time of the Twenty-Seventh Congress of the Communist Party of the Soviet Union, they were ready to launch a foreign-policy initiative that would change the international atmosphere and end the Cold War. Gorbachev had met Reagan in Geneva the previous November, matched him for charm, and impressed him with his liberal intentions. It had long been clear that Stalinism was dead, but now the reins holding member countries of the Bloc in line seemed to be loosening.

In foreign policy Gorbachev gave priority to rapprochement with the countries of the European Union as well as the United States. The rationale of his approach was soon to become apparent: improving East–West relations and increasing trust between the superpowers would allow large cuts in military budgets – what was to become known as 'the peace dividend' – a prospect that reason suggested would be as desirable in the White

House as it was in the Kremlin. The first fruits were to be seen in the agreement to limit the deployment of intermediate-range ballistic missiles and some troop withdrawals from member countries of the Bloc. Gorbachev's popularity abroad had soared, and cheering crowds greeted him in every capital he visited.

Meanwhile he was introducing Soviet citizens to democratic practices which chimed with Western conceptions. At the Party congress in February 1986, when the policies of *glasnost* and *perestroika* were proclaimed, Gorbachev not only undertook to promote individual legal rights but also announced that electors would in future be allowed a choice of candidates (a practice already introduced in Hungary). The idea was also mooted of creating a two-party system by splitting the Communist Party of the Soviet Union between its liberal and conservative wings and sharing the assets between them.[7] In private apartments, bars and hotel lobbies across the Soviet Union crowds gathered round television sets to watch the proceedings. They were not accustomed to the sight of democracy in action, after all, and they watched with quiet fascination, wondering what it boded.[8]

On 26 April 1986 came news of the Chernobyl disaster. The cause has been attributed to incompetent managers, who should have shut the overheating reactor down immediately instead of trying to cool it,[9] but Gorbachev's 'speeding-up' policy may also have contributed. The power industry had been set a target of a 20 per cent increase in output under the current Plan, and managers were under pressure to attain it. This may have persuaded some to take risks. The outcome was radioactive emissions on a catastrophic scale. Extensive evacuation and decontamination programmes had to be carried out, distress alleviated, and a huge wave of concern ridden out abroad as well as at home. Moreover the incident implied systemic failures in training and procedures which had to be addressed. Nor was this the only unwelcome news. Income from the state liquor monopoly had slumped since the introduction of the anti-alcohol campaign. And government expenditure on housing and health, as well as on the military and scientific establishments, was rising strongly, threatening a sizeable budgetary deficit. Most of the production targets under the Plan seemed to be within reach in the first months of 1988, but then world oil prices, which had hit a high in 1986, began to fall, reducing hard-currency earnings and opening up a balance-of-payments deficit which began to increase with disconcerting speed.

None of this was allowed to reduce the momentum of reform, however. In 1988 a law on enterprise was passed and Gorbachev introduced the concept of separation of powers between the executive, legislature and judiciary. But the reformers were already beginning to face stiffening resistance within the Party, and Yegor Ligachev, the second-ranking man in the Party and up to this point Gorbachev's most important ally, was near the point of breaking with him. Ligachev was of the view that the reforms had gone far enough, that any more would be destabilizing. As *Moscow News* reported, leaflets were being circulated which claimed that *perestroika* would lead to 'economic disaster and social upheaval and then to the country's enslavement by imperialist states'.[10]

Support for the challenge came not only from conservative 'Stalinists' but from officialdom generally, especially in the provinces, and from others who found the prospect of further radical change unnerving. The challenge was faced down at a meeting of the Party's Central Committee. Even though most members probably felt as Ligachev did, the conditioning of decades led them to stifle their misgivings, show solidarity, and rally behind the leader. The chance of a genuine democracy had been lost when it was decided not to split the Party, and now perhaps the last chance for stability had gone too.

The final act of the Soviet tragedy was heralded in December 1988 by an earthquake in Soviet Armenia which killed 25,000 people, made many more homeless, and required massive spending on relief. With the strain on the budget mounting higher than ever, the decision had already been taken to cut the expenses of empire. It was announced that from 1 January 1989 world market prices would be charged for Soviet oil and gas exported to members of the Bloc. No longer able to pay the piper, Moscow would no longer be entitled to call the tune. So the satellites in Eastern Europe were freed from their slavish obligation to follow the Kremlin's directions. Nevertheless, Gorbachev hoped that they would follow his line voluntarily and accept reformed Communism, or at least coalition governments, with a gradual transition from authoritarianism to democracy.

Continuing withdrawals of Soviet troops from Poland, Hungary, Czechoslovakia and East Germany pleased the inhabitants. So did the advent of democracy in the first two countries. At the election held in June 1989 Poles celebrated by voting overwhelmingly for opposition Solidarity candidates. But for the fact that they had been guaranteed 173 of the 460 seats in parliament, the Communists would not have been represented there at all.[11] Then in July, at a Warsaw Treaty Organization meeting in Bucharest, Gorbachev proclaimed a reversal of the Brezhnev Doctrine.

The politically correct principle henceforth was to be non-interference in the affairs of the countries of the Bloc. In East Germany a committee was formed to consider changes to the constitution, while in the Soviet Union itself political reforms proceeded apace, though not without reverses.

Gorbachev was open, and apparently somewhat uncertain, as to the form the new Soviet democracy should take. 'The existence of a particular number of political parties does not represent a solution,' he remarked in the early spring of 1989. '[But] we shall open up the possibilities of our system.'[12] Not only the Party but 'social organizations' were to be able to field candidates for elections, and he pledged continuing improvements to electoral practices. At the elections to the Congress of People's Deputies held a few days later the public reacted by rejecting some candidates who had not been opposed.

As the economic position deteriorated over the summer, Gorbachev began to sound increasingly desperate about political and constitutional reform. At a plenary session of the Party Central Committee in mid-July his concern was chiefly about the Party itself and how to restructure its organization from the top. It was his most efficient instrument of government, but it was becoming increasing loath to follow him into these unfamiliar waters. 'It is impossible to decree the Party's authority,' he warned. The Party was 'lagging behind society', and a 'dangerous discrepancy' would arise if it proved itself to be 'less dynamic than the people'.[13] However, it was difficult to know how interested the people really were in constitutional reform.

On 3 August Professor Vorontsov, a technocrat who was not a Party member, was appointed to membership of the Council of Ministers. Eleven days later a draft law to make suffrage 'genuinely direct' was tabled.[14] To those who argued that democracy threatened solidarity, Gorbachev retorted that 'a plurality of views cannot be an obstacle to unity of action.'[15] The debates continued into late September. But the focus on 'constitutional construction' was distracting attention from looming economic and political problems. Striking miners in Siberia were bought off by pay hikes. Indeed money was thrown at every problem, demanding considerable increases in the money supply which fuelled inflation. Estonia reserved the right to veto Union legislation; there were signs of restiveness among other groups, and opposition was voiced not only by those who wanted to put brakes on the reform processes, but by some who urged a faster pace.

Foremost of these was Boris Yeltsin. Promoted to the Secretariat of the Central Committee, he was put in charge of the Moscow Party, and soon proved himself to be both dynamic and unreliable. He urged faster reform, but seemed to be devoid of political ideas or policies. He enjoyed power, but behaved in a domineering manner. To some he was the image of an heroic, patriotic man of action, to others the model of what had once been called a Party 'careerist', and to others again he was an alcoholic maverick. Given to offering his resignation in the expectation that it would not be accepted, he offered it once too often and was not allowed to withdraw it. So it was that in 1987 Yeltsin entered the political wilderness. He was full of resentment. But after two years of marginalization the fates were to offer him the chance of revenge.

Meanwhile the satellite countries, too, were in a state of political turmoil. Instead of gliding towards freedom, Poland had lurched into it. The transition had been smoother in Hungary, but elsewhere it was resisted. Chiefly the resistance came from established leaders who were reluctant to relinquish power, but in Czechoslovakia and Bulgaria there was a wide measure of popular indifference to the issue except among intellectuals and they were a minority. Gorbachev was placed in a strange position. He had either to breach his own principle of non-interference and force the conservatives out of office, or else allow them to continue in their unreformed ways, letting them trail behind as anomalous and unwanted appendages, like rattling cans at the back of the Soviet wedding car. Rather than be embarrassed by them, he chose to prise them out of office. How this was done using Party and KGB connections is one of the strangest stories of the late Soviet period.[16]

The process began in East Germany, where word suddenly began to spread that a new, safe, way of escaping to the West was to take a holiday in Hungary and then cross the frontier into Austria. Hungary had opened its frontier with Austria on 2 May 1989. By 1 July 25,000 people, including many East Germans, were waiting to cross. On 22 August unaccountably lax Czech security allowed crowds of East Germans to occupy the West German embassy in Prague. On 11 September Hungary removed restrictions on all its frontiers, and over the next few days 20,000 East Germans poured across them. By the end of the month thousands were escaping to the West through Czechoslovakia and Poland too. The Polish and Czech governments then urged the East German leader, Erich Honecker, to let would-be migrants leave for the West directly rather than across their frontiers. Late in August he finally agreed to allow those now trapped in West German embassies to leave, though on sealed trains that would travel through East Germany only at night. But security was breached, and on the night of 4 October crowds stormed Dresden railway station trying to board the train as it passed through.

Honecker was about to celebrate the fortieth anniversary of the regime. On 7 October Gorbachev himself arrived in East Berlin, the guest of honour at the celebrations, and proceeded to rack the pressure up on his host several notches more. The fact that he received a warmer reception than his host from the crowds that turned out to see him was not surprising – Gorbachev was very popular outside the Soviet Union. But the broad hints he dropped to Honecker in public were unexpected. 'Life punishes those who lag behind the times,' he warned. As if on cue, large crowds of demonstrators gathered in Leipzig as well as East Berlin, and Honecker was left in no doubt that he should not expect the Soviet troops stationed in his country to save him. On the night of 18/19 October he was abandoned as Party leader and replaced by Egon Krenz, who was responsible for public order and the secret police. The appointment had received Gorbachev's imprimatur. Honecker himself subsequently attributed his downfall to Gorbachev.[17]

The spotlight moved in quick succession from East Berlin to Prague and back again, and then to Sofia. In Prague, on 28 October, the seventy-first anniversary of the country's foundation, a patriotic demonstration was held in Wenceslas Square. The police broke it up, and there were no obvious repercussions. A professor at Charles University who passed through Wenceslas Square regularly in the days that followed observed dissident activists trying to drum up support for another demonstration, but people walked on past them, apparently indifferent.[18] In Berlin, however, excitement rose again when, on 6 November, the East German government finally lifted restrictions on foreign travel. This precipitated a popular craze to leave the country. Sometimes this meant only a few days' sightseeing in the West; nevertheless, there was a haemorrhage of trained professionals, and health services were soon at the point of breakdown.

Three days after restrictions had been lifted there was fresh excitement when crowds began to tear down the Berlin Wall. On 12 November it was announced that eleven of the twenty-four ministries in East Germany's government were being allotted to members of non-Communist parties. This accorded with the Kremlin's latest political line favouring coalition governments, but the fact that Krenz had allowed himself to be overtaken by events did not please Moscow. On 10 November the Bulgarian leader, Todor Zhivkov, was voted out of office by a majority of one in the Central Committee. His successor, Petar Mladenov, had only just returned from a meeting with Gorbachev in Moscow, and the critical vote was thought by some to have been that of Dobri Dzurov, who was reputed to be very close to Moscow.

Circumstantial evidence suggested that the Kremlin was engineering the political changes taking place in the Bloc, and this was shortly to be confirmed in the case of the Czech revolution. The critical incident – recorded on camera – took place in Prague on 17 November, when police apparently attacked demonstrating students, beating one up so badly that he died. This prompted a storm of public outrage and immense crowds bearing banners soon filled Wenceslas Square. The very next day an umbrella opposition movement called Civic Forum headed by Havel was formed, and within ten days there were changes of government and of Party leader, the Party having surrendered its political monopoly. Images of the police killing the student, the inception the Prague Revolution, and the crowd scenes that followed were seen by millions the world over, giving rise to the idea that the people had toppled Communism.

Yet the images were deceptive. A Czech parliamentary inquiry into the police violence of 17 November was quietly discontinued once it was learned that no one had been killed and that the blood spilled had been stage blood. The 'victim' turned out to be a member of the secret police. The public had been treated to a piece of political theatre, staged by Czech security in conjunction with the KGB – a drama worthy of Havel himself. But it had served to launch a genuine revolution. Early in December Civic Forum transformed itself into a political party; on 7 December Communist Party leader Adamec resigned. By the end of the year Havel was installed in the Hradshin Castle as provisional president pending elections. Meanwhile only Ceausescu, of all the old Communist leaders, remained to be disposed of – and Gorbachev and the KGB had a discreet hand in the resolution of that problem too.

The critical date in Bucharest was 22 December. Ceausescu, just returned from a state visit to Iran, appeared on the balcony of the Party headquarters building to make a speech and receive the dutiful plaudits of the crowd assembled in the open space below, as he had done on several occasions in the past. Only this time, instead of applauding, the crowd began to jeer. As the situation became threatening, the dictator and his wife were taken to the roof and flown away by helicopter. But they were soon caught, tried by a summary court martial, and shot. As it transpired, leading figures in the regime which replaced his were already in the building when Ceausescu had begun to speak. In what had been, until the last instalment, a series of bloodless revolutions Gorbachev had cut the satellites loose. He had yet to ensure the security of the Soviet Union in its new circumstances, however, and to shore up his own, increasingly fragile, position as its leader.

The Soviet standard of living deteriorated steadily during 1989. Food rationing became commonplace in many areas, political protests more frequent, and in April there were nineteen fatal casualties in Tbilisi, the capital of Georgia, when troops fired on a crowd of demonstrators. In August, on the anniversary of the Nazi–Soviet Pact, there were demonstrations in the Baltic republics too, and nationalists soon began to organize in Ukraine. Averting his eyes from the deterioration in the economy and from the threat of dynamic nationalism, Gorbachev persevered with political and constitutional reform. In February 1990 he asked the Central Committee to discontinue the Soviet Party's political monopoly, and, true to its tradition of obedience to the leader, it complied, albeit unhappily. In foreign affairs, however, matters did not go well for Gorbachev.

He had hoped for an orderly transition from authoritarian Communism in the countries of the Bloc but, except in Bulgaria and Romania, the reformed socialism that he promoted was rejected and, rather than the gradualism which he envisaged, change came in a rush. Gorbachev also intended to maintain the strategic balance in Europe but with excitement at the prospect of reunification running high on both sides of the German divide Chancellor Kohl moved to absorb East Germany and so reunite his country. The United States affected indifference, Britain disliked the idea and so did France; but neither was disposed to invoke its powers under the Four Power Treaty to prevent German reunification. Gorbachev was entitled to send in troops to maintain the divide and might well have received some support from the West had he done so. But he shrank from it. It would have ended the détente with West Germany, which had become a pillar of Soviet foreign policy. So Gorbachev, who might have prevented unification, allowed it to happen, and confined himself to seeking economic concessions from Kohl to help bolster the now tottering Soviet economy. It was a modest price to pay for Soviet complaisance, and a major political triumph for the German leader.[19]

So it was that by the end of 1990 the unification of Germany, which had been unimaginable even a year before, became a fact. Concerns emerged in west Germany about the cost of absorbing the east, and in the east about the loss of full employment, the erosion of cultural values in which many East Germans had taken some pride, and the inflow of carpetbaggers. But by then it was too late.

There were to be other disappointments in what had been the outer fringes of the Soviet Empire. In June 1991 COMECON was precipitately wound up, at which regional trade ground almost to a standstill. The new regimes in Poland, Hungary and Czechoslovakia tried to reorient their commerce from the East to the West but failed. The Warsaw Treaty Organization, linchpin of the Bloc's defences, was also to become a dead letter, allowing the United States to lead its allies towards an eastward expansion of NATO. In Yugoslavia, deteriorating economic conditions were already fostering nationalist breakaway movements in Slovenia and Croatia, setting the country on a slide to dissolution and bloody civil war, while in the Soviet Union itself the unpredictable Boris Yeltsin, who had so recently been excluded from the political arena, contrived to find a new political space for himself by posing as a Russian patriot.

He had argued that if constituent republics of the Soviet Union like Lithuania or Kazakhstan had an autonomous political life it was anomalous that Russia, the Union's largest constituent by far, should not. Gorbachev could not challenge his logic, and so in March 1990 Yeltsin was able to stand for election to the Supreme Soviet of the Russian Federal Republic. He was elected, and soon chosen to be its chairman. Having created a new political platform, he proceeded to claim sovereignty for Russia and to encourage the Baltic republics and others to claim their independence too. Yeltsin contributed to the dissolution of the Union. But the sharp economic deterioration had given him and the other nationalist politicians their opportunity.

In June 1990 Estonia, one of the more prosperous Soviet republics, proclaimed itself independent in the economic sphere. Lithuania went further, claiming a right to veto all Union legislation, and Uzbekistan, one of the most populous Soviet republics, declared itself sovereign. The once stable Soviet economy was descending into chaos as social distress and inflation rose. Shopping was becoming more and more difficult, necessities of life increasingly expensive, while many employees suddenly lost employment perks and privileges which they had come to take for granted. In August 1990 Gorbachev reacted by setting up a commission of the Supreme Soviet to draft a plan for economic recovery. There were deep divisions of opinion about what should be done, and the argument soon crystallized into a struggle between radical reformers and those who wanted to revert to the old ways. Yeltsin, an instinctive politician, agreed to co-operate. He supported the radicals and was politically helpful to Gorbachev for a time. A 500-day plan for the regeneration of the country, largely the work of an economist called Stanislav Shatalin, was tabled. It called for measures to control inflation, the stabilization of the ruble, the end of price controls, and privatization of the huge state sector.

Similar to the 'shock therapy' advocated by the Harvard economist Jeremy Sachs in Poland, it implied a devolution of economic control which was problematical in the Soviet Union as it had not been in Poland. This was not only because it threatened the interests of powerful *apparatchiki* and to trigger popular discontent, but because the Soviet economy was several times larger than Poland's as well as more complex, and its geographical spread immense. It demanded some careful co-ordination if it were not to become dysfunctional. Furthermore, the isolation of many enterprises made them as vulnerable as Canadian 'company towns', threatening a series of local social disasters if they should suddenly become bankrupt. The plan also threatened the disintegration of the Union. So the weight of opinion began to shift towards the conservatives. Gorbachev sent the Plan back to be redrafted in a less extreme form. This angered those who wanted the speedy implementation of radical reforms, and several ministers resigned. It also bolstered the separatist cause in some republics, especially those adjacent to the West.

Gorbachev, who had failed to grasp one nettle, now reached out to snatch at another: he sanctioned the use of force against the national movement in Lithuania. On 17 March 1991 special units of Soviet forces stormed the television tower in Vilnius, capital of Lithuania, which had been occupied by separatists. There were fifteen fatalities. Intended to be a discreet and bloodless operation which would deter nationalists across the Union, the implementation had been clumsy. Gorbachev moved quickly to disown it; Yeltsin, perhaps afraid that he might be purged or eliminated if the leader's new 'hard line' prevailed,[20] called for a 'declaration of war' against the Soviet leader. On 28 March he mobilized a large crowd of demonstrators in Moscow in defiance of a ban on demonstrations.

With strikes and calls for his resignation flaring up right across the country, Gorbachev changed tack yet again. He accepted the idea of allowing the constituent republics an autonomy verging on independence, and joined forces with Yeltsin. Seventy per cent of Russian voters who turned out for a referendum on 17 March endorsed the idea of 'the preservation of the Union of Socialist Republics as a renewed federation of equal sovereign republics in which the rights and freedom of the individual of any nationality will be guaranteed'.[21] The contorted language of the document reflected Gorbachev's disposition to be all things to all men, but it could not quite disguise the contradiction in terms. Nevertheless, on 23 April 1991 representatives of nine constituent republics agreed that there should be a new Union treaty. Four months later it was ready for signing. Meanwhile Yeltsin's hand had been strengthened further by a substantial victory in the Russian elections held that June.

The same month the Soviet premier, supported by the ministers of Defence and the Interior, went to the Supreme Soviet asking for Gorbachev's presidential powers to be transferred to them. The country was on the brink of disaster, they argued, and Gorbachev's inadequate leadership was central to the problem. Retrospect lends some credence to their claims. Nevertheless, the leader once again succeeded in talking his way out of trouble. He said he was working to create a socialism which was both humane and democratic. Vague rather than convincing, he nevertheless persuaded enough members to endorse the idea of another Party congress, to be held in December. At that point, he conceded, the question could be raised of his being constitutionally removed from office.

The loss of the European satellites had done the Soviet president no good politically, but what really undermined his position were the fast-deteriorating economic and social conditions, and the fact that, to an increasing extent, he was held responsible for the deterioration. The unfortunate public looked about for a figure that might save them and, since Gorbachev had lost credence and most of the other Soviet ministers and officials seemed colourless, Boris Yeltsin became the chief beneficiary of this change of mood. His popularity seemed to be founded less on the 'liberal' cause which he espoused than on the fact that he seemed decisive. But other decision-makers believed that the country would be ruined unless strong action was taken urgently.

Gorbachev was on holiday in the Crimea when, on 18 August, an 'Emergency Committee' of leading ministers tried to carry out a *coup d'état*. Unfortunately for them, the army was divided and, though Gorbachev was placed under house arrest, some KGB and army units ordered to arrest Yeltsin and other oppositionists refused to do so. In the hours of uncertainty that followed Yeltsin rallied the opposition, called for Gorbachev's release, and posed on a tank for the benefit of the cameras. He was backed by several figures of political substance including the mayor of Leningrad. Together they called for Gorbachev's restoration. The organizers of the coup might well have prevailed had they been ruthless. But, like Gorbachev himself, most of them shrank from shedding blood. The only fatal casualties were two conspirators, including the Minister of Defence, who committed suicide in the wake of the coup's failure. At that point no one sought to take the poisoned chalice of the leadership from Gorbachev's weak grasp. However Yeltsin had used the interregnum and his position of Russian president to suspend the Russian Communist Party and seize its assets. He then stood by like an *éminence grise* while the tragedy played on to its conclusion

Gorbachev returned to Moscow as a spent force. He joined forces with Yeltsin again, but was now the junior partner. Yeltsin, who held the initiative, would not declare his hand. He denied that he was against the 'Union of Sovereign States', whose constitution was being drafted, but as the negotiations over the new form of union continued he did his best to weaken its powers. When Gorbachev offered him the presidency if he backed the project, he demurred; and when a governmental crisis arose in September he pretended to be ill. The republics were demanding ever-increasing expenditure, but on 16 October it was announced that the government was spending twice the amount of its revenue. Next day Ukraine backed out of the proposed economic union and within a week repudiated responsibility for a share in any future Soviet debt. Having refused to agree to a common army, it reinforced its point by withholding food coupons to units which would not take orders from the new Ukrainian Ministry of Defence. Three other republics, of the remaining fourteen, also refused to agree to a common army.

Output (GNP) fell by an eighth between mid-January and September 1991. The budget deficit was ballooning, unemployment was soaring, and inflation – which the International Monetary Fund estimated to have reached 150 per cent in 1990 – was rising by 2 or 3 per cent a week. The IMF urged long-term help but the Group of Seven, the world's richest countries, refused to rush into any rescue plan. Then the Russian government seized the Soviet gold reserves and suspended oil exports. As investors got the scent of another Russian catastrophe, on 15 November 1991 stock-market values round the world plummeted. And, as at moments of national emergency since medieval times, the Patriarch of the Russian Church addressed the Russian people. 'The old structures have collapsed', Aleksei II said bleakly, 'and new ones are not yet in place . . . People are losing faith in the future and in their political leaders.'

It was a form of political extreme unction, but the death throes of the Soviet Union were not yet quite complete. When Ukraine voted for independence in a referendum held at the beginning of December Yeltsin moved immediately to create an association which would be weaker still. This 'Commonwealth of Independent States', centred on Minsk, capital of Belarus, would constitute a single market and co-operate in military matters but have very little real power. However, the Baltic republics and Georgia refused to endorse even this shadow of a union.

Recognizing the failure of his last mission, and the impossibility of his position, Gorbachev went on television a few days later to announce his resignation and a formal end to the entity of which he was president. At midnight on 31 December 1991 the Union of Soviet Socialist Republics, Russia's fourth empire, would cease to exist.[22] He spoke with sadness and with dignity. Not so Boris Yeltsin. He moved into the presidential offices in the Kremlin before Gorbachev had time to clear his desk, and threw a party there.

The end was untidy and brought benefit only to the scavengers of the dead state. Ukraine gained independence but lost the assured Russian market for its grain and coal, on which it had depended. Its huge Russian minority suddenly found themselves in an alien state. Kazakhs formed only 40 per cent of the population of newly independent Kazakhstan; indeed, they barely outnumbered Russians, who formed 38 per cent of its population.[23] As the Soviet Union disintegrated there were widespread uncertainties not only about trade and the currency, but about the law and its enforcement, about what was licit and illicit. Lithuania tried to rehabilitate those condemned by Soviet courts for collaboration with the Nazis during the war, only to backtrack when Western countries indicated that this was politically incorrect. Concern spread abroad too – about the repayment of Soviet debt, nuclear proliferation, even about a possible nuclear holocaust.

The Soviet system need not have collapsed so precipitately, nor indeed at all. As Yeltsin subsequently remarked, the Soviet Union could have survived for many years, if not indefinitely. What, then, caused its dramatic collapse? Few of the explanations that were popular at the time hold much credence in retrospect. The Pope's moral support and diplomacy may have helped speed the break-up of Yugoslavia, but he had little influence in the Soviet Bloc proper outside Poland, Lithuania and western Ukraine. The 'Star Wars' project put a strain on the Soviet budget by demanding increased military expenditure for a time but, though debilitating, it was no death blow. There is no evidence to support the idea put about by resentful Communists that the Soviet Union was murdered thanks to a conspiracy by the capitalist West. Nor was nationalism the cause. Nationalism was indeed the banner beneath which several Soviet republics left the Union, yet it turned out to be an excuse for leaving, rather than the cause. The spread of electronic communication may have rendered conventional censorship and political control futile, but only in the long term, and the regime had ceased to be Stalinist in its oppressions long before Gorbachev came to power.

Since the 1960s the Soviet economy had been unable to compete with capitalism. Its inefficiencies had been recognized in Brezhnev's time, but cautious efforts to improve the system had met with little success. The entrenched interests of the Soviet managerial class, the *apparatchiki*, obstructed systemic reform. The difficulties attending this option led Gorbachev repeatedly to avoid it and address political reform instead. Yet the people had become disillusioned with democracy even before Gorbachev lost power. Communist China engineered a better solution in the light of his experience. It adopted a mixed economy, part planned, part free, and gave priority to economic, rather than political, reform. That prescription might well have worked in Russia too.

As it was, the attempts to decentralize decision-taking, encouraging regional officialdom and managers to take more power into their hands, drove the system towards a precipice. After some initial confusion, managers and officials began to take Gorbachev at his word. In doing so they undermined the authority of the central institutions on which the leadership depended for the execution of its policies. Furthermore Yeltsin's assault on the Communist Party removed Gorbachev's most effective lever of government. But, perhaps Gorbachev was the architect of his own failure. As he admitted in retrospect, he had certainly been remiss in failing to keep the money supply in check. As a result, inflation gathered speed, destroying savings and creating increasing distress. Communist Russia was an essentially makeshift contraption. Born of war and revolution, it had been shaped by necessity and hardened by time into a fixed, rigid and ultimately brittle system.

Gorbachev deserves credit for positive achievements.[24] He, more than anyone else, was responsible for changing Russia's political configuration – albeit in a way he had neither foreseen nor intended. He also did great harm, though without intending to. Unlucky and incautious, he was soon overwhelmed by the rush of events and by successive crises. Having bravely begun the dangerous process of radical reform, he suddenly found the machine careering onward and downward out of his control. In the end, then, the verdict must be death by misadventure.

The rejoicing over the collapse was great. Yet the advent of democracy was to solve no problems, and many who rejoiced at the time were to regret the Soviet Union's demise. Most of the good things which both the dissidents and Western politicians and ideologues forecast would emerge from the collapse of Communism did not materialize. Indeed, most Russians were to find the first fruits of the freedom they had been promised very sour indeed. It is on this aftermath – the condition of Russia in the post-Communist era – that we must now focus, for that is the soil in which any future expansion will be rooted.

15
Reinventing Russia

When the Soviet Union collapsed, crowds swarmed out on to the streets of central Moscow and St Petersburg to greet the new order. They were mostly younger people and their expectations matched their excitement. Russia was free. The stern face of authority was fast fading away; political correctness and restrictions were things of the past. Untrammelled now by empire, Russians would no longer be isolated from the world. They would be ruled by democracy instead of tsars and commissars, and join the global economy. Western statesmen and economists had forecast that investment would flow in from Wall Street, the London Stock Exchange and all the other bourses of the free world. A vibrant free economy would rise up in place of the moribund, now crumbing, bureaucratic economy. People would have opportunity and choice instead of dull predictability.

A handful of Russians were soon to become wealthy beyond dreams, as in a fairy tale, though a few were to perish at the hands of contract killers, and one or two even ended up in jail for fraud. Shops in city centres were filled with an amazing variety of expensive goods. Mercedes limousines, Cardin dresses, blue jeans and Macdonald hamburgers proclaimed the coming of the new age. But for most people the euphoria was momentary, the aftertaste bitter.

More and more old ladies stood patiently in lines outside metro stations hoping to sell a treasured possession, a cigarette or two, or a wilting posy of wild flowers to buy some food. Infants died of malnutrition; young women and children were recruited for the prostitution and pornography industries, and not a few of them exported. The use of drugs increased, forgotten diseases like typhus returned and new ones like AIDS, virtually unknown in the Soviet era, began to spread. The welfare system that had for so long sheltered the population steadily deteriorated. The birth rate rapidly declined; the death rate soared.

As in the Time of Troubles four centuries earlier (See Chapter 6), disaster struck six years out of seven, in the form not of unusual weather and crop failure this time, but of precipitous industrial decline. By 1998 the country's gross national product was less than half what it had been in 1990. Young scientists emigrated, and capital, desperately needed for investment, flowed out to foreign bank accounts. One of the brighter spots in the new, dark world, was shone by schoolteachers who continued to turn up in their classrooms even though some had not been paid for months.

What was the source of the disaster? Was it the inevitable consequence of an inevitable transition? Was it due to Communism and the bad habits it encouraged; or, as many Russians believed, the work of the United States? Washington certainly wished former Communist states to join the free-trade system and, as Bismarck had noticed a century and a half earlier, free trade favours robust economies, not vulnerable ones like Russia's. Could it have been the fault of Russia's own corrupt elite, the so-called *nomenklatura*, many of whom had also occupied important positions under Communism? Or were misconceived policies of the new men led by Boris Yeltsin and their advisers to blame?

The decline had begun under Gorbachev but little had been done to stop it. Inflation continued to spiral upward, reaching an annual rate of over 2,000 per cent before it eventually abated. The social impact of this factor alone was immense. Savings were wiped out; investment ceased. The International Monetary Fund advanced loans with conditions attached and some of the richer countries pitched in, notably Germany, which advanced Russia the equivalent of over $24 billion between 1989 and 1993,[1] but most of these loans fell into the wrong hands and eventually disappeared into numbered Swiss bank accounts and American stocks.[2] All that accumulated for Russians in Russia was foreign debt, which had hardly existed in the Soviet era. On the other hand Russia was no longer burdened by empire. It had shrunk almost to the frontiers of 1700 in Asia and of 1600 in Europe, and its population was now no more than 150 million. This was a manageable size for an economy, and Boris Yeltsin now proceeded to dismantle and rebuild according to a new model.

Yeltsin's understanding of economics was limited, but he followed the advice urged upon him by the West and set young Russian economists to the task. American free-market theory provided the framework, and shock therapy was favoured over gradualism. The ideas of the Harvard economist Jeremy Sachs, which had recently accomplished an apparent miracle in Poland, were particularly influential, and the revolution was implemented in a hurry. It seemed that this would make the transition painful but short, but according to Anatolii Chubais, one of those chiefly responsible for the manner in which the transformation was undertaken, there was another, political, motive. Yeltsin was anxious to destroy the base for any Communist revival in the future.[3] So was Washington. Together they succeeded.

On 2 January 1992, the day after Russia began its separate existence, most prices were freed from state controls – though those for oil and other natural resources were kept so low that vast quantities were sold on abroad for profit. To make the new, higher, prices in the shops more affordable wages were raised, which meant further increases in the money supply. So did the huge subsidies doled out to public utilities. Together they led to a further spurt in inflation. This was eventually curbed by high interest rates, but investment dried up as a result. Furthermore, it suddenly became apparent that the lack of adequate financial institutions was a serious impediment. As the chief IMF economist remarked, the government had 'tried to take a short cut to capitalism, creating a market economy without the underlying institutions, and institutions without the underlying institutional infrastructures'.[4]

Capitalism cannot work its miracles without capital, and with foreigners reluctant to invest and newly rich Russians spiriting their assets away to foreign banks, no miracle was possible. Before long about $2 billion was leaving the country each month – more than all the aid, loans, credit and investment that were coming in.[5] So far things had gone very badly wrong. It seemed that the only way to create the elusive economic miracle was to stimulate appetites and let greed off the leash.

This was soon done. In August 1992 Yeltsin signed a decree disposing of state property to raise money. Vouchers were issued entitling every adult in the country to 10,000 rubles-worth of shares in the enterprise or institution with which they were associated. Alternatively they could sell their vouchers. Voucher auctions would be arranged. The randomness of the method met with the approval of Western economic theorists. Most people might have no idea of value, they said, but the vouchers would surely end up in the hands of people who did. And so it turned out. Most Russians, bemused by the process, sold their vouchers – many of them to touts who offered ready money for them on the street. Managers and new businessmen, who had a better understanding of values than the general public, made killings and manoeuvred themselves into positions to make more. The proceeds, intended to reduce the state's massive deficit, turned out to be disappointing, however, because during the interval that passed before they reached the treasury their value had been savaged by inflation. On the other hand gigantic windfall profits went to a handful of sharp-eyed and unscrupulous operators who exploited the reformers' mistakes.

The beneficiaries were mainly young men in the know. Since there were so few of them, and the industries they came to control dominated the Russian economy, they were soon wielding political power as well as financial clout. Aside from Viktor Chernomyrdin, a government functionary who was no longer young, the first generation of multimillionaires included Mikhail Khodorkovskii, Vladimir Gusinskii, Petr Aven, Roman Abramovich and Boris Berezovskii. Able youngish, civil servants, city functionaries, economic advisers, scientific researchers, they turned themselves into *biznesmeny* and swiftly graduated to become tycoons dominating important industries – aluminium, natural gas, air transport, banks, the media, and oil. Several of them came to be closely connected with organized crime as well as with government, for the atmosphere, in Moscow particularly, closely resembled that of Chicago during prohibition and they needed protection, whether from former KGB operatives or from the Chechen and other organized mobs.[6]

While the plutocrats counted their assets, the masses counted the costs of the transition. At least a third, and probably over half, the population had been forced below the poverty line, and the health statistics of the first years of post-communist freedom told their own story. Between January 1992, when the switch from a planned to a market economy began, and June 1994 the death rate in Russia rose by over 30 per cent, to a level unknown in any country that was not at war or suffering from famine. The rise in mortality among males of working age was particularly steep. They died from heart attacks, strokes, alcohol poisoning, suicide and murder. A UNICEF study attributed the sharp increase in adult deaths to stress arising from fear of unemployment, although despair at the collapse of a familiar world seems also to have played a part. A dramatic increase in infant mortality, which more than doubled in the period 1991–3, was no less alarming. Child health had been improving steadily until 1990.[7] Now, suddenly, health-care services and education were in danger of collapse. They would have done so had conscientious teachers, doctors and nurses not continued to work even when their modest salaries were unpaid. And unpaid workers isolated amid the vast wastes of the north also worked on for lengthy periods without reward simply because they and their families could not afford the costs entailed in moving and starting a new life elsewhere.

In December 1993 President Yeltsin approved a new coat of arms for Russia. It took the form of a Byzantine eagle with two heads surmounted by three crowns.[8] It might seem odd that Yeltsin, who had played a key role in stripping Russia of empire, should have adopted this imperial symbolism for the new, truncated Russia, but it was not the only irony. A former Communist *apparatchik*, he was now the scourge of Communism. This and his pious commitment to the cause of democracy, which he paraded as religiously as any seventeenth-century tsar paraded his commitment to Christ and all the saints, commended him to Washington and London, despite the fact that only two months before adopting the imperial insignia he had ordered troops to launch a bloody attack on parliament and shut it down.

A clash between the democratically elected President and the democratically elected parliament was, perhaps, inevitable. The social cost of transition had been causing great distress and alienating people from economic reform. Many Russians who had believed the promises that market reforms would conjure up an economic miracle were now disenchanted; nostalgia was growing fast for the past that had been lost, and the change in mood was reflected by parliament. The truth was that, given Russia's circumstances, democracy was incompatible with a market economy.

It made for a fraught political scene. Accusations of corruption had been flying; an attempt was launched to impeach President Yeltsin. Despite the frantic efforts of his political staff, he received only a narrow endorsement in a national referendum, which had also rejected his proposal to dissolve parliament. At this point one of his staunchest supporters, the former air-force general Aleksandr Rutskoi, suddenly joined the opposition. Appointed by Yeltsin to chair a commission on corruption in government, he had found evidence of unlawful dealings leading straight to the door of the President's office and implicating several of his associates. Rutskoi denounced him on television, and was himself accused in his turn. So the President's stand-off with parliament continued.

Negotiations on the constitution made some progress, but on 21 September Yeltsin announced that he was dissolving parliament. The Supreme Court declared this to be illegal, and demonstrators, some of them armed, gathered in the parliament building. Security troops then surrounded the building and cut off all services to it. An ultimatum was delivered: the parliament building must be cleared by Monday 4 October. On 3 October crowds marched to the television tower and the parliament building. There were exchanges of fire, and at least 100 casualties. Yeltsin had won. It has been suggested that the parliament and its defenders were partly to blame for the bloodshed. However, Roy Medvedev has found evidence of Yeltsin's intent to abolish parliament, if necessary by force, whether it was defended or not.[9] So the people's defenders were defeated, and a constitution which increased Yeltsin's powers as president was imposed. In the words of a leading Western historian of the post-communist period, Yeltsin had got his way only by the use of 'methods involving electoral fraud. The birth of the new Russia was induced by anti-constitutionality, violence and corruption.'[10] Despite this, the United States issued no protest. As the leading proponent of both market economies and democracy, it regarded the former as much the more important.

By now Yeltsin was hardly popular among Russians, but the media were supportive of him, as were most Western governments. No challenger of any political stature was visible, and he did not yet have to seek re-endorsement. So he continued to preside over Russia's transformation and its decline both at home and abroad. Auctions of state enterprises now took place. However, which huge enterprises would go to whom and at what prices was to a great extent determined by a small group of officials and businessmen in advance of the auctions, and the auction process itself was fraudulent. Competitors were bought off or threatened, and sometimes the successful bid was the only one.[11] Then the government introduced a new scheme to raise money: offering the new industrial oligarchs shares in lucrative industries as security against loans. If the government was unable to repay the loans, as seemed likely, then the lenders were entitled to take possession of the shares.

So the connection between economic power and politics became ever closer. Viktor Chernomyrdin, who bought a major stake in the huge natural-gas enterprise Gazprom, which he had run, was to serve twice as prime minister. He also made a personal fortune estimated at $5 billion. This was hardly surprising given that Gazprom's value grew from $250 million in 1993/4, when it was auctioned, to $40,483 million by 1997.[12] Others made similar killings. The new billionaires, on visits abroad, wore innocent expressions: they admitted to having occasionally done things normally regarded as wrong, but claimed they had had no choice. The law was not always clear, and they had had to protect themselves. They were playing a game not of their making, and played it according to the uncertain rules of the time.[13]

Russia had suffered almost as serious a decline in international standing as it had economically. Its strategic position had been weakened by the loss of empire, and its rival was exploiting its advantage. Disregarding undertakings it had given to Gorbachev, who had represented a state which no longer existed, the United States decided that NATO should after all expand eastward and, having effectively excluded Russia's navy from the Black Sea, it declared the Caspian to be a region affecting vital US interests – an indication that it was prepared to intervene there militarily. The Caspian was strategically important. It was a hinge between Russia, the Caucasus and Central Asia, and it contained considerable oil and natural gas deposits. But Russia's interests there were no less vital than America's, and Yeltsin was determined to preserve them. These circumstances help to explain the war in Chechnya which began in December 1994 and continued into 1996.

This war has often been explained in terms of a classic struggle between an imperial power (Russia) and a new nation striving to be free (the Chechens). This view derives in large measure from the propaganda issued by Chechnya's president of the time, Djokar Dudaev. Dudaev beat the nationalist drum. Yet his own legitimacy as president was questioned and his declaration of independence, like his commitment to the Koran as the basis of his regime, breached the 1993 Constitution of the Russian Federation of which Chechnya was a part. However, they brought him financial aid and volunteers from Afghanistan and Saudi Arabia who saw him now as a potential leader of jihad. Dudaev's regime was corrupt, associated with organized crime in both Chechnya and Russia, and less than popular among the Chechens themselves. A leading Western historian of post-Soviet Russia has gone so far as to call Dudaev's rule 'a disgrace to minimal standards of political decency'.[14] But there were other dimensions to the coming struggle in Chechnya.

Chechnya was a transit centre for oil from western Siberia as well as the Caspian, and Dudaev and his associates were reselling a great deal of it abroad for foreign currency to their own considerable profit and that of their Russian friends. Chechnya was formally a semi-autonomous province of Russia, so the trade was illegal. The losses to the exchequer were serious, yet they did not precipitate Yeltsin's decision to intervene militarily in Chechnya. Rather it was another, more traditional, form of Chechen piracy: kidnapping. In May 1994 a Chechen war band descended on the quiet resort town of Mineralnye Vody not far to the north. They proceeded to kidnap busloads of Russians and hold them to ransom for several million dollars. Security forces eventually succeeded in thwarting the attempt, but meanwhile a storm of outrage had been raised in Russia. In any case the Kremlin was becoming concerned that Chechnya might become a base for militant Muslim fundamentalism, and so in August the Kremlin decided to move troops in and take Dudaev out.

It was easier said than done. Despite their tanks and helicopter gunships, the Russian forces were unprepared for such a conflict. Too many raw recruits were used, and they suffered heavy casualties. The war was dirty, and the government deserved the bad press it got both at home and abroad for the cruelties inflicted on the Chechens. However, the atrocities were by no means one-sided.[15] The insurgents fought viciously, slitting the throats of Russian prisoners they had taken in view of cameras, and the army responded as viciously. The army eventually secured the ruins of Chechnya's capital, Grozny, but the war had become unpopular in Russia. Then in June 1995 a Chechen commander, Shamil Basaev, hitherto a political rival of Dudaev and reputed to have fought alongside the *mujahidin* in Afghanistan, penetrated the town of Budennovsk in southern Russia with a band of guerrillas. After a shoot-out resulting in over a hundred deaths, he and his men occupied the local hospital, taking patients, staff and visitors hostage. This crisis brought Prime Minister Chernomyrdin to the scene and the negotiations were televised. Most of the 1,600 hostages were released, but the guerrillas were allowed to withdraw to Chechnya taking the rest with them, and Russia's premier was exposed to public humiliation.

If 1995 had been disappointing, 1996 was hardly better. Russia's gross national product fell by 6 per cent that year – the fifth consecutive year it had fallen. Total production was half of what it had been in 1990, and the government was able to collect only 65 per cent of the taxes due to it. In 1988–9 it had withdrawn Soviet forces from Afghanistan, but now, seven years later, Russia had commitments there again, backing at least one faction in the north; the war in Chechnya ground expensively on; and NATO proceeded with its plan for eastward expansion to Russia's frontiers. Having received no pay for five months, the miners of Vorkutka finally went on strike; Russia was forced to conclude an agreement with France, undertaking to compensate the descendants of those who had invested in Russian bonds since 1830; the police registered 574 contract killings, of which only 64 were solved; and the Vatican, egged on by Cardinal Ratzinger, launched a missionizing campaign to give desperate Russians the consolation of the Catholic Church.[16] There were, it is true, some more promising developments. Inflation was cut to 22 per cent a year, and the tax police became more aggressive in pursuing defaulters; the state's traditional money-spinner, the liquor monopoly, was restored; and several Central Asian states drew closer to Russia for fear of the Taliban. As in the early seventeenth century, the Catholic missionizing campaign met with obdurate, though less violent, resistance, and public opinion began to call for the state to reassert itself.[17]

Since it was also an election year, policy sails were trimmed accordingly. The loss of an entire armoured regiment, ambushed in a mountain pass by Chechen guerrillas led by an Arab incomer called Khattab,[18] hastened a resolution and in April 1996 the war was brought to an uneasy end. Dudaev himself was killed by Russian special forces on the last day of that month. The following January Aslan Maskhadov was elected to replace him. But he proved unable to control either the Muslim fundamentalists organizing for war or the Chechen gangs, whose kidnapping targets soon included schoolchildren and British communication workers. Maskhadov subsequently accused Boris Berezovskii of abetting the kidnappers by arranging ransom payments to them. Whether this allegation was true or not, Berezovskii's contacts fitted him for the role,[19] and he was also to play a key role in Yeltsin's re-election.

Despite growing indifference to the democratic process, opinion polls suggested that the President's chances were poor, and so he thought of postponing the election. The Chechen war had brought no glory; the scandalous shares-for-loans scheme had necessitated the dismissal of Anatolii Chubais, the key official in charge of the privatization programme; and Yeltsin's own health was deteriorating. His drinking problem became all too obvious on an official visit to Germany, and he was developing serious heart problems. Nevertheless, he had a small number of very powerful political helpers, all of them beneficiaries of privatization, and all of them terrified that a resurgent Communist Party might gain an electoral victory and destroy their business empires. Berezovskii brought them together to fund Yeltsin's re-election campaign; Chubais was drafted in to be campaign manager, and Yeltsin's daughter was included in the committee to ensure ready communication with the President's office.[20]

The law limited funding for every presidential candidate to $3 million, but Yeltsin's re-election committee soon gathered at least $500 million and perhaps as many as $1 billion.[21] Those who contributed were to be richly rewarded for their generosity. The Communist campaign could count on up to 500,000 workers, but it could not get access to television in order to transmit its message. Yeltsin, on the other hand, enjoyed a virtual monopoly of television exposure. Leading American and British public-relations and advertising experts were also recruited to help his campaign. Everything was done to promote a favourable image of the President; every dirty trick was used against his Communist rival, Gennadii Ziuganov. Soft-sell, sentimental advertisements were particularly effective and teams of hecklers went everywhere that Ziuganov went, in order to disrupt his meetings. When a bomb killed four people in the Moscow metro the Communists were blamed and the electorate was invited to vote for Yeltsin, civic peace and stability. On 3 July Yeltsin won the second round of voting with 54 per cent of the poll. This was not an overwhelming endorsement, even though the election had been a travesty of constitutional democratic process. However, relieved that the Communists had been defeated, Western governments did not protest.

Moves soon began to remove the President on grounds of his ill health. He had undergone a quintuple heart bypass operation in 1996, and many felt that his health was too poor to sustain the burdens of office. Yeltsin soldiered on nevertheless. Troops were being withdrawn from Chechnya but there were troubles enough on other fronts. Reports were arriving from Latvia that the authorities there were discriminating against the country's substantial Russian minority on linguistic grounds. Similar complaints were being voiced in Estonia and other formerly Soviet states. Public opinion was exercised about the issue: surely the government had a responsibility to those 20 million Russians who, though no fault of their own, had suddenly found themselves classified as aliens in another state.[22]

Nor were these the only problems. There were difficulties reaching agreement with Iran and the former Soviet republics of Azerbaydzhan, Kazakhstan and Turkmenistan over rights to the Caspian oilfields, and negotiations with Ukraine over how to divide up what had formerly been the Soviet Black Sea fleet proved both hard and protracted. Agreement was finally reached in May after more than five years of talks. In August, US warships visited the Crimea and joined others from Turkey, Romania and Bulgaria – all three now aligned with the USA – for exercises in the Black Sea. This flag-waving outside Russia's new back door was resented. As the weeks passed it also became clear that extremists were taking over in Chechnya. In January 1997 Boris Berezovskii was appointed deputy head of Russia's Security Council, perhaps as a reward for his help in getting Yeltsin re-elected, but Berezovskii had interests in Chechnya and contacts with Chechens.

By 1997 the outlook seemed to be brightening. For the first time since the collapse the economy grew a little. But black clouds soon gathered once again. A financial crisis in Asia was soon to affect Russia, and 1998 showed the economic upturn of the previous year to have been a false dawn. More than one Russian in four was now living below the poverty line; the government was still short of revenue, and the financial system was close to collapse. That January interest rates rose to over 40 per cent. Worse was to come. In the first half of the year world oil prices fell 40 per cent below the average for 1997, and in April the value of the ruble tumbled as Russia's indebtedness soared. In May the parliament, which Yeltsin had been forced to reinstate, passed a motion impeaching Yeltsin for treason by a vote of three to one. However, the constitution demanded a two-thirds vote in the Federal Council too before the President could be forced out. The delay saved Yeltsin for the moment.

In July the IMF advanced almost $5 billion to support the ruble, but the currency could not be saved. In August the government was forced to devalue it sharply, declare a moratorium on foreign creditors, and default on its domestic debt. Banks collapsed, and crowds of worried, angry people crowded round their bolted doors in the vain hope of trying to withdraw their savings. Yeltsin had no alternative but to appoint a premier whom parliament would find acceptable. The least objectionable to Yeltsin himself was an experienced foreign-affairs specialist, Yevgeny Primakov. At the same time Vladimir Putin, who had been a KGB operative in East Germany before the collapse and had since worked for the city of St Petersburg, became chief of security. But Yeltsin was already overdrawn on his political account. His days in power were numbered.

That year the ruble had lost nearly three-quarters of its value, the economy contracted by another 5 per cent, and inflation rose to 80 per cent. Parliament's impeachment vote of May 1998 proclaimed that Yeltsin had betrayed his country. It could indeed be argued that, whatever his intentions, he had served the interests of the United States rather better than he had served those of Russia, and he had certainly broken trust with the people. According to Stiglitz, an American economist who had held senior office in the IMF:

> The [Russian] government was virtually giving away its valuable state assets, yet was unable to provide pensions for the elderly or welfare payments for the poor . . . [It] was borrowing billions from the IMF, becoming increasingly indebted, while the oligarchs who received such largesse from the government were taking billions out of the country.
>
> The IMF had encouraged the government to open up its capital accounts, allowing a free flow of capital. The policy was supposed to make the country more attractive for foreign investors; but it was virtually a one-way door that facilitated a rush of money out of the country.

It was Washington that most feared a revival of Communism; Washington that had encouraged Yeltsin to take that disastrous short cut; Washington that wanted no debate on economic policy in Russia. As Stiglitz put it, Washington was 'afraid of democracy'. And, when the ruble crisis of 1998 came, it was the Clinton administration that pressured the World Bank into lending Russia money, even though many of the bank's own officials were against it. As a result a 'rescue' was launched. Within days, billions of dollars appeared in Cypriot and Swiss bank accounts. In addition to the Russian oligarchs themselves, the beneficiaries were 'the Wall Street and other Western investment banks who had been . . . pressing hardest for a rescue package'. Their investments in Russia had seemed lost, but when the IMF rescue came through they seized the opportunity of getting as much of their money as possible out. In destroying the last vestiges of the Communists' planned economy, America had gained a major victory for private enterprise and open markets. The poor Russians (of whom almost half had to live on less than $4 a day) were left to bear the heavy costs of the operation.[23]

A Russian anti-Communist intellectual wrote what might have been Yeltsin's obituary. He thought Yeltsin to be 'the perfect incarnation of the most repellent traits of the Russian psyche, of the most shameful features of the Russian national character: irresponsibility . . . ignorance, boorishness . . . servility towards the strong . . . [and with an] inferiority complex to the West'.[24] Already in decline when he took office, most of the economy's remaining strength had been dissipated during Yeltsin's tenure of the presidency. And the population had fallen by 6 million in ten years. Now, belatedly, there were some signs of an improvement. GNP began to rise, inflation to fall, and the balance of trade to improve. True, Russia was heavily in debt to the West (it was soon to reach eight times the size of the national budget), but it was owed money by India, Cuba, North Korea, Mongolia, Poland and various other former members of the Soviet Bloc. The new premier, Primakov, steered a judicious course but decided, at last, to crack down on the corrupt. The prosecutor-general, who rejoiced in the name of Ivan the Terrible's notorious hatchet man, Skuratov, was instructed to prepare for the prosecutions of Berezovskii and of Pavel Borodin, Yeltsin's Chief of Staff. However, Yeltsin quickly intervened to dismiss both Skuratov and then Primakov.[25] Democracy is no guarantee of good government. The election had given Yeltsin a mandate. Now he exploited it using his authority, which was in effect unlimited.

Yeltsin's economic policies were by now being characterized as 'a crime against national security' by anti-Communist newspapers which had once supported him; according to an opinion poll, the President was now distrusted by nine Russians out of ten.[26] He tried desperately to deflect his regime's unpopularity by dismissing one prime minister after another. Stepashin, who replaced Primakov in May 1999, was himself replaced by Vladimir Putin in August. Meanwhile the President played the patriot and defender of Orthodoxy on the international stage. He gave moral support to the Orthodox Serbs in the former Yugoslavia, and ordered a small Russian force, stationed in Bosnia as part of the international peace-keeping operation there, to seize Sarajevo airport, enraging NATO's American commander. The gesture did not affect the outcome in Bosnia, however.[27] Yeltsin also gave support to Serbia in its repression of the Kosovo Albanians, following nationalist (KKL) threats to the Serb minority in Kosovo, but Washington saw the Serbs rather than the Albanian nationalists as guilty and bombed Serbia into submission. He showed concern, too, for Russians suffering discrimination in the Baltic states, but thinly veiled threats from Western agencies that discrimination against minorities might effect these states' applications to join NATO and the EU were more effective. Yeltsin's bluster could not disguise his lack of clout on the international stage.

His concessions over the Kurile Islands, which had long been a bone of contention with Japan, at least improved relations with that country, and he also contributed to better relations with China, which had been managing its economic transition so much more skilfully than Russia had done. In October 1999 he was constrained to approve Putin's decision to send Russian forces back into Chechnya. The soft line there which Berezovskii had advocated had not been effective. The bandit gangs were out of control, and Islamic fundamentalism was gaining strength. Early in August, Khattab and Shamil Basaev had led a group of armed fundamentalists into neighbouring Dagestan. Russian military operations in Dagestan turned out to be much more succesful than they had been in Chechnya itself in the earlier war – partly, perhaps, because the Americans, alarmed now about the Muslim fundamentalism in the region, offered help to disrupt the insurgents' communications. However, the principal reason was that the Dagestanis, who had voted for the Communists in the recent elections, disliked fundamentalism.[28]

But by now even Yeltsin understood that he had run out of options. At the end of the year he suddenly announced that he was stepping down. Elections for a new president would be held in March 2000. In the meanwhile, in accordance with the constitution, the Prime Minister would act as caretaker. Before he stepped down, however, Yeltsin elicited an assurance from Putin that he would not be prosecuted. Putin moved into office on 1 January 2000.

★

Although most of the Western press regarded Putin with suspicion, characterizing him as authoritarian, and repeatedly reminding the public of his KGB past, his popularity rating among Russians climbed steadily. After a decade of misery and disorder, the prospect of firm government now seemed very welcome. Now that opinion had turned against terrorism, the new war in Chechnya was popular too. Even the KGB – now called the Federal Security Service (FSB) – was coming to be well regarded, thanks partly to a public-relations campaign presenting it as Russia's shield against its foreign enemies. One of Putin's first presidential actions was to restore Yuri Andropov's bust to prominence at FSB headquarters – a shrewd move, since Andropov, himself a former KGB chief, had been the godfather of radical reform and also represented the good, stable times before the collapse. In March 2000 Putin was duly elected.

A greater contrast with his predecessor could hardly be imagined. Putin was as slight and fit as Yeltsin was burly and ailing; as collected and deliberate as Yeltsin was erratic and unbridled; as discreet and measured as Yeltsin was ebullient and greedy – and a good deal more knowledgeable about the wider world. The article he published on the government's web site on the eve of becoming interim president presented a realistic summation of Russia's position and a well-judged statement of his priorities. Nor did he fail to project a personal image to the public. In an autobiography by interview he spoke about having been 'a hooligan' at school, and of his passions for the martial arts and for books and films about spies. He also spoke frankly about his previous career, not concealing an acquaintance with Boris Berezovskii and saying one or two pleasant things about Yeltsin while firmly distancing himself from both. And what he said in public struck an immediate chord with the people. 'We are a rich country of poor people,' he told them. He spoke of his 'pride in the fatherland', and told them straightforwardly that 'for Russia a strong state . . . is . . . the guarantee of order, the initiator and main driving force for change.'[29]

Although realistic about his country's capabilities and the strengths of its adversaries, he contrived to take a positive line in foreign affairs. Claiming that 'a power with a geopolitical position like Russia has national interests everywhere', he reasserted Russia's claims in the Caspian, took a tougher line on Ukrainian and Georgian debt, adopted a bolder position in Transcaucasia and Central Asia, worked towards a 'strategic partnership' with China and improved relations with Iran and India. But he also tried to reach an accommodation with NATO,[30] and after 11 September 2001 he co-operated with the USA over terrorism, while preserving a sphere for Russia's ally in Afghanistan, the Northern Alliance.

At home, Putin emphasized the importance of the rule of law, encouraged property-ownership, sponsored legislation facilitating the purchase and sale of land, but set his face against what he saw as the abuse of press freedom. When the media magnate Vladimir Gusinskii refused to suppress lampoons of Putin appearing in his papers, he was pursued; when he fled to Greece, extradition proceeding were instituted on the grounds that he had committed fraud. The President, Russia's representative figure, was not considered to be a suitable subject for mockery in Russia's present sensitive state.

In 2001, 28 per cent of Russia's budget had to be earmarked for debt-repayment. Recovery from the disastrous Yeltsin decade was slow, but at least it had begun. In 2002 both GNP and the balance-of-payments situation improved. Foreign investment was also rising and 700 American companies were doing business in Russia, though its best trading partners were Germany, India, Japan, which consumed enormous quantities of Russian-caught fish, and Cyprus. However, the country's demographic decline was giving rise to concern. The population had fallen to 143 million and was still in decline. Moreover, part of the decline was associated with a 'brain drain'. This was doubly damaging because it lost the country much expertise as well as energetic people in their prime.

There were periodic reminders that Russia had lost its superpower status. The Vatican decided the time was ripe to take a higher profile in Russia, and four new dioceses were created there; Ukraine defied its larger neighbour by declaring Russian to be a minority language, even though at least half its subjects spoke it;[31] and Russia's isolation in Europe increased with the enlargement of both NATO and the European Union eastward.

On coming to power, Putin had emphasized the importance of the state as a guarantor of order and a driving force for change, and he made the defence of the state his first priority in office. The measures he took to this end were certainly authoritarian, but they were not directed towards a restoration of an all-encompassing state sector nor to the suppression of democracy as some suggested. His pursuit of billionaire oligarchs like Vladimir Gusinskii, a former theatre director, of Boris Berezovskii, once a mathematician at the Academy of Sciences, and Mikhail Khodorkovskii, chemistry graduate and former Komsomol activist, suggested that they might have been. Certainly these people and their like were highly unpopular, and widely thought to have stolen public property. But while their unpopularity facilitated Putin's attempt to bridle them, it did not occasion it. The fundamental reason was that these plutocrats threatened the state.

Had privatization spawned several hundred wealthy oligarchs there might not have been a problem, but only a handful of incredibly wealthy billionaires emerged. There was very little competition: the common interests of the owners encouraged the formation of cartels.[32] Between them, the billionaires enjoyed virtual control of most of Russia's major industries: oil, gas, aluminium, banking, communications, copper, steel and coal; and control of these implied control of the entire economy. If a few industrial oligarchs wielded more power than the state, the state could not fulfil its primary functions of guaranteeing the rule of law and defending the general good.

This posed a fundamental problem. The fact that some of the billionaires had been buying into politics and that Khodorkovskii, head of the huge oil company Yukos, had blithely concluded an agreement to build a strategic pipeline from eastern Siberia to China without reference to Moscow,[33] made it an urgent matter to address. The mayhem associated with the rise of the oligarchs was a warning of what unbridled free enterprise could lead to. Furthermore, Yeltsin's re-election had demonstrated how effective money could be in securing a virtual media monopoly for one candidate and in distorting the democratic process. At a very early stage, therefore, Putin had called some of the bigger players together and promised to steer clear of business provided they kept out of politics. Gusinskii and Berezovskii, who may have seen political influence as a defence against prosecution for serious crimes, fled abroad. The rest complied – except for Khodorkovskii, by now reputed to be the wealthiest Russian of all. He decided to defy Putin. The state prosecution service now poured resources into an investigation of the man, his companies, and their activities.

On 27 October 2003 a police special unit met Khodorkovskii's plane as it landed on a Siberian airfield, disarmed his bodyguards and arrested him for tax evasion and fraud.[34] Shortly afterwards the British government granted political asylum to both Berezovskii and one of his associates, Akhmed Zakaev, a proponent of Chechen sovereignty.

In December 2003 Putin won an overwhelming endorsement from the electorate. Managed democracy was working. It might not be meeting meet the highest standards of constitutional politics, but was no worse a travesty than the American presidential election of 2000 had been, and even American businessmen in Russia preferred Putin's careful authoritarianism to anarchic rule by oligarchs and mafias.[35] In March 2004 the President dismissed his prime minister, Mikhail Kasianov, and in so doing severed the last prominent link with the corrupt Yeltsin regime. The fact that a diplomat, Mikhail Fradkov, was appointed to succeed Kasianov suggested that, having steadied developments within Russia, Putin was intent on developing Russia's position in the wider world.

The frontiers with what Russians now termed 'the near abroad' were still contested in some areas. The gates of Europe had been closed against it, but Russia had clung on to the important Baltic naval base of Kaliningrad, formerly Konigsberg. It had held on by force to Moldova, and, though Georgia was lost, its support for the Abkhazian rebels and the Ossetinians secured it influence in the vicinity. The change in mood in the United States following the disasters of 11 September meant that its attempts to suppress nationalism in Chechnya drew no formal American protest. However, the assassination of a Chechen premier and the bloody seizure of schoolchildren in Beslan by Basaev's people in the summer of 2004 showed that anti-terrorist operations there were not yet effective.

The changing mood also helped Moscow in Central Asia. Although the United States had been able to penetrate the region, it now needed Russian help in its global campaign to keep militant Islam and terrorism at bay. Russia was well equipped to help. It was experienced in fighting terrorists. It also had better intelligence on the Islamic world, and many more experts in its languages and cultures. And it retained influential friends in the former Central Asian republics and Afghanistan.

Under Putin, Russia was developing relations in Asia that promised to stand it in good stead. Its arms exports to India and China were buoyant, it was respected in the Middle East, and the unpopularity of the American-led invasion of Iraq presented it with worldwide opportunities.

Putin's progress was no less deliberate abroad than at home. In the opinion of at least one Western international-relations expert, he rapidly succeeded in revolutionizing Russia's position in the world. Displaying a clear sense of strategic realities and steadiness in the pursuit of his priorities, Putin was quick to appreciate opportunities and skilful in exploiting them. Unlike Yeltsin, he was concerned with realities, not gestures. He made it clear that, even in its reduced state, Russia had teeth, and its ability to cut off gas or oil supplies to a near neighbour or to withdraw from the agreement on limiting conventional forces in Europe could indeed be effective negotiating points. He made a realistic but advantageous accommodation with NATO, changed a forced retreat in the face of America's power into a strategic partnership with the USA against the forces of terrorism, and transformed defeat over strategic disarmament into 'the spearhead of Russia's global resurgence'.[36]

The springboard for any resurgence depends on the economy, and Russia's has been growing steadily at a rate of 6 per cent a year. Though it is overly dependent on commodities, it is likely to meet Putin's stated aim of doubling GDP by 2011. The budget shows a surplus, the national debt is shrinking, and unemployment is relatively low. Much ground remains to be made up, but analysts suggest that the recovery is likely to continue. The fact that the Russians are recovering from the collapse of their fourth empire is not to suggest that they will create a fifth. But nor can the prospect be entirely written off. To make an informed assessment of its chances, however, they must be reviewed in relation to both the current world situation and the historical record.

Conclusion

THE RUSSIANS CREATED four empires, each of a different kind, and each of the four collapsed for different reasons. The first was a trading empire based on co-operation between indigenous Russians and Varangian adventurers which developed into an association of city states governed by a grand prince. Though heavily influenced by Christian Byzantium and in awe of it, the rulers of Kievan Rus had imperial ambitions of their own, and held sway over a multi-ethnic, multilingual population, Finno-Ugrian and Turkic as well as Slavonic. This first Russian empire collapsed in the face of the invading Mongols, but also because the breakdown of its succession system made it easier prey than it might otherwise have been.

The origins of the second empire lay in the continuation of the northward migratory trend prompted by global warming described in Chapter 1. The Mongol invasion intensified the trend, and in due course the originally spontaneous movement of population came to be organized and directed by the monasteries in conjunction with the Grand Prince. The ascendancy of Moscow owed much to its strategic, and profitable, position in Russia's river system, to its ruler's role as chief intermediary between the Russians and their Tatar overlords, and to his success in persuading the head of the Russian Orthodox Church to move his base from Kiev to Moscow. Expanding into the forests of the north and east, which were rich in valuable furs, it grew wealthy through trade with the west and the south, and its rulers were eventually able to claim pre-eminence as grand princes of all Russia and shake off what remained of Mongol domination.

Muscovy's progress towards imperial status, claiming heritance from the later Roman Empire, was facilitated by the centralizing efforts of the grand princes of Vladimir-Moscow, who held sway over what was by then the most prosperous part of Russia. Their strategy of creating one very populous commercial centre, Moscow, in that underpopulated country, even at the expense of other cities, aided the process. So did a growing sentiment among the Russian elite that one strong state was preferable to several weak principalities. St Sergius's father was only one of many princely servitors who transferred his allegiance to Moscow in the period. Later, Ivan III's marriage to the niece of the last Byzantine emperor seemed to set the seal on the imperial claim, and it was this Ivan, not Ivan IV, who established the principle of hereditary autocracy.[1]

This empire later collapsed, partly because Ivan IV had dissipated its strength with his incessant wars and domestic upheavals, and partly because of the untimely death of his immediate successor, the last of his line, but chiefly because of a sharp and unpredictable change of climate. The upshot was a series of disastrous harvests, epidemics and migrations, widespread starvation and consequent social troubles. Their combination deprived the incumbent Tsar Boris of legitimacy, despite all his conscientious efforts. As this second empire crumbled, Poland and Sweden enlarged their empires at Russia's expense, although Ivan's biggest acquisition, Siberia, remained firmly in Russian hands.

The Romanov Empire, established in 1613, was a more conventional, dynastic, entity. It survived for three centuries, during which time it expanded its territory significantly – not only in Europe and Central Asia, but in the Far East too. This was a more difficult task for a land-based empire than for its latter-day rivals Britain, France or even Germany, which had easier access to the sea. Yet all these empires continued to expand until they encountered rivals and limits were imposed by agreement or by force. Only the United States succeeded in creating an imperial space for itself on the two continents of the western hemisphere without the need to expand territorially and to control alien populations directly. It also secured immense markets for itself, trade, preferably exclusive, having always been an imperial goal.

But though Russia was not so advantaged, the Romanovs made impressive enough gains, extending their territory into central Europe and the Balkans, across the Caucasus, and to the heights of Central Asia. This empire too fell eventually, partly because its autocratic ruler, Nicholas II, was incompetent, but also because its economy had developed relatively late in comparison with its rivals' and was insufficiently industrialized to sustain participation in a modern total war. The same might be said of Austria-Hungary and the Ottoman Empire, both of which collapsed soon afterwards, along with their supporter, Imperial Germany. The First World War also impoverished France and Britain, ending their prospects of maintaining imperial status far into the future. But events were to show that ruined Russia was not done yet.

The Soviet regime which built Russia's fourth empire noted the lessons of its predecessor's failure. This new emergent empire was more deeply ideological than any of its predecessors, and therefore better equipped to build a great sphere of influence. It was based on the novel principle of a centrally planned economy and followed the practices of a wartime economy. The organizational core of the state hierarchy was supplemented however by an efficient Party organization that was ramified into every town, village, enterprise and professional organization. Like the modernizing precedents of Ivan IV and Peter I, the revolution presided over by Stalin was immensely costly in human life and happiness. But it worked in terms of world power. The economy was transformed, a powerful military machine was constructed, its enemies were defeated, and an empire created which was more extensive than any of its predecessors. Moreover, in addition to extensive territorial gains, the Soviet regime also ran an informal empire, the Communist Bloc, which embraced the Balkans, east–central Europe and half of Germany as well as Mongolia and Cuba; and it exerted immense influence in the world beyond through the Communist Party, and among many non-aligned countries both as a nuclear superpower and as a model of how to escape the toils of economic backwardness.

It eventually fell partly because the burdens of empire became too expensive to maintain; partly because the planned economy, which had helped to make the Soviet system so successful, eventually proved insufficiently supple to accommodate the new technology; and partly because its leader, Mikhail Gorbachev, under pressure to provide ever greater social benefits and beset by misfortune, made unnecessary mistakes. He promoted galloping inflation by default, and realized too late that the bureaucratic and Party hierarchies played essential roles in co-ordinating the system and ensuring that central policies were implemented. Once regional administrators were invited to make their own decisions without reference to Moscow, the system collapsed into chaos. The collapse was both hastened and exploited by nationalist politicians who inherited the ruins of the once mighty state. Russia itself was reduced in Europe and the Caucasus to the frontiers of c. 1600, and in Asia to those of the mid eighteenth century. Under Boris Yeltsin (1992–9) Russia's remaining strengths continued to flow away. The state weakened, its authority eroded and Russia's voice in the world faded.

Russia has been reduced territorially. In Europe it is contained by NATO;[2] in Asia it is contained albeit rather less securely by China and the local allies of the United States. But though Russia is no longer a superpower, it remains formidable in terms of nuclear power as well as conventional forces, and continues to occupy the vast region of northern Eurasia which makes it virtually impregnable. Invading Swedish, French and German armies, all of them rated superior to the Russian army of their time, have advanced far into the interior, but to their own destruction. No power today is likely to contemplate another attempt. Russia is most vulnerable strategically in sparsely populated eastern Siberia – to peaceful infiltration by the burgeoning Chinese population. Indeed, Russia generally has become demographically weak. Nevertheless, though its empires have gone, Russia and Russians remain. To assess their prospects we need to consider their historical experience as well as current indicators and developments.

The natural conditions with which they have always had to contend have had a profound effect on them. The harshness of the climate has made them hardy and enduring; the immensity of their landscape and the low density of settlement, as well as the brevity of the growing season, have encouraged both co-operation and coercion in social relationships, for Russians have needed a greater degree of organization than most peoples in order to survive and prosper. In the past this need has favoured centralized, authoritarian forms of government and discouraged more participatory forms.

Whether or not Montesquieu's judgement that very large countries need authoritarian government still holds in the technologically advanced twenty-first century, recent attempts to graft Western institutions and managerial methods on to the Russian polity and economy have proved disappointing. This is partly because their proponents have failed to take sufficient account of Russian conditions and the traditions deriving from them. They have applied theoretical solutions to a country and a people they did not understand sufficiently well. Outsiders from a different habitat with different historical experience should not expect prescriptions which work in the worlds they know to succeed anywhere else even if they have the help of a few enthusiastic helpers in the country concerned. The attempt to impose a Western form of liberal democracy on Russia in conditions of economic and social collapse merely had the effect of making liberal democrats unelectable. Democracy may best suit comparatively rich countries, but if that is the case what are the prospects of an economic recovery which might provide more fertile ground for it?

After Yeltsin they were distinctly unpromising. In Putin's first five years of office, however, the annual growth rate was in the region of 8 per cent a year, thanks largely, though by no means completely, to burgeoning oil revenues. If such a rate were to be maintained, GNP might well double within a decade. Since Yeltsin's departure progress has been made to bring order to the disorderly state of affairs that was his legacy. The ruble has been stabilized, and Russia's credit ratings have risen; corrupt localism has been restricted, social conditions have improved, and the new regime has committed itself to the rule of law. But problems remain. The media are not as free as they were, the limits of centralization have yet to be established, and the as yet unresolved Khodarkovskii case has raised doubts about the relationship between government and big business, between the state and the forces of free enterprise. Though often presented as incompatible, these are in fact complementary. Russia needs investment capital which only the world market can provide; but companies need to operate within a legal framework which only the state can maintain. If an accommodation between them is reached, the economic recovery should continue. If not, Russia will face unpleasant alternatives: either a return of the over-mighty state or untrammelled corporate greed.

In the long term, Russia's economic power is contingent on the extent of its market and the size of its population. Perhaps the most serious consequence of the collapse was demographic weakness. Russia's population continued to fall for more than ten successive years at the end of the last century. The climbing death rate of the Yeltsin years eventually eased off, but the birth rate failed to recover. According to the preliminary results of the 2002 census, the population in October of that year was 145.2 million – almost 2 million fewer than in 1989.[3] And there is a qualitative as well as a quantitative problem. Russia has been suffering from a 'brain drain'. Many able young Russian scientists and economists, entrepreneurs and engineers who might otherwise have contributed to the new Russia now live and work in the West.

Not since the first Time of Troubles, at the beginning of the 1600s, have Russia's fortunes been so low. Yet its recovery then was amazingly rapid, and it was soon on the expansionist path again. What, then, of Russia's prospects now?

Emerging from their second Time of Troubles, the Russians themselves have been less interested in empire than in political stability, economic regeneration and the elimination of social distress. Putin has understood this. In his address to the country on 26 May 2004 he stated his priorities: 'A stable democracy and developed civil society . . . the strengthening of Russia's international positions. But . . . [above all] substantial growth in the well-being of our citizens.'[4] The social objectives at least may soon be attained. Even if they are not, Russia's status as a major power, though not as a superpower, will be maintained.

In the opinion of a Western analyst, the idea that the collapse of the Soviet Union implied the end of Russia's great-power status is mistaken. All that happened was that 'One of the world's undisputed great powers temporarily subordinated its foreign and domestic policies to the West's capricious preferences. This state of affairs was never likely to last long.'[5] Russia is still the only power that stretches right across the land mass of Eurasia, and it is vital to the stability of every country situated there.[6] The prospects of building an empire of the dimensions of its last two predecessors lie far beyond its present reach, of course. Nevertheless the Russians still possess a number of advantages that could lead to their building a new sphere of influence, and even territorial enlargement, in the more distant future.

One obvious advantage Russia has over most countries in the modern world is its large reserves of every kind of strategic commodity from diamonds to natural gas, and from aluminium to uranium. Another lies in the superior quality of its educational system, which is geared to detect special talents in young children and develop them in special schools. Despite the brain drain, Russia will not lack for learning and expertise to exploit its material advantages, and with its tradition of careful planning it should make the best of them. However, a strong state cannot be based on a shrinking or static population and until now, as we have seen, Russia's demographic situation has been very weak indeed. Only in 2003, for the first time since the collapse, did Russia's birth rate rise, and then only very slightly.[7] If this should mark the beginning of an upward demographic trend, however, the prospects for longer-term revival will be strengthened. Furthermore, Russia's strategic position has been improving fast of late, thanks partly to circumstances, partly to Moscow's adroit exploitation of them.

The collapse of the Soviet Union left some successor states even worse off than Russia. Belarus has ever since been seeking reunion, and Ukraine, despite chances of being accepted into NATO's protective embrace, needs the Russian market and therefore remains ambivalent about the West, keeping its options open. Both states have large numbers of Orthodox communicants as well as other historic ties which make many of their citizens sympathetic to Moscow. Russia may yet prove the preferable option for Ukraine both for trading purposes and to ensure energy supplies. Russia's ability to interrupt or cut off the flow of oil and natural gas not only to what Russians call 'the near abroad' but to Western Europe and the Balkans too gives it considerable clout. So does its continuing occupation of Kaliningrad, the Baltic port once called Konigsberg which it acquired in the eighteenth century and contrived to hold on to both in 1945 and in 1991.

This powerful naval base wedged in between Lithuania and Poland on the Baltic frightens its neighbours and is a serious nuisance for NATO, but when the withdrawal of Russian troops from Lithuania in August 2003 prompted demands for its demilitarization Moscow refused. The retention of the enclave provides it with a powerful lever, and it is not the only one at Moscow's disposal. The presence of large Russian-speaking minorities in the Baltic states provides another. The states which host them distrust them, and, as we saw in Chapter 15, there have been charges that Russians in the 'near abroad' are denied civil and political rights. Moscow can exploit and even manipulate this situation to its advantage.

Russia's position in the Caucasus is no less strong, though the commitment is expensive because of the need to contain Chechen extremism. Since 11 September, however, the Western Powers have become more sympathetic to Moscow's point of view. The troubles will eventually subside for a time when the insurgents tire, as has always happened in the past. Meanwhile, despite the dreadful costs, no Russian government dare give in. The safety of the northern Caucasus, of oil pipelines from the Caspian Sea, and of communications to the south is an interest which Moscow cannot afford to jeopardize.

Georgia has become an American client – though an unstable one – but with allies in the Georgian provinces of Abkhazia and Ossetia, which dislike rule from Tbilisi, Russia can still exert influence there. Armenia, to the south of Georgia, still aligns with Russia and, thanks to careful nurturing over many years, Russia's relations with Iran are good. Along with the other states bordering the Caspian Sea, the two countries have agreed the bases of exploiting its oil and gas reserves, but Russia's position is stronger than the rest because of its pipeline facilities.

In Central Asia Russia's position is stronger still. Kazakhstan, the largest state in the region, is a firm ally, and Russia maintains test sites, an air base and a cosmodrome on its territory. The Uzbeks and the Kyrgyz as well as the Kazakhs know the Russians well and trust them more than other outsiders. Turkmenistan exports its natural gas through Russia, and Tajikistan has so far allowed Russian troops to patrol its frontiers with Afghanistan. A common concern to combat Islamic fundamentalism and to stabilize Afghanistan have recently brought Russia and the United States closer than for decades, but Russia now seems to be the preponderant strategic influence in Central Asia once again.

In May 2003 Russia, Kazakhstan, Kyrgyzstan and Tajikistan, as well as Belarus and Armenia, agreed to set up a collective security organization with headquarters in Moscow, a rapid-reaction force for Central Asia under

Russian command, and a common air-defence system. They also agreed to co-ordinate foreign policy and security.[8] The Collective Rapid Deployment Force was set up within a year, and, in return for rescheduling part of that country's sizeable debt,[9] Russia also obtained a permanent lease on a military air-base at Kant in Kyrgyzstan, at the heart of the region and within range of Afghanistan, Pakistan, India and China.

Russo-Chinese relations since the collapse have prospered. Trade between the two countries almost tripled during Putin's first term. Both powers are involved together with three Central Asian states in the 'Shanghai Forum', and their common interests include anti-terrorism and counter-insurgency (China approves of Moscow's policy in Chechnya, Russia of Chinese policy in Taiwan and Tibet), international conflict management, and Iraq. China implicitly recognizes Russia's leading role in Central Asia. Divergent interests may divide them in future, but for the moment the Russo-Chinese entente holds.[10] Furthermore, as in the Soviet period, relations with India are good, and India remains a major importer of Russian arms and military technology. In Asia, then, Russia's power and influence have been growing again.

The United States is the world's only superpower, but even a superpower's ability to control territory and peoples has its limitations, as the intervention in Iraq has demonstrated. Russia lacks the strength to challenge America in the foreseeable future, yet nothing is immutable. The world changes, and the strategic order will change with it. Russia has begun to recover. Its military capability is considerable albeit much reduced, and its tradition of careful diplomacy based on superior intelligence, realism and understanding of other cultures gives it advantages which others lack, and will stand it in good stead. History provides no sure guide of things to come, but, as I write in September 2004, it would be unwise to write off Russia's chances of future power.

Chronology

Date	*Geology/climate and selected events in European/world history*	*Russian history and imperial development*
Before present		
20,000–26,000	Age of mammoths	Sungir remains
24,000	Onset of the Ice Age	
7,000–8,000	Global warming; ice retreats	Aspen, birch, hazel, willow, hornbeam, linden, oak, elm, etc.
		Animals, wildfowl
6,000	Palaeolithic era	Agriculture and animal husbandry
4,000	Babylonia	Tripolye settlements
3,500		Hunter-gatherers in Finland
3,000	Iron Age	Swidden agriculture
	Persian Empire	Cimmerians, Scythians, Sarmatians
	Alexander the Great	
2,000	Roman Empire	
Common Era (CE)		
330 CE	Constantine the Great founds Constantinople	Khazar kaganate
c. 650–	Spread of Islam: Baghdad Caliphate	
c. 856		Riurik at Ladoga
858		Askold and Dir take Kiev
860	Vikings raid Constantinople	
882	Alfred the Great	Oleg defeats Askold and Dir
		Khazar hegemony over Kiev
c. 955		Olga visits Constantinople
		Sviatoslav conquers Khazars
		Christianization of Rus

		Vladimir builds St Sofia in Kiev
		Iaroslav the Wise (d. 1054)
1066	Normans conquer England	
1068		Rus defeated by Polovtsians (Cumans)
1113		Vladimir Monomakh, Prince of Vladimir-Suzdal
1204	Crusaders sack Constantinople	
1232		Baty Khan routs Russians
		Mongol era begins
1240		Collapse of Kievan Rus
		Alexander Nevskii beats off Swedes and German Knights
c. 1300		Rise of Vladimir-Moscow
1325		Metropolitan of Kiev moves to Moscow
1331		Ivan I (Money-Bag) becomes grand prince
1380		Dmitrii defeats Tatars at Kulikovo
1400		St Sergius. Monastic colonization
1413	Treaty of Horodlo	Catholicization in Lithuania
1425	Growth of Inca Empire	Vasilii II
1441	Council of Ferrara	Ivan III (the Great)
	Louis XI of France	
1453	Constantinople falls to Turks	
	Lorenzo de' Medici	
	Henry the Navigator	Novgorod subjected to Moscow
1472		Ivan III m. Zoe Palaeologue
1485	Henry VII of England	
	Aztec Empire	
1547		Ivan IV (the Terrible)
1550	Spain and Portugal build empires	Law book issued
		Kazan captured
		First Russian outposts in Caucasus
		Conquest of Siberian khanate
		Livonian war
		English merchants discover Russia
		Archangel established
		Boris Godunov

1601	Onset of Little Ice Age	Mangazeia founded
1605		Russia in turmoil
		Collapse of Muscovite state
		Pretender Dmitrii takes Moscow
1606		Swedes invade
1612		Moscow recaptured
1613		Michael Romanov crowned tsar
1630–31		War with Poland
		Smolensk recaptured
1648	Fronde in France	Dezhnev reaches Pacific
	English Civil War	Ukrainian Cossacks rebel against Polish rule
1654		War with Poland
		Ukrainian Cossacks submit to Tsar Alexis
1660	Restoration of monarchy in England	
1667		Peace of Andrusovo: Russia gains eastern Ukraine
1676		Death of Alexis, accession of Fedor
1689		Treaty of Nerchinsk with China
1689–1725		Peter I (the Great)
		Great Northern War
1703		Foundation of St Petersburg
1709		Russians rout Swedes at Poltava
1711		Russians defeated by Turks on river Pruth
1716		Orenburg Line begun (base for future expansion into Central Asia)
		Annexation of Baltic states
1724		War with Persia
1725		Catherine I
1726		Alliance with Habsburg Emperor
1727		Peter II
1730		Anna Iovanovna
1741		Elizabeth Petrovna
1756–63	Seven Years War	
1761		Peter III
1762		Catherine II
1769–73	American Revolution	War with Turks
		First partition of Poland

1783		Annexation of Crimea
1787–93	French Revolution	War with Turks
1793		Second partition of Poland
1795	Revolutionary Wars	Third partition of Poland
1800	Napolean	A Russian fleet enters the Mediterranean
1803		A Russian ship circumnavigates the globe
1808		Finland annexed
1811		Bessarabia annexed
1812		Russia invaded by Napoleon's *Grande Armée*
1815	Waterloo	Russian troops in Paris
1820s		War in Chechnya
		Russia sponsors Greek independence
1828–9		Russians take Tabriz and Erzurum
		Russia penetrates Central Asia and Far East; gains access to Mediterranean
		Russia sponsors autonomous Serbia
		Russian colonization of Alaska
1837–1901	Queen Victoria	
1853–6		Crimean War
1864	American Civil War	Russians take Chimkent
1865		" " Samarkand
1873		" " Khiva
		" " Kokand
1877–8		War with Turks
		Russia sponsors Bulgarian independence
		Railway-building
1885	Heyday of British Empire	Russians defeat Afghans at Pendjeh
1890s		Russia industrializes
		Trans-Siberian Railway
1896		Russia–China accord
1904		War with Japan
1905		Battle of Tsushima
1914–18	First World War	

1917		Nicholas II abdicates; end of Romanov Empire
		Bolsheviks remove Provisional Government
1918–		Civil War
		War with Poland
		Loss of Baltic states, Ukraine, etc.
1924		Death of Lenin; power gravitates to Stalin
1928–9	Great Depression	Stalin launches Collectivization and first Five-Year Plan
1933	Hitler in power in Germany	
1934–8		Purges and show trials
1938	Munich Agreement	
1939	Second World War begins in West	
1940		Occupation of Baltic states
1941		Hitler invades Soviet Union
	Pearl Harbor; US enters WWII	
1942		Battle of Stalingrad
1943		Battle of Kursk; Germans in retreat
1944	Invasion of Normandy	Yalta Conference
1945	Atomic bomb dropped on Japan	Soviet forces take Berlin
		Potsdam agreement
1947	Marshall Plan	Onset of the Cold War
	Chinese Communists defeat Nationalists	Soviet Bloc formed
1949		Soviet Union acquires atom bomb; breach with China
1953		Death of Stalin
1954		COMECON becomes active
1955		Warsaw Pact
1956		Soviet intervention in Hungary
1959		Cuba aligns with Moscow
1961		Soviet Union puts first astronaut into space
1964		Brezhnev replaces Khrushchev
1968		Soviet intervention in Czechoslovakia
1979		Soviet intervention in Afghanistan

1982		Andropov becomes Party Secretary
1984		Death of Andropov; Chernenko succeeds him
1985		Death of Chernenko; Gorbachev becomes Party Secretary; détente with West
1986		Chernobyl disaster
1988–91	Reunification of Germany	Collapse of Bloc
		Dissolution of Soviet Union
1992		Yeltsin as Russian president
		Catastrophic decline
		Russia reverts to frontiers of *c.* 1650
1994–6	NATO extends eastward	First Chechen War
		US warships enter Black Sea
2000		Putin becomes president
		Reassertion of Russian interests
		Economic recovery

Notes

INTRODUCTION

1. One of the few exceptions is Basil Sumner's masterly *Survey of Russian History* (2nd edn, London, 1947).

1: THE RUSSIANS: WHO ARE THEY?

1. B. M. Fagan, *The Journey from Eden: The Peopling of Our World* (London, 1990), p. 183. At one time mammoth tusks had been plentiful enough to use as building frames or tent poles.
2. O. Semino et al., 'The genetic legacy of palaeolothic *Homo sapiens sapiens* in extant Europeans', *Science*, 290 (5404), 10 November 2000, 1155–9, and the interview with Peter Underhill in *Montreal Gazette*, 11 November 2000, p. D-9. Also L. Cavalli-Sforza, P. Menozzi and A. Piazza, *The History and Geography of Human Genes* (Princeton, 1994), pp. 3–59 (for the principles) and map 5.2.7, pp. 262–3, and atlas C-5 (for the geographic spread). Despite subsequent intermarriage with Mongols and other peoples of different genetic heritage, the evidence shows Russians to be of predominately Caucasian stock. There was a discursive but interesting discussion on genetics relevant to history on the Marshall Poe e-mail connection (mpoe@fas.harvard.edu) in September 2002. It centred on haplotype M17, which distinguishes eastern from western Europeans.
3. V. Bunak, 'Antropologicheskie tipy russkago naroda i voprosy istorii ikh formirovanie', *Kratkie soobshcheniia Instituta etnografii AN/SSR*, 36 (1962), 75–82.
4. L. and F. Cavalli-Sforza, *The Great Human Diaspora* (Reading, Mass., 1995), especially pp. 115–16. For indications of genetic differences between Russians and other Europeans, see Cavalli-Sforza et al., *History and Geography of Human Genes*, p. 270.
5. G. Vernadsky, *Ancient Russia* (New Haven, 1947, repr. 1973), pp. 21–2; D. Christian, *A History of Russia, Central Asia and Mongolia*, vol. 1 (Oxford, 1998), pp. 77–8; J. Mallory, *In Search of Indo-Europeans. Language, Archaeology and Myth* (London, 1989), p. 196.

6. P. Dolukhanov, *The Early Slavs: Eastern Europe from the Initial Settlement to Kievan Rus'* (London, 1996), p. 70. Sredny Stog is associated with the domestication of the horse.
7. Christian, *Russia, Central Asia and Mongolia*, vol. 1, p. 40.
8. Dolukhanov, *The Early Slavs*, pp. 101–2.
9. Ibid., pp. 109–15.
10. See C. Renfrew, *Archaeology and Language* (London, 1987) – but also his critic J. Mallory, who concludes that Renfrew's idea of the spread of the first Indo-Europeans 'is not congruent with either the linguistic or archaeological evidence' (*In Search of Indo-Europeans. Language, Archaeology and Myth*). I am grateful to my former colleague Bruce Trigger for guidance in this area. While haplotype U entered the bloodstream of Europeans some 40,000 years ago, and haplotypes H and V more than 10,000 years ago, bearers of haplotype J 'may well have descended from . . . women who came to Europe 8,000 years ago from Anatolia' – *Times Literary Supplement*, May 2001, in a review of B. Sykes's *The Seven Daughters of Eve*.
11. 'At that time there was only one Slavic people, including those along the Danube who were subject to the Hungarians, the Moravians, Czechs, Poles and Polanians, who are now called Russians' (adapted from the translation by S. Cross and P. Olgerd, eds., of *The Russian Primary Chronicle* (Cambridge, Mass., 1953), p. 62).
12. Baedeker, *Russia: A Handbook for Travellers* (Leipzig, 1914), pp. xxxviii–xxxix.
13. L. Milev, *Velikorusskii pakhar' i osobennosti rossiiskogo istoricheskogo protsessa* (Moscow, 1998), pp. 554–6. Milev's theory will receive some attention later in the book.
14. Dolukhanov, *The Early Slavs*, pp. 117–19; M. Gimbutas, *The Slavs* (London, 1971), pp. 24–5; Vernadsky, *Ancient Russia*, pp. 48–50.
15. Dolukhanov, *The Early Slavs*, pp. 119–25; Gimbutas, *The Slavs*, pp. 44, 46–9.
16. See V. Levasheva in *Trudy gosudarstvennogo istoricheskogo muzeia*, vyp. 32 (Moscow, 1956), pp. 20ff., and B. Grekov, *Die Bauern in des Russlands von den ältesten Zeiten bis den 17 Jahrhundert* (2 vols., Berlin, 1959), *passim*.
17. Christian, *Russia, Central Asia and Mongolia*, vol. 1, pp. 331–3.
18. See the maps in P. Barford, *The Early Slavs: Culture and Society in Early Medieval Eastern Europe* (Ithaca, 2001), pp. 376, 378.
19. On the properties of Russian rye and the lore associated with it see R. Smith and D. Christian, *Bread and Salt: A Social and Economic History of Food and Drink in Russia* (Cambridge, 1984), pp. 5–6 and *passim*; Christian, *Russia, Central Asia and Mongolia*, vol. 1, p. 331 (and inference therefrom).
20. Barford, *The Early Slavs*, especially the maps on pp. 387, 399.
21. See the suggestive passage in ibid., pp. 189–91. Also W. Ryan, *The Bathhouse at Midnight* (University Park, Pa., 1999), ch. 2, esp. p. 37.
22. Christian, *Russia, Central Asia and Mongolia*, vol. 1, p. 340. For a translation of the passage from Ibn Khurdadhbih see G. Vernadsky et al., *A Source Book for*

Russian History from the Earliest Times to 1917 (3 vols., New Haven, 1972), vol. 1, p. 9. On Khazar metrology and money economy see O. Pritsak, *The Origins of the Old Rus' Weights and Monetary Systems* (Cambridge, Mass., 1998), esp. p. 32. On taxes paid to Khazar towns see Barford, *The Early Slavs*, p. 237.

23. The remains at Old Ladoga, like the first settlements at Novgorod, have been carefully investigated by archaeologists – see M. Brisbane, ed., *Archaeology of Novgorod: Recent Results from the Town and its Hinterland*, Society for Medieval Archaeology, monograph 13 (Lincoln, Nebr., 1992); for the broader background S. Franklin and J. Shepard, *The Emergence of Rus' 750–1200* (London, 1996), pp. 12ff. On the early association of Vikings and Slavs, see M. Liubavskii, *Obzor istorii russkoi kolonizatsii*, ed. A. Ia. Degtarev et al. (Moscow, 1996), p. 55.
24. Brisbane, ed., *Archaeology of Novgorod*, pp. 90ff. See also E. Nosov, 'The problem of the emergence of early urban centres in northern Russia', in J. Chapman and P. Dolukhanov, *Cultural Transformations and Interactions in Eastern Europe* (Aldershot, 1993), pp. 236–56, and A. Kuza, 'Sotsial'no-istoricheskaia tipologiia drevnerusskikh gorodov x–xiii vv', in *Russkii gorod: issledovania i materially*, no. 176 (Moscow, 1983), pp. 4–36. On the phenomenon of 'paired' towns, see Nosov, 'Early urban centres in northern Russia', and the references therein.
25. Ibn Rusta is quoted in Franklin and Shepard, *The Emergence of Rus'*, p. 45.
26. I. Dubov, 'The ethnic history of northwestern Rus' in the ninth to the thirteenth centuries', in D. Kaiser and G. Marker, eds., *Reinterpreting Russian History* (New York, 1994), pp. 14–20. Also A. Sakharov, 'The main phase and distinctive features of Russian nationalism', in G. Hosking and R. Service, eds., *Reinterpreting Russian Nationalism* (London, 1995), pp. 7–18.

2: THE FIRST RUSSIAN STATE

1. See A. Ya. Degtarev's rationalization of the legend that the men of Novgorod summoned Riurik to rule as their prince in Liubavskii, *Obzor istorii russkoi kolonizatsii*, p. 55.
2. The importance of the Khazars is suggested by the fact that Viking rulers of the early tenth century styled themselves 'kagan', the title of the Khazar ruler – see Barford, *The Early Slavs*, pp. 238–9. The Khazars were successful commercially, and even developed money economy and coinage – see O. Pritsak, 'Did the Khazars possess a monetary economy?', in his *Origins of the Old Rus' Weights and Monetary Systems*, pp. 21–32.
3. Constantine VII Porphyrogenitus, *De Administrando Imperio*, ed. Gy. Moravcik and R. Jenkins (2 vols., London, 1962), section 9: 'On the coming of the Russians in "monolykha".' See also Franklin and Shepard, *The Emergence of Rus'*.
4. C. Mangö, trans., *The Homilies of Photius* (Cambridge, Mass, 1958), pp. 95ff.
5. See Vernadsky's chronology in his *Ancient Russia*, pp. 394–5; Franklin and Shepard, *The Emergence of Rus'*, p. 57.

6. M. McCormick, *Origins of the European Economy: Communications and Commerce, A.D. 300–900* (Cambridge, Mass., 2001), pp. 610, 743, 760.
7. Christian, *Russia, Central Asia and Mongolia*, vol. 1, p. 342; Franklin and Shepard, *The Emergence of Rus'*, pp. 103–4; O. Pritsak, *Origins of Rus'*, vol. 1: *Old Scandinavian Sources other than the Sagas* (Cambridge, Mass., 1981), p. 583.
8. I have adapted this passage from the Laurentian Chronicle from the translation in Vernadsky et al., *Source Book*, vol. 1, pp. 22–3.
9. The account of Olga that precedes and follows is derived from several sources, including Ye. A. Kivlitskii, 'Sv. Ol'ga [Helen]', *Entsiklopedicheskii slovar'* (Brockhaus-Efron), vol. 21A (St Petersburg, 1897), pp. 910–11, Barford, *The Early Slavs*, p. 147; Franklin and Shepard, *The Emergence of Rus'*, pp. 134–9.
10. For an account of taxation in Kievan Rus', see G. Vernadsky, *Kievan Russia* (New Haven, 1948, repr. 1973), pp. 190–92.
11. I. Dubov, *Voprosy istorii*, 5 (1990), 15–17, translated in part in D. Kaiser and G. Marker, eds., *Reinterpreting Russian History: Readings 860–1862* (New York, 1994), pp. 13–20. Dubov discusses the contributions of Vikings, Slavs and others to the development of society in the forest zone of central Russia.
12. See the translated excerpts from Ouranos and Liutprand in D. Geanakoplos, *Byzantium: Church Society and Civilization seen through Contemporary Eyes* (Chicago, 1984), pp. 112–13.
13. Yngvar's saga, see Palsson and Edwards, *Vikings in Russia*, pp. 52, 55–6.
14. Constantine VII, *De Administrando Imperio*, section 9.
15. See Barford, *The Early Slavs*, p. 237.
16. Franklin and Shepard, *The Emergence of Rus'*, pp. 370–71.
17. A. Kazhdan and A. W. Epstein, *Change in Byzantine Culture in the Eleventh and Twelfth Centuries* (Berkeley, 1990), p. 81.
18. Constantine VII, *Le Livre des cérémonies*, ed. A. Vogt (Paris, 1935, 1939–40); Liutprand, *Relatio de legatio Constantinopolitana*, ed. J. Becker (Hanover and Leipzig, 1915); H. Evand and W. Wixom, eds., *The Glory of Byzantium* (New York, 1977); A. Kazhdan and M. McCormick, 'The social world of the Byzantine courts', in H. Maguire, ed., *Byzantine Court Culture from 829 to 1209* (Washington, 1997), pp. 167–98.
19. I follow the interpretation in Kivlitskii, 'Sv. Ol'ga [Helen]', rather than Franklin and Shepard (*The Emergence of Rus'*, p. 137), who think that Olga was seeking legitimation for the new Russia from as many sources as possible. On the question of her baptism see G. Ostrogorsky, *History of the Byzantine State* (Oxford, 1980), p. 283, n. 1.
20. Another translation of this excerpt from the Laurentian Chronicle is to be found in Vernadsky et al., *Source Book*, vol. 1, p.25.
21. For example, the recurring refrain 'Dunai, Dunai' in historical songs about Stepan Razin.
22. Vernadsky, *Kievan Russia*, p. 42; Ostrogorsky, *History of the Byzantine State*, pp. 292–6.

23. Franklin and Shepard, *The Emergence of Rus'*, p. 163.
24. I. Sevcenko, *Ukraine between East and West* (Edmonton, 1996).
25. G. H. Hamilton, *The Art and Architecture of Russia* (Harmondsworth, 1954), pp. 10–14.
26. Pritsak, *Origins of Rus'*, vol. 1, p. 32.
27. F. Dvornik, 'Byzantine political ideas in Kievan Russia', *Dumbarton Oaks Papers*, 9–10 (1956), 76–94.
28. F. Dvornik, *Byzantine Missions among the Slavs* (New Brunswick, 1970), p. 277.
29. See D. Obolensky, 'Vladimir Monomakh', in his *Six Byzantine Portraits* (Oxford, 1988), pp. 83ff.; Palsson and Edwards, *Vikings in Russia*, p. 32.
30. See J. Fennell, *The Crisis of Medieval Russia 1200–1304* (London, 1983), p. 163, on the consequences two and a half centuries later.
31. The Laurentian Chronicle, translation adapted from Vernadsky et al., *Source Book*, vol. 1, p. 27.
32. Obolensky, 'Vladimir Monomakh', pp. 83ff.
33. Ibid.
34. See Christian, *Russia, Central Asia and Mongolia*, vol. 1, p. 368.
35. Fennell, *The Crisis of Medieval Russia*, pp. 20, 22.
36. S. Belokurov, ed., *Snosheniia Rossii s Kavkazom*, Moskovskogo glavnogo arkhiva Ministerstva Inostrannykh Del (now the Russian State Archive), vyp. 1 (Moscow, 1889), pp. iiiff.
37. F. Dvornik, 'Byzantine influences in Russia', in M. Huxley, ed., *The Root of Europe* (London, 1952), pp. 95–106, and his 'Byzantine political ideas' *loc. cit.*
38. Fennell, *The Crisis of Medieval Russia*, p. 57.
39. The Novgorod Primary Chronicle as quoted in Fennell, *The Crisis of Medieval Russia*, p. 74.
40. Well organized in tens, hundreds, thousands, and units of ten thousand, they were well equipped too. Every soldier had two horses and carried an axe, a bow and three quivers full of arrows. Some were more heavily armed and carried armour. They were also well trained: their bows had a range of 300 yards, and they could shoot as they rode. Their discipline was fierce but effective: a man who fled from battle was executed; if a section of ten men fled, the remaining ninety men of their hundred would be slaughtered. See Christian, *Russia, Central Asia and Mongolia*, vol. 1, pp. 397–415.
41. For a balanced assessment of the Mongol impact, see C. J. Halperin, *Russia and the Golden Horde: The Mongol Impact on Russian History* (London, 1987).

3: REINCARNATION

1. In his *The Crisis of Medieval Russia*, John Fennell concludes that this was not an immediate consequence of the invasion. However, by the second half of the thirteenth century Moscow had become the safest part of Rostov-Suzdal

and was a magnet for the displaced and vulnerable – see M. Liubavskii, *Obrazovanie osnovnoi gosudarstvennoi territorii velikorusskoi narodnosti. Zaseleniia i ob"edieniia tsentra* (Moscow, 1929, repr. 1996), p. 33.

2. M. Rywkin, 'Russian colonial expansion before Ivan the Dread: a survey of basic trends', *Russian Review*, 32 (1973), 286–93; also R. Kerner, *The Urge to the Sea: The Course of Russian History: The Role of Rivers, Portages, Ostrogs, Monasteries and Furs* (Berkeley and Los Angeles, 1942), pp. 33–5. Janet Martin's *Treasure of the Land of Darkness: The Fur Trade and its Significance for Medieval Russia* (Cambridge, 1986) gives Kerner's thesis a new twist.
3. A. N. Mouravieff, *A History of the Church of Russia*, trans. R. W. Blackmore (Oxford 1842), p. 47.
4. See the laudatory account in ibid., pp. 51–6.
5. See the discussion in Halperin, *Russia and the Golden Horde*.
6. A. A. Gorskii, *Russkie zemli v xiii–xiv vekakh: puti politicheskogo razvitiia* (Moscow, 1996), pp. 58–62, 66–7, 56.
7. His history of Russian colonization was completed in the early 1930s, but remained unpublished till almost the end of the century – see A. Ia. Degtarev's introduction to Liubavskii, *Obzor istorii russkoi kolonizatsii* (Moscow, 1996).
8. Liubavskii, *Obzor*, pp. 51–6.
9. See J. Fennell's *The Emergence of Moscow 1304–1359* (London, 1968), *passim*, for a repeated struggle to extract a credible explanation from the sources. Fennell's work has contributed much to the account which follows. For a more positive if less painstaking treatment see also N. Borisov, *Ivan Kalita* (Moscow, 1997).
10. Fennell, *The Emergence of Moscow*, pp. 4, 90–93.
11. Ibid., p. 112.
12. Borisov, *Ivan Kalita*, pp. 6–7.
13. R. Howes, ed., *The Testaments of the Grand Princes of Moscow* (Ithaca, 1967), pp. 182ff.
14. J. Meyendorff, *Byzantium and the Rise of Russia* (Crestwood, NY, 1989), p. 185.
15. See R. Crummey, *The Formation of Muscovy 1304–1613* (London, 1987), pp. 43ff.
16. 'The Wanderer of Stephen of Novgorod', in G. Majeska, trans. and ed., *Russian Travellers to Constantinople in the Thirteenth and Fourteenth Centuries* (Chicago, 1970), pp. xxxi, xxxiii; Liubavskii, *Obzor istorii russkoi kolonizatsii*, p. 39.
17. See the discussion by M. Klimensko in his introduction to *The 'Vita' of St. Sergii of Radonezh* (Boston, Mass., n.d.), pp. 15–16.
18. As well as Klimensko's edition of *The 'Vita'*, see R. G. Skrynnikov, *Gosudarstvo i tserkov' na Rusi xiv–xvi vv* (Novosibirsk, 1991), pp. 43ff.
19. Liubavskii, *Obzor istorii russkoi kolonizatsii*, pp. 190–92, 542–44.
20. Ibid., p. 19.
21. Ibid., p. 22.

22. Liubavskii, *Obrazovanie osnovnoi gosudarstvennoi territorii velikorusskoi narodnosti*, pp. 42–4 et seq., and his *Obzor istorii russkoi kolonizatsii*, pp. 22–3.
23. E.g. the testament of Vasilii I, in Howes, ed., *Testaments of the Grand Princes of Moscow*, p. 219. On the apanage, see A. E. Presniakov, *The Formation of the Great Russian State: A Study of Russian History in the Thirteenth and Fourteenth Centuries* (Chicago, 1970), pp. 392–3.
24. Crummey, *The Formation of Muscovy*, gives a convenient account of this.
25. For details of this unedifying period, see A. Zimin, *Vitiaz' na rasput'e: feodal'naia voina Rossii xv v* (Moscow, 1991). Zimin devoted most of his career to the political history of fifteenth- and sixteenth-century Russia and produced six books on it. Of the remaining five, two deal with the periods 1480–1505 (which he calls 'the birth of Russia') and 1505–33 (Russia's ascent), and the remaining three with the reign of Ivan IV (see Chapter 5).
26. See G. Pickhan, 'The incorporation of *Gospodin Pskov* into the Muscovite state', in L. Hughes, ed., *New Perspectives in Muscovite History* (Basingstoke, 1992), pp. 51–8.
27. See A. A. Zimin, *Formirovanie boiarskoi aristokratii v Rossii vo vtoroi polovine xv – pervoi treti xvi v* (Moscow, 1988), p. 283.
28. A. E. Moorhouse, in his introduction to Presniakov, *The Formation of the Great Russian State*, pp. xxxi–xxxiii.
29. Liubavskii, *Obzor istorii russkoi kolonizatsii*, p. 39.

4: THE FOUNDATION OF AN EMPIRE

1. Presniakov, *The Formation of the Great Russian State*, pp. 381–2.
2. J. Fennell, *Ivan the Great of Moscow* (London, 1961), pp. 37–54; also Presniakov, *The Formation of the Great Russian State*, pp. 364–7, especially on the Church and the constitutional position. The parallels with Henry VII, Louis XI and others are suggested by L. Cherepnin, *Obrazovanie russkogo tsentralizovannogo gosudarstva v xiv–xv vv* (Moscow, 1966), p. 7; on financial policy, insofar as it has been reconstructed, see S. Kashtanov, *Finansy srednevekovoi Rusi* (Moscow, 1988), chs. 2–4.
3. N. Sinitsyn, *Tretii Rim: istoki i evolutsiia russkoi srednevekovoi konseptsii (xv–xvii vv)* (Moscow, 1998), pp. 213 – a thorough analysis of the Italian and Austrian sources for this development.
4. See plates f. 1v and f. 31r between pp. 416 and 417 in N. Borisov, *Ivan III* (Moscow, 2000).
5. Sinitsyn, *Tretii Rim*, p. 116.
6. The account of events which follows is based chiefly on Fennell, *Ivan the Great of Moscow*, pp. 37–54.
7. Translated passage from the Nikon Chronicle, Kaiser and Marker, eds., *Reinterpreting Russian History*, p. 91.

8. On the subjection of Pskov, see Pickhan, 'The incorporation of *Gospodin Pskov*'; on Ivan's reception in Moscow, Iu. G. Alekseiev, *Gosudar' vseia Rusi* (Novosibirsk, 1991), p. 85. The term 'boyar' has often been misunderstood. It originally denoted a member of a prince's war band, but under Ivan it came to refer to a handful of close advisers to the Grand Prince – in effect a ministerial elite. (See V. Kliuchevskii, *Boiarskaia duma drevnei Rusi* (Moscow, 1909), and in particular Zimin, *Formirovanie boiarskoii aristokratii.*)
9. Aside from Fennell, *Ivan the Great of Moscow*, see H. Birnbaum, 'Did the 1478 annexation of Novgorod by Muscovy fundamentally change the course of Russian History?', in Hughes, ed., *New Perspectives in Muscovite History*, pp. 37–50.
10. On the institution of *pronoia* in the Byzantine Empire, see Ostrogorskii, *History of the Byzantine State*, pp. 330–31.
11. See Presniakov, *The Formation of the Great Russian State*, pp. 376–7; Fennell, *Ivan the Great of Moscow*, pp. 64–6.
12. Zimin, *Formirovanie boiarskoii aristokratii*, pp. 283ff.
13. See R. M. Crosskey, *Muscovite Diplomatic Practice in the Reign of Ivan III* (New York, 1987), app. J, p. 84.
14. Ibid., pp. 238–42, 43.
15. Ibid., pp. 84, 98–9. On the first Russian embassy to the Ottoman Turks, led by Pleshcheev, see A. V. Nekliudov, ed., *Nachalo snoshenii Rossii s Turtsiei* (Moscow, 1883).
16. Magdolna Agoston on Ivan III's wax seal of 1497 in Gy. Szvak, ed., *Proceedings of the 3rd International Conference on Russia* organized by the University of Budapest (Budapest, forthcoming).
17. Fennell, *Ivan the Great of Moscow*, pp. 37–84; Presniakov, *The Formation of the Great Russian State*, pp. 364–7.
18. Adapted from Crosskey's translation of the instruction of 17 May 1503, in Crosskey, *Muscovite Diplomatic Practice*, pp. 292–3.
19. See G. Mattingly, *Renaissance Diplomacy* (Harmondsworth, 1965). For Russia's early relations with Poland, the Balkan principalities and Turkey, see V. Ulianitskii, ed., *Materialy o Rossii, Pol'shi, Moldavii, Vlachi v 14–16 st, Chteniia v obshchestve istorii i drevnostei rossiiskikh*, vol. 3 (Moscow, 1887), pp. 1–24.
20. Fennell, *Ivan the Great of Moscow*, pp. 129, 117; instruction dated May 1493 in Crosskey, *Muscovite Diplomatic Practice*, p. 294.
21. N. N. Bantysh-Kamenskii, *Obzor vneshnykh snoshenii Rossii (po 1800)*, Pt 1 (Moscow 1894), pp. 1–2; also Sinitsyn, *Tretii Rim*, p. 118, quoting Ivan's instructions to his own envoy and Habsburg ambassador Herberstein's report.
22. Fennell, *Ivan the Great of Moscow*, pp. 117–18.
23. Trakhaniot's account in the Milan State Archive, see Crosskey, *Muscovite Diplomatic Practice*, p. 64 and n. 23 on that page.
24. P. P. Epifanov, 'Voiska i voennaia organizatsiia', in A. V. Artsikhovskii et al., *Ocherki russkoi kul'tury xvi v*, vyp. 1 (Moscow, 1976), p. 344.

25. Ibid., pp. 354–5.
26. M. Khodarkovsky, *Russia's Steppe Frontier: The Making of a Colonial Empire 1500–1800* (Bloomington, 2002), pp. 74–8; B. Nolde, *La Formation de l'Empire Russe* (2 vols., Paris, 1952–3), vol. 2, p. 16.
27. K. V. Bazilevich, *Vneshnaia politika russkogo tsentralizovannogo Gosudarstvva, vtoraia polovina xv veka* (Moscow, 1952), pp. 16, 29–30.
28. The words of Dmitrii Gerasimov, interpreter to the mission, in A. V. Kartashev, *Ocherki po istorii russkoi tserkvi* (2 vols., Moscow, 1992), vol. 2, p. 7.
29. On the burning of Kobyle, Fennell, *Ivan the Great of Moscow*, p. 70; on the war of 1501, see E. Christiansen, *The Northern Crusades* (London, 1997), pp. 255–7.
30. J. Tazbir, *Poland as the Rampart of Christian Europe* (Warsaw, n.d.), p. 32.
31. See M. Poe, *Foreign Descriptions of Muscovy: An Analytic Bibliography of Primary and Secondary Sources* (Columbus, Ohio, 1995), p. 11.
32. Fennell, *Ivan the Great of Moscow*, pp. 325–6.
33. Crummey, *The Formation of Muscovy*, pp. 134–5.
34. Mouravieff, *The Church of Russia*.
35. On the Kuritsyns' careers, S. B. Veselovskii, *D'iaki i pod'iachie xv–xvii vv* (Moscow, 1975), pp. 278–80.
36. Crummey, *The Formation of Muscovy*, p. 87 and the maps in Bazilevich, *Vneshnaia politika russkogo tsentralizovannogo Gosudarstvva, vtoraia polovina xv veka*; on Dolmatov, Veselovskii, *D'iaki i pod'iachie xv–xvii vv*, pp. 155–6.
37. Pickhan, 'The incorporation of *Gospodin Pskov*'.
38. Sinitsyn, *Tretii Rim*, pp. 215–20.
39. M. Rywkin, ed., *Russian Colonial Expansion to 1917* (London, 1988).
40. Skrynnikov, *Gosudarstvo i tserkov' na Rusi xiv–xvi vv*, p. 362.
41. S. von Herberstein, *Rerum Moscoviticarum Commentarii* (Vienna, 1549). On the significance of Russians shaving off their beards, see Cornelia Soldat's and others' contributions of 2 February 2003 to Sergei Bogatyrev's e-mail site sergei-bogatyrev@helsinki.fi.

5: IVAN IV AND THE FIRST IMPERIAL EXPANSION

1. See the account in the Nikon Chronicle as translated by Vernadsky et al., *Source Book*, vol. 1, pp. 133–4. Ivan's legitimacy was to be reinforced by a charter issued by the Patriarch of Constantinople in 1561, which traced Ivan's descent through Monomakh's sister Anna to Constantine the Great, asserting his legitimacy by 'lineage and blood'. The genetic association was, however, a political fiction. See ibid., p. 171.
2. See Poe, *Foreign Descriptions of Muscovy*, pp. 12–13; R. Frost, *The Northern Wars 1558–1721* (London, 2000), pp. 78–80, 91; P. Longworth, 'Russia and the Antemurale Christianitatis', in Gy. Szvak, ed., *The Place of Russia in Europe* (Budapest, 1999). See also a paper warning of the danger to central Europe if

Russia should become strongly entrenched along the southern shoreline of the Baltic: G. V. Forsten, *Akty i pis'ma k istorii Baltiiskogo voprosa v xvi i xvii stoletiakh* (St Petersburg, 1889), pp. 14–28.

3. See the contrasting views of R. Hellie, 'What happened? How did he get away with it? Ivan Groznyi's paranoia and the problem of institutional restraints', *Russian History*, 14 (1987), 199–224; A. A. Zimin, *Reformy Ivana Groznogo* (Moscow, 1960), R. Skrynnikov, *Ivan Groznyi* (Moscow, 1980), and A. Dvorkin, *Ivan the Terrible as a Religious Type* (Erlangen, 1992).
4. Nikon Chronicle excerpted in Vernadsky et al., *Source Book*, vol. 1, p. 133.
5. See B. Floria, *Ivan Groznyi* (Moscow, 1999), p. 17. Tales about the infant Ivan pulling the wings off a butterfly resemble (and are probably of the same German provenance) as the tales of Dracula – see M. Cazacu, *L'Histoire du Prince Dracula en Europe Centrale et Orientale* (Geneva, 1998).
6. For Moscow's dealings with the various Mongol factions see Khodarkovsky, *Russia's Steppe Frontier*, pp. 106–11. For the implications for further southward expansion see C. Lemercier-Quelquejoy, 'Co-optation of the elites of Kabarda and Daghestan in the sixteenth century', in M. Bennigsen Broxup, ed., *The North Caucasus Barrier: The Russian Advance towards the Muslim World* (London, 1992), pp. 18–42.
7. Communication from Jukka Korpela posted on M. Poe site, 29 March 2000.
8. R. Hakluyt, *The Principal Navigations Voyages Traffiques and Discoveries of the English Nation* (12 vols., Glasgow, 1908), vol. 3, p. 384.
9. Nolde, *La Formation de l'Empire Russe*, vol. 1, pp. 77–8.
10. J. Martin, 'Peculiarities of the *pomest'e* system', in Gy. Szvak, ed., *Muscovy: Peculiarities of its Development* (Budapest, 2003), pp. 76–87.
11. See Floria, *Ivan Groznyi*. Also Khodarkovsky, *Russia's Steppe Frontier*, pp. 102–45.
12. Nolde, *La Formation de l'Empire Russe*, vol. 2, pp. 303–5.
13. Bantysh-Kamenskii, *Obzor vneshnykh snoshenii Rossii (po 1800)*, Pt 1, vol. 1, pp. 9–7.
14. A. Kappeler, *Russland als Vielvölkerreich* (Munich, 1992), p. 43; and see ch. 8 below.
15. Vernadsky et al., *Source Book*, vol. 1, 1972, p. 142; B. Rudakov, *Entsiklopedicheskii slovar'*, vol. 3 (St Petersburg, 1900), pp. 803–5; Nolde, *La Formation de l'Empire Russe*, vol. 1, pp. 132–3.
16. For translations of the basic Russian account, see T. Armstrong, ed., *Yermak's Campaign in Siberia* (London, 1975), and W. Coxe, *Account of the Russian Discoveries between Asia and America* (4th edn, London, 1803), pp. 418ff.
17. E. Winter, *Russland und das Papstum* (Berlin, 1960), p. 179; Longworth, 'Russia and the Antemurale Christianitatis'; on England, see S. Baron, *Muscovite Russia* (London, 1980), Essay III, pp. 42–63; also M. Anderson, *Britain's Discovery of Russia* (London, 1958).
18. See Frost, *The Northern Wars*, pp. 24 and 77. Russia's administrative policy in

Livonia has been examined by N. Angermann, *Studien zur Livlandpolitik Ivan Groznyjs* (Marburg, 1972); see particularly pp. 25ff.

19. *The Russian Invasion of Poland in 1563* – a translation by J. C. H[otten] of *Memorabilis et perinde stupenda de crudeli Moscovitarum Expeditione narratio* (Douai, n.d.).
20. Among the most useful contributions to the huge literature on the *oprichnina* are S. B. Veselovskii, *Isledovaniia po istorii oprichniny* (Moscow, 1963), esp. here pp. 133ff., and Zimin, *Reformy Ivana Groznogo*. My account also draws on Floria's *Ivan Groznyi*. It is worth noting that Vipper, the leading apologist for Ivan, was an anti-Bolshevik who fled Russia at the Revolution and consented to return only at the approach of war in 1941.
21. See I. Pryzhkov, *Istoriia kabakov v Rossii* (Moscow, 1991). On the origins of the commune, see R. E. F. Smith, *Peasant Farming in Muscovy* (Cambridge, 1977).
22. Floria, *Ivan Groznyi*, pp. 172f., 168ff.
23. Ibid., p. 179.
24. This is argued by Janet Martin in her *Medieval Russia 980–1584* (Cambridge, 1996), pp. 347–8.
25. That the Duma (the Russian word for 'council') was a formalized institution at this stage is a construct of historians who assume too much.
26. Floria, *Ivan Groznyi*, p. 393.
27. Adapted from J. L. I. Fennell's translation of Ivan's letter of 1564 in his *The Correspondence between Prince A. M. Kurbsky and Tsar Ivan IV of Russia 1564–1579* (Cambridge, 1955).
28. Floria, *Ivan Groznyi*, pp. 393–4.
29. S. B. Veselovskii, *Trudy po istochnikovedenii i istorii Rossii v periode feodalzma* (Moscow, 1978), p. 153.
30. See Dvorkin, *Ivan the Terrible as a Religious Type*, p. 105. Chapter 8 of this work, which draws on recent as well as older scholarship, is helpful on the *oprichnina*.
31. Floria, *Ivan Groznyi*, pp. 233–43.
32. E. Chistiakova, ed., N. Rogozhin, compiler, et al., *'Oko vsei velikoi Rossii': ob istorii rossiiskoi diplomaticheskoi sluzhby xvi–xvii vekov* (Moscow, 1989), pp. 54ff.
33. See the contributions of D. Kayser, J. Kollman and others to the Marshall Poe web site http://www.people.fas.harvard.edu for June 2001, etc.
34. A. A. Zimin, *V kanun groznykh potriasenii: predposylki pervoi krest'ianskoi voiny v Rossii* (Moscow, 1986), p. 5.
35. 'The Testament of Ivan IV, the Terrible', in Howes, ed., *Testaments of the Grand Princes of Moscow*, p. 307–8.

6: THE CRASH

1. See Zimin, *V kanun groznykh potriasenii.*
2. Chistiakova, Rogozhin et al., *'Oko vsei velikoi Rossii'*, pp. 71ff. Vasilii Shchelkalov took charge of the Foreign Office on his brother's death.
3. See W. E. D. Allen, ed., *Russian Embassies to the Georgian Kings (1589–1605)* (2 vols., Cambridge, 1970), vol. 1, p. 60.
4. Zimin, *V kanun groznykh potriasenii*, p. 237.
5. M. Raeff, *Siberia and the Reforms of 1822* (Seattle, 1956), p. xiv.
6. On frontier defences, see Khodarkovsky, *Russia's Steppe Frontier*, pp. 131ff. *passim.*
7. Hakluyt, *Voyages*, vol. 3, p. 384.
8. V. Klein, *Uglichskoe sledstvennoe delo i smerti Tsarevicha Dmitriia* (Moscow, 1913), and Veselovskii, *Trudy po istochnikovedenii i istorii Rossii v periode feodalzma*, pp. 156–89. See also R. G. Skrynnikov, *Boris Godunov* (Moscow, 1979), pp. 67–84.
9. For the Romanovs' role in promoting, and exploiting, the cult, see A. Kleimola, 'The Romanovs and the cult of the Tsarevich Dmitrii', in *Religiia i tserkov' v kul'turno-istoricheskom razvitiei russkogo severa* (Kirov, 1996), pp. 230–3.
10. On Boris himself, apart from Skrynnikov, *Boris Godunov*, see Chester Dunning's compendious history of the Time of Troubles, *Russia's First Civil War: The Time of Troubles and the Founding of the Romanov Dynasty* (University Park, Penn., 2001), pp. 91ff. and *passim.*
11. Nolde, *La Formation de l'Empire Russe*, vol. 2, p. 317.
12. Allen, ed., *Russian Embassies to the Georgian Kings*, vol. 1, pp. 87ff. for translations of the diplomatic record; the preceding introduction for the background, and the apparatus in vol. 2 for explanations of people, places etc. The list quoted appears in the embassy's instructions: vol. 1, p. 98.
13. B. Gudziak, *Crisis and Reform: The Kievan Metropolitanate, the Patriarch of Constantinople and the Genesis of the Union of Brest* (Cambridge, Mass., 1998), is scholarly and helpful and, though by a Uniate, is not unsympathetic to Orthodox sentiments. See also M. Dmitriev, B. Floria and S. Iakovenko, *Brestskaia uniia 1596g i obshchestvenno-politicheskaia bor'ba na Ukraine i v Belorussii v xvi–nachale xvii v*, Pt 1 (Moscow, 1996), on the causes. However, an adequate account of how the religious divide between Orthodox, Uniate and Catholic came to be drawn has yet to be written.
14. Mouravieff, *A History of the Church of Russia*, p. 145.
15. Zimin, *V kanun groznykh potriasenii*, p. 238.
16. Iu. Got'e, ed., *Akty otnosiashchiesia k istorii zemskikh soborov*, vyp. 1 (Moscow, 1909), pp. 12ff.
17. C. Bussow, *The Disturbed State of the Russian Realm*, trans. and ed. G. Orchard (Montreal, 1994), pp. 13–14. The account is confirmed by other sources.
18. Ye. Borisenkov and V. Piasetskii, *Tysiachiletnaia letopis' neobychnykh iavlenii prirody* (Moscow, 1988), pp. 323–4.

19. Bussow, *The Disturbed State of the Russian Realm*, pp. 32–3.
20. Smith to Cecil, 25 February 1606, Cecil Papers 104/47, Hatfield House Library.
21. P. Longworth, 'Political rumour in early modern Russia', in Szvak, ed., *Muscovy: Peculiarities of its Development*, pp. 27–33.
22. The standard source for these events is Dunning, *Russia's First Civil War*, pp. 131ff.
23. The New Chronicle quoted in Vernadsky et al., *Source Book*, vol. 1, p. 183.
24. References to most of these can be found in Dunning, *Russia's First Civil War*; on Dmitry's 'magic with devils', Ryan, *The Bathhouse at Midnight*, p. 39.
25. Dunning, *Russia's First Civil War*, ch. 14.
26. The New Chronicle quoted in Vernadsky et al., *Source Book*, vol. 1, p. 183.
27. Dunning, *Russia's First Civil War*, pp. 412–13.
28. Instructions for King Sigismund's envoy to the Pope, 22 September 1611, Vernadsky et al., *Source Book*, vol. 1, pp. 201–2.
29. Iaroslavl to Vologda letter, February 1611, Vernadsky et al., *Source Book*, vol. 1, p. 197.
30. Dunning, *Russia's First Civil War*, p. 421.
31. Archimandrite Dionysius's appeal of 6 October 1611, Vernadsky et al., *Source Book*, vol. 1, p. 204; Letters from Kazan to Perm and from Tobolsk to Narym, September and October 1611, Vernadsky et al., *Source Book*, vol. 1, pp. 201–4.
32. Pozharskii to Solvychegodsk, 7 April 1612, Vernadsky et al., *Source Book*, vol. 1, pp. 205–7.
33. Ibid., pp. 199–200.
34. See R. Hellie, *The Economy and Material Culture of Russia 1600–1725* (Chicago, 1999), p. 498.
35. Dunning, *Russia's First Civil War*, pp. 438–9.
36. See the now rich literature on pretenders in the seventeenth and eighteenth centuries – Perrie, Skrynnikov, Longworth et al.
37. G. Hosking has argued that Russia's development was impeded by a lack of national self-consciousness. Yet the mobilization letters quoted above suggest otherwise. The Russians had a clear sense of who they were at the beginning of the 1600s, and other ethnic groups in Russia seem to have shared that sense to some extent.

7: RECOVERY

1. N. Rogozhin, 'Mesto Rossii xvi–xvii vekov v Evrope po materialam posolskikh knig', in Szvak, ed., *The Place of Russia in Europe*, pp. 88–96.
2. There was a rebellion in Moscow in 1648, serious riots in other major cities in 1650–51; the 'Copper Riots' of 1660–61, the huge uprising led by the

Cossack Stepan Razin in southern Russia in 1670–71; the musketeer riot of 1682, etc.

3. The estimate is based on figures in D. Moon, *The Russian Peasantry 1600–1930* (London, 1999), table 1.3 and p. 21, n. 17. Moon draws his data from Ye. Vodarskii, *Naselenie Rossii za 400 let* (Moscow, 1973), p. 27, and his *Naselenie Rossii v kontse xvii–nachale xviii veka* (Moscow, 1977), pp. 134, 192. I have adjusted Moon's figures to take account of seventeenth-century frontier changes. The estimate in C. McEvedy and R. Jones, *Atlas of World Population History* (London, 1980), p. 79, seems somewhat inflated.
4. Hellie, *The Economy and Material Culture of Russia*, pp. 635–9.
5. Ibid., pp. 643, 637.
6. I have argued the point in *Alexis, Tsar of All the Russias* (London, 1984), p. 160.
7. Even the English-language literature on the conquest of Siberia is too considerable to list here, but I refer to the works I found useful in the references which follow.
8. See the instructions to the governor of Tsivylsk in Cheremis country near Kazan in Nolde, *La Formation de l'Empire Russe*, vol. 1, p. 75, quoting *Dopolneniia k aktam istoricheskim* (4 vols., 1846–72), vol. 2, doc. 79.
9. Tsar Vasilii Shuiskii to the governor of Pelym, 6 August 1609, in Vernadsky *et al.*, *Source Book*, vol. 1, p. 263.
10. R. Fisher, ed., *The Voyage of Semen Dezhnev in 1648* (London, 1981), pp. 107–8. For graphic evidence of the dangers and privations Stadukhin and other explorers confronted, see also pp. 74–84.
11. A well-informed defector to Sweden in the 1660s, G. Kotoshikhin (*O Rossii v tsarstvovanii Alekseia Mikhailovicha*, ed. A. Pennington (Oxford, 1980), p. 106, estimated the treasury's annual income from Siberian tribute at over 600,000 rubles.
12. K. Serbina, ed., *Kniga bol'shemu chertezha* (Moscow and Leningrad, 1950).
13. Petition from servicemen at Fort Verkholensk to Tsar Michael, in J. Forsyth, *A History of the Peoples of Siberia: Russia's North Asian Colony 1581–1990* (Cambridge, 1992), pp. 87–8.
14. Forsyth in A. Wood, ed., *The History of Siberia: From Russian Conquest to Revolution* (London, 1991), Table 5-1, p. 71. For more on the native peoples of Siberia see Christian, *Russia, Central Asia and Mongolia*, vol. 1, pp. 54–7, Forsyth, *A History of the Peoples of Siberia*, and T. Armstrong, *Russian Settlement in the North 1581–1990* (Cambridge, 1992).
15. Instruction to the governor of Iakutsk, 10 February 1644, Vernadsky et al., *Source Book*, vol. 1, pp. 266–7. The same principle informs similar orders dating back at least twenty years.
16. [Olearius], *The Voiages and Travels of the Ambassadors sent by Frederick, Duke of Holstein, to the Great Duke of Muscovy and the King of Persia* (2nd edn, London, 1669), pp. 117, 136.

17. On units of 'new formation', see J. Keep, *Soldiers of the Tsar: Army and Society in Russia 1462–1874* (Oxford, 1985), pp. 80–1.
18. *Uchenie i khitrost' ratnago stroieniia pekhotnykh liudei [Kriegskunst der Fuss]* (Moscow [State Printing Court], 1647). Over 1,000 copies of the book were printed; fewer than 200 were sold. However, its influence would have been greater than the number suggests in an age when copyists' services were cheap.
19. P. Gordon, *Dnevnik 1659–1667*, ed. D. Fedosov (Moscow, 2002), p. 100.
20. Longworth, *Alexis*, pp. 144, 266 (n. 26), 267 (n. 61).
21. *Tula: materialy dlia istorii goroda xvi–xviii stoletii* (Moscow 1884), pp. 2–29.
22. Longworth, *Alexis*, pp. 260–61, n. 42.
23. For the Ukrainian background, see S. Lep'iavko, *Kozats'ki viini kintsya xvi st. v Ukraini* (Chernihiv, 1996).
24. P. Longworth, *The Cossacks* (London, 1969), ch. 4.
25. Vernadsky et al., *Source Book*, vol. 1, p. 296.
26. Ibid., pp. 300–301. Recent publications by some Ukrainian historians repeat the claim that Pereiaslav was a treaty rather than a submission.
27. Longworth, *Alexis*, p. 96.
28. On Cossack democracy etc. see Longworth, *The Cossacks*, ch. 1. On Khmelnytsky and his successors, ibid., ch. 4.
29. Vernadsky et al., *Source Book*, vol. 1, pp. 202–4.
30. W. E. D. Allen, *The Ukraine: A History* (Cambridge, 1940), pp. 152–58; also Frost, *The Northern Wars*, pp. 186–8.
31. See Longworth, *Alexis*, ch. 7, especially the Tsar's letter to his chief negotiator at Andrusovo, p. 176.
32. Nolde, *La Formation de l'Empire Russe*, vol. 1, pp. 194–5.
33. On the advent of the Kalmyks, see Khodarkovsky, *Russia's Steppe Frontier*, pp. 133–5.
34. On Poland's foreign service in the critical period of the late seventeenth century, see A. Kaminsky, *Republic vs. Autocracy: Poland-Lithuania and Russia 1686–1697* (Cambridge, Mass., 1994), which demonstrates the amateurishness of Polish diplomacy by contrast to Russia's. See also my review in *American Historical Review*, December 1995, pp. 1622–3.
35. I. Kozlovskii, *Pervye pochty i pervye pochtmeistery v Moskovskom gosudarstve*, vol. 1 (Warsaw, 1913), pp. 86–7.
36. See L. Hughes, *Sophia, Regent of Russia 1657–1704* (New Haven, 1990), pp. 43–5 and generally on the period 1676–89.
37. Khodarkovsky, *Russia's Steppe Frontier*, p. 71.
38. Veselovskii, *D'iaki i pod'iachie xv–xvii vv*, pp. 203, 45–6, 531–2. See also Chistiakova, Rogozhin et al., *'Oko vsei velikoi Rossii'* on Ivanov (pp. 92–108) and pp. 108ff. on Matveyev and Golitsyn.

8: PETER THE GREAT AND THE BREAKTHROUGH TO THE WEST

1. Vernadsky et al., *Source Book*, vol. 2, p. 343 (with adaptation).
2. On the first campaign of the Swedish war, see Frost, *The Northern Wars*, pp. 229ff.; D. Kirby, *Northern Europe in the Early Modern Period: The Baltic World, 1492–1772* (London, 1990), pp. 299ff.
3. For the early, as well as the later, history of St Petersburg, see J. Bater, *St Petersburg: Industrialization and Change* (London, 1976).
4. G. Adlerfelt, *The Military History of Charles XII* (3 vols., London, 1740), vol. 3, pp. 197, 235.
5. Kirby, *Northern Europe in the Early Modern Period*, p. 325. The terms were interesting in that, in trying to prevent Russia interfering in Swedish affairs, the treaty also insisted that Russia prevent any change to Sweden's 1720 constitution or the succession to the throne, which gave Russia a legal reason to interfere.
6. N. N. Molchaninov, *Diplomatiia Petra Velikogo* (Moscow, 1986).
7. E. Schuyler, *Peter the Great* (2 vols., London, 1884), vol. 2, p. 478.
8. Ibid., pp. 238–39 (revised).
9. On the Khiva expedition, see T. Barrett, *At the Edge of Empire: The Terek Cossacks and the North Caucasus Frontier 1700–1860* (Boulder, 1999), p. 31; on Peter's strategy in Central Asia, A. Donnelly, *The Russian Conquest of Bashkiriya 1552–1840* (New Haven, 1968), ch. 4 and its references.
10. Khodarkovsky, *Russia's Steppe Frontier*, p. 7.
11. M. Olcott, *The Kazakhs* (Stanford, 1995), p. 30.
12. J. Bell (of Antermony), *Travels from St Petersburgh in Russia to Diverse Parts of Asia* (2nd edn, London, 1764), vol. 1, pp. 132–316, and vol. 2, pp. 1–155.
13. Coxe, *Russian Discoveries*, pp. 442–45; for an account of the China negotiations see the account by de Lange, the embassy's secretary, in Bell, *Travels from St Petersburgh*, vol. 2, pp. 166ff.
14. Schuyler, *Peter the Great*, vol. 2, p. 593.
15. Khodarkovsky, *Russia's Steppe Frontier*, pp. 159, 161–2.
16. Vernadsky et al., *Source Book*, vol. 2, p. 345.
17. S. Krashennikov, *The History of Kamschatka and the Kurilski Islands* (Glocester [*sic*], 1764), pp. 224, 172, 176, 202, 224; Forsyth, *A History of the Peoples of Siberia*, p. 101.
18. Forsyth, *A History of the Peoples of Siberia*, pp. 137, 139.
19. Coxe, *Russian Discoveries*, p. 22.
20. R. Fisher, ed., *The Voyage of Semen Dezhnev*, pp. 257–72 for maps illustrating how understanding of the geography of north-eastern Siberia developed. Also Forsyth, *A History of the Peoples of Siberia*, p. 101.
21. See P. Longworth 'Ukraine: history and nationality', *Slavonic and East European Review*, 78, 1 (January 2000), pp. 115–24.

22. Kappeler, *Russland als Vielvölkerreich*, esp. p. 69.
23. See E. Thaden, *Russia's Western Borderlands 1710–1870* (Princeton, 1984), pp. 7–14.
24. Rywkin, ed., *Russian Colonial Expansion*, p. xv.
25. Schuyler, *Peter the Great*, vol. 2, p. 464.
26. A. Kahan, *The Plow, The Hammer and the Knout: An Economic History of Eighteenth Century Russia* (Chicago, 1985), table 1.1, p. 8, and pp. 9–10.
27. Schuyler, *Peter the Great*, vol. 2, p. 464.
28. Hellie, *The Economy and Material Culture of Russia*, pp. 9–11; Kahan, *The Plow, The Hammer and the Knout*, pp. 7–16.
29. H. Ragsdale, 'Russian projects of conquest in the eighteenth century', in H. Ragsdale, ed., *Imperial Russian Foreign Policy* (Cambridge, 1993), pp. 75ff.

9: GLORIOUS EXPANSION

1. Milev, *Velikorusskii pakhar' i osobennosti rossiiskogo istoricheskogo protsessa* (Moscow, 1998), p. 565.
2. Rondeau to Harrington, 4 January 1731 in Vernadsky et al., *Source Book*, vol. 2, p. 379, col. 2.
3. E. Finch to Harrington, 2 June 1741 in Vernadsky et al., *Source Book*, vol. 2, pp. 381–2.
4. Nolde, *La Formation de l'Empire Russe*, vol. 2, pp. 20–23.
5. Ye. Anisimov, 'The imperial heritage of Peter the Great in the foreign policy of his early successors', in Ragsdale, *Imperial Russian Foreign Policy*, p. 21.
6. C. von Manstein [chief ADC to Marshal Münnich], supplement to his *Memoirs of Russia* (London, 1770), pp. 404–8, 391 (quotation), 295ff., 304, 109ff.
7. Ibid., p. 131.
8. Kahan, *The Plow, The Hammer and the Knout*, p. 15, table 1.11.
9. Manstein, *Memoirs of Russia*, p. 417.
10. *An Authoritative Narrative of the Russian Expedition against the Turks by an Officer in the Russian Fleet* [possibly Admiral Greig himself] (London, 1772), pp. 9–16; N. Saul, *Russia and the Mediterranean 1797–1807* (Chicago, 1970), pp. 5–7.
11. Kahan, *The Plow, The Hammer and the Knout*, tables 3.17 and 3.18, pp. 92–3.
12. J. Hanway, *An Historical Account of the British Trade over the Caspian Sea* (2nd edn, 2 vols., London, 1754), vol. 1, pp. 9ff; for Elton's journal, see pp. 11–27. Also Olcott, *The Kazakhs*, pp. 31–33; Donnelly, *The Russian Conquest of Bashkiriya*, pp. 105–6, 116, 158.
13. Hanway, *British Trade over the Caspian Sea*, vol. 1, pp. 281, 301, 308, 310–11, 349, 364–5; P. Longworth, 'The role of Westerners in Russia's penetration of Asia, 17th–18th century', in Gy. Szvak, ed., *The Place of Russia in Eurasia* (Budapest, 2001).

14. Olcott, *The Kazakhs*, p. 33; Khodarkovsky, *Russia's Steppe Frontier*, pp. 159, 165, 204.
15. Donnelly, *The Russian Conquest of Bashkiriya*, pp. 57ff. (the quoted passage is on p. 76; the casualty figures are on p. 138).
16. Ibid., p. 156.
17. P. Longworth, *The Three Empresses* (London, 1972), pp. 144–5.
18. J. Forsyth, 'The Siberian native peoples before and after the Russian conquest', in Wood, ed., *The History of Siberia*, pp. 69–89.
19. Coxe, *Russian Discoveries*, p. 330.
20. For the impact of smallpox on the population, Kahan, *The Plow, The Hammer and the Knout*, p. 14; Forsyth, *A History of the Peoples of Siberia*, pp. 189, 128, 95, 162 (the quotation is from Shelekhov); Coxe, *Russian Discoveries*, pp. 280–81.
21. Chappe d'Auteroche, *A Journey into Siberia* (2nd edn, London, 1774), pp. 392–4.
22. A. Fisher, *The Russian Annexation of the Crimea 1772–1783* (Cambridge, 1970), pp. 52ff.
23. P. Pallas, *Travels through the Southern Provinces of the Russian Empire in 1793 and 1792* (2 vols., London, 1802–3), vol. 2, p. 361.
24. P. Longworth, *The Art of Victory* (London, 1966), pp. 127–131; Nolde, *La Formation de l'Empire Russe*, vol.1, ch. 10, and A. Fisher, *The Russian Annexation of the Crimea*, pp. 137, 156.
25. Broxup, ed., *The North Caucasus Barrier*, p. 3.
26. Pallas, *Travels*, vol. 2, p. 343. Pallas carried out a thoroughgoing survey at the behest of P. A. Zubov, then chief administrator of the Crimea; E. Lazzerini, 'The Crimea under Russian rule', in Rywkin, ed., *Russian Colonial Expansion*, pp. 13–38; and J. Reuilly, *Travels in the Crimea* (London, 1807), pp. 63–84.
27. I. de Madariaga, *Russia in the Age of Catherine the Great* (London, 1982), pp. 361–4. On the establishment of Greek and Armenian colonies around the Sea of Azov, see Nolde, *La Formation de l'Empire Russe*, vol. 2, pp. 140–52; also M. Raeff, 'Patterns of Russian imperial policy towards the nationalities', in M. Raeff, ed., *Political Ideas and Institutions in Imperial Russia* (Boulder, 1994), p. 163.
28. For the whereabouts of German, Swiss, Greek, Bulgarian, Jewish and other settlers in southern Russia in the late eighteenth and particularly the early nineteenth century, see J. Pallot and D. Shaw, *Landscape and Settlement in Romanov Russia* (Oxford, 1990), p. 83, fig. 4 (map of settlement). On the development of the ports, Reuilly, *Travels in the Crimea*, pp. 82–4.
29. R. Bartlett, *Human Capital: The Settlement of Foreigners in Russia 1762–1804* (Cambridge, 1972). Also Pallot and Shaw, *Landscape and Settlement in Romanov Russia* and the other sources already mentioned.
30. The English version of Catherine's manifesto of 1763 inviting foreigners is reproduced in Bartlett, *Human Capital*, pp. 237–41, 264–7. The quoted passages are from a handbill, ibid., pp. 243–4.

31. G. Reinbeck, *Travels from St. Petersburg through Moscow, Grodno, Warsaw, Breslaw, etc. to Germany in the Year 1805* (London, 1807), p. 147.
32. Thaden, *Russia's Western Borderlands*, p. 43.
33. An interesting discussion of these issues is provided by Kappeler, *Russland als Vielvölkerreich*, pp. 74–78.
34. Z. Kohut, 'The Ukrainian elite in the eighteenth century and its integration into the Russian nobility', in I. Banac and P. Bushkovich, *The Nobility of Russia and Eastern Europe* (New Haven, 1983), pp. 65–85.
35. Longworth, *The Cossacks*, pp. 224–34.
36. S. Lavrov's archival research has also shown that at least one Russian governor-general – V. N. Tatishchev, Kirillov's successor as governor of Orenburg – was bilingual in Russian and German.
37. Madariaga, *Russia in the Age of Catherine the Great*, pp. 323–34.
38. Kappeler, *Russland als Vielvölkerreich*, pp. 105f, 96, 116; J. Hartley, *A Social History of the Russian Empire, 1650–1825* (London, 1999), p. 75.
39. Thaden, *Russia's Western Borderlands*, pp. 33–4.
40. Raeff, ed., *Political Ideas and Institutions*; Madariaga, *Russia in the Age of Catherine the Great*, ch. 18.
41. Saul, *Russia and the Mediterranean*, pp. 42–4.
42. Coxe, *Russian Discoveries*, p. 306.
43. N.-G. Le Clerc, *Histoire physique, morale, civile et politique de la Russie moderne* (2 vols., Paris–Versailles, 1783–5), vol. 1, pp. 475–86 et seq.
44. R. Hellie, 'The costs of Muscovite military defence and expansion', in E. Lohr and M. Poe, eds., *The Military and Society in Russia 1450–1917* (Leiden, 2002), pp. 41–66.
45. Kahan, *The Plow, The Hammer and the Knout*, table 1.1, p. 8.

10: THE ROMANTIC AGE OF EMPIRE

1. The estimates of land area are Liubavskii's, in his *Obzor istorii russkoi kolonizatsii*, p. 539.
2. M. Atkin, *Russia and Iran 1780–1828* (Minneapolis, 1980), pp. 73ff; General Tornau's account in J. Baddeley, *The Russian Conquest of the Caucasus* (London, 1908), pp. 272–4; M. Atkin, 'Russian expansion in the Caucasus to 1893', in Rywkin, ed., *Russian Colonial Expansion*, pp. 139–87 (I have adapted his translation of Tsitsianov's words).
3. Baddeley, *The Russian Conquest of the Caucasus*, p. 76.
4. Proclamation of 18 February 1808 issued by Count Bouxhoevden in [General Sprengtporten], *Narrative of the Conquest of Finland by the Russians in the Years 1808–9*, ed. General Monteith (London, 1854), pp. 225–7.
5. The quoted passage is in Vernadsky et al., *Source Book*, vol. 2, p. 490. See also Kappeler, *Russland als Vielvölkerreich*, pp. 87–8.

6. See G. Jewsbury, *The Russian Annexation of Bessarabia 1774–1828* (Boulder, 1976), pp. 26–66.
7. The size of the *Grande Armée* is the estimate of C. von Clausewitz, *The Campaign of 1812 in Russia* (London, 1843). For the campaign itself, aside from Clausewitz see L. Tolstoy's *War and Peace*. Tolstoy based his account of operations on the archive of the Russian quartermaster-general, his uncle.
8. Kutuzov to Alexander I, 4 September 1812, Vernadsky et al., *Source Book*, vol. 2, pp. 497–8.
9. F. Vigel's memoirs quoted in Vernadsky et al., *Source Book*, vol. 2, p. 511.
10. Clausewitz, *The Campaign of 1812*, p. 100.
11. [Sir R. Wilson], *A Sketch of the Military and Political Power of Russia in the Year 1817* (2nd edn, London, 1817).
12. H. Seton-Watson's *The Russian Empire 1801–1917* (Oxford, 1967) is still useful. For an account of the diplomacy *c.* 1815, Poland in the context of the settlement, and the strategic implications of Russia's expansion in the early nineteenth century, see pp. 142–52.
13. Ibid., pp. 172–4; Kappeler, *Russland als Vielvölkerreich*, pp. 71ff.
14. A. Pushkin, 'Klevetnikam Rossii' ('To the Slanderers of Russia'), 1831.
15. Thaden, *Russia's Western Borderlands*, p. 231.
16. On the fundamental problem see G. von Rauch, *Russland: Staatliche Einheit und nationale Vielfalt* (Munich, 1953). Vigel is quoted on the title page of Raeff's, *Siberia and the Reforms of 1822*. On communications, J. Gibson, 'Tsarist Russia and colonial America', in Wood, ed., *The History of Siberia*, p. 105.
17. J. Cochrane, *Narrative of a Pedestrian Journey through Russia and Siberian Tartary to the Frozen Sea and Kamtchatka* (3rd edn, London, 1825), pp. 346–7. So far from being prejudiced against native people Captain Cochrane married one, a Kamchadale woman.
18. Raeff, *Siberia and the Reforms of 1822*, pp. 85, 7; Armstrong, *Russian Settlement in the North*, pp. 104–205 *passim*; extracts from Speransky's Statute for the Administrative Organization of Siberia of 1822 are provided in Vernadsky, *Source Book*, vol. 2, pp. 506–8; Forsyth, *A History of the Peoples of Siberia*, p. 164.
19. See R. Hovannisian, 'Russian Armenia: a century of rule', *Jahrbücher für Geschichte Osteuropas*, Neue Folge, 19, 1 (1971), 31–48.
20. Lazzerini, 'The Crimea under Russian rule', pp. 131–2.
21. Yermolov is quoted in Baddeley, *The Russian Conquest of the Caucasus*, p. 97. I have modernized the translation.
22. See for example, M. Gammer, 'Russian strategies in the conquest of Chechnia and Daghestan 1825–1859', in M. Broxup, ed., *The North Caucasus Barrier: The Russian Advance Towards the Muslim World* (London, 1992).
23. Barrett, *At the Edge of Empire*, p. 23.
24. Pallas, *Travels*, vol. 1, p. 405; see also [G. Ellis?], *Memoir of a Map of the Countries Comprehended between the Black Sea and the Caspian* (London, 1788), not only

for the map, which is of the Caucasus, itself but for the useful compilation from the works of Guldenstaedt, Reinegg and others on the customs of the peoples of the Caucasus, their languages etc.

25. *The Russian Journal of Lady Londonderry*, ed. W. Seaman and J. Sewell (London, 1973), p. 80.
26. Pallas, *Travels*, vol. 1, p. 438.
27. F. von Gille, *Lettres sur le Caucase et la Crimée* (Paris, 1859), p. 109.
28. E. Spencer, *Travels in the Western Caucasus* (2 vols., London, 1838), vol. 1, pp. 96–7.
29. Baddeley, *The Russian Conquest of the Caucasus*, pp. 272–4.
30. For estimates of Chechen population, see M. Wagner, *Travels in Persia, Georgia and Koordistan* (3 vols., London, 1856), vol. 1, pp. 253–4; Gille, *Lettres sur le Caucase et la Crimée*, p. 111.
31. W. E. D. Allen and P. Muratoff, *Caucasian Battlefields* (Cambridge, 1953), ch. 3; for an analysis of these campaigns, see Gammer, 'Russian strategies'.
32. On the Tsar's interest in the Ardebil Library see L. Kelly, *Diplomacy and Murder in Teheran: Alexander Griboyedov and Imperial Russia's Mission to the Shah of Persia* (London, 2002), pp. 157–8; *passim* for a lively account of the negotiations with the Persians and the career of the playwright Griboyedov, who played a key role in them (and met his death as a result).
33. R. Pinkerton, *Russia, or Miscellaneous Observations of the Past and Present of that Country and its Inhabitants* (London, 1833), pp. 135–6.
34. Baron von Haxthausen, *Transcaucasia* (London, 1854), pp. 45–6.
35. 'Declaration of Circassian Independence Addressed to the Courts of Europe', in E. Spencer, *Travels in Circassia, Krim Tartary, etc.* (2 vols., London, 1837), vol. 1, pp. 293–7, reproducing [D. Urquhart], *The Portfolio*, vol. 1.
36. See J. Bell, *Journal of a Residence in Circassia during the Years 1837, 1838 and 1839* (2 vols., London, 1840).
37. See Gammer, 'Russian strategies'; also Allen and Muratoff, *Caucasian Battlefields*.
38. See X. Hommaire de Hell, *Travels in the Steppes of the Caspian Sea* (London, 1847), pp. 201ff.
39. Baron von Haxthausen, *The Russian Empire, its People, Institutions and Resources* (2 vols., London, 1856), vol. 2, pp. 292–4.
40. Census returns reproduced in R. Venables, *Domestic Scenes in Russia* (London, 1839), p. 349.
41. The Alaska Company had its headquarters in Petropavlovsk on Kamchatka, but Russian naval Captain A. von Krusenstern (*Voyage Round the World*, trans. R. Hoppne (2 vols., London, 1813), vol. 2, pp. 105, 110) reported that the Company's ships were ill-built and equipped, and its employees tyrannical not only to the Kodiaks and Aleuts but to Russians too.
42. H. D. Seymour, *Russia on the Black Sea and the Sea of Azov, being a Narrative of Travels in the Crimea and the Bordering Provinces* (London, 1855), pp. 91–2.

43. L. Oliphant, *Russian Shores of the Black Sea* (London, 1854), p. 261.
44. Vernadsky et al., *Source Book*, vol. 2, p. 551.
45. Ibid., pp. 552–3, 560.

11: DESCENT TO DESTRUCTION

1. Goncharov's novel is available in English translation.
2. The statistical surveys published by the government are impressive in both their extent and their quality. There are, besides, both many good accounts by contemporaries (e.g. D. Mackenzie Wallace, *Russia* (London, 1912)) and several good scholarly studies.
3. Decree of 26 January 1857, Vernadsky et al., *Source Book*, vol. 3, p. 607; see also V. Grossman, 'The industrialization of Russia', in C. Cipolla, ed., *The Fontana Economic History of Europe* (London, 1973), vol. 4, section 7; Seton-Watson, *The Russian Empire*, pp. 406–7.
4. McEvedy and Jones, *Atlas of World Population History*, pp. 79, 159, 161.
5. Vice-Chancellor (Foreign Secretary) A. M. Gorchakov to his opposite numbers, 1864, quoted in Vernadsky et al., *Source Book*, vol. 3, p. 610. For the implications see A. Tuminez, *Russian Nationalism since 1856: Ideology and the Making of Foreign Policy* (London, 2000).
6. O. Alexander, 'Tiutchev's political memorandum rediscovered', *Elementa*, 1 (1933), 91ff.
7. V. Grigorev, 1840, quoted in M. Bassin, *Imperial Visions: Nationalist Imagination and Geographical Expansion in the Russian Far East 1840–65* (Cambridge, 1990), p. 54.
8. Kappeler, *Russland als Vielvölkerreich*, pp. 215–17.
9. B. Manz, 'Central Asian uprisings in the nineteenth century', *Russian Review*, 46, 3 (1987), 267–81.
10. See S. Becker, 'Russia's Central Asian Empire 1885–1917', in Rywkin, ed., *Russian Colonial Expansion*, pp. 235–40.
11. See D. Mackenzie, 'The conquest and administration of Turkestan, 1860–85', in Rywkin, ed., *Russian Colonial Expansion*, pp. 208ff.
12. R. Leslie, *Reform and Insurrection in Russian Poland 1856–1865* (London, 1963), is still the fullest and most balanced account in English.
13. Vernadsky et al., *Source Book*, vol. 3, pp. 612–13.
14. The point is made by Thaden in his *Russia's Western Borderlands*, p. 239.
15. B. Sumner, *Russia and the Balkans 1870–1880* (Oxford, 1937), pp. 60ff.
16. Translated, with some omissions, from the text in M. Baring and D. Costello, eds., *The Oxford Book of Russian Verse* (Oxford, 1944), pp. 130–31.
17. Sumner, *Russia and the Balkans*, pp. 580–82.
18. See J. Le Donne, *The Russian Empire and the World 1700–1917: The Geopolitics of Expansion and Containment* (New York and Oxford, 1997), esp. map 5, p. 134.

19. B. Sumner, *Tsardom and Imperialism in the Far East and Middle East, 1880–1914* (London, 1940), pp. 21–31.
20. I have adapted T. von Laue's translation in *Journal of Modern History*, 26 (March 1954), 64–73.
21. See B. Mitchell in Cipolla, ed., *Fontana Economic History of Europe*, vol. 4, pt 2, pp. 793–4, 773, 775; A. Gerschenkron's contributions to *The Cambridge Economic History of Europe*, vol. 6 (Cambridge, 1965); also his *Europe in the Russian Mirror* (Cambridge, 1970).
22. For the significance of this rare concession without constraint, see N. Bolkhovitinov, 'The sale of Alaska in the context of Russian–American relations in the 19th century', in Ragsdale, *Imperial Russian Foreign Policy*, pp. 193–21; on the background, see Muravev's memorandum to Alexander II of March 1854 in G. Lensen, *The Russian Push towards Japan: Russo-Japanese Relations, 1697–1875* (Princeton, 1959), pp. 300–301.
23. Adapted from Vernadsky et al., *Source Book*, vol. 3, p. 694, col. 2.
24. M. Baring, *What I Saw in Russia* (London, n.d. [*c.* 1905]), p. 40. Also pp. 41–42.
25. For a convenient summation of these developments see Seton-Watson, *The Russian Empire*, pp. 581–85; also Sumner, *Tsardom and Imperialism*, pp. 9f.
26. See E. Zabriskie, *American–Russian Rivalry in the Far East* [1895–1914] (Philadelphia, 1946).
27. For the raw numbers, see McEvedy and Jones, *Atlas of World Population History*, pp. 81, 79; for an interesting discussion of the reasons and a good introduction to the complexities of and literature on the agrarian problem see Moon, *The Russian Peasantry*, pp. 165–83, *passim*.
28. See S. O'Rourke, *Warriors and Peasants: The Don Cossacks in Late Imperial Russia* (Basingstoke, 2000), ch. 4.
29. See N. Hans, *History of Russian Educational Policy* (London, 1931), p. 184.
30. See, *inter alia*, P. Semenov-Tyanshanskii and V. Lamanskii, *Russia*, 10 vols (St Petersburg, 1899–1914).
31. Kerner, *The Urge to the Sea*, ch. 5, pp. 94ff.
32. P. Rich, *The Tsar's Colonels: Professionalism, Strategy and Subversion in Late Imperial Russia* (Cambridge, Mass., 1998), esp. pp. 7–17 *passim.*
33. From 83.67 per cent in 1857 to 86.01 per cent in 1897 – see Moon, *The Russian Peasantry*, table 1.3, p. 21.
34. Figures supplied to the Russian ambassador in London by Foreign Minister N. D. Sazonov in coded telegrams dated 29 June and 10 August 1909, in Vernadsky et al., *Source Book*, vol. 3, p. 750.
35. Sumner, *Tsardom and Imperialism*, pp. 39–40.
36. Wood, ed., *The History of Siberia*, p. 2.
37. V. Maklakov was a leading Kadet and a future commissioner (minister) of justice in the provisional government. I have slightly adapted the translation in Vernadsky et al., *Source Book*, vol. 3, p. 781.

38. Polovtsev, quoted in Vernadsky et al., *Source Book*, vol. 3, p. 698. Again I have adapted the translation.
39. See Seton-Watson, *The Russian Empire*, pp. 588–9; also Sumner, *Tsardom and Imperialism*, p. 5.
40. G. Vitarko, 'Aviation . . . and imperatives of modernization', in Lohr and Poe, eds., *The Military and Society in Russia*, pp. 273–91.
41. Durnovo to Nicholas II, February 1914, has been widely published. I have based these extracts on the text in Vernadsky et al., *Source Book*, vol. 3, pp. 793–8.
42. Seton-Watson, *The Russian Empire*, p. 700.
43. G. Buchanan, *My Mission to Russia and Other Diplomatic Memories* (2 vols., London, 1923), vol. 2, pp. 48–9.
44. The term *bol'sheviki* denotes members of the 'majority' Social Democrats, as distinct from the *mensheviki* who would not follow Lenin's line.

12: THE CONSTRUCTION OF A JUGGERNAUT

1. W. Chamberlin, *Russia's Iron Age* (London, 1935), p. 253.
2. A. Brusilow, *A Soldier's Note-Book 1914–1918* (London, 1930), p. 326.
3. L. Pazvolsky and H. Moulton, *Russian Debts and Russian Reconstruction* (New York, 1924), pp. 20–22, 43–4, 166–7.
4. Grossman, 'The industrialization of Russia'.
5. The most thorough source on this, as for most of the early history of the USSR, is E. H. Carr, *The Bolshevik Revolution, 1917–1923* (3 vols., London, 1950–54); for a continuation of the account, see E. H. Carr, and R. Davies, *Socialism in One Country, 1924–1926* (London, 1950) and *Foundations of a Planned Economy, 1926–1929* (London, 1969).
6. E. H. Carr, *The Soviet Impact on the Western World* (London, 1947), p. 23.
7. The declaration is reproduced in English translation as app. 4 of Armstrong, *Russian Settlement in the North*, pp. 192–3.
8. Allen, *The Ukraine*, pp. 318–19. The standard work on the inception of Soviet nationality policy is R. Pipes, *The Formation of the Soviet Union: Communism and Nationalism* (Cambridge, Mass., 1964).
9. R. Service, *A History of Twentieth-Century Russia* (Cambridge, Mass., 1997), pp. 113–14; Broxup, ed., *The North Caucasus Barrier*, p. 6.
10. Allen, *The Ukraine*, pp. 320–4.
11. Olcott, *The Kazakhs*, pp. 134–56.
12. See Forsyth, *A History of the Peoples of Siberia*, p. 232.
13. V. Kabuzan, *Russkii etnos v 20–80–kh godakh xx veka*, p. 273.
14. *Statistical Handbook of the USSR for 1928*, cited in V. Timoshenko, *Agricultural Russia and the Wheat Problem* (Stanford, 1932), p. 504 and table II, p. 520.
15. The figures for Britain and the United States are for 1923. See *The Works of Nikolai D. Kondrat'ev*, ed. N. Maklasheva et al., vol. 3 (London, 1998), p. 366.

16. Ibid., p. 295 (I have slightly adapted S. Wilson's translation).
17. Timoshenko, *Agricultural Russia and the Wheat Problem*, pp. 26, 28–9.
18. Ibid., table V, p. 527.
19. Quoted in E. Rees, 'Stalin and Russian nationalism', in Hosking and Service, eds., *Russian Nationalism Past and Present*, p. 85.
20. V. Zhiromaksia, *Demograficheskaia istoriia rossii k 1930–e gody* (Moscow, 2001), p. 66.
21. Ibid., table 12, pp. 80–81, and pp. 83–4.
22. See the report (to Congress) of the Commission on the Ukraine Famine, Washington, DC, 1988. Also R. Conquest, *Harvest of Sorrow: Soviet Collectivization and the Terror Famine* (London, 1986). Service, *Twentieth-Century Russia*, pp. 202, 207, disposes of the accusation temperately and economically.
23. Allen, *The Ukraine*, pp. 321, 324–5.
24. Ibid., pp. 327–8, quoting *Pravda*, 3 April 1930.
25. I. N. Kiselev, 'Estestvennoe dvizhenie naseleniia v 1930–kh godakh', in Iu. Poliakov et al., eds., *Naselenie Rossii v 1920–1950-e gody: chislennost', poteri, migratsii* (Moscow, 1994), pp. 59–65, esp., pp. 57–8; V. Zemskov, 'Spetsposolentsy (1930–1959gg.)', in ibid., pp. 145–69. See also n. 29 below.
26. On conditions for ordinary people, methods of coping and prevailing optimism in the 1930s, see S. Fitzpatrick, *Everyday Stalinism* (Oxford, 1999), p. 75 and *passim*; on support for the transformation in society, p. 224. For a critical view of Fitzpatrick's new approach to the Stalinist years, see M. Malia, 'Revolution fulfilled', *TLS*, 15 June 2001, pp. 3–4.
27. Chamberlin, *Russia's Iron Age*, p. 49.
28. Ibid., pp. 52–3.
29. R. Conquest, *The Great Terror* (London, 1968).
30. Quoted in M. Lewin, *Russian Peasants and Soviet Power* (London, 1968), p. 516.
31. See V. Zhiromskaia, 'Chislennost' naseleniia Rossii v 1939g.: poisk istiny', in Poliakov et al., eds., *Naselenie Rossii v 1920-1950-e gody*, pp. 27–47; Chamberlin, *Russia's Iron Age*, pp. 364–6.
32. J. Erickson, *Stalin's War with Germany*, vol. 1: *The Road to Stalingrad* (London, 1998), pp. 63–4.
33. See ibid., ch. 1.
34. On the Khalkin-Gol campaign see J. Erickson, *The Soviet High Command* (London, 1961), pp. 532–57.
35. Ibid., pp. 542–7.
36. The point is made by A. J. P. Taylor, *The Origins of the Second World War* (London, 1969), pp. 316–19.
37. Erickson, *The Road to Stalingrad*, ch. 2.
38. For good accounts of the early operations, see Erickson's *The Soviet High Command*, chs. 17 and 18, and his *The Road to Stalingrad*, pp. 99–222.
39. Quoted in Erickson, *The Road to Stalingrad*, p. 5.
40. Ibid., p. 235.

41. C. Andrew and V. Mitrokhin, *The Mitrokhin Archive: The KGB in Europe and the West* (London, 2000), p. 135.
42. Ibid., p. 433.
43. J. Erickson, *Stalin's War with Germany*, vol. 2: *The Road to Berlin* (New Haven, 1999), pp. 45–6.
44. Ibid., ch. 3, esp. p. 135.
45. Longworth, *The Cossacks*, pp. 329–39.

13: THE HIGH TIDE OF SOVIET IMPERIALISM

1. For details of the operation see J. Erickson, *The Road to Berlin*, pp. 139–42, and *passim* for subsequent operations.
2. Quoted in J. Haslam, *Vices of Integrity* (London, 1999), p. 107.
3. J. Mackintosh, *Strategy and Tactics of Soviet Foreign Policy* (London, 1962), p. 10.
4. M. Djilas, *Conversations with Stalin* (Harmondsworth, 1969), p. 90.
5. O. Gordievsky claims that the Germans lost 9 million men in the fighting on all fronts, whereas the Soviet Union lost between 20 and 30 million on its western front alone – see his letter in the *TLS*, 4 May 2001.
6. Primo Levi, *The Voice of Memory: Interviews 1961–1987*, ed. M. Belpoliti, trans. R. Gordon (New York, 2001), p. 52.
7. For a concise account of the circumstances at the conclusion of the war and events up to the onset of the Cold War, see P. Longworth, *The Making of Eastern Europe* (2nd edn, London, 1997), pp. 69–82 and nn. 1–13, pp. 92–3.
8. O. Jaszi, 'The economic crisis in the Danubian states', *Social Research* (New York, New School of Social Research), 2 (1935), 98–116. The extract quoted is on p. 116.
9. See Longworth, *The Making of Eastern Europe*, pp. 80–81.
10. M. Perrie, *The Image of Ivan the Terrible in Russian Folklore* (Cambridge, 1987), p. 117.
11. Personal communication from the daughter.
12. R. Slusser and J. Triska, *Calendar of Soviet Treaties* (Stanford, 1959), pp. 304, 323. The work gives an impression of intense diplomatic activity round the world in the post-war years.
13. Mackintosh, *Strategy and Tactics of Soviet Foreign Policy*, pp. 130–32.
14. Ibid., pp. 205ff.
15. *Pravda*, 28 January 1959.
16. Service, *Twentieth-Century Russia*, p. 351.
17. See Bugai, N., 'Pravda o deportatsii chechenskogoï ingushetskogo narodor' [The Truth about the Deportation of the Chechen and Ingush Peoples], *Voprosy istorii*, 7 (1990), pp. 32–44.
18. Kappeler, *Russland als Vielvölkerreich*, pp. 310–12.
19. V. Kabuzan, *Russkie v mire: dinamika, chislennost' i rasselenniia 1719–1989* (St Petersburg, 1996), p. 271.

20. Grossman, 'The industrialization of Russia'.
21. Olcott, *The Kazakhs*, pp. 238–40.
22. Armstrong, *Russian Settlement in the North*, p. 170.
23. Kabuzan, *Russkie v mire*, p. 274.
24. Kappeler, *Russland als Vielvölkerreich*, p. 313.
25. Andrew and Mitrokhin, *The Mitrokhin Archive*, pp. 651–5.
26. Longworth, *The Making of Eastern Europe*, pp. 51–2 *passim* and n. 12, p. 66.
27. M. Sicker, *The Strategy of Soviet Imperialism* (New York, 1988), p. 13.
28. The standard source for this is M. Kaser, *COMECON* (London, 1967); see also his (ed.) *The Economic History of Eastern Europe* (3 vols., Oxford, 1986).
29. Service, *Twentieth-Century Russia*, p. 388.
30. Sicker, *The Strategy of Soviet Imperialism*, pp. 145–7.
31. Ibid., p. 69; Andrew and Mitrokhin, *The Mitrokhin Archive*, pp. 508–11.
32. Andrew and Mitrokhin, *The Mitrokhin Archive*, pp. 149–77, *passim*. For a Russian account of these activities based on archives preserved by the Association of Veterans of Russia's Foreign Intelligence Service, see *Ocherk istorii rossiiskoi vneshnei razvedki*, vol. 6: *1945–1965* (Moscow, 2003).
33. A. Reid, *The Shaman's Coat: A Native History of Siberia* (London, 2002), pp. 133 passim; 160–61.

14: AUTOPSY ON A DECEASED EMPIRE

1. See Tuminez, *Russian Nationalism since 1856*, p. 42. As she points out, this policy of 'rooting' (*korenizatsiia*) also encouraged nepotism, cronyism, corruption and the creation of virtual fiefdoms, but then nationalism has always been used as a means of accessing political power and economic advantage.
2. V. Shlapentokh, 'A normal system? False and true explanations for the collapse of the USSR', *TLS*, 15 December 2000, pp. 11–13. The author herself conducted several of the surveys referred to.
3. Boris Aristov to Moscow, 18 October 1978, quoted in Andrew and Mitrokhin, *The Mitrokhin Archive*, p. 666.
4. Described by a sociologist involved – T. Zaslavakaia, 'Novosibirsk report', *Survey*, 28, 1 (1984), 88–108.
5. I have described the processes of collapse before in the context of the Soviet Bloc states themselves – Longworth, *The Making of Eastern Europe*, ch. 1, especially pp. 11ff.
6. It was reported that Soviet scientists eventually concluded that a mirror system fitted to their missiles could divert missiles sent against them. In practice it was unnecessary for all Soviet missiles to get through: the prospect of only two or three of them succeeding in destroying as many large American cities would have constituted an effective deterrent (and the fear of one reaching its target might have been enough). Meanwhile the cost of the arms race, some scholars

argue, contributed to the destabilization. For an interesting account of Soviet science and references to some useful literature on the subject, see Y. Rabkin and E. Mirskaia, 'Science and scientists in the post-Soviet disunion', *Social Science Information*, 32, 4 (1993), 553–79.

7. In retrospect this turned out to be the best opportunity to create a genuine democracy that was to be offered, but at that moment it was too radical even for Gorbachev, and the chance was missed – cf. Archie Brown's lecture at the School of Slavonic Studies, London, 1 March 2004.
8. The author's observation. He was in Moscow and Kiev at the time.
9. See Service, *Twentieth-Century Russia*, pp. 445–6.
10. Quoted by David Remnick reviewing F. Chuyev's interviews with Molotov and Ligachev's autobiography in *New York Review*, 25 March 1993, pp. 33–8.
11. From this point on the text reflects BBC transcripts of broadcasts from the Soviet Union and the Bloc countries, SU/0472 i etc. and EE/0457 etc.
12. Gorbachev, 28 March 1989, BBC, SU 0419 i.
13. Gorbachev, 18 July 1989, BBC, SU/0515 C1/1–4, 22 July 1989.
14. BBC, SU/0527 i and 0536 i.
15. BBC, SU/0528 c1/1–6/.
16. I have told the story before in Longworth, *The Making of Eastern Europe*, pp. 12–15.
17. Interview of 25 February 1991 reported in the press.
18. Private communication confirmed by another eyewitness.
19. See A. Stent, *Russia and Germany Reborn: Unification, the Soviet Collapse and the New Europe* (Princeton, 1999), esp. pp. 11ff.
20. The point is suggested by M. Malia, 'The August revolution', *New York Review*, 26 September 1991, pp. 22–6. The account of the coup which follows also draws on this source, though the interpretation of events is mine,.
21. Service, *Twentieth-Century Russia*, p. 495. Service provides an account of the last days of the old regime which is sympathetic to Gorbachev.
22. For a useful summary of the economic decline and the political collapse consequent upon it, see the *Quarterly Reports* issued by The Economist's Intelligence Research Unit for 1990 and 1991.
23. Tuminez, *Russian Nationalism since 1856*, pp. 239, 241.
24. See A. Brown, *The Gorbachev Factor* (Oxford, 1996).

15: REINVENTING RUSSIA

1. Stent, *Russia and Germany Reborn*, p. 211.
2. J. Stiglitz, *Globalization and its Discontents* (London, 2002), p. 56. Generally on the reforms see R. Service, *Russia: Experiment with a People* (London, 2002), ch. 9.
3. *The Times*, 18 July 2001, p. 20.

4. Stiglitz, *Globalization and its Discontents*, p. 139.
5. S. Cohen, *Failed Crusade. America and the Tragedy of Post-Communist Russia* (New York, 2000), p. 150.
6. P. Klebnikov, *Godfather of the Kremlin* (New York, 2000), is informative on the subject, particularly the links with the 'Chechen mob'. The author was subsequently murdered.
7. J. Nell and K. Stewart, *Death in Transition: The Rise in the Death Rate in Russia since 1992*, UNICEF Occasional Papers: Economic Policy Series, no. 45 (Florence, 1994), pp. 36, table 22, pp. 20, v, 12–13.
8. B. Kagarlitsky, *Restoration in Russia: Why Capitalism Failed*, trans. R. Clarke (London, 1995), p. 24.
9. R. Medvedev, *Post-Soviet Russia* (New York, 2000).
10. Service, *Russia: Experiment with a People*, p. 107.
11. See Klebnikov, *Godfather of the Kremlin*, pp. 200–210 *passim*.
12. Ibid., pp. 135, 325.
13. Personal observation.
14. Service, *Russia: Experiment with a People*, p. 156 and *passim*. On the connections with organized crime, its abetters among Russian officials, and with Boris Berezovskii see also Klebnikov, *Godfather of the Kremlin*, pp. 40–2.
15. For an account of the war see A. Lieven, *Chechnya: Tombstone of Russian Power* (New Haven, 1998).
16. *Rossiia v tsifrakh* (Moscow, 1997), p. 262; *Financial Times*, 18 December 1996 and 22 and 24 January 1997.
17. G. Smith, ed., *State-Building in Russia: The Yeltsin Legacy and the Challenge of the Future* (New York, 1995), pp. 217–25.
18. See G. Derluguian, 'Che Guevaras in turbans', *New Left Review*, 237 (September/October 1999), 3–27.
19. Klebnikov, *Godfather of the Kremlin*, p. 265.
20. For a full account of the election and the means by which it was won based on the researches of an able journalist, see ibid., ch. 8.
21. The lower estimate is cited by Service, *Russia: Experiment with a People*, p. 156, the higher by Klebnikov, *Godfather of the Kremlin*.
22. For reports on the Latvian issue, see Reuters reports, 9 March 1998. More generally, see J. Taylor in *Atlantic Monthly*, February 2002, pp. 69ff.
23. Stiglitz, *Globalization and its Discontents*, p. 145 et seq.
24. Kagarlitsky, *Restoration in Russia*, p. 58.
25. The Swiss government was to issue a warrant for Borodin's arrest on charges of money-laundering late the following year.
26. Cohen, *Failed Crusade*, pp. 136, 141.
27. B. Yeltsin, *Midnight Diaries* (London, 2000), p. 266.
28. Derluguian, 'Che Guevaras in turbans'.
29. V. Putin, 'Russia at the Turn of the Millennium', has been translated as an appendix (pp. 209–19) to N. Gevorkian, N. Timakova, A. Kolesnikov [and V.

Putin], *First Person*, trans. G. Fitzpatrick (London, 2000); see also L. Shvetsova, *Putin's Russia* (New York, 2003), and Tuminez, *Russian Nationalism since 1856*, pp. 297–8.

30. B. Lo, *Russian Foreign Policy in the Post-Soviet Era* (Basingstoke, 2002), pp. 157–67.
31. O. Skrypnyk on the Senkus web site. Most other unreferenced sources in this chapter are from the press, particularly the *Financial Times*.
32. See the World Bank's report *From Transition to Development* (New York, 2004).
33. See S. Kotkin, *Financial Times Magazine*, 6 March 2004, p. 19.
34. For an interesting, not unsympathetic, article on Khodorkovskii see C. Freeland in *Financial Times Magazine*, 1 November 2003, pp. 17–22. The business is still violent, however. The death of a London lawyer who headed Yukos's holding company in an unexplained helicopter crash in March 2004 has been attributed to his reported willingness to co-operate with the prosecution – see *Private Eye*, 1102 (19 March 2004), 28.
35. For an example, see Freeland, *Financial Times Magazine*, 1 November 2003, pp. 17–22.
36. Lo, *Russian Foreign Policy*, p. 125.

CONCLUSION

1. Presniakov, *The Formation of the Great Russian State*, p. 381.
2. Against undertakings given by Washington and Bonn at the time, and against the advice of George Kennan, Paul Nitze and others – see Stent, *Russia and Germany Reborn*, p. 221.
3. Russian census statistics posted on UN website, 9 June 2004, p. 3.
4. As reported by J. Page in *The Times*, 27 May 2004, p. 50.
5. M. Walker in *World Policy Journal*, 11, 1 (1994), 1.
6. I. Prizel, *National Identity and Foreign Policy: Nationalism and Leadership in Poland, Russia and Ukraine* (Cambridge 1998), p. 272.
7. Personal communicaton of Dr V. Zhiromskaia at ELTE seminar, Budapest, May 2004.
8. R. Allison, 'Regionalism, regional structures and security management in Central Asia', *International Affairs*, 80, 3 (May 2004), 463–83.
9. A. Bohr, 'Regionalism in Central Asia: New geopolitics, old regional order', *International Affairs*, 80, 3 (May 2004), 485–502.
10. B. Lo, 'The long sunset of strategic partnership: Russia's evolving China policy', *International Affairs*, 80, 2 (March 2004), 295–309.

Bibliography

Adlerfelt, G., *The Military History of Charles XII* (3 vols., London, 1740)

Agoston, M., 'Voskovaia pechat' Ivana III 1497g' ['Ivan III's wax seal of 1497'], in Gy. Szvak, ed., *Muscovy: Peculiarities of its Development* (Budapest, 2003)

Alekseiev, Iu., *Gosudar' vseia Rusi* [*Sovereign of All Russia*] (Novosibirsk, 1991)

Allen, W. E. D., *The Ukraine: A History* (Cambridge, 1940)

—— ed., *Russian Embassies to the Georgian Kings (1589–1605)* (2 vols., Cambridge, 1970)

Allen, W. E. D., and Muratoff, P., *Caucasian Battlefields* (Cambridge, 1953)

Allison, R., 'Regionalism, regional structures and security management in Central Asia', *International Affairs*, 80, 3 (May 2004), 463–83

Andreev, A., *Istoriia Kryma: khronika vekov* [*A History of the Crimea: A Chronicle of the Ages*] (Moscow, 2000)

Andrew, C., and Mitrokhin, V., *The Mitrokhin Archive: The KGB in Europe and the West* (London, 2000)

Angermann, N., *Studien zur Livlandpolitik Ivan Groznyjs* [*Studies in Ivan the Terrible's Livonia Policy*] (Marburg, 1972)

Anisimov, Ye., 'The imperial heritage of Peter the Great in the foreign policy of his early successors', in Ragsdale, ed., *Imperial Russia's Foreign Policy*, *q.v.*

Armstrong, T., *Russian Settlement in the North 1581–1990* (Cambridge, 1992)

—— ed., *Yermak's Campaign in Siberia* (London, 1975)

Atkin, M., *Russia and Iran 1780–1828* (Minneapolis, 1980)

—— 'Russian expansion in the Caucasus to 1893', in Rywkin, ed., *Russian Colonial Expansion*, pp. 139–87

Baddeley, J., *The Russian Conquest of the Caucasus* (London, 1908)

Bantysh-Kamenskii, N. N., *Obzor vneshnykh snoshenii Rossii (po 1800)* [*Survey of Russia's Foreign Relations to 1800*], 4 pts (Moscow, 1894–1902)

Barford, P., *The Early Slavs: Culture and Society in Early Medieval Eastern Europe* (Ithaca, 2001)

Baring, M., *What I Saw in Russia* (London, n.d. [*c.* 1905])

Barnett, V., *Kondratiev and the Dynamics of Economic Development: Long Cycles and Industrial Growth in That Context*, March 1998

Barrett, T., *At the Edge of Empire: The Terek Cossacks and The North Caucasus Frontier 1700–1860* (Boulder, 1999)

Bartlett, R., *Human Capital: The Settlement of Foreigners in Russia 1762–1804* (London, 1979)

Bassin, M., *Imperial Visions: Nationalist Imagination and Geographical Expansion in the Russian Far East 1840–1865* (Cambridge, 1990)

Bazilevich, K., *Vneshnaia politika russkogo tsentralizovannogo gosudarstvva, vtoraia polovina xv veka* (Moscow, 1952)

Becker, S., 'Russia's Central Asian Empire 1885–1917', in Rywkin, ed., *Russian Colonial Expansion*, pp. 235–40

—— *Russia's Protectorate in Central Asia: Bukhara-Khiva 1865–1924* (Cambridge, Mass., 1968)

Bell, J., *Journal of a Residence in Circassia during the Years 1837, 1838 and 1839* (2 vols., London, 1840)

Bell, J. (of Antermony), *Travels from St Petersburgh in Russia to Diverse Parts of Asia*, (2nd edn, 2 vols., London, 1764)

Belokurov, S., ed., *Snosheniia Rossii s Kavkazom 1568–1613* [*Russia's Relations with the Caucasus 1568–1613*], Moskovskogo glavnogo arkhiva Ministerstva inostrannykh del, vyp.1 (Moscow, 1889)

Bogatyrev, S., 'Battle for divine wisdom. The rhetoric of Ivan IV's campaign against Poland', in Lohr and Poe, eds., *The Military and Society in Russia 1450–1917*, pp. 325–63

Bohr, A., 'Regionalism in Central Asia: New geopolitics, old regional order', *International Affairs*, 80, 3 (May 2004), 485–502

Bolkhovitnikov, N., 'The sale of Alaska in the context of Russian–American relations in the 19th century', in Ragsdale, *Imperial Russian Foreign Policy*, pp. 193–21

Borisenkov, Ye., and Piasetskii, V., *Tysiachiletnaia letopis' neobychnykh iavlenii prirody* [*A Thousand-Year Chronicle of Unusual Phenomena in Nature*] (Moscow, 1988)

Borisov, N., *Ivan III* (Moscow, 2000)

—— *Ivan Kalita* [*Ivan Money-Bag*] (Moscow, 1997)

Bremner, R., *Excursions in the Interior of Russia* (2 vols., London, 1839)

Brisbane, M., ed., *Archaeology of Novgorod: Recent Results from the Town and its Hinterland*, Society for Medieval Archaeology, monograph 13 (Lincoln, Nebr., 1992)

British Broadcasting Corporation, Transcripts of broadcasts from the Soviet Union and Eastern Europe, series SU and EE

Brown, A., *The Gorbachev Factor* (Oxford, 1996)

Broxup, M. Bennigsen, ed., *The North Caucasus Barrier: The Russian Advance towards the Muslim World* (London, 1992)

Brudny, Y., *Reinventing Russia: Russian Nationalism and the Soviet State 1953–1991* (Cambridge, Mass., 1998)

Brusilow, A., *A Soldier's Note-Book 1914–1918* (London, 1930)

Buchanan, G., *My Mission to Russia and Other Diplomatic Memories* (2 vols., London, 1923)

Bunak, V., 'Antropologicheskie tipy russkago naroda i voprosy istorii ikh formirovanie' ['Russian anthropological types and the question of their historical formation'], *Kratkie soobshcheniia Instituta etnografii AN/SSR*, 36 (1962), 75–82

Bushev, P., *Istoriia posolstv i diplomaticheskikh otnoshenii Russkogo i iranskogo gosudarstv v 1613–1621gg* [*History of the Embassies and Diplomatic Relations of the Russian and Iranian States from 1613 to 1621*] (Moscow, 1987)

Bussow, C., *The Disturbed State of the Russian Realm*, trans. and ed. G. Orchard (Montreal, 1994)

Cameron, G. Poulett, *Personal Adventures and Excursions in Georgia, Circassia and Russia* (2 vols., London, 1845)

Campenhausen, L. von, *Travels through Several Provinces of the Russian Empire with an Account of the Zaporog Cossacks and of Bessarabia, Wallachia and the Crimea* (London, 1808)

Carr, E. H., *The Bolshevik Revolution 1917–1923* (3 vols., London, 1950–54)

—— *The Soviet Impact on the Western World* (London, 1947)

Carr, E. H., and Davies, R., *Socialism in One Country, 1924–1926* (London, 1950)

—— *Foundations of a Planned Economy, 1926–1929* (London, 1969)

Cavalli-Sforza, L. and F., *The Great Human Diaspora* (Reading, Mass., 1995)

Cavalli-Sforza, L., Menozzi, P., and Piazza, A., *The History and Geography of Human Genes* (Princeton, 1994)

Cecil Papers 104/47 (Hatfield House Library)

Chamberlin, W., *Russia's Iron Age* (London, 1935)

Chapman, J., and Dolukhanov, P., *Cultural Transformations and Interactions in Eastern Europe* (Aldershot, 1993)

Chappe d'Auteroche, *A Journey into Siberia* (2nd edn, London, 1774)

Cherepnin, L., *Obrazovanie russkogo tsentralizovannogo gosudarstva v xiv–xv vv* [*The Formation of the Russian Centralized State in the Fourteenth and Fifteenth Centuries*] (Moscow, 1966)

Chistiakova, E., ed., N. Rogozhin, compiler, et al., *'Oko vsei velikoi Rossii': ob istorii rossiiskoi diplomaticheskoi sluzhby xvi–xvii vekov* [*'The Eyes of All Great Russia': On the History of the Russian Diplomatic Service in the Sixteenth and Seventeenth Centuries*] (Moscow, 1989)

Christian, D., *A History of Russia, Central Asia and Mongolia*, vol. 1 (Oxford, 1998)

Christiansen, E., *The Northern Crusades* (London, 1997)

Clausewitz, C. von, *The Campaign of 1812 in Russia* (London, 1843)

Cochrane, J., *Narrative of a Pedestrian Journey through Russia and Siberian Tartary to the Frozen Sea and Kamtchatka* (3rd edn, 2 vols., London, 1825)

Cohen, S., *Failed Crusade. America and the Tragedy of Post-Communist Russia* (New York, 2000)

Conquest, R., *Harvest of Sorrow: Soviet Collectivization and the Terror Famine* (London, 1986)

Constantine VII Porphyrogenitus, *De Administrando Imperio* [*On the Administration of the Empire*], ed. Gy. Moravcik and R. Jenkins (2 vols., London, 1962)

—— *Le Livre des cérémonies* [*The Book of Ceremonies*] ed. A. Vogt (Paris, 1935, 1939–40)

Coxe, W., *Account of the Russian Discoveries between Asia and America* (4th edn, London, 1803)

Cross, S., and Olgerd, P., eds., *The Russian Primary Chronicle* (Cambridge, Mass., 1953)

Crosskey, R. M., *Muscovite Diplomatic Practice in the Reign of Ivan III* (New York, 1987)

Crummey, R., *The Formation of Muscovy 1304–1613* (London, 1987)

Demidova, N., *Sluzhebnaia Biurokratiia v Rossii v xvi v* [*The Service Bureaucracy in Russia in the Sixteenth Century*] (Moscow, 1987)

Derluguian, G., 'Che Guevaras in Turbans', *New Left Review*, 237 (September/ October 1999) 3–27

Dimnik, M., *Mikhail, Prince of Chernigov and Grand Prince of Kiev 1224–1246* (Toronto, 1981)

Djilas, M., *Conversations with Stalin* (Harmondsworth, 1969)

Dmitriev, M., Floria, B., and Yakovenko, S., *Brestskaia uniia 1596g i obshchestvenno-politicheskaia bor'ba na Ukraine i v Belorussii v xvi-nachale xvii v* [*The Union of Brest of 1596 and Social-Political War in Ukraine and Belarus in the Sixteenth and Early Seventeenth Century*], Pt 1 (Moscow, 1996)

Dolukhanov, P., *The Early Slavs: Eastern Europe from the Initial Settlement to Kievan Rus'* (London, 1996)

Donnelly, A., *The Russian Conquest of Bashkiriya 1552–1740* (New Haven, 1968)

Drozdov, I., and Fartyshev, V., *Iurii Andropov i Vladimir Putin: na puti k vozrozhdeniia* [*Yuri Andropov and Vladimir Putin: On the Road to Regeneration*] (Moscow, 2001)

Dubov, A., *Geograficheskaia sreda i istoriia Rossii konets xv-seredina xix v* [*The Geographical Setting and History of Russia from the Fifteenth to the Mid Nineteenth Century*] (Moscow, 1983)

Dubov, I., 'The ethnic history of northwestern Rus' in the ninth to the thirteenth centuries'.

Dunning, C., *Russia's First Civil War: The Time of Troubles and The Founding of the Romanov Dynasty* (University Park, Pa., 2001)

Dvorkin, A., *Ivan the Terrible as a Religious Type* (Erlangen, 1992)

Dvornik, F.,'Byzantine influences in Russia', in M. Huxley, ed., *The Root of Europe* (London, 1952), pp. 95–106

—— *Byzantine Missions among the Slavs* (New Brunswick, 1970)

—— 'Byzantine political ideas in Kievan Russia', *Dumbarton Oaks Papers*, 9–10 (1956), 76–94

Economist Intelligence Unit, *Country Reports: USSR/Russia* (London, 1987–2002)

[Ellis, G.?], *Memoir of a Map of the Countries Comprehended between the Black Sea and the Caspian* (London, 1788)

Epifanov, P., 'Voiska i voennaia organizatsiia' ['The armed forces and military organization'], in A. V. Artsikhovskii, et al., *Ocherki russkoi kul'tury xvi v*, vyp. 1 (Moscow, 1976)

Erickson, J., *The Soviet High Command* (London, 1961)

—— *Stalin's War with Germany*, vol. 1: *The Road to Stalingrad* (London, 1998)

—— *Stalin's War with Germany*, vol. 2: *The Road to Berlin* (New Haven, 1999)

Erman, A., *Travels in Siberia* (2 vols., London, 1848)

Evans, J., ed., *The Mission of N. P. Ignat'ev to Khiva and Bukhara in 1858* (Newtonville, 1984)

Fagan, B. M., *The Journey from Eden: The Peopling of Our World* (London, 1990)

—— *People of the Earth* (7th edn, New York, 1992)

Fennell, J., *The Crisis of Medieval Russia 1200–1304* (London, 1983)

—— *The Emergence of Moscow 1304–1359* (London, 1968)

—— *Ivan the Great of Moscow* (London, 1961)

—— ed. and trans., *The Correspondence between Prince A.M. Kurbsky and Tsar Ivan IV of Russia 1564–1579* (Cambridge, 1955)

Fisher, A., *The Russian Annexation of the Crimea 1772–83* (Cambridge, 1970)

Fisher, R., *The Russian Fur Trade 1550–1700* (Berkeley, 1943)

—— *The Voyage of Semen Dezhnev in 1648* (London, 1981)

Fitzpatrick, S., *Everyday Stalinism* (Oxford, 1999)

Fletcher, G., *Of the Russe Commonwealth*, ed. R. Pipes (Cambridge, Mass., 1966)

Floria, B., *Ivan Groznyi* [*Ivan the Terrible*] (Moscow, 1999)

Forsten, G., *Akty i pis'ma k istorii Baltiiskogo voprosa v xvi i xvii stoletiakh* [*Documents Relating to the History of the Baltic Question in the Sixteenth and Seventeenth Centuries*] (St Petersburg, 1889)

Forsyth, J., *A History of the Peoples of Siberia: Russia's North Asian Colony 1581–1990* (Cambridge, 1992)

—— 'The Siberian native peoples before and after the Russian conquest', in Wood, ed., *The History of Siberia*, pp. 69–89

Franklin, S., and Shepard, J., *The Emergence of Rus' 750–1200* (London, 1996)

Frost, R., *The Northern Wars 1558–1721* (London, 2000)

Gammer, M., 'Russian strategies in the conquest of Chechnia and Daghestan 1825–1859'.

Geanakoplos, D., *Byzantium: Church Society and Civilization seen through Contemporary Eyes* (Chicago, 1984)

Gerschenkron, A., 'Agrarian policies and industrialization: Russia 1861–1917', in H. Habbakuk and M. Postan, eds., *The Cambridge Economic History of Europe*, vol. 6 (Cambridge, 1965), pp. 706–800

—— *Europe in the Russian Mirror* (Cambridge, 1970)

Gevorkian, N., Timakova, N., Kolesnikov, A. [and Putin, V.], *First Person*, trans. G. Fitzpatrick (London, 2000)

Gimbutas, M., *The Slavs* (London, 1971)

Gille, F. von, *Lettres sur le Caucase et la Crimée* [*Letters on the Caucasus and the Crimea*] (Paris, 1859)

Goldfrank, D., 'Policy, tradition and the Menshikov mission of 1853', in Ragsdale, ed., *Imperial Russia's Foreign Policy*, pp. 119ff.

Goncharov, I., *The Voyage of the Frigate* Pallada, trans. N. Wilson (London, 1965)

Gordon, P., *Dnevnik 1659–1667* [*Diary 1659–1667*], ed. D. Fedosov (Moscow, 2002)

Gorskii, A., *Russkie zemli v xiii–xiv vekakh: puti politicheskogo razvitiia* [*The Russian Lands in the Thirteenth and Fourteenth Centuries: Routes of Political Development*] (Moscow, 1996)

Got'e, Iu., ed., *Akty otnosiashchiesia k istorii zemskikh soborov* [*Historical Acts Relating to the History of Assemblies of the Land*], vyp. 1 (Moscow, 1909)

[?Greig, Admiral S.], *An Authoritative Narrative of the Russian Expedition against the Turks by an Officer in the Russian Fleet* (London, 1772)

Grossman, G., 'The industrialization of Russia', in C. Cipolla, ed., *The Fontana Economic History of Europe* (London, 1973), vol. 4, section 7

Gudziak, B., *Crisis and Reform: The Kievan Metropolitanate, the Patriarch of Constantinople and the Genesis of the Union of Brest* (Cambridge, Mass., 1998)

Hakluyt, R., *The Principal Navigations Voyages Traffiques & Discoveries of the English Nation*, vols. 2 and 3 (Glasgow, 1903)

Halen, J. von, *Memoirs of his Journey to Russia, his Campaign with the Army of the Caucasus, etc.* (2 vols., London, 1830)

Halperin, C. J., *Russia and the Golden Horde: The Mongol Impact on Russian History* (London, 1987)

—— 'The Russian land and the Russian tsar: the emergence of Muscovite ideology', *Forschungen zur osteuropäische Geschichte* [*Researches into East European History*], 23 (1976), 23–82

Hamilton, G., *The Art and Architecture of Russia* (Harmondsworth, 1954)

Hans, N., *History of Russian Educational Policy 1701–1917* (London, 1931)

Hanway, J., *An Historical Account of the British Trade over the Caspian Sea* (2nd edn, 2 vols., London, 1754)

Hartley, J., *A Social History of the Russian Empire 1650–1825* (London, 1999)

Haslam, J., *Vices of Integrity* (London, 1999)

Haxthausen, Baron von, *The Russian Empire, its People, Institutions and Resources* (2 vols., London, 1856)

—— *Transcaucasia* (London, 1854)

Hell, X. Hommaire de, *Travels in the Steppes of the Caspian Sea* (London, 1847)

Hellie, R., 'The costs of Muscovite military defence and expansion', in Lohr and Poe, eds., *The Military and Society in Russia 1450–1917*, pp. 41–66

—— *The Economy and Material Culture of Russia 1600–1725* (Chicago, 1999)

—— 'What happened? How did he get away with it? Ivan Groznyi's paranoia and the problem of institutional restraints', *Russian History*, 14 (1987), 119–224

Herberstein, S. von, *Rerum Moscoviticarum Commentarii* [*Commentaries on Muscovite Affairs*] (Vienna, 1549)

Hosking, G., 'Empire and nation-building in late imperial Russia', in Hosking and Service, eds., *Russian Nationalism Past and Present*, pp. 19–34

—— *Russia and the Russians* (London, 2001)

Hosking, G., and Service, R., eds., *Reinterpreting Russia* (London, 1999)

—— eds., *Russian Nationalism Past and Present* (London, 1998)

Hovannisian, R., 'Russian Armenia: a century of rule', *Jahrbücher für Geschichte Osteuropas* [*Yearbooks for the History of Eastern Europe*], Neue Folge, 19, 1 (1971), 31–48

Howes, R., ed., *The Testaments of the Grand Princes of Moscow* (Ithaca, 1967)

Hughes, L., *Sophia, Regent of Russia 1657–1704* (New Haven, 1990)

—— ed., *New Perspectives in Muscovite History* (Basingstoke, 1992)

Ignat'ev, N. P., *see* Evans, J., ed.

Jaszi, O., 'The economic crisis in the Danubian states', *Social Research* (New York, New School of Social Research), 2 (1935), 98–111

J. C. H[otten], trans., *The Russian Invasion of Poland in 1563*, a translation of *Memorabilis et perinde stupenda de crudeli Moscovitarum Expeditione narratio* (Douai, n.d.)

Jewsbury, G., *The Russian Annexation of Bessarabia 1774–1828* (Boulder, 1976)

Kabuzan, V., *Russkie v mire: dinamika, chislennost' i rassellenniia 1719–1989* [*The Dynamics, Numbers and Distribution of Russians in the World*] (St Petersburg, 1996)

—— *Russkii etnos v 20–80-kh godakh xx veka* [*Ethnic Russians in the '20s to the '80s of the Twentieth Century*]

Kagarlitsky, B., *Restoration in Russia: Why Capitalism Failed*, trans. R. Clarke (London, 1995)

Kahan, A., *The Plow, the Hammer and the Knout: An Economic History of Eighteenth Century Russia* (Chicago, 1985)

Kaiser, D., and Marker, G., *Reinterpreting Russian History: Readings 860–1862* (New York, 1994)

Kaminsky, A., *Republic vs. Autocracy: Poland-Lithuania and Russia 1686–1697* (Cambridge, Mass., 1994)

Kappeler, A., *Russland als Vielvölkerreich* [*Russia as Multinational Empire*] (Munich, 1992)

Kartashev, A., *Ocherki po istorii russkoi tserkvi* [*Essays on the History of the Russian Church*] (2 vols., Moscow, 1992)

Kaser, M., *COMECON* (London, 1967)

——*The Economic History of Eastern Europe* (3 vols., Oxford, 1986)

Kashtanov, S., *Finansy srednevekovskoi Rusi* [*The Finances of Medieval Russia*] (Moscow, 1988)

Kazhdan, A., and Epstein, A. W., *Change in Byzantine Culture in the Eleventh and Twelfth Centuries* (Berkeley, 1990)

Kazhdan, A., and McCormick, M., 'The social world of the Byzantine courts', in H. Maguire, ed., *Byzantine Court Culture from 829 to 1209* (Washington, DC, 1997), pp. 167–98

Keep, J., *Last of the Empires: A History of the Soviet Union, 1945–91* (Oxford, 1995)

—— *Soldiers of the Tsar: Army and Society in Russia 1462–1872* (Oxford, 1985)

Kelly, L., *Diplomacy and Murder in Teheran: Alexander Griboyedov and Imperial Russia's Mission to the Shah of Persia* (London, 2002)

Kerner, J., *The Urge to the Sea: The Course of Russian History: The Role of Rivers, Portages, Ostrogs, Monasteries and Furs* (Berkeley and Los Angeles, 1942)

Khodarkovsky, M., *Russia's Steppe Frontier: The Making of a Colonial Empire 1500–1800* (Bloomington, 2002)

Kirby, D., *Northern Europe in the Early Modern Period: The Baltic World 1492–1772* (London, 1990)

Kiselev, I. N., 'Estestvennoe dvizhenie naseleniia v 1930-kh godakh' ['The natural movement of population in the 1930s'], in Poliakov et al., eds., *Naselenie Rossii v 1920–1950-e gody*, pp. 68ff.

Kivlitskii, Ye., 'Sv. Ol'ga [Helen]' ['St Olga (Helen)'], *Entsiklopedicheskii slovar'*, vol. 21A (St Petersburg, 1897), pp. 910–11

Klaproth, J. von, *Reise in den Kaukasus und nach Georgien* [*Travels in the Caucasus and Georgia*] (2 vols., Halle and Berlin, 1812)

Klebnikov, P., *Godfather of the Kremlin* (New York, 2000)

Kleimola, A., 'The Romanovs and the cult of the tsarevich Dmitrii, in *Religiia i tserkov' v kul'turno-istoricheskom razvitiei russkogo severa* (Kirov, 1996), pp. 230–3

Klein, V., *Uglichskoe sledstvennoe delo i smerti Tsarevicha Dmitriia* [*The Uglich Inquiry and the Death of the Tsarevich Dmitrii*] (Moscow, 1913)

Klimensko, M., ed., *The 'Vita' of St. Sergii of Radonezh* (Boston, Mass., n.d.)

Kliuchevskii, V., *Boiarskaia duma drevnei Rusi* [*The Goyar council of old Russia*] (Moscow, 1909)

Kohl, J., *Russia and the Russians in 1842* (2 vols., London, 1842)

Kohut, Z., 'The Ukrainian elite in the eighteenth century and its integration into the Russian nobility', in I. Banac and P. Bushkovich, *The Nobility of Russia and Eastern Europe* (New Haven, 1983), pp. 65–85

Kondrat'ev, Nikolai D., *The Works of Nikolai D. Kondrat'ev*, ed. N. Maklasheva et al., vol. 3 (London, 1998)

Kotoshikhin, G., *O Rossii v tsarstvovanii Alekseia Mikhailovicha* [*On Russia in the Reign of Tsar Aleksey Mikhailovich*], ed. A. Pennington (Oxford, 1980)

Kozlovskii, I., *Pervye pochty i pervye pochtmeistery v Moskovskom gosudarstve* [*The First Posts and the First Postmasters in the Russian State*], vol.1 (Warsaw, 1913)

Krashennikov, S., *The History of Kamtschatka and the Kurilski Islands* (Glocester [*sic*], 1764)

Krusenstern, A. von, *Voyage round the World*, trans. R. Hoppner (2 vols., London, 1813)

Kuza, A., 'Sotsial'no-istoricheskaia tipologiia drevnerusskikh gorodov x–xiii vv' ['A socio-historical typology of Russian towns in the tenth to the thirteenth century'], in *Russkii gorod: issledovaniia i materiali*, no. 176 (Moscow, 1983), pp. 44–36

Labaume, E., *A Circumstantial Narrative of the Campaign in Russia* (London, 1815)

Lantzeff, G., *Siberia in the Seventeenth Century: A Study of the Colonial Administration* (Berkeley, 1943)

Le Clerc, N.-G., *Histoire physique, morale, civile et politique de la Russie moderne* [*The Physical, Moral, Civil and Political History of Modern Russia*] (2 vols., Paris–Versailles, 1783–85)

Le Donne, J., *The Russian Empire and the World 1700–1917: The Geopolitics of Expansion and Containment* (New York and Oxford, 1997)

Lensen, G., *The Russian Push towards Japan: Russo-JapaneseRelations 1697–1875* (Princeton, 1959)

Lep'iavko, S., *Kozats'ki viini kintsya xvi st. v Ukraini* [*The Cossack Wars in Ukraine at the End of the Sixteenth Century*] (Chernihiv, 1996)

Leslie, R., *Reform and Insurrection in Russian Poland 1856–1865* (London, 1963)

Lesseps, J. de, *Travels in Kamtshatka during the Years 1787 and 1788* (2 vols., London, 1790)

Lewin, M., *Russian Peasants and Soviet Power* (London, 1968)

Lieven, A., *Chechnya: Tombstone of Russian Power* (New Haven, 1998)

Lieven, D., *The Russian Empire and its Rivals* (London, 2000)

—— *Russia's Rulers under the Old Regime* (New Haven, 1989)

Liubavskii, M., *Obrazovanie osnovnoi gosudarstvennoi territorii velikorusskoi narodnosti. Zaseleniia i ob"edieniia tsentra* [*The Formation of the Original State Territory of the Great Russian People*] (Moscow, 1929, repr. 1996)

—— *Obzor istorii russkoi kolonizatsii* [*A Survey of the History of Russian Colonization*], ed. A. Ia. Degtiarev et al. (Moscow, 1996)

Lo, B., 'The long sunset of strategic partnership: Russia's evolving China policy', *International Affairs*, 80, 2 (March 2004), 295–309

—— *Russian Foreign Policy in the Post-Soviet Era* (Basingstoke, 2002)

Lohr, E., and Poe, M., eds., *The Military and Society in Russia 1450–1917* (Leiden, 2002)

Longworth, P., *Alexis, Tsar of All the Russias* (London, 1984)

—— *The Art of Victory* (London, 1972)

—— *The Cossacks* (London, 1969)

—— *The Making of Eastern Europe* (2nd edn, London, 1997)

—— 'Political rumour in early modern Russia', in Gy. Szvak, ed., *Muscovy: Peculiarities of its Development* (Budapest, 2003), pp. 27–33

—— 'Russia and the Antemurale Christianitatis', in Gy. Szvak, ed., *The Place of Russia in Europe* (Budapest, 1999)

—— 'Ukraine: history and nationality', *Slavonic and East European Review*, 78, 1 (January 2000), 115–24

McCormick, M., *Origins of the European Economy: Communications and Commerce, A.D. 300–900* (Cambridge, Mass., 2001)

McEvedy, C., and Jones, R., *Atlas of World Population History* (London, 1980)

Mackenzie, D., 'The conquest and administration of Turkestan, 1860–85', in Rywkin, ed., *Russian Colonial Expansion*, pp. 208ff.

Mackintosh, J., *Strategy and Tactics of Soviet Foreign Policy* (London, 1962)

Madariaga, I. de, *Russia in the Age of Catherine the Great* (London, 1982)

Majeska, G., trans. and ed., *Russian Travellers to Constantinople in the Thirteenth and Fourteenth Centuries* (Chicago, 1970)

Mallory, J., *The Archaeology of the Proto-Indo-Europeans* (London, 1997)

—— *In Search of Indo-Europeans. Language, Archaeology and Myth* (London, 1989)

Mangö, C., trans., *The Homilies of Photius* (Cambridge, Mass., 1958)

Man'kov, A., *Tseny i ikh dvizheniia v russkom gosudarstve xvi v* [*Prices and their Movements in the Sixteenth-Century Russian State*] (Moscow, 1951)

Manstein, C. von, *Memoirs of Russia* (London, 1770)

Manz, B., 'Central Asian uprisings in the eighteenth century', *Russian Review*, 46, 3 (1987), 267–81

[Marbault], *Essai sur le commerce de Russie* [*Essay on Russia's Commerce*] (Amsterdam, 1777)

Marigny, T. de, *Three Voyages in the Black Sea to the Coast of Circassia* (London, 1837)

Martens, F. de, *Recueil de traits et conventions conclus par la Russie avec les puissances étrangères* [Collection of Treaties and Conventions Concluded by Russia with Foreign Powers] (15 vols., St Petersburg, 1874–1909)

Martin, J., *Medieval Russia 908–1584* (Cambridge, 1996)

—— 'Peculiarities of the *pomest'e* system', in Gy. Szvak, ed., *Muscovy: Peculiarities of its Development* (Budapest, 2003), pp. 76–87

—— *Treasure from the Land of Darkness: The Fur Trade and its Significance for Medieval Russia* (Cambridge, 1986)

Mattingly, G., *Renaissance Diplomacy* (Harmondsworth, 1965)

Medvedev, R., *Post-Soviet Russia* (New York, 2000)

Meyendorff, J., *Byzantium and the Rise of Russia* (Crestwood, NY, 1989)

Milev, L., *Velikorusskii pakhar' i osobennosti rossiiskogo istoricheskogo protsessa* [*The Ploughman of Great Russia and Peculiarities of the Russian Historical Process*] (Moscow, 1998)

Milner-Gulland, R., *The Russians* (Oxford, 1997)

Molchaninov, N. N., *Diplomatiia Petra Velikogo* [*The Diplomacy of Peter the Great*] (Moscow, 1986)

Moon, D., *The Abolition of Serfdom in Russia, 1762–1907* (London, 2001)

—— *The Russian Peasantry 1600–1930* (London, 1999)

Mouravieff, A., *A History of the Church of Russia*, trans. R. W. Blackmore (Oxford, 1842)

Nekliudov, A., ed., *Nachalo snoshenii Rossii s Turtsiei* [*The Beginning of Russia's Relations with Turkey*] (Moscow, 1883)

Nell, J., and Stewart, K., *Death in Transition: The Rise in the Death Rate in Russia since 1992*, UNICEF Occasional Papers: Economic Policy Series, no. 45 (Florence, 1994)

Nolde, B., *La Formation de l'Empire Russe* (2 vols., Paris, 1952–3)

Norman, H., *All the Russias: Travels and Studies in Contemporary European Russia, Finland, Siberia, the Caucasus and Central Asia* (New York, 1903)

Nosov, E., 'The problem of the emergence of early modern urban centres in northern Russia', in Chapman and Dolukhanov, *Cultural Transformations and Interactions in Eastern Europe*, pp. 236–56

Obolensky, D., *The Byzantine Commonwealth* (Crestwood, NY, 1991)

—— *Byzantium and the Slavs* (Crestwood, NY, 1994)

—— 'Vladimir Monomakh', in his *Six Byzantine Portraits* (Oxford, 1988), pp. 83–114

Ocherk istorii rossiiskoi vneshnei razvedki [*An Outline History of Russia's Foreign Intelligence Service*], vyp. 6: *1945–1965* (Moscow, 2003)

Olcott, M., *The Kazakhs* (Stanford, 1995)

[Olearius], *The Voiages and Travels of the Ambassadors sent by Frederick, Duke of Holstein, to the Grand Duke of Muscovy and the King of Persia* (2nd edn, London, 1669)

Oliphant, L., *Russian Shores of the Black Sea* (London, 1854)

O'Rourke, S., *Warriors and Peasants: The Don Cossacks in Late Imperial Russia* (Basingstoke, 2000)

Ostrogorsky, G., *History of the Byzantine State* (Oxford, 1980)

Ostrowski, D., *Muscovy and the Mongols* (Cambridge, 1998)

Paleologue, M., *An Ambassador's Memoirs* (3 vols., London, 1923)

Pallas, P., *Neue Nordische Beitrage* [*New Contributions on the North*] (3 vols., St Petersburg and Leipzig, 1793–6)

—— *Travels Through the Southern Provinces of the Russian Empire in 1793 and 1794* (2 vols., London, 1802–3)

Pallot, J., and Shaw, D., *Landscape and Settlement in Romanov Russia* (Oxford, 1990)

Palsson, H., and Edwards, P., eds., *Vikings in Russia: Yngvar's Saga and Eymund's Saga* (Edinburgh, 1989)

Pamiatniki diplomaticheskikh snoshenii drevnei Rossii s derzhavami inostrannymi [*Monuments of Old Russia's Diplomatic Relations with Foreign Powers*] (10 vols., St Petersburg, 1851–71)

Parker, W., *An Historical Geography of Russia* (London, 1968)

Pazvolsky, L., and Moulton, H., *Russia's Debts and Russian Reconstruction* (New York, 1924)

Perrie, M., *The Image of Ivan the Terrible in Russian Folklore* (Cambridge, 1987)

Pickhan, G., 'The incorporation of *Gospodin Pskov* into the Muscovite state', in Hughes, ed., *New Perspectives on Muscovite History*

Pinkerton, R., *Russia, or Miscellaneous Observations of the Past and Present of that Country and its Inhabitants* (London, 1833)

Pipes, R., *The Formation of the Soviet Union: Communism and Nationalism* (Cambridge, Mass., 1964)

Poe, M., *Foreign Descriptions of Muscovy: An Analytic Bibliography of Primary and Secondary Sources* (Columbus, Ohio, 1995)

—— *The Russian Moment in World History* (Princeton, 2003)

Poliakov, Iu., et al., eds., *Naselenie Rossii v 1920–1950-e gody: chislennost', poteri, migratsii* [*Russia's Population in the 1920s to the 1950s: Numbers, Losses, Migrations*] (Moscow, 1994)

Porter, R. Ker, *A Narrative of the Campaign in Russia during the Year 1812* (London, 1814)

Presniakov, A., *The Formation of the Great Russian State. A Study of Russian History in the Thirteenth and Fourteenth Centuries* (Chicago, 1970)

Pritsak, O., *The Origins of the Old Rus' Weights and Monetary Systems* (Cambridge, Mass., 1998)

—— *Origins of Rus'*, vol. 1: *Old Scandinavian Sources other than the Sagas* (Cambridge, Mass., 1981)

Prizel, I., *National Identity and Foreign Policy: Nationalism and Leadership in Poland, Russia and Ukraine* (Cambridge, 1998)

Pryzhkov, I., *Istoriia kabakov v Rossii* [*A History of the Pot-house in Russia*] (Moscow, 1991)

Raeff, M., 'Patterns of Russian imperial policy towards the nationalities', in M. Raeff, ed., *Political Ideas and Institutions in Imperial Russia* (Boulder, 1994)

—— *Siberia and the Reforms of 1822* (Seattle, 1956)

Rabkin, Y., and Mirskaia, A., 'Science and scientists in the post-Soviet disunion', *Social Science Information*, 32, 4 (1993), 553–79

Ragsdale, H., 'Russian projects of conquest in the eighteenth century', in Ragsdale, ed., *Imperial Russian Foreign Policy*, pp. 75ff.

—— ed., *Imperial Russia's Foreign Policy* (Cambridge, 1993)

Rauch, G. von, *Russland: Staatliche Einheit und nationale Vielfalt* [*Russia: State Unity and National Diversity*] (Munich, 1953)

Reid, A., *The Shaman's Coat: A Native History of Siberia* (London, 2002)

Reinbeck, G., *Travels from St. Petersburg through Muscovy, Grodno, Warsaw, Breslaw, etc. to Germany in the Year 1805* (London, 1807)

Renfrew, C., *Archaeology and Language* (London, 1987)

Reuilly, J., *Travels in the Crimea* (London, 1807)

Rich, D., *The Tsar's Colonels: Professionalism Strategy and Subversion in Late Tsarist Russia* (Cambridge, Mass., 1998)

Rogger, H., *National Consciousness in Eighteenth Century Russia* (Cambridge, Mass., 1960)

Rogozhin, N., 'Mesto Rossii xvi–xvii vekov v Evrope po materialam posolskikh knig' [Russia's place in sixteenth- and seventeenth-century Europe according to the material in the diplomatic books], in Gy. Szvak, *The Place of Russia in Europe* (Budapest, 1999), pp. 89–96

Rozhdestvenskii, S., *Sluzhiloe zemlevladenie v Moskovskom Gosudarstve xvi veka* [*Service Agriculture in the State of Muscovy*] (St Petersburg, 1897)

Russell, W., *General Todleben's History of the Defence of Sebastopol 1854–5: A Review* (London, 1865)

Ryan, W., *The Bathhouse at Midnight* (University Park, Pa., 1999)

Rywkin, M., 'Russian colonial expansion before Ivan the Dread: a survey of basic trends', *Russian Review*, 32 (1973), 286–93

—— ed., *Russian Colonial Expansion to 1917* (London, 1988)

Sarytchew [Sarychev], G., *Account of a Voyage of Discovery to the North-East of Siberia, the Frozen Ocean, and the North-East Sea* (London, 1806)

Saul, N., *Russia and the Mediterranean 1797–1807* (Chicago, 1970)

Schuyler, E., *Peter the Great* (2 vols., London, 1884)

Semenov-Tyanshanskii P., and Lamanskii, V., *Rossiia: polnoe geograficheskoe opisanie nashego otochestva* [*Russia: A Complete Geographical Description of Our Fatherland*] (*x* vols., St Petersburg, 1899–1914)

Semino, O. et al., 'The genetic legacy of palaeolothic *Homo sapiens sapiens* in extant Europeans', *Science*, 290 (5404), 10 November 2000, 1155–9

Serbina, K., ed., *Kniga bol'shemu chertezha* [*The Great Book of Routes*] (Moscow and Leningrad, 1950)

Service, R., *A History of Twentieth-Century Russia* (Cambridge, Mass., 1997)

—— *Russia: Experiment with a People* (London, 2002)

Seton-Watson, H., *The Russian Empire 1801–1917* (Oxford, 1967)

Sevcenko, I., *Ukraine between East and West* (Edmonton, 1996)

Seymour, H. D., *Russia on the Black Sea and the Sea of Azov, being a Narrative of Travels in the Crimea and the Bordering Provinces* (London, 1855)

Sicker, M., *The Strategy of Soviet Imperialism* (New York, 1988)

Shlapentokh, V., 'A normal system? False and true explanations for the collapse of the USSR', *TLS*, 15 December 2000, pp. 11–13

Shvetsova, L., *Putin's Russia* (New York, 2003)

Sinitsyn, N., *Tretii Rim: istoki i evolutsiia russkoi srednevekovoi konseptsii (xv–xvii vv)* [*The Third Rome: The Sources and Development of a Medieval Conception (Fifteenth to Seventeenth Centuries)*] (Moscow, 1998)

Skrynnikov, R. G., *Boris Godunov* (Moscow, 1979)

——*Gosudarstvo i tserkov' na Rusi xiv–xvi vv* [*State and Church in Fourteenth- to Sixteenth-Century Russia*] (Novosibirsk, 1991)

——*Ivan Groznyi* [*Ivan the Terrible*] (Moscow, 1980)

——*Samozvantsy v Rossii v nachale xvii veka* [*Pretenders in Russia at the Beginning of the Seventeenth Century*] (Novosibirsk, 1990)

Slusser, R., and Triska, J., *Calendar of Soviet Treaties* (Stanford, 1959)

Smith, G., ed., *State-Building in Russia: The Yeltsin Legacy and the Challenge of the Future* (New York, 1995)

Smith, R., and Christian, D., *Bread and Salt: A Social and Economic History of Food and Drink in Russia* (Cambridge, 1984)

Spencer, E., *Travels in Circassia, Krim Tartary, etc.* (2 vols., London, 1837)

——*Travels in the Western Caucasus* (2 vols., London, 1838)

[Speranskii, M.], *Zapiska o monetnom obrashchenii Grafa Speranskogo s zamechaniiami Grafa Kankrina* [*Count Speranskii's Memorandum on Monetary Circulation with Remarks by Count Kankrin*] (St Petersburg, 1895)

[Sprengtporten, Colonel], *Narrative of the Conquest of Finland by the Russians in the Years 1808–9*, ed. Gen. Monteith (London, 1854)

Stent, A., *Russia and Germany Reborn: Unification, the Soviet Collapse and the New Europe* (Princeton, 1999)

Stiglitz, J., *Globalization and its Discontents* (London, 2002)

Sumner, B., *Russia and the Balkans 1870–1880* (Oxford, 1937)

—— *Survey of Russian History* (London, 1947)

—— *Tsardom and Imperialism in the Far East and Middle East, 1880–1914* (London, 1940)

Taylor, A. J. P., *The Origins of the Second World War* (London, 1969)

Tazbir, J., *Poland as the Rampart of Christian Europe* (Warsaw, n.d.)

Thaden, E., *Russia's Western Borderlands 1710–1870* (Princeton, 1984)

—— *Russification in the Baltic Provinces and Finland 1855–1914* (Princeton, 1981)

Theen, R., 'Quo vadis Russia? The problem of national identity and state-building', in G. Smith, ed., *State-Building in Russia*, pp. 40–80

Timoshenko, V., *Agricultural Russia and the Wheat Problem* (Stanford, 1932)

Todleben, General, *see* Russell, W.

Tooke, W., *View of the Russian Empire during the Reign of Catharine the Second and to the Close of the Present Century* (3 vols., London, 1799)

Tula: materialy dlia istorii goroda xvi–xviii stoletii [*Materials Relating to the History of the Town of Tula from the Sixteenth to the Eighteenth Century*] (Moscow, 1884)

Tuminez, A., *Russian Nationalism since 1856: Ideology and the Making of Foreign Policy* (London, 2000)

Ulianitskii, V., ed., *Materialy o Rossii, Pol'shi, Moldavii, Vlachi v 14–16 st* [*Materials on Russia, Poland, Moldavia and Walachia from the Fourteenth to the Sixteenth Century*], Chteniia v obshchestve istorii i drevnostei rossiiskikh, vyp. 3 (Moscow, 1887), pp. 1–24

[US Congress], *Commission on the Ukrainian Famine: Report* (Washington, DC, 1988)

Venables, R., *Domestic Scenes in Russia* (London, 1839)

Vernadsky, G., *Ancient Russia* (New Haven, 1947, repr. 1973)

—— *Kievan Russia* (New Haven, 1948, repr. 1973)

—— et al., eds., *A Source Book for Russian History from the Earliest Times to 1917* (3 vols., New Haven, 1972)

Veselovskii, S. B., *Isledovaniia po istorii oprichniny* [*Researches into the History of the Oprichnina*] (Moscow, 1963)

—— *D'iaki i pod'iachie xv–xvii vv* [*Russian Civil Servants of the 15th to 18th Centuries*] (Moscow, 1975)

—— *Trudy po istochnikovedenii i istorii Rossii v periode feodalzma* [*Work on the Sources for and the History of Russia in the Medieval Period*] (Moscow, 1978)

Vigilev, A., *Istoriia Otechestvennoi pochty* [*A History of Russia's Postal Service*] (Moscow, 1977)

Vitarko, G., 'Aviation . . . and imperatives of modernization', in Lohr and Poe, eds., *The Military and Society in Russia 1450–1917*, pp. 273–91

Vodarskii, Ye., *Naselenie Rossii za 400 let* [*The Population of Russia over the Last 400 Years*] (Moscow, 1973)

—— *Naselenie Rossii v kontse xvii–nachale xviii veka* [*Russia's Population at the Turn of the Seventeenth and Eighteenth Centuries*] (Moscow, 1977)

Wagner, M., *Travels in Persia, Georgia and Koordistan* (3 vols., London, 1856)

[Walhausen, J.], *Uchenie i khitrost' ratnago stroieniia pekhotnykh liudei* [*Infantry Drill and Technique*] (Moscow, 1647)

Wallace, D. Mackenzie, *Russia* (London, 1912)

[Wilson, Sir R.], *A Sketch of the Military and Political Power of Russia in the Year 1817* (2nd edn, London, 1817)

Winter, E., *Russland und das Papstum* [*Russia and the Papacy*] (Berlin, 1960)

Wood, A., ed., *The History of Siberia: From Russian Conquest to Revolution* (London, 1991)

World Bank, *From Transition to Development* (New York, 2004)

Wortman, R., *Scenarios of Power* (Princeton, 1995)

Yeltsin, B., *Midnight Diaries* (London, 2000)

Zabriskie, E., *American–Russian Rivalry in the Far East* [1895–1914] (Philadelphia, 1946)

Zaslavakaia, T., 'Novosibirsk report', *Survey*, 28, 1 (1984), 88–108

Zemskov, V., 'Spetsposolentsy (1930–1959gg)' ['Forced labour settlement (1930–1959)'], in Poliakov et al., eds., *Naselenie Rossii v 1920–1950-e gody*, pp. 145ff.

Zhiromskaia, V., 'Chislennost' naseleniia Rossii v 1939g: poisk istiny' ['The size of Russia's population in 1939: a search for the truth'], in Poliakov et al., eds., *Naselenie Rossii v 1920–1950-e gody*, pp. 27ff.

—— *Demograficheskaia istoriia Rossii v 1930-e gody* [*The Demographic History of Russia in the 1930s*] (Moscow, 2001)

Zimin, A. A., *Formirovanie boiarskoi aristokratii v Rossii vtoroi poloviny xv-pervoi treti xvi v* [*The Formation of the Boyar Aristocracy in Russia from the Second Half of the Fifteenth to the First Third of the Sixteenth Century*] (Moscow, 1988)

—— *V kanun groznykh potriasenii: predposylki pervoi krest'ianskoi voiny v Rossii* [*On the Eve of Terrible Shocks: The Origins of Russia's First Peasant War*] (Moscow, 1986)

—— *Reformy Ivana Groznogo* [*The Reforms of Ivan the Terrible*] (Moscow, 1960)

—— *Vitiaz na rasput'e: feodal'naia voina Rossii xv v* [*Knight Errant at the Parting of the Ways: Feudal War in Fifteenth-Century Russia*] (Moscow, 1991)

Index